The
Nature of
Cape Cod

The
NATURE of
CAPE COD

Beth Schwarzman

Illustrated by Sandra Hogan McDermott

UNIVERSITY PRESS OF NEW ENGLAND
HANOVER AND LONDON

University Press of New England, Hanover, NH 03755
Text and maps © 2002 by Elisabeth C. Schwarzman;
figures 102 (p. 122) and 124 (p. 129) © 1977 by Mabel Crittenden;
all other illustrations © 2002 by Sandra Hogan McDermott

Printed in the United States of America

5 4 3 2 1

Library of Congress Cataloging-in-Publication Data
Schwarzman, Beth.
  The nature of Cape Cod / Beth Schwarzman ; illustrated by Sandra Hogan
McDermott.
    p.   cm.
Includes bibliographical references (p.   ).
  ISBN 1–58465–270–5 (cloth : alk. paper) — ISBN 1–58465–107–5 (pbk. :
alk. paper)
  1. Natural history—Massachusetts—Cape Cod. I. Title.
QH105.M4 S39 2002
508.744'92—dc21   2002001446

To my parents,
Max D. Crittenden, Jr., geologist, and
Mabel B. Crittenden, botanist

CONTENTS

PROLOGUE: STORIES ON THE LAND

Cape Cod did not always have fudge shops and beach parking lots, or even roads and houses. Beneath the amenities it has always been nature—beaches or Cod, warm waters, shellfish or forests—that attracted people here. Although today it is possible to live on the Cape and never see a Herring, dig a clam, or walk a sand road, nature and natural processes still operate as they have for millennia, and still affect the lives of residents and visitors alike. The evidence of those natural processes is written on the landscape for all to read, if they look. So, too, are the stories of the people who, attracted by the nature of Cape Cod, lived here before us.

The native peoples on the Cape knew a heavily forested landscape inhabited by deer, elk, wolves, and Turkeys. They lived in small villages and burned clearings in the forest to grow corn and beans. They hunted along well-used trails, caught ducks in the marshes, and collected shellfish along the shore. Nights were dark and winters cold.

To the first European settlers, the Cape Cod landscape looked like wilderness, and they set themselves to tame it. They cleared fields and planted rye and barley; they pastured their livestock on the salt marshes and dammed the streams to provide water power for gristmills. They hunted whales for oil and cut forest trees for wood.

By the 1850s Henry David Thoreau, perhaps the first tourist, saw a landscape denuded and eroded by the work of those settlers and their descendants. He commented that many villages held only women, children, and the elderly because the men were at sea fishing, whaling, or trading; the land no longer provided a living. Young people soon began moving west in search of better prospects and warmer climes.

Immigrants to the Cape in the early 1900s found areas of abandoned farmland and cut-over cedar swamps. They turned their hands to commercial agriculture and, with the availability of fertilizer, soon made the Cape a major exporter of strawberries and asparagus as well as the traditional cranberries, firewood, and shellfish. Paved roads, electric light, and central heat soon followed.

Those here before us took the nature of Cape Cod as they found it, and they left it changed. We inherit the landscape they created from the forests, streams, and hills—the kitchen middens, millponds, woodlots, cranberry bogs, and abandoned fields. The evidence for their interaction with nature is visible, but to see it you must peer around, between, and beneath the houses, sidewalks, lawns, shopping centers, and pavement where we, unlike our predecessors on the Cape, spend most of our time.

As always, nature and natural processes have been at work all the while. Ice, sun, waves, wind, storms, frost, and growing seasons have all written their signatures on the land. Look and you will see their marks, some overwritten by recent human stories, others as obvious as a new break through a barrier beach. Behind these you will find the fainter lines of thousands of years of earlier stories.

I hope you will see the Cape and the natural world differently after using this book, and that the book will be your companion for many pleasant and illuminating hours as you explore the nature of Cape Cod.

A NOTE ON NAMES

I have chosen to capitalize the proper common names of species (Greater Black-backed Gull, Red Oak) and to lowercase the more general references (gulls, oaks).

I hope that this choice will make unfamiliar species names easier to read. When I write Narrow-leaved Cattail, for instance, the term clearly refers to a species, not just a cattail with narrow leaves. (In a few cases, such as Sphagnum Moss, the term refers to a group of species that have no common names. In other cases, such as Eel and Kingfisher, the capitalized name refers to the only species of that kind to be found on Cape Cod.

The maps follow U.S. Geological Survey conventions in eliminating punctuation from names.

The

NATURE *of* CAPE COD

SETTING

CAPE COD AND THE SEA AROUND US

A Sense of Place

Cape Cod juts eastward into the Atlantic Ocean from a sharp bend in the coast of North America. To the north are Cape Cod Bay and Massachusetts Bay; to the east are the famous fishing grounds of Georges Bank; to the south are Vineyard and Nantucket Sounds, bounded by

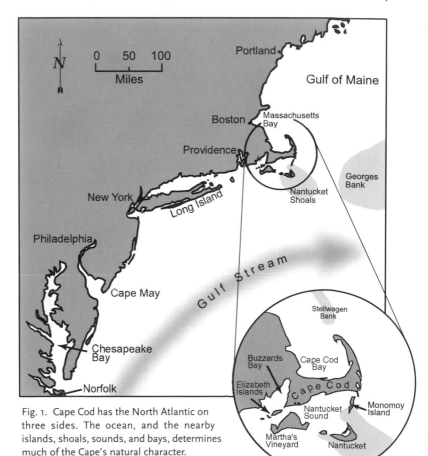

Fig. 1. Cape Cod has the North Atlantic on three sides. The ocean, and the nearby islands, shoals, sounds, and bays, determines much of the Cape's natural character.

the islands of Martha's Vineyard and Nantucket; and to the west are Buzzards Bay and Block Island Sound. Although the waters around the Cape are shallow, the ocean determines the weather here, just as it has dominated the Cape's history and the livelihoods of its inhabitants.

The cold North Atlantic Ocean is part of the weather story on the Cape, but the other part is the Gulf Stream. This ocean current brings Caribbean water as warm as 80°F north along the coast. In spring, as the northerly winds of winter give way to summer southwesterlies, we feel the warming effect of the Gulf Stream even though it is offshore. The coastal waters warm slowly, but by late summer, water south of the Cape can be 73°F. That's as much as 8° warmer than water in Cape Cod Bay, where the ocean is chilled by the Labrador Current that brings northern water south along the coast.

Summers are cooler and breezier here on the Cape than inland (that's the effect of the North Atlantic) and winters warmer, with less snow and more rain. The Cape feels the ocean in high humidity from spring through fall. Being near the ocean also means that spring comes late; in some years summer doesn't seem to arrive until July. In the fall, however, we get back the warmth that we missed in spring; weather warm enough for sailing can linger into mid-November, a benefit of the Gulf Stream.

The warm Gulf Stream also has a downside; it is responsible for fog. South or southeasterly winds blowing across the warm Gulf Stream water pick up quantities of water vapor. In spring and early summer, when those moist winds pass over the still-cool water around the Cape, the water vapor condenses to form fog. Fog is most frequent and thickest over water and near the south coast, especially in Chatham on the southeast corner of the Cape. The fog tends to evaporate as it passes over the warmer land, though it may form again when it reaches the cold waters of Cape Cod Bay. Later in the summer, warmer water means fewer foggy days.

Cape Cod lies in the belt of westerly winds (the names of winds reflect the direction *from* which they blow) that flow all the way around the earth in the north temperate zone. The prevailing summer winds here tend to blow from south of west, and the average winter winds from north of west. These general wind patterns are altered locally by the shape of land and water. In the summer the daily heating of the land draws cooler ocean air inland, causing our characteristic afternoon sea breezes. But those characteristic breezes differ from place to place. On Sandy Neck, which faces north toward Cape Cod Bay, for instance, the sea breeze is northeasterly. This local wind counteracts the prevailing southwesterly wind and may result in little wind on the beach. On the Buzzards Bay beaches, on the other hand, the onshore sea breeze adds to the prevailing wind, often making for strong, gusty breezes. Onshore sea breezes also help to explain why Chatham has more fog than other south-coast towns—the onshore winds in Chatham are southeasterly, and the warm Gulf Stream is closest in that direction.

Storms also alter the general westerly pattern as they pass over. Many winter storms come from the west, across the continent. The low-pressure center of those storms, therefore, is west of us, and draws winds into it from the east and northeast, producing the typical winter northeaster (traditionally pronounced "no'th eastah," not "nor'easter") along the coast. After the storm center has passed, the wind backs around to the northwest and blows hard and cold for a time. Summer weather, usually more benign, also generally comes from the west, sometimes bringing afternoon thunderstorms. In spring and summer the northwest winds after a front can seem warm, bringing us the inland heat instead of the cool sea breezes.

An exception to the pattern of weather from the west is hurricanes. These revolving storms form in the tropical Atlantic off Africa and move west toward the Caribbean on the trade winds; some then turn northeast and track along the coast. Hurricanes have had significant effects on the Cape even though one comes this way only every few years. The rotting trunks of trees felled by the Great Hurricane of 1938 can still be seen in some woodlands. The trees, shorelines, and boats of the Cape have been damaged repeatedly since 1938 in fairly direct hits by the Great Atlantic Gale of 1944 and by named hurricanes Carol and Edna (1954), Donna (1960), Gloria (1985), and Bob (1991). Fewer lives are lost in hurricanes here today than in earlier years due to better weather forecasting, but accurate forecasts don't reduce the battering of the waves or the steeple- and tree-toppling force of the wind. So many people have moved to the coast in the years since the powerful hurricanes of the 1940s and 1950s that property damage will be very high when the next big one comes.

Because Cape Cod lies on a corner of the coast that forms a boundary between natural environments, it also straddles a border between

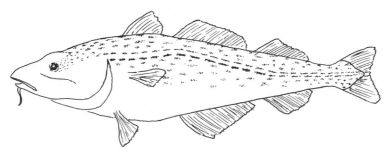

Fig. 2. Atlantic Cod (*Gadus morhua*), Cape Cod's namesake. After 500 years of sustained fishing, the Cod population collapsed in the late 1980s under the pressure of mechanized trawlers. Although the fishery is restricted and there are some signs of an increase, the Cod population is still far below historic levels.

communities of organisms. To the north are the rocky coasts, cold waters, and dark spruce woods of Maine; to the south lie the sandy shores, warmer waters, and oak and pine woods of New Jersey. Cape Cod shares characteristics of both zones. American Holly, at its northern limit on the Upper and Mid-Cape, shows green in the bare winter woods because the warmth of the Gulf Stream allows plants more common in the New Jersey Pine Barrens, 120 miles to the south, to grow here. On the other hand, some plants of more northerly climes grow here and not farther south. Birch trees and cranberries, more common in Maine, may be remnants of the plant communities that grew here at the end of the Ice Age. In salt marshes you'll find Fiddler Crabs that teem in the marshes in Georgia but are not found north of Cape Cod. Underwater this relationship holds true as well: the Bay Scallop reaches its northerly limit on Cape Cod, and the eponymous Cod goes no farther south.

Tides and Currents

The tides in the open Atlantic, east of Cape Cod, rise and fall 5 to 9 feet twice every twenty-four hours, in response to the gravitational pull of the moon and the sun. Every two weeks, at about the times of the full and new moons, the so-called spring or moon tides rise higher and fall lower than the tides during the intervening weeks. The east-facing beaches of the Lower Cape have tides similar to those in the open ocean.

But the tides that wash the rest of the Cape are more complicated, even though they are pulled by the same gravitational forces. Cape

Cod and its shoals create an enormous blockage in the path of the tides, slowing the water and forcing it to detour around the land. The effects of the detours are seen every day in the height and the timing of the tides around the Cape. For example, in Cape Cod Bay at the east end of the canal, high tide occurs approximately three hours before high tide at the west end only 7 canal miles away. The tide in Cape Cod Bay rises and falls about 9 feet; at the head of Buzzards Bay the range is only about 4 feet, and it's as little as 1½ feet at Woods Hole.

These complicated tidal differences create strong currents as large volumes of water try to squeeze through narrow passages or shallow sounds. In the Cape Cod Canal the current can flow as fast as 5.2 knots (about 6 miles an hour), and even in the relatively wide-open waters of Vineyard and Nantucket Sounds the currents often reach 3 knots. These currents were important to sailing vessels around the Cape from the time of the earliest explorers and fishermen. Even today sailboats time their passages through the canal and the sounds to use rather than fight the currents.

Upper? Cape

On Cape Cod people talk about the Upper Cape and the Lower Cape as though there were some obvious up and down. The Upper Cape is the part closest to the mainland (Bourne, Falmouth, Mashpee, and Sandwich), and its elevations are higher than those of the Lower Cape; these facts might be the reason for the name. But probably in the old days people went "Down Cape" in the same sense that they went "Down East" to Maine— they sailed downwind in the prevailing westerly winds. Someone traveling by sailboat has reason to notice whether the trip to the next town will be upwind. The terms have stuck even though today's travelers don't decide whether they are going to work or the grocery store depending on which way the wind is blowing.

AT THE BOTTOM OF IT ALL: GEOLOGY OF CAPE COD

Seeing like a Geologist

In your mind's eye peel away the surface layer of Cape Cod, the zone where we live: the veneer of houses and streets, the lawns and lawn ornaments, tomato plants and sewage treatment plants, the flagpoles, the trees and towns. Now you are seeing Cape Cod as geologists see it: a massive ridge of rocks, gravel, and sand dumped here by a glacier.

Cape Cod was built by a glacier between 15,000 and 20,000 years ago as the Ice Age came to an end. That fact explains many of the Cape's notable features—beaches and bluffs, porous soil, rocky hills and sandy plains, many ponds, and the few freshwater streams. These Cape Cod landscapes were built of materials brought by the glacier and shaped by glacial processes, then rearranged around the edges by the sea.

In order to understand how the Cape was formed, it is useful to understand something about the way a glacial ice sheet works. Here's an explanation; then we'll get back to what it means for Cape Cod.

How Glaciers Operate

To picture the glacier that formed Cape Cod, think of Greenland. Greenland today is covered by a glacier up to 11,000 feet thick (that's more than 2 miles from top to bottom). Each year for thousands of years, more snow has fallen on Greenland than has melted. As the snow piled up, the snowflakes were crushed and recrystallized into pellets of ice, just as they are when you pack snow in your hands to make a snowball. As snow continued to pile up, the weight of the pile increased until it compacted the ice pellets at the bottom of the pile into solid ice.

We think of ice as hard and brittle, but surprisingly, ice can flow when it is under pressure—pressure such as the weight of several thousand feet of ice and snow. As the pile of snow and ice grew deeper, and the pressure increased, the ice at the bottom of the pile began to flow. Slowly but inexorably it flowed out from under the greatest weight, out from under the area of greatest snow accumulation. The speed of glacial flow varies tremendously, but most often falls in the range of a few inches to a few feet per day.

If it is too difficult to imagine ice flowing, picture Jell-O instead. A cube of Jell-O is strong enough to support a small paperback book, but imagine what happens if you pile volumes A through F of an encyclopedia on that same Jell-O cube…. Now picture what happens if you make a pile of Jell-O so high that the Jell-O in the top of the pile weighs as much as those encyclopedia volumes—the same thing, the Jell-O at the bottom will squash. If you keep adding Jell-O to the top of the pile, the squashing Jell-O at the bottom will spread wider. Ice, of course, is much stronger than Jell-O; it takes more weight to make ice flow, and it flows more slowly. But with enough weight and time, ice will flow.

In Greenland today we see the result of these processes. Snow has piled up to great depths and has compacted into ice over an area of about 750,000 square miles. That ice flows slowly outward at the bottom of the glacier until it reaches the ocean, where it breaks up into icebergs. Ice continually develops and flows away from the center as long as more snow falls than melts. As large as the Greenland ice sheet is, it is only a small fraction of the size of the glaciers of the Ice Age. These glaciers were truly continental in size. One of them covered two-thirds of the width of North America, and another covered northern Europe, including most of the British Isles.

The flowing ice of a continental glacier is a mighty force. It moves slowly but has great erosive and carrying power. Moving ice can carry rocks as big as small houses—rocks that are much too heavy to be carried by moving water—as well as the smallest grains of sand or silt, and everything in between, all mixed together and frozen into the ice. This great sheet of ice, as much as 1,000 miles wide and several miles thick, flows across the land, acting like a herd of giant bulldozers and a huge and proportionately powerful piece of sandpaper. The glacier pushes and carries loose rocks; it tears blocks of rock from the bedrock below and carries them along. Some of these blocks of rock may freeze into the bottom of the glacier, where they become tools that shape the bedrock beneath the moving glacier. The "tools" get ground down themselves, sometimes developing flat, polished surfaces.

8

The glacier grinds up and over any hill or mountain that is lower than the top of the ice. The rounded 3,100-foot-high summit of Mt. Monadnock in southern New Hampshire shows the polish and deep grooves carved by the glacier passing over it; those features demonstrate that the ice was thick enough to completely cover that peak. The ice keeps moving, collecting and carrying rocks and scraping and smoothing the bedrock it crosses.

The edges of a growing continental glacier eventually reach either the ocean or warm weather. Where the glacier moves out into the ocean, it progressively breaks up into icebergs that float away, dropping their loads of rock debris onto the ocean floor as they melt. Where the weather is warm enough to melt the glacier before it reaches the ocean, it creates characteristic deposits of rock and sand on land. A melting glacier releases vast amounts of meltwater, of course, and it also releases the sand, rocks, and silt it has been carrying.

Even though the front of the glacier is melting, the glacier itself continues to spread outward as long as snow continues to accumulate at its center; so ice continues to flow toward the melting edge. Sometimes the rate of melting just about equals the speed of forward movement. In that case the front edge of the glacier stays in roughly the same place for a time while the body of the glacier keeps bringing in more material and releasing it. As the glacier front melts, rocks and gravel are stranded, and they accumulate in front of the glacier in linear hills called moraines. If the glacier surges or re-advances, it can override those materials or bulldoze them into higher and steeper hills.

Streams of meltwater issuing from the melting edge of the glacier carry great quantities of the gravel, sand, and silt that the glacier has transported. As these sediment-choked streams meander across the land in front of the glacier, they gradually drop their load, creating gently sloping plains that build toward the sea. These gently sloping deposits of sand and gravel are called outwash, and the land they form is called an outwash plain.

A continental glacier like this is the result of colder climates than the earth experiences today. In the 1990s evidence began to accumulate that changes from glacial to nonglacial climate conditions, and back again, may be correlated with altered water circulation in the oceans. Evidence also indicates that the climate can switch from one state to the other during a glacial episode, in time spans that are short even in human terms: less than ten years. The ultimate cause of such dra-

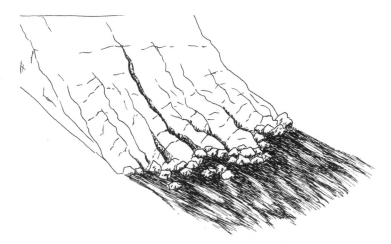

Fig. 3. The surface of a continental glacier looks like nothing more exciting than a snowfield. But at its melting edge the ice is riven with crevasses and diminished to a thin, ragged wedge. Torrents of meltwater carry sand, silt, and gravel out across the outwash plain, leaving the larger rocks where they melted free of the ice.

matic climate changes may be small, periodic variations in the earth's orbit and the amount of sunlight reaching earth. Questions remain, but it is clear that the earth's climate cooled as the Ice Age began and warmed up again as it ended. Could it happen again? In a word, yes. Glacial conditions have occurred repeatedly in the earth's history and could recur. Human activity, such as burning fossil fuels and cutting forests, does warm the earth. How that human-induced warming will interact with the natural cycles is still unclear. Climate change is an active field of research; we can expect frequent reports that will lead to a better understanding of the mechanisms of the earth's climate.

A climate cold enough to create continent-size glaciers has another effect on the world. In today's climate virtually all the snow that falls on land in the temperate zone melts within a few months and runs as water back into the oceans. During an ice age the winter snow in these areas does not all melt during the next summer; it becomes ice, locking water into the glaciers on the continents. All this snow originated as water that evaporated out of the oceans. Because the oceans continue to lose water through evaporation and little of it returns, sea level drops worldwide. Sea level around the entire earth dropped hundreds of feet during the Ice Age and remained low until the glaciers melted.

Glaciation and Cape Cod

The glacier that formed Cape Cod was the last advance of the ice sheet that repeatedly flowed across and melted off North America during the Ice Age—geologically speaking, very recently: between about 1,800,000 and 10,000 years ago. About 75,000 years ago a fluctuation toward a cold climate began the process that led to the creation of Cape Cod. As the climate grew cold, more snow accumulated and turned to ice, the glacier began to advance, and the level of the oceans fell.

One center of snow accumulation at that time was east of Hudson Bay, and the ice spread in all directions from there. This glacier eventually accumulated to as much as 2 miles thick. It is hard to imagine the power of such a huge volume of moving ice. It scraped across the country, grinding over mountains and gathering and carrying vast amounts of rock in all sizes, from house-size blocks to particles so fine they are called "rock flour." The ice moved south across Canada and, about 25,000 years ago, into New England (which wasn't named then, of course) and toward the area where Cape Cod is today.

When the front of the glacier approached, this area looked completely different than it does today. It was all dry land, more than 100 miles inland from what was then the coast. Because so much water was trapped in ice sheets, the worldwide sea level was about 400 feet lower than it is today. Any area that today is under less than 400 feet of water was dry land. Buzzards Bay, Cape Cod Bay, Nantucket and Vineyard Sounds, Georges Bank, all were part of a gently sloping coastal plain cut by a few valleys. Cape Cod, the Elizabeth Islands, Martha's Vineyard, and Nantucket did not yet exist.

As the ice moved across southern New England toward the place Cape Cod is today, it came into regions with warmer weather. Although the glacier continued to advance, the southern edge of the ice began to melt. Streams of meltwater carried sediment away from the front of the ice and deposited it on the coastal plain to the south. Despite the thinning of the southern edge by melting, the ice sheet continued to be pushed from behind by the accumulation of more snow in the far north, and it continued to flow south across southern New England. About 21,000 years ago the front of the glacier reached its farthest points south: about where Martha's Vineyard and Nantucket are now. The front of the glacier extended east across Georges

Bank and the basin that is now the Gulf of Maine to Newfoundland, and west across the location of Long Island (which was also made by this glacier) and northern New Jersey, through Pennsylvania and Ohio and on into the Upper Midwest.

This description might give you the mental image of uniform ice advancing evenly all across that 2,000-mile front. But we know from studies of modern ice caps that glaciers generally don't move forward

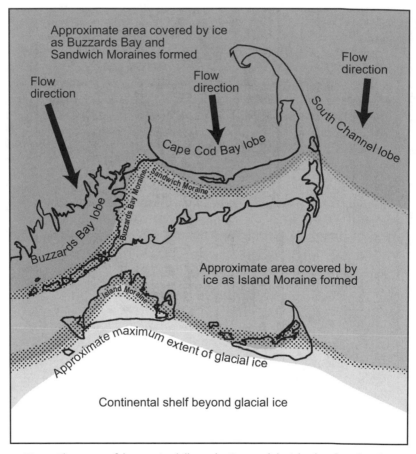

Fig. 4. The curves of the moraine hills on the Cape and the Islands reflect their formation by three ice streams, which fed the scalloped lobes at the edge of the ice. Each ice stream brought to Cape Cod a distinctive mix of rocks collected from the land across which it traveled.

all at once. Instead, ice in some areas can move more rapidly than the ice around it, forming "ice streams." Such streams of fast-moving ice probably fed large curving ice bulges along the glacier front. Three bulges, or "lobes," of ice formed Cape Cod, each named for the low area it occupied: the Buzzards Bay lobe, the Cape Cod Bay lobe, and the South Channel lobe. These lobes crossed different country to get to the Cape, and each apparently advanced at its own pace.

WHAT'S UNDERNEATH?

Beneath the sand and gravel of Cape Cod there is clay, more sand, and more gravel, deposited during previous glacial advances. These older deposits form the cliffs at Gay Head on Martha's Vineyard, but here on the Cape the older deposits lie deep beneath the surface. The solid bedrock on which all the glacial deposits lie is buried even deeper—200 to 700 feet below sea level—and is not exposed on the Cape or Islands. The closest exposures of bedrock are to the north at Marshfield and to the west at Fort Phoenix at the mouth of New Bedford Harbor. At Fort Phoenix the smoothed granite headland bears the telltale tool marks and polish left by the glacier.

Sand and gravel from the melting (but still advancing) glacier built an outwash plain across the area and far out to the southeast. As the glacier front approached the site of Martha's Vineyard and Nantucket, the ice rode over the new outwash plain, bulldozing gravel and sand up ahead of it. The rate of melting and the forward motion of the glacier apparently reached a rough balance at this time. Although the ice continued to move forward, its southern edge melted back at roughly the same rate; so the ice front stayed in about the same place. The ice melted back during warm spells or where the advance rate was slower, and it bulldozed forward during colder times or where the ice advanced faster, building up a ridge of hills that forms the high land on Martha's Vineyard and Nantucket. You can think of this ridge of moraine as the Island Moraine, although it was just a line of low hills on the coastal plain at the time. The glacier continued to melt at a great rate; the sand and rock transported from the north melted out of the ice and accumulated in front of the glacier. Meltwater streams continued to build the outwash plain far out to the southeast of present-day Nantucket.

About 18,000 years ago the climate began its current warming trend, causing the glacier to melt back faster than it was pushed forward. (Glaciers only flow forward, away from the center of accumulation. When a glacier "retreats," what really happens is that the ice melts faster than it flows forward; a glacier never backs up.) The front of the glacier dwindled and melted; soon ice was gone from the area of the Islands. Blocks of ice were stranded in the areas now occupied by Vineyard and Nantucket Sounds and Cape Cod, and were covered by sediment released from the melting front of the glacier just to the north. Except for these buried blocks, all the ice south of Cape Cod melted. Then the climate cooled, and the ice advanced again. Along the northern and western edges of what is now Cape Cod the glacier reached a balance again, piling up rocks and boulders as they melted free of the ice, depositing extensive outwash plains that further buried the stranded blocks of ice to the south, and forming a temporary lake in Nantucket Sound. The ice occasionally re-advanced briefly after episodes of faster melting. These re-advances piled the moraine materials higher, forming the moraine hills of the Upper Cape and Mid-Cape. The Buzzards Bay Moraine (formed by the Buzzards Bay lobe of the glacier) runs in a great curve from Cuttyhunk Island in the southwest through Woods Hole to the village of Buzzards Bay. The Sandwich Moraine, formed by the Cape Cod Bay lobe, runs from Bournedale east into Dennis.

STONECUTTING

The boulders on the moraines were a resource to locals through the early 1900s, supplying the stone that forms the foundations and doorsteps of many an old Cape Cod building. Today stone is usually cut with saws; modern granite curbstones show the semicircular scratches and sharp, square edges that indicate power saws. But these are modern tools. Until the 1930s stone was cut using only hand tools; these tools left their own marks on the cut stones and on the boulders from which pieces were cut.

The hand tools are simple and age-old: a heavy hammer, a set of steel wedges, and a star drill. This last is an impact drill, the kind John Henry was hitting with his 9-pound hammer. Such a drill makes a hole by crushing the rock directly beneath its sharp edges; it is rotated one-eighth of a turn after each hammer blow, and the crushed rock must be removed from the bottom of the hole from time to time with a long-handled "spoon."

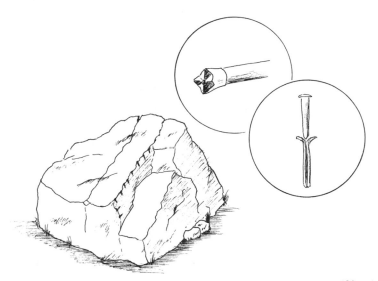

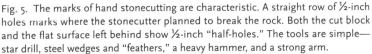

Fig. 5. The marks of hand stonecutting are characteristic. A straight row of ½-inch holes marks where the stonecutter planned to break the rock. Both the cut block and the flat surface left behind show ½-inch "half-holes." The tools are simple— star drill, steel wedges and "feathers," a heavy hammer, and a strong arm.

To cut a block of stone, a stonecutter drilled a series of ½-inch-diameter holes about 3 inches deep and 8 inches apart along the line where he wanted the stone to break. Into each hole he inserted a pair of steel "feathers"—half cylinders with finger grips on the top—aligning them parallel to the desired break. A steel wedge was driven between each pair of feathers until the strain cracked the rock along the line of holes. The resulting block of rock has a rough but relatively flat surface with a row of ½-inch diameter half-holes along one or two edges; the block left behind has the same imprint. Today, you will see many of these rocks still in use. You may also see some rocks that were drilled but never broken free. Seeing such cut stones everywhere on the Cape, you have to admire the strength, patience, and tenacity of the stonecutters, who were often farmers or fishermen in other seasons.

In the last of the glacial re-advances here the Cape Cod Bay lobe of the glacier rode over the northern end of the Buzzards Bay Moraine, depositing its distinctive collection of rocks on top, and sending quantities of sand and gravel southwestward to form the relatively flat land west of the Buzzards Bay Moraine in Bourne and Falmouth. This re-advance also pushed up a small moraine ridge in Cape Cod Bay west of Wellfleet Harbor. The South Channel lobe, east of the Lower Cape, lingered longest, shedding outwash to the west, forming the uplands and plains now stretching from Chatham to Truro. Stellwagen Bank, north of the Lower Cape, also formed in the angle between the Cape Cod Bay lobe and the South Channel lobe as the glacier re-advanced.

But this period of re-advances was only a brief halt in the warming trend. (Geologists have a long view—brief in this case means perhaps 2,000 to 3,000 years.) The climate continued to warm, and the glacier melted rapidly. By about 15,000 years ago the ice had melted to points north of what is now Boston, and by 13,000 years ago most of New England was free of ice.

As the ice melted, some of the meltwater was trapped in short-lived lakes between the glacier and the new moraine ridges. One such lake was in what is now Cape Cod Bay. The centers of Sandwich and Barnstable are built on the gently sloping deltas of sand and gravel deposited at the edge of this temporary lake. Steeper deltas and outwash fans were deposited into the lake from the South Channel lobe to the east, forming parts of the Lower Cape. The lake didn't last long; soon the water found low spots and cut channels in the glacial deposits as it drained back to the ocean. Another lake formed east of the Lower Cape, but it also quickly drained, toward the west and south. With the ice and lakes gone and the ocean still several hundred feet lower than it is today, the new ridge of sand and gravel—now called Cape Cod—was left bare, high and dry.

The Sea Returns

At the glacial maximum, 21,000 years ago, sea level was about 400 feet lower than today. When the glacier began to melt away, the water ran into the ocean, and sea level began to rise. The edge of the ice sheet across southern New England was thin; the melting that exposed a large area of land returned relatively little water to the seas, and sea level rose slowly at first. As the thicker ice to the north began to melt, much greater volumes of water were released, and sea level began to rise more rapidly. By about 10,000 years ago sea level had risen to approximately 110 feet below present levels. Cape Cod was still just a ridge of sand and rocks on the coastal plain, and the shoreline was miles to the southeast. By 6,000 years ago sea level was only 50 feet

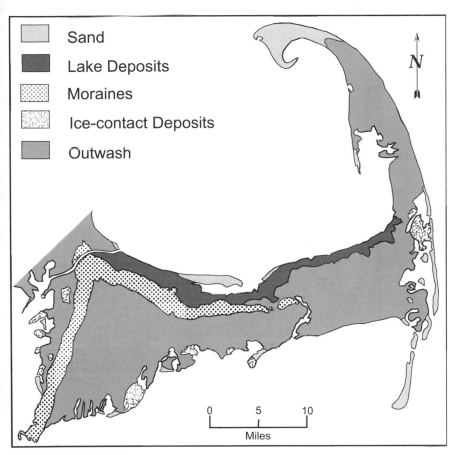

Sand

Lake Deposits

Moraines

Ice-contact Deposits

Outwash

N

0   5   10
Miles

Fig. 6. Geologic map of Cape Cod. A geologic map is a summary of thousands of observations about the shape of the land and the character of the materials it is made of. With this map you can determine the geologic nature of any place on the Cape and know whether to expect, for instance, sandy plains or bouldery hills. Marsh deposits are not shown. The map is generalized from maps by Oldale and others and published by the U.S. Geological Survey.

below today's level; the sea was reaching into bays north and south of the Cape. By this time most of the glacial ice had already melted, so the rate of sea level rise was slowing. About 3,500 years ago, with sea level only 20 or so feet below present level (and the rate of rise slowing further), the sea had risen up around the moraines and outwash plains and had turned our ridge of rocks and sand into a peninsula. Farther to the south only the tops of the highest hills of the Island Moraine and nearby outwash stuck up above water to form the islands of Martha's Vineyard and Nantucket. Since that time the worldwide sea level has gradually risen to its present level.

Meanwhile, the blocks of ice buried under the outwash plains and moraines had been melting. As the blocks of ice melted, the sand and gravel above them collapsed into the spaces where the ice had been. Eventually, when the buried ice had completely melted, hollows were left on the surface. Some of these hollows are now bays flooded by the sea; others, higher on the glacial deposits, are on land. Those land-locked hollows that filled with water, either from rain or groundwater, formed ponds and other wetlands.

As the sea approached its current level, the ocean took over the shaping of Cape Cod: waves eroded the sandy hills along the shore and created bluffs, rapidly cutting back exposed shorelines, especially those facing the open Atlantic. The eroded sand was carried along the foot of the bluffs to form beaches and on across the mouths of bays to form barrier spits. Winds off the water carried beach sand inland to form dunes. Rainwater that previously had sunk deep into the sandy ground and moved underground off to the southeast now began to find seawater filling the spaces between the sand grains all along the shores. Because fresh water is lighter than salt water, it was forced to the surface along the new shoreline as springs.

Fig. 7. These small faceted rocks—ventifacts (the word means made or shaped by the wind)—were once larger and rounded. They were sandblasted into this characteristic shape by the strong winds that swept across the barren landscape after the glacier melted but before vegetation stabilized the surface. These specimens range from 1 to 4 inches across, in the usual size range for ventifacts on the Cape.

Until pioneer plants established themselves here, the wind must have whipped across this expanse of bare, rocky sand and gravel, picking up sand and silt from hills and plains, using it to abrade and polish rocks on the surface, then depositing it in low, protected areas. The rains must have cut deeply into the highest hills and steep slopes, eroding more fine-grained material and depositing it in the swales, leaving boulders exposed on hills and ridges. We don't know how long it was after the ice left that the first plants grew here and began to slow the wind and protect the surface. The oldest known plant remains are pollen of spruce, pine, and *Hudsonia*, among others, from 12,000-year-old freshwater peat deposits. But plants likely grew here before that time, particularly the pioneer grasses and lichens that can grow in bare sand.

SOILS

The soil on the Cape has been much disturbed by farming and deeply eroded in some areas because of land clearing, but where it remains it is the characteristic soil of cool, forested areas with a sandy parent material. Below the uppermost layer of black, decaying plant material, the soil is white or gray—it is mostly quartz sand from which most other minerals, especially the iron-bearing ones, have been leached by water. Below the white zone is a tough, rusty-brown zone where the iron and clays carried down from higher in the soil have been deposited. The white soil layer looks like beach sand, especially where it is carried into a trail by rain. The similarity reflects the weathering and leaching processes, which have removed most minerals other than quartz from both beach sand and the upper layer of the Cape's soil.

Soon after the glacier melted away, but before the buried ice blocks melted, the long, narrow valleys that form the inlets on the south side of the Upper Cape developed. You may not have noticed the upper parts of these valleys, but if you drive between Hyannis and Falmouth on Route 28 you cross twenty-one of them. Watch for a place where the road dips down 20 to 50 feet: it may cross cranberry bogs or a bridge over a small stream, then climb back up to the level of the outwash plain. Though generally shorter and shallower, nine similar valleys occur on the Mid-Cape in Yarmouth and Dennis, and other somewhat similar ones, including the Pamet River, cut the Lower Cape. These unusual valleys are narrow, straight, and without tribu-

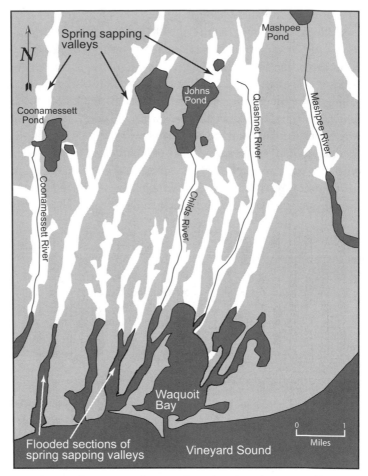

Fig. 8. The straight, narrow valleys in Falmouth and Mashpee are unlike ordinary stream valleys. They were formed by the action of springs undermining the land surface. Waquoit Bay formed where a number of such valleys coalesced at their mouths.

taries, unlike valleys cut by surface rivers. They are also much too big for such small streams as the Red River (in Chatham) or the Quashnet (between Falmouth and Mashpee) that now occupy them. These valleys share many characteristics, indicating that they formed in the same way.

These valleys were cut by water coming out of springs rather than by water running off the surface. At the time these valleys formed, sea level was lower than it is today, but it was rising. Little or no vegetation stabilized the sandy soil, and the ground may have been frozen much of the time. Groundwater came to the surface in springs, just as it does today near the shore, but the shoreline was in areas now below sea level. A valley began where a spring came to the surface; here the sand around the spring was softened by the flowing springwater. The softened sand was easily carried away by the flowing water, allowing the springwater to come to the surface and weaken more sand, a bit farther uphill. Over time, this process of softening and carrying away sand (called spring sapping) caused the spring to reach the surface farther and farther inland. As the springs moved up the groundwater gradient, this process carved narrow, straight valleys.

As these spring-sapping valleys were cut 30 to 50 feet deep in sand, their sides gradually collapsed, widening the valleys and making the slopes less steep. The groundwater table is higher than the floors of these valleys, so the rivers in them generally do not flow out of ponds; they rise where groundwater seeps into the valley and gather additional water as they run to the sea. Rising sea level flooded the lower ends of these valleys, forming inlets such as Great Pond in Falmouth, the Mashpee River estuary in Mashpee, and Bumps River in Centerville.

Today sea level continues to rise. On the Cape, part of the "sea level rise" is actually the land sinking (it is still readjusting after the changes wrought by the glacier); but global sea level has risen between 4 and 8 inches in the last 100 years. Those two factors add up on the Cape to at least 12 inches of sea level rise in the last century. Over the past 60 years global sea level has risen about three times as fast as it did in the previous 2,000 years. Estimates for the future range from 5 to 37 additional inches of rise by 2100—the best estimate is about 19 inches. The current increase in the rate of sea level rise is probably due to the many and increasing human activities that warm the earth. As this accelerated rise in sea level continues, we must expect faster erosion of the land along shorelines, more rapid rearrangement of beaches and sand spits, and the gradual encroachment of seawater into marshes, streams, and coastal ponds. Although similar changes happened during the past 18,000 years, we now have both a stake in the outcome and a front-row seat.

For Cape Cod, Geology Is Destiny

Cape Cod is an irregular ridge of sand, rock, and gravel only a little above sea level. Its soil is thin, acidic, and sandy. In the coastal bluffs are the mixed rocks and sand of the glacial deposits, exposed by the work of the rising sea. The sea also makes, reshapes, and moves beaches and barrier islands. The boulder-strewn hills from the Elizabeth Islands to Bourne and on to Barnstable are the piles of rocks and sand dropped by the glacier and pushed up by the ice into high moraines. The gently sloping plains are the outwash, formed of sand and gravel carried away from the front of the glacier by streams of water. Both the hills and the plains are pitted with hundreds of ponds and wetlands. Now you know why this is so.

The rocks, sand, and gravel that make up Cape Cod all came from somewhere else; they were collected by the glacial ice as it moved south across eastern North America. The great variety of rock types that you will find here is the result of this eclectic collecting. But the bulk of the rocks on the Cape are various types of granite. Granite is a very common rock across New England and is also strong and resistant to wear. As a result, lots of granitic rocks were picked up by the glacier, and many of them survived to melt out into the moraines and outwash plains of the Cape and Islands. You can recognize granites when you see them on the beach, as the boulders on the moraine or in a breakwater, or in the foundation of an old building: they are the speckled rocks, made mostly of pale gray and white minerals (quartz and feldspar), usually with some small grains of black, iron-bearing minerals, and often with some pink feldspar crystals. Granites form deep in the earth's crust from melted rock. These bodies of molten rock cool and crystallize slowly, giving time for the crystals to grow large. Later erosion exposed such granites at the surface across the Northeast. Eventually some were picked up and transported here by the glacier.

Whether we are thinking of the shape of the land, the nature of the ground, the environment that determines which plants live here, or where our drinking water comes from, an understanding of the glacial origin of the Cape underpins all our knowledge of the nature of Cape Cod.

How Do We Know?

Geologists have learned the geologic story of Cape Cod by looking at the evidence left by its formation—the shape of the land and the materials it is made of. By comparing this evidence with places around the globe where land is being shaped and new surfaces are being formed, geologists have found that only glaciers produce the kinds of features we see here on Cape Cod. The dates of the parts of the story come from measuring the radioactive decay of one or another element in shells, plants, and other organic materials, a modern technique that early geologists did not have available. As with all stories reconstructed from scraps of circumstantial evidence left behind after the action is over, the story of the glacial formation of Cape Cod can only be partially confirmed. Although we certainly believe that the basic story is correct, our understanding must always be open to changes and additions as evidence is found or reinterpreted.

ENVIRONMENTS

WOODLANDS

Today so much of the Cape is wooded that one might think that it was always so. But a walk in any woodland here will show you that this is not the forest primeval; the spindly trees in many places suggest that this is not even the forest medieval. In the almost four hundred years since the first European colonists arrived, all the original forests have been cut, and cut again. Trees were cut for firewood, to clear fields for farming, for lumber to build houses and ships, for fence posts, and for fuel for local industries such as making salt, glass, pine tar, and brick. The woods we see today have grown only after those uses of the land ended. (See page 96 for drawings and descriptions of Cape Cod's trees.)

Many parts of Cape Cod, especially on the outwash plains, are covered with a scrubby woods of Pitch Pine and oak. Because these "pine barrens" are characteristic of such large areas, it is tempting to think of these woods as a regrowth of the original forest of Cape Cod. The reports of early explorers and settlers suggest otherwise. In 1602 the English explorer Bartholomew Gosnold named Cape Cod for the

Fig. 9. Pitch Pine (*Pinus rigida*). The 3-inch needles of this small native pine grow in bundles of three, surrounded by a papery wrapper at the base.

Codfish that sustained his expedition, and on the Elizabeth Islands found

> High timbered oaks…, cedars, straight and tall; beech, elm,
> holly; walnut trees in abundance … hazelnut trees, cherry
> trees, sassafras trees in great plenty all the island over … also
> divers other fruit trees.

William Bradford reported that the hills surrounding Provincetown harbor, where the *Mayflower* anchored in 1620, were "all wooded with oaks, pines, sassafras, juniper, birch, holly, some ash, walnut…."

Even allowing for hyperbole and misidentification, it is clear that from the exposed Elizabeth Islands in the southwest to the sandy hills of Provincetown on the east, the Cape bore a forest similar to that on the mainland of New England: a mixture of hardwood (deciduous) and softwood (evergreen) trees. No one mentions "scrub" anything.

In the 1850s, after the Cape had been subjected to two hundred years of farming and woodcutting, Henry David Thoreau did find scrubby trees, where he found any trees at all. He commented repeatedly on the barren sand plains of the Lower Cape. He also reported the beginnings of reforestation on the denuded hills:

> The country was, for the most part, bare, or with only a little
> scrubby wood left on the hills. We noticed in Yarmouth and
> … Dennis large tracts where pitch-pines were planted four or
> five years before.

On the Upper and Mid-Cape more wooded areas remained, especially on the moraine hills—Thoreau heard of a "large tract of wood running down the centre of the Cape from Sandwich, three miles wide and thirty long…," but in many areas there was deforestation on the same scale as on the Lower Cape. Photos from as late as the 1890s show wide sweeps of treeless pasture or "mowing" in areas that are woodland today. Although woodlots remained, most of the land was treeless, and views of the sea could be had from almost every hillock.

By the end of the 1800s, however, trees were beginning to return. In Falmouth in the 1870s "summer people" bought farms and woodlots and started planting trees on the estates they created. Trees were planted around village greens and houses all across the Cape. Pitch Pines, White Pines, and Black Locusts were planted to slow soil erosion or the encroachment of dunes. Subsistence farming became less important by the late 1800s, and farm fields were abandoned to trees. Over time these various trees grew into the woodlands on the Cape today.

What the Trees Tell Us

Today's woodlands give evidence of the history of land use in the area, and the trees tell us something about their individual histories. At any wooded location, looking closely at the species of trees and the sizes, shapes, and growth patterns of both the trees and the forest can reveal some of the history of that patch of woods.

The shape of the crown of a tree can show whether it grew in thick woods or in a field. Trees with wide-spreading crowns and branches low on the trunk grew in the open, with no competition for sunlight. Trees that have few low branches and a tall, narrow crown grew in a forest where they had to grow tall to find the sun. In some places you can see an occasional wide-spreading old tree (most often White

Fig. 10. Large American Beech (*Fagus grandifolia*) in forest of younger trees. The tree in the foreground grew in an open field with no competition for sun, as shown by the low, wide-spreading branches. The thin younger trees had to compete with each other and the big Beech for sunlight, so they grew tall, shed their lower branches, and produced upward-reaching upper branches.

Environments

Pine, beech, or oak) surrounded by narrow younger trees. The wide-spreading tree may have been left for shade in a pasture or it might have grown along a fence that protected it from grazing or mowing. When pastures were abandoned and coal replaced firewood as the major heat source, trees reclaimed the area; they grew up around the old "wolf tree," competing with it and each other for sunlight.

Many of the largest-diameter White Pines have forked trunks beginning 10 or 15 feet above the ground. When these trees were younger their tops were damaged by insects or high winds, and several side branches grew upward, forming new trunks. These forked trees were sometimes left when other trees were cut because they didn't provide much useful lumber; now they are larger than their younger compatriots.

Trees with multiple trunks also hold evidence of the past. Many locust, maple, and oak trees have two or three trunks beginning close to the ground. These trees sprout new branches from cut stumps, and those branches grow into trunks. You can estimate how long ago a tree was cut by the age of the sprouted trunks, and you can sometimes get an idea of the size of the tree that was cut by estimating the diameter of the stump from which the new shoots grew.

Here and there in the woods you may find a cluster of saplings with long, toothed leaves, perhaps 20 to 25 feet tall, growing near a standing, dead trunk. These are remnants of the mighty American Chestnuts that once constituted a significant proportion of the woods of the East. These saplings are root sprouts, growing from the roots of the trees whose aboveground portions were wiped out by the chestnut blight that spread across the United States starting in the early 1900s. Such young sprouts are infected also, and probably do not live long enough to produce seed. But they are here, putting out the large, striking leaves that most people never expected to see in their lives, and giving evidence of the forest's former glory. Over time these sprouts may develop resistance to the blight, but research is trying to speed the process and bring back those graceful, wide-spreading trees.

Most Sassafras trees on the Cape are hardly more than saplings; the biggest have trunks only 6 to 8 inches in diameter. We tend to think of the trees that produce those varied mitten leaves as the 97-pound weaklings of the forests. But wait until they grow up! Sassafras does not grow tall, reaching only 40 feet or so, but there are records of Sas-

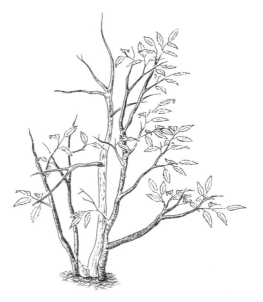

Fig. 11. American Chestnut (*Castanea dentata*). These sprouts grow from the roots of a tree whose aboveground parts were killed back by the chestnut blight.

safras trees with trunks 3 feet in diameter. So what do the spindly Cape Cod Sassafrases tell us? Probably that Sassafras was harvested here until recently for the aromatic bark of its roots. This was long used as a tonic (packets of Sassafras are still sold in health food stores here) and for perfume in soap and cosmetics. Sassafras was one of the precious products of the New World that Gosnold took home to England; it supposedly was a cure for various terrible diseases, including syphilis. Although it hasn't been thought of as a miracle cure for a long time, its other uses produced a small income for the local farmers. Today's thickets of Sassafras are root sprouts just attaining tree size after centuries of cutting for those uses.

Other than the trees that sprout from stumps or roots, the earliest trees to colonize abandoned fields are the Red Cedars and the pines. The seedlings of these trees need direct sunshine to survive; they will have none of the filtered shade of the deep woods. That is why pine and Red Cedar seedlings often cover a road cut just a few years after road construction—they will only sprout in open areas. A stand of Red Cedars and pines may indicate that the ground they occupy is an abandoned field or pasture.

Fig. 12. Leaves of the Sassafras tree (*Sassafras albidum*). Most Sassafras trees have leaves of all three types, but older trees have a higher proportion of the simple oval leaves.

Forest Dynamics

Because farming ended within the last hundred years on much of the Cape, there are many areas where pine woods have recently taken over abandoned fields. But if you look in the shade of those pines you will not find young pines. You will find hardwoods like oaks, beeches, and maples. Pine seedlings may not like shade, but those of hardwoods do. This means that (barring a forest fire or a destructive infestation of human beings with axes or chain saws) as the pioneer pines die they will be replaced by a mixture of the hardwood trees that have been growing in their shade. Pines will seed in a clearing caused by a hurricane or the aforementioned plague of humans, but they are unlikely to become the dominant tree again unless the land is completely cleared.

Some parts of the Cape may have had fire-adapted Pitch Pine forests well before Europeans arrived. Both anecdotal and archaeological evidence indicates that fires were set or used by native peoples to provide clearings for agriculture and to improve the hunting. The land-use practices of the European settlers stripped the soil and may have contributed to the expansion of Pitch Pine forests, even without the planting that Thoreau noticed. Pitch Pines are flammable trees, but they are also well adapted to surviving and regrowing after fire; burned areas are more likely to return as pure stands of Pitch Pine. Pitch Pines can sprout from their roots, they can put out new branches and needles from their trunks, and some of their cones do not open until heated by a fire. The South Mashpee Pine Barrens (see site 13) are an example of the pine barrens that result from fire; there are many others, especially on the Lower Cape. Fire is actually necessary for the continued existence of pine barrens; given enough time without fire, other trees will shade out the Pitch Pines.

The moraine hills of the Upper and Mid-Cape have more varied trees than the outwash plains. The soil is somewhat richer, few areas were plowed, and the hills were never completely cleared, providing a wider variety of seeds to reestablish forests when the fields were abandoned. In some of these areas woods have been growing for more than a hundred years. That has not been long enough to give us back all the features of the mature forests of yore, but at least we see many of the species that grew here before the wholesale clearing: American Chestnut, American Beech, Sassafras, Hop-hornbeam, hickory, ash, and birch well as the more common oaks and pines.

One of the reasons that it is possible to read land-use history in the plants of a wooded area is that different plants respond differently to various kinds of disturbances. Pitch Pines become dominant in response to repeated fires, for instance, whereas hickories and maples may not survive. Similarly, pines quickly reclaim abandoned fields, followed by some of the oaks, but other oaks may not return, or may return only slowly and sparsely, to fields that were plowed. Dwarf Chinquapin Oak and Bear Oak are of this latter type; the presence of numbers of these small trees suggests the area has not been plowed. Some of the understory plants are also good indicators of whether a field was plowed: Wintergreen, Trailing Arbutus, Black Huckleberry, and several of the low blueberry species colonize plowed ground very slowly. Their absence in many areas on the Cape strongly suggests plowing, though severe soil erosion may also prevent their growth.

Life among the Trees

A forest is not just a stand of trees. The trees create a microclimate around and beneath them that cuts the wind and reduces the amount of sunshine reaching the ground, as well as changing the soil and the availability of water and nutrients. The invisible parts of the trees—the roots—move water and nutrients, knit the soil together, and provide a substrate for the crucial decomposing fungi whose threads permeate the soil. Because the fungi are visible only when they produce their fruiting bodies—mushrooms—we tend to forget their presence. Plants, however, have constant relationships with these fungi; some can not live without them. Many other plants and many animals live preferentially in, under, and around the trees of a forest, taking advantage of the conditions and habitat made by the trees. Some of these forest dwellers are obvious, such as the understory of shrubs that makes cross-country walking difficult, or the jays and squirrels that bring themselves noisily to your attention. Others, both animal and vegetable, are more obscure. Each of these organisms lives in the woods instead of in open country for its own good reasons, and each has developed ways of taking advantage of that environment.

WOODLAND PLANTS

A number of attractive flowering plants grow most commonly in the woods. Some leaf out and bloom early in the season while the ground is moist and sun warms the forest floor through the bare branches. Others, generally shrubs, bloom later, even at the end of summer, after months of warmer but shaded growth beneath the trees. (See page 120 for illustrations and details of Cape Cod's common plants.)

One of the earliest-blooming flowers is Trailing Arbutus, also known as Mayflower, despite its early April flowers. (The English Mayflower, for which both the Pilgrims' ship and this plant were named, does bloom in May.) Trailing Arbutus has fragrant pink or white flowers tucked among its fuzzy evergreen leaves on plants 1 or 2

Fig. 13. Trailing Arbutus (*Epigaea repens*). You may have to crouch down and peer beneath the fuzzy leaves of this low plant to find the fragrant flowers.

inches high. It grows especially well on banks where it doesn't get buried in dead leaves. Another woodland flower with a similar name, Canada Mayflower, has a single rolled leaf that looks like a tiny Tulip as it comes up, but the small spike of flowers is more like a minuscule white Hyacinth. It blooms in late May or early June. To further confuse the "May———" flower story, Maystar is a small starlike white flower, usually with seven petals. It does bloom in May, its delicate stem rising above a whorl of lance-shaped leaves.

Wintergreen may be the most common ground cover in the woods. This low plant, also called Teaberry and Checkerberry, has shiny inch-long oval evergreen leaves. The blossoms are not showy—white bells beneath the leaves—but the red berries that follow persist all winter. Wintergreen flavoring is named for this plant, and the plant was named because it is ... green in winter. Both berries and leaves contain wintergreen oil—taste the berries and smell a crushed leaf. Spotted Pipsissewa is common in areas where Wintergreen grows. Its 1- to 3-inch toothed, white-marked leaves also grow close to the ground; its small white flowers rise several inches higher.

Late spring brings the Pink Lady's Slipper, an orchid that is quite abundant in many woodlands despite the disturbances of the past three hundred years; the rootstocks of Lady's Slipper can survive woodcutting, fire, and grazing, and may return after plowing. Their presence suggests an area that was not stripped of vegetation to the point of major soil loss. In shady woods these plants rarely bloom two years in a row, needing several years to build up the resources to flower. In dense woods they may cease to bloom until fire, wind, or insects reduce the shade. The two distinctively pleated basal leaves last all summer. The Lady's Slipper needs the network of fungus in its native soil and rarely survives transplantation. It doesn't do well if picked, either.

Sheep Laurel blooms from late May into summer. Its red-pink flowers are shaped like half-size versions of the commonly cultivated Mountain Laurel. The flowers of these plants are built to ensure cross-pollination; spring-loaded stamens flip up when touched and stick their pollen onto the back of the bee (or the tip of your finger—try it). Sheep Laurel is also known as Lambkill because its foliage is poisonous to domestic animals.

Swamp Azalea is one of the most fragrant flowers on the Cape. The trumpet-shaped white blossoms attract the eye against the dark back-

Fig. 14. Sheep Laurel (*Kalmia angustifolia*). When not in bloom this small shrub is recognizable by the drooping, gray-green leaves.

ground of leaves, but more often people find this tall shrub by following its fragrance. It tends to grow in damp places, as the name would indicate, but can also be found in drier parts of the woods. Swamp Azalea is also called Clammy Azalea because the outside of the blossom is covered with sticky hairs.

Sweet Pepperbush is a large shrub that produces fragrant spikes of small white flowers in July and August. The peppercorn-size seed capsules persist all winter, making the plant easy to identify even when it has no leaves. It, too, will grow in damp areas but also is found in dry ground.

Blueberries and huckleberries (they are difficult to tell apart except by how many seeds the berries have) grow thickly as understory in many woods and produce their small pink or white bell-shaped flowers in late spring. If you want berries, however, you should find bushes growing in the sun; they will grow in the shade but produce few berries there. This is why the blueberry barrens in Maine and Nova Scotia are burned over every few years.

Another common group of plants in the understory is the viburnums, tall shrubs with flat clusters of small white flowers followed by blue or red berries. Arrowwood, one of the most common, grows long straight shoots that were reputedly used by native peoples for making arrow shafts.

In some woodland plants the flowers are small and are not the most obvious characteristic. One of the most assertive of these is Catbrier, which with the similar Greenbrier is sometimes called "Devil's Tangle" and other less polite names. These are native vines with roundish leaves, smooth green bark, and wicked thorns. The branches of Catbrier can grow to 30 feet, clinging to trees or bushes with tendrils like those of pea plants. Old vines can be as much as ⅜ of an inch in diameter; young vines are sometimes so thin that they are hardly noticeable until you try to walk through them, when the thorns bring them forcibly to your attention. A thick growth of Catbrier can knit trees together into an impenetrable barrier; heavy snow on such a mass of vines may break the supporting trees. Despite its thorns, this green vine is browsed by deer and rabbits, especially in the winter—look for the neatly clipped stubs left by rabbits and ragged ones left by deer.

Sweet Fern is a 2- to 3-foot shrub related to Bayberries that forms thickets in open woods and along the edges of woods. The name is half right—the leaves have a spicy-sweet fragrance, but this is not a fern. The misnomer gives a clue to the shape of the leaves, however: long and narrow with many lobes on each side, like a fern. Unlike ferns, this is a woody shrub with leathery leaves. The catkins look something like the ones on birch trees. The fragrant leaves were used to stuff mattresses before the days of innersprings.

Lichens (pronounced "lye′ ken") are so common that they may go unnoticed. According to the old mnemonic, lichens are "algae that took a *likin'* to a fungus"—get it? That is, algae and fungus living together, making a new composite plant. The algae make food by photosynthesis, and the transparent threads of the fungus protect the algae and attach to the rock or tree. Flat-growing or leafy lichens form white, orange, gray-green, or black patches on trees or rocks, and tufts of fibrous gray-green lichen grow on many hardwood trees, where they are most visible in winter. Lichens also grow on rock walls and brick and stone buildings (the orange *Xanthoria* lichen is quite common near the seashore), and pale-gray mounds of the lichen known as Reindeer Moss sprout on bare ground. Lichens can colonize new surfaces within a year or two, and some may grow visibly from month to month, but growth is often very slow. Lichens can grow on bare soil and rock; they produce acids that break down the minerals in rock and thus are a part of the process of soil formation. Once you notice lichens, you will see them everywhere on the Cape and will never again think of tree trunks as plain brown.

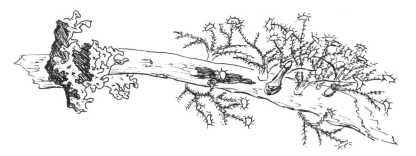

Fig. 15. Lichen on twig. *Right*, Old Man's Beard (*Usnea* sp.); *left*, a leafy type. Few lichens have common names.

Another group of interesting plants in the woodlands is the club mosses. These ancient evergreen plants suggest miniature pine trees—none is more than 8 inches high. The club mosses, which go by common names such as Ground Pine and Creeping Jenny, have trailing stems with short, upright branches and fine, shiny green needles. They are most noticeable in the fall and winter when the bright green needles shine among the fallen leaves. Club mosses were once much collected for Christmas decorating. Because they reproduce by spores (a process that is chancier than seed reproduction) and may take twenty years from spore to tiny new plant, club mosses grow back slowly, if at all, when plants are damaged or removed. In the fall the spores are borne at the tops of the branches in upright yellowish-brown spore bodies like candles in candelabra. The spores are extremely light and flammable; in the early days of photography they were one of the main constituents of flash powder.

WOODLAND ANIMALS

Birds are the most common and visible animals in woodlands, especially in spring as they stake out territories. (An annotated list of birds frequently seen on the Cape is on page 136.) In woodlands you may see or hear Bobwhites or Towhees on the ground, sparrows in the thickets, and birds as different as the elusive Brown Creeper, the noisy Blue Jay, and singing warblers in various parts of the trees. The size of a patch of woods has a big effect on what birds can live successfully there. For many birds the woodland edges are unattractive, especially as nesting sites, because they are more exposed to weather and predators. These "edge effects" make large, unbroken blocks of conservation land particularly valuable to many creatures. Some of the most familiar birds, of course, prefer the edge habitats and successfully live around towns: Cardinals, Blue Jays, and Robins are examples.

Most woodland animals other than birds are nocturnal; although White-tailed Deer, Skunks, Opossums, Flying Squirrels, Red Foxes, Raccoons, and Coyotes live in or near woodlands, they are not seen reliably. The most likely time to see them is in early morning or at dusk, but you may see their footprints in mud, sand, or fresh snow any time of day. Coyotes are relatively recent arrivals on the Cape, having been known to breed here only since the early 1980s. They have adapted quickly to the broken-up woods and towns of the Cape. Coyotes are omnivores and eat everything from berries and grasshoppers to rabbits and mice, when they can catch them. They have been known to hunt cats and other small pets.

Squirrels, on the other hand, can be seen at almost any time. Look high in the trees for the brown leafballs that are the Gray Squirrels' winter houses. You may see the "kitchen midden" beneath a squirrel's favorite dining branch: broken acorn hulls, hickory nutshells carefully gnawed open, and the scales and "cone cobs" of pinecones that have been chewed apart to extract the seeds. (How do they get the pitch off the roofs of their mouths?) In late summer it is common to find cut-off tips of pine branches on the ground beneath pine trees.

Fig. 16. Squirrel kitchen midden. The squirrel that made this midden had access to a variety of trees including pine, hickory, and oak. Most middens consist of piles of chewed-off scales and cone cobs—there is much more waste per nut with pinecones than with acorns or hickory nuts.

They were dropped by squirrels harvesting the cones growing on them. Red Squirrels live commonly along the north side of the Cape but are local elsewhere; they are most common in White Pines. (Flying Squirrels also make middens of hulls and shells, but these nocturnal creatures are rarely seen.) Chipmunks, small tan ground squirrels with black and white stripes down their backs, live in burrows under rocks or logs and whisk busily about on the ground. They seem to be unevenly distributed, more common on the hills of the moraine than on the outwash plains, perhaps because burrow sites are easier to find on the moraine. They sleep during the winter but do not hibernate, waking up occasionally to eat from their stashes of nuts and seeds.

Red-backed Salamanders are sometimes found under logs or drifts of leaves in the woods (or in a backyard if it is not too civilized). Unlike their wetland kin, Red-backed Salamanders can live in dry woods. They survive by being active mostly at night, when it is cool and dewy. If you find one under a log, be sure to put the log back just as it was when you are finished looking. No lizards live on Cape Cod.

MOORS AND GRASSLANDS

The harsh, treeless moors and grasslands are populated by tough, low plants. On moors the plants are chiefly members of the heath family: Bearberry, Broom Crowberry, and Poverty Grass; in grasslands, grasses. These environments developed on the Cape as the result of fire, dry, sandy soils, strong, sometimes salty winds, grazing, and logging. Today only the soils and the wind remain as significant factors in plant distribution—fire, logging, and grazing being generally incompatible with housing developments. As a result, grasslands and moors are much reduced from their historic extent.

Grasslands still survive in a few farm fields and old cemeteries, along the edges of airports and old roads, and in areas burned or mowed by wildlife managers to provide habitat for species such as Sandplain Gerardia and Bobwhites. Moors survive, where they have not reverted to woods or been displaced by buildings, mostly on the dunelands of the Lower Cape and in a few similar coastal areas.

Fig. 17. Butterfly Weed (*Asclepias tuberosa*). This member of the milkweed family grows to about 2 feet and produces brilliant orange flowers in the typical milkweed shape.

Grasslands are defined by the presence of grasses, but flowers like Butter-and-Eggs, Queen Anne's Lace, Blue-eyed Grass, asters, violets, goldenrods, and milkweeds are commonly seen in meadows. Because grasslands are an unusual habitat on the Cape, some grassland plants are rare. One of the most beautiful is the orange Butterfly Weed, which indeed is much frequented by butterflies. If you see some, don't pick them; collect some seeds and grow the plant in your garden or meadow—it grows easily from seed. (Despite the fact that they are mowed, lawns and golf greens do not qualify as meadows—the grass monoculture provides little food or habitat for creatures, and most native grassland plants are treated as weeds.)

Butterflies and other insects that are attracted to meadow flowers are more common in the open habitats of moors and grasslands than in woodlands. A number of birds also prefer these environments, in part because of the insects. In summer Bobolinks, Bluebirds, Horned Larks, and Eastern Kingbirds nest or feed around grasslands and moors. Sparrows, Horned Larks, and Redpolls frequent them in winter. Foxes and Coyotes hunt the birds, Meadow Voles, Short-tailed Shrews, and Cottontail Rabbits through the grass and shrubs. Hawks often patrol here looking for the same prey, as do Short-eared Owls, which can sometimes be seen in daylight.

Before humans arrived on the Cape, small areas of native grasslands and moors were probably maintained by occasional natural fires or drifting sand. The native peoples created more grasslands and moors through their use of fire to clear agricultural fields, increase forage for game animals, and maintain areas of food plants such as blueberries.

European settlers rapidly increased the amount of both grassland and moors on the Cape by clearing forested land for pastures and farm fields. From colonial times to the middle of the 1800s meadow birds such as Bluebirds and Meadowlarks were familiar in farmlands. But as farms were abandoned during the past 150 years, these habitats have reverted to woods to such an extent that Bluebirds and other field creatures have become uncommon. Over this same period the Heath Hen, a relative of the Prairie Chicken that lived in open habitats along much of the East Coast, was driven to extinction. A small population survived into the 1900s on Martha's Vineyard, but such remnant populations are especially vulnerable to disturbance and reduced fertility, and this one was no exception.

Coastal moors are more likely to be replaced by human landscaping than by trees, because a corollary of their unique environment is the splendid ocean views that attract development. The inland moors and blueberry barrens on the Cape, however, were largely artifacts of human disturbance; blueberries and huckleberries survived in areas denuded by the felling of the forests and the grazing of sheep. Those moors have rapidly reverted to forest.

WATER, WATER EVERYWHERE: FRESHWATER ENVIRONMENTS

To the visitor from the mountains of the Northeast or the arid West, Cape Cod has one startling feature: water. It is not the ocean that is surprising (writers from Thoreau to Rachel Carson have talked about the sea around us, and visitors expect it); rather it is the more immediate and pervasive fresh water. Ponds, marshes, and swamps are everywhere.

The Cape shares this characteristic with Minnesota, the "Land of Ten Thousand Lakes," and has wetlands for the same reason—both areas were covered by the southern edge of the last glacier of the Ice Age. In both places the melting of the glacier left irregular terrain with deep depressions where buried blocks of ice melted at last, allowing the ground on top to collapse. These depressions are called "kettle holes" for their round, steep-sided shape. Some kettle holes are dry, but many are filled with water.

Where Does the Water Come From?

The ponds and other wetlands on the Cape contain more water than falls as rain or snow into each little basin. But few surface streams run out of the wetlands here, and even fewer run in. The water in Cape Cod wetlands comes mainly from groundwater, not runoff.

On the Cape most of the rain that falls sinks into the ground—the Cape, after all, is made of porous sand and gravel deposits. Underground, the water fills the spaces among the sand grains—this is what is known as groundwater. A cup full of dry sand has room for about ¼ cup of water among the grains—try it. Water seeps slowly down among the grains until it reaches something that keeps it from going deeper, like the bottom of your cup of sand. Across most of the Cape this bottom is either bedrock or a layer of impermeable clay generally less than 250 feet down. Around the shores of the Cape the bottom is salt water, on which the fresh groundwater floats. The groundwater

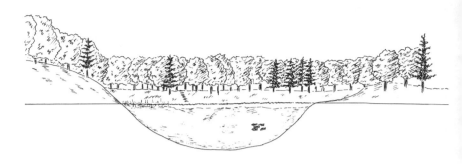

Fig. 18. Where a kettle hole dips beneath the water table, groundwater fills the depression and forms a pond. This pond shows characteristic steep slopes above the water.

moves down and outward along this bottom toward the shoreline, where it runs out into streams, estuaries, and coastal waters. The top surface of the layer of fresh water is called the water table.

Anywhere that the water table is higher than the bottom of a kettle hole, water will flow into the kettle and form a pond or other wetland. So wetlands on Cape Cod are windows on the groundwater: they allow us to see the groundwater at that point. During a prolonged drought the level of water in ponds and other wetlands drops, because the water below ground keeps moving down and little new water is added from precipitation. Pond levels also drop during very cold winters when most of the precipitation is snow; during the spring melt the ponds and wetlands fill again. Conversely, during extended periods of very heavy rainfall the wetlands can fill above their usual levels, to the consternation of those who have burrows or basements too close to water level.

The water table of the Cape is not all connected. The groundwater is separated into six lenses, so called because the water-filled area is shaped something like a simple lens: thicker at the center with gently curving surfaces. The edges of each lens are low areas where the fresh water emerges above the surface and runs into streams or bays. The largest body of groundwater is the Sagamore lens, which underlies the Upper Cape and the Mid-Cape towns of Barnstable and Yarmouth; it runs from Woods Hole and Bourne east to Bass River. Dennis, Brewster, Harwich, Chatham, and Orleans share the Monomoy lens, while the Lower Cape has a series of small lenses. These bodies of groundwater, small and large, all work the same way, though the details of ele-

Environments

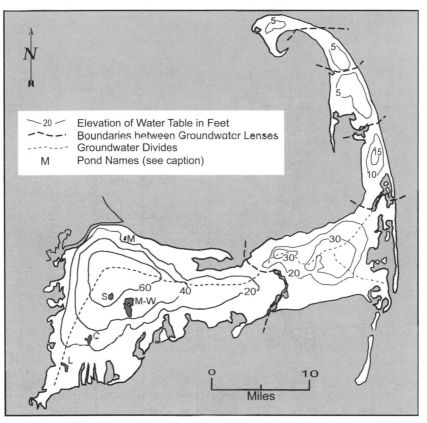

ENVIRONMENTS

Fig. 19. All the water on the Cape comes from groundwater—water in municipal water systems, water from private wells, and the water in ponds, wetlands, and streams. The contour lines show the elevation of the water table in the six Cape groundwater lenses. The ponds shown are S, Snake Pond, Sandwich; M, Shawme Lake (also called Mill Pond), Sandwich; M-W, Mashpee-Wakeby Ponds; C, Coonamessett Pond, Falmouth; and L, Long Pond, Falmouth. Adapted from U.S. Geological Survey Hydrographic Atlas 692.

vation and distance vary among them. The water table is highest where the land is highest. The highest part of the Sagamore lens is on the northern section of the Massachusetts Military Reservation, where the land is about 150 to 200 feet above sea level. The surface of Snake Pond in Sandwich, and of the groundwater at that point, is 68 feet above sea level. The water table drops in all directions from the high land, as does the elevation of pond surfaces. Mashpee-Wakeby Ponds are 55 feet above sea level, Coonamessett Pond is 33 feet, Falmouth's Long

Pond 11 feet, and Shawme or Mill Pond, in Sandwich Center, only 16 feet above sea level.

The groundwater in the Sagamore lens moves down and away from its highest elevation toward the shores at a rate of about 1 foot per day. That means that some of the water that people are drinking today from Long Pond, Falmouth's reservoir, may have fallen as rain or snow on the highest land 8 miles inland more than a hundred years ago. The situation is similar in the other lenses.

Ponds

Cape Codders outdo even the laconic Minnesotans in understatement by labeling the extensive and varied bodies of water on the Cape "ponds." Some are, indeed, small and shallow, no more than duck ponds, but many are deep and large enough to be called lakes anywhere else. Perhaps as recompense for this slight, ponds larger than 10 acres carry the more dignified title of "great pond," and are owned by the state even if the land surrounding them is private.

WHY "ROUND POND"?

Nearly every town on the Cape has a Round Pond, and there are a dozen others just as round but with more historic names like Hog, Hoxie, Nye, or Shubael Pond. These ponds are so nearly round that they gave the general name of "kettle pond" to ponds formed by buried blocks of glacial ice. Why are there so many round ponds?

The smallest ponds probably were fairly round when the little block of ice that formed them first melted, because loose sand and gravel falls into a smooth slope. But many of the ponds that are now round started out as irregular depressions formed by large, irregular blocks of ice. These ponds have become round by the action of wind-driven waves. Waves carry sand and silt along a pond's shore and deposit it on the lee sides of points or in shallow water, thus filling depressions and building smooth, curved sand spits across coves. Look for evidence of this history at the edges of many rounded ponds.

DEEP POND AND OTHER IMPONDERABLES

Cape Codders gave their ponds practical, no-nonsense names: there are at least ten Long Ponds (long and narrow), eight Flax Ponds (Flax was soaked in standing water preparatory to making linen for weaving), uncounted Mill Ponds (look for the dams), a number of Round

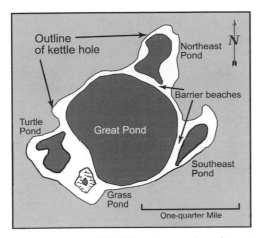

Fig. 20. Great Pond, Wellfleet, is a round pond in an irregular kettle hole. That kettle hole originally held an irregular pond, but barrier beaches built across the coves, creating the round central pond and the small peripheral ponds.

Ponds (any doubt about their shape?), three Spectacle Ponds (two round ponds connected by a narrow strait), and a sprinkling of Fresh, Sandy, Shallow, Crooked, Grassy, and Muddy Ponds. Most of these names are descriptive and well earned, but pay no mind to the Deep Ponds. There are some very deep ponds on the Cape and not a one of them is called Deep Pond. Mashpee Pond is 87 feet deep, Long Pond in Falmouth is 77 feet deep, and Cliff Pond in Brewster is 88 feet deep. By contrast, one of the Deep Ponds in Falmouth is 28 feet deep, and the greatest depth of the other is only 13 feet; other Deep Ponds are hardly more impressive.

The true deep ponds tend to have colder water than shallower ponds, and most are "two-story" ponds, that is, ponds that have warm water on top and colder water below. Fishermen are interested in the water structure of a pond because different kinds of fish live preferentially in different water temperatures. Shallow ponds tend to warm all the way to the bottom in the spring through a combination of mixing by the wind and "density mixing"; these processes warm only the surface layer of deep ponds. Density mixing occurs when surface water warms after the winter. Because water actually gets denser as it warms from 32°F to 39°F, the warming water at the surface sinks, exposing more cold water to be warmed. As the water column warms toward

Freshwater

47

39°F (doesn't sound very warm, does it?) the density difference decreases and density mixing stops, leaving the deep water at about 39°F while the surface water warms toward swimming temperatures.

The layer of dense, cold (and in brackish ponds, salty) water at the bottom of deep ponds can become depleted of oxygen. In this water decomposition is carried on by anaerobic bacteria, which give off hydrogen sulfide. Every few years, usually because of strong winds oriented along the length of the pond, the water in such a pond may "turn over," or mix all the way to the bottom. That this has happened becomes quite clear downwind, because of the rotten-egg smell of hydrogen sulfide. Siders Pond in Falmouth is one such pond. It has turned over twice in the past fifteen years, becoming brackish top to bottom and releasing a truly impressive sulfurous smell.

WHITHER THE POND

Like all holes in the ground, ponds tend to collect whatever is going around. Leaves and dust blow in, mud and sand wash in, dead algae and plants sink to the bottom. Even without human help ponds eventually fill in. Shallow ponds may become bogs or swamps, and then woods, in a few hundred years. Deep ponds will take thousands of years. As long as there is land higher than the pond, that land will shed sediment and organic material into the pond and gradually fill it. This is a natural process.

Human activity may speed up the process. Agriculture, foot traffic, or grazing may strip plants from the bank, increasing erosion. Ponds have sometimes been filled in for roads or buildings, and thoughtless disposal of yard waste or trash in or around ponds can fill them more quickly. But human activity may damage or destroy these fragile habitats by increasing the nitrogen and phosphorus in the water, causing an unusual growth of algae. In pristine ponds the growth of algae is limited by the availability of these nutrients. The ecosystem of the pond is adapted to that limitation; fish, plants, and all the other members of the community are in balance under those conditions. But in the last few decades development has added phosphorus and nitrogen to many of our ponds from the gray water and sewage output of thousands of houses. Most houses direct their sewage into septic tanks where the solids are broken down by bacteria, and the liquids, laden with nitrogen and phosphorus, leach into the ground and thence into . . . the ponds and bays of the Cape via the groundwater.

Fig. 21. Buttonbush (*Cephalanthus occidentalis*). This characteristic shrub of pond edges may grow to 10 feet.

This large new input of nutrients overwhelms the ecosystem of the pond. The only organisms that can take advantage of such fertilization are some previously uncommon fast-growing algae. These algae multiply rapidly, shading out slower-growing plants and clogging the water for the fish and birds. In addition, the algae can deplete the oxygen in the water and cause fish kills. This overfertilized condition, which you may hear referred to as "eutrophication," is now a fact or a concern for almost every pond on the Cape.

LIVES AT THE POND

Growing around ponds is a characteristic group of plants that will tolerate occasionally or continuously wet feet. The trees include Red Maple, Tupelo, willow, and alder. Unless there is a path, many ponds may be hard to reach or even see because of a dense understory of Highbush Blueberries, Swamp Azalea, Sweet Pepperbush, viburnum, and Buttonbush, laced together with Catbrier. Once you reach the edge of the water you may find Blue Flag Iris, Pickerelweed, rushes, sedges, cattails, water lilies, and Swamp Loosestrife, as well as the introduced Purple Loosestrife and Yellow Iris. In late summer Rose Coreopsis, Virginia Meadow Beauty, and the rare Plymouth Gentian bloom around the sandy or peaty margins of coastal-plain ponds where fluctuations of water level prevent the establishment of woody plants. Until we came along, the abundance of these lovely flowers was determined mostly by pond water level. Today, the beauty of ponds has attracted so many of us that we have become the major factor determining their survival.

The most numerous plants in a pond are the algae, which form the basis for most of the food web. These are some of the same algae which, when oversupplied with nutrients, can reproduce dramatically and overwhelm other parts of the ecosystem.

Activity in ponds starts in very early spring, when the water still seems cold to us but density mixing is bringing nutrients to the surface. Longer days, and nutrients in surface water, encourage more photosynthesis by the algae, which are food for the creatures about to become active after the winter slowdown. You can see the result of the spring growth of algae in the color and clarity of the ponds—the clear water of winter rapidly turns green and cloudy. It is a sign of spring (and, unfortunately, nutrient loading).

Real spring seems assured when the Herring "run" up the streams from the sea and the Ospreys return from the tropics to eat them. Ospreys, black-and-white raptors sometimes called Fish Hawks, with

Fig. 22. Ospreys catch a great many Herring, especially in spring. These fish-eating raptors have a wingspan of more than 5 feet; the soles of their feet have bristles that help them stabilize their slippery prey during flight.

a wingspan of about 5 feet, hover or soar above ponds, looking for fish. Sometimes you can hear their distinctive "chirp" from where they hover, high in the sky, sounding like giant Robins. When an Osprey spots a fish it plunges downward talons first, sometimes going underwater in its attempt to grab the potential meal. Ospreys arrive first on the Upper Cape, usually by the middle of March; they reach the Lower Cape near the end of the month and are ready and waiting when the Herring begin to arrive in numbers during April.

"Herring runs" (the phrase can refer to the river or stream and to the migration of the fish) are mostly composed of Alewives (called Herring hereabouts) but also include other fish that live most of their lives in salt water but spawn in fresh water, including Shad and Blue-back Herring. These fish come into the ponds as soon as the water is consistently a degree or two warmer than the salt water. They spawn early because large fry have a better chance to survive when they swim out to sea in late summer. The Ospreys, too, return to reproduce as early as possible so that their offspring will be well grown and flying before winter. So the warming water brings Herring to the ponds, where Ospreys (and Kingfishers, gulls, and cormorants) await them.

Also about this time the young Eels come into ponds from the sea. These fish, in a pattern opposite from Herring, spawn in the open ocean and grow up in our ponds and bays. The larvae spend several years growing in the ocean before entering fresh water as transparent 3-inch-long elvers (sometimes called Glass Eels). They may spend as many as twenty years growing to adult size (2 to 4 feet) in the ponds before returning to the Sargasso Sea to spawn. A bit of a mystery still exists about Eels, for once the adults leave the shore they are never seen again. The next generation of juveniles are found in the Sargasso Sea, but the intervening step is not known. Of course, Eels and Herring only reach the ponds that have an outlet to tidewater. Although many of the ponds on the Cape are isolated, a surprising number do connect to the sea.

In summer those Herring fry which escaped being eaten as eggs or as tiny fish spend their time searching for food in schools along the shores, just like the minnows of the landlocked fish. These small fry are food for larger fish such as Pickerel and for turtles and cormorants. Some ponds are home to the native Pumpkinseed Sunfish; others have various introduced bass, perch, and trout. Toads and frogs and their tadpoles are sometimes seen in ponds, especially shallow ones.

In June the female Snapping Turtles come out of the ponds and sometimes travel far from the water looking for a good place to lay eggs. These "Snappers" can be up to two feet across, with heavy ridged and spiked shells that look positively prehistoric—it's a little like seeing a dinosaur in your yard. If you find one just leave her alone (and keep the dog away); she'll quietly lay her eggs and go back to the pond. Painted Turtles also lay their eggs ashore, but they don't go as far from the water and are most likely to be seen in ponds, basking in the sun on logs or rocks.

Insects abound around ponds. Water boatmen, water striders, and whirligig beetles live in and on the water, as do midges and mosquitoes. Hunting these insects are predatory dragonflies and damselflies, underwater as juveniles and in the air as adults. Few hunters are more efficient than a dragonfly. If you can find one perched on a twig or grass stem it is well worth a few minutes to watch it. They are fast flyers and rarely return to their perch without prey.

Birds are attracted to ponds by the plants, insects, and fish. Swallows swoop over the water, picking up insects on the fly. Flycatchers and Eastern Kingbirds grab insects by darting briefly from a branch. Kingfishers nest in burrows in steep banks and perch on overhanging branches to spot small fish before diving in to catch them. Black-

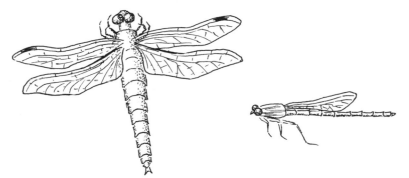

Fig. 23. Typical dragonfly (*left*) and damselfly (*right*) represent the many species. These mighty hunters eat large quantities of mosquitoes. Dragonflies range in size from 1 to 3 inches. They always perch with their wings outstretched. Damselflies are on average smaller; they perch with folded wings. Some species of dragonflies flock and migrate south in fall.

crowned Night-Herons hunt fish, tadpoles, and frogs along pond shore, mostly in the low light of early morning and late afternoon; they make an unmistakable "graawk" if startled into flight. Canada Geese, swans, and Mallards often nest in the vegetation around ponds. Swans (these are the introduced European Mute Swans) are territorial and aggressive, actively chasing away other swans and geese that try to nest on the same pond, and threatening dogs and people who come too close. By sometime in June strings of goslings, ducklings, and cygnets follow their parents about, each kind piping its version of the universal juvenile chorus: "Where's the food?"

In late summer the young Ospreys are catching their own fish, the gawky gray juvenile swans have begun to grow white feathers, and baby birds of all feathers finally have given up demanding to be fed by their tired parents. The small Herring fry move down the outlets of the ponds to salt water, running a gauntlet of Herring Gulls and predatory fish. By the middle of October most Osprey have left for points south.

In the fall the ponds cool again, and the summer activity slows. Turtles hibernate, cormorants migrate, and plants from algae to water lilies die back. Most ponds on the Cape freeze every winter, for a month or more, beginning in late December and lasting into early February. Winter is the time you are most likely to see a River Otter around a partially frozen pond. They dive for fish—even Eels—and sit on the ice to eat them; in summer their diets are more varied and include turtles, shellfish, and frogs.

About Groundwater

Because Cape Cod drinks its groundwater, it is important to keep that water clean. It is both difficult and expensive to clean groundwater if it becomes contaminated. Unfortunately, that is exactly what happened to the Sagamore groundwater lens at the Massachusetts Military Reservation, beginning around the time of World War II. Spills and leaks of fuel and solvents and improper disposal of chemicals have contaminated the groundwater. Each of the contaminated sites is the source of a "plume" of contaminated water, moving, as the groundwater moves, down the groundwater gradient. The plumes of contaminated water are thin; they have not affected the entire depth of the groundwater. Nevertheless these plumes of toxic materials have contaminated a number of private and town water wells and some cranberry bogs, necessitating their closure. There are now questions about the effects of contaminants on fish and shellfish in the ponds and bays that the plumes are approaching. These plumes of contaminated water are being studied, and some cleanup has begun, but completing the job will take many more years and cost more millions of dollars. It is a reminder that on the Cape we have only this one source of water. Better to keep potential pollutants out of the ground than to try to remove them later.

More Standing Water

Most of the irregular depressions the glacier left us are not deep enough to be ponds. Wetlands—bogs, swamps, and marshes—occupy many of these swales and are also found in spring-sapping valleys, and at the edges of ponds and streams. Wetlands are important for groundwater recharge, storm water filtration and storage, and as habitats for plants and animals. Characteristic groups of plants occupy each type of wetland, but they all have standing water in common, red-brown water that looks like tea or ale. In fact these two brown beverages and the brown swamp water get their color from the same source: plant materials steeped in water. In marshes, bogs, and swamps, as in teapots, dead plants soak in water. The colors (and the flavors) of the plants are soluble and end up in the water. What does it taste like? Read on.

MARSHES

Freshwater marshes form where fresh water stands for all or most of the year but does not stagnate. These environments occur along streams in low-gradient valleys, around ponds with gently sloping sides, and in shallow kettle holes whose floors are just barely below the water table. Like many transitional environments, freshwater marshes are transitory. Shallow ponds with marshes around them will gradually fill with sediment and plant material and become all marsh, but sediment will continue to collect. Once the floor of a kettle is above the water table, dry-land trees, shrubs, and plants will take over. In estuaries, as sea level rises, the seaward edge of freshwater marshes can be drowned by salt water; rising sea level may create new marsh upstream, however, because the freshwater lens on the Cape floats on the salt water and rises with it.

The plants of freshwater marshes are typically tall and thin—cattails, reeds, rushes, and sedges that live with their roots or tubers in the muddy marsh bottom and quickly push their leaves up above the

Fig. 24. Freshwater wetlands come in a wide variety of types, from bogs to ponds to marshes, but cattails, sedges, and wading birds are typical of many of them. Great Blue Herons are a common sight on the Cape during fall, winter, and spring.

water in the spring. Among these plants live a number of tall, thin birds such as herons and bitterns. These birds hunt fish, frogs, insects, and aquatic invertebrates among the plants and in the open pools. The bitterns and the smaller rails are hard to see because of their protective coloration and their habit of freezing and then slipping away through the stems as an observer moves on. Herons are more visible and tend to fly when disturbed.

The birds you are most likely to see in freshwater marshes in spring and summer are the male Red-winged Blackbirds, perching on tall cattails and advertising their territories by singing and showing their red wing patches. The voice of the Red-winged Blackbird, an early harbinger of spring, is sometimes heard as early as late February.

Muskrats live in many freshwater marshes as well as the marshy edges of shallow ponds, building their mounded den houses of the reeds and cattails from the marsh, and eating the roots and stems of the same plants. They can sometimes be seen swimming, sculling with their vertically flattened tails.

A spectacular plant of marshes is Rose Mallow, which can turn a green marsh into a sea of pink in the late summer. The flowers are large, up to 7 inches across, and look as if they escaped from the tropics, which is essentially true—Rose Mallow belongs to the same family as Hibiscus. Like its tropical cousins, each of the showy blossoms of the Rose Mallow lasts only one day.

VERNAL POOLS

Vernal pools are temporary ponds that form in the spring from snowmelt and spring rains. The irregular surface of the glacial deposits on Cape Cod provides many closed depressions that hold water in the spring. The fact that vernal pools are temporary creates both challenges and advantages for the creatures that depend on them. Because these pools have water only a few months of the year, fish do not live in vernal pools, and so one whole class of predators is eliminated. That is the advantage. The disadvantage is the short period in which to hatch, grow, and either reproduce or metamorphose into a form that can live out of the water, before the pool dries up.

Wood Frogs and Spotted Salamanders rely on vernal pools for breeding; they live in the nearby upland during the rest of the year and breed in the pools where they were hatched. Spotted Salamanders gather in large numbers around some of these pools to breed at the time of the first warm spring rains. Their eggs hatch, and the young grow up enough to go ashore before the pool dries up, at least in most

Fig. 25. Vernal pools occur where a depression holds water for a few months in the spring, anywhere from swales in otherwise dry woods to old gravel pits.

Environments

years. Wood Frogs can often be heard at quite a distance from the pool, but it is difficult to believe that a small frog is making the sound, which sounds like a cross between a "quack" and a "bark." These small frogs are diurnal but shy, so they retreat into the water at your approach, and the sound stops.

Fairy Shrimp, which are small relatives of true shrimp, have no terrestrial phase but live their whole short lives in vernal pools. In the two months or so that the typical vernal pool has water, the Fairy Shrimp hatch from eggs from a previous year, grow to adulthood, lay the eggs that will perpetuate the species, and die. Fairy Shrimp eggs survive the drying of the pool in which they were laid and can stay viable for many years. These eggs can apparently be carried by birds or the wind to other sites, but the eggs do not hatch until the pool has water in spring.

Other animals such as Spring Peepers and Painted Turtles may use vernal pools, but they do not rely exclusively on them; they can also be found in other wet areas.

SPHAGNUM BOGS

Bogs are probably the most unusual environment to be found on the Cape; they have rare plants growing in uncommon conditions. First, the conditions: standing acidic water, low oxygen, and very few nutrients (don't even try growing tomatoes in a bog). Because these conditions are harsh and quite unusual, the plants that have adapted to live there are likewise rare, or at least limited. Most of the bog vegetation, however, is one type: Sphagnum Moss, sometimes called peat moss. This plant is not rare, but as a simple plant that has no vascular system it can live only in very wet places. Sphagnum Moss can grow in acidic water having no more nutrients than rainwater, and it perpetuates these conditions in areas where it grows because it makes the water more acidic as it absorbs the few available nutrients.

Sphagnum Moss forms pale green mats and mounds of fuzzy, branching stems sometimes tinged with yellow or red, which can hold as much as twenty times their weight of water, creating soggy conditions that exclude many other plants. The living plants grow upward, year after year, burying the growth of previous years. The dead vegetation is preserved by the acidic water and compacted by the weight above, forming an inch or so of peat a year. This is how the well-

Fig. 26. Sphagnum Moss (*Sphagnum* sp.). Commonly known as peat moss, these plants perpetuate the conditions that favor their growth: acidic standing water.

known Irish peat bogs formed, from which peat is cut and dried for fuel. Peat bogs on the Cape were also mined for fuel in this way in the eighteenth and nineteenth centuries, once the forests were depleted. The bogs that remain today are protected by wetlands regulations.

A word of caution: in "quaking bogs" the mat of Sphagnum Moss is floating on water; it is possible to fall though. Although many bogs quiver when you walk on them, the rubbery undulations of quaking bogs may indicate that the plant mat is not very strong.

Many of the other plants of bogs are indeed rare. (They were less so two hundred years ago, before bogs were mined for peat or converted to cranberry cultivation.) Plants that grow in bogs have adapted to the low levels of nutrients in a variety of ways, including having small, tough, evergreen leaves, but the method that attracts the most interest is catching and eating animals. We tend to think of it the other way around: usually the animals eat the plants. But in bogs, nutrients are so limited that some plants have developed ways to trap and digest insects to get more. The carnivorous plants you are most likely to see on the Cape are the sundews. The leaves of these small plants are covered with sticky red hairs that trap insects and then digest them and absorb the nutrients, leaving only the exoskeleton. Pitcher Plants, which trap insects in liquid in deep tubular leaves, also occur on the Cape but are quite uncommon.

A number of flowering orchids grow in bogs. They are all rare and some are threatened; take lovely photos if you should find one, but don't pick. Orchids, like Sphagnum Moss, can survive in low-nutrient conditions. They are very effective at extracting dilute nutrients from their surroundings. The bright pink Arethusa, and paler Grass Pink and Rose Pogonia (also called "Snake Mouth"—you'll know why if you see it), bloom in early to midsummer. These flowers may occasionally be seen in inactive cranberry bogs, but the agricultural activities have greatly reduced their numbers.

Few animals large enough to see live in bogs—a few insects, some secretive voles or shrews, and sometimes frogs or salamanders. You may sometimes see deer tracks in bogs, and the occasional warbler or sparrow, but overall these areas provide little to attract most animals.

PLANTS OF THE HEATH FAMILY

Although the name "heath" may not be familiar, the plants of this family are. Azaleas, Mountain Laurel, Trailing Arbutus, rhododendrons, cranberries, and blueberries all belong to this family of tough, versatile plants. Many heath family members are evergreen; others produce notable flowers or fruit, making them attractive garden plants. They are well adapted to live in the Cape's acid soils. Most will tolerate wet feet, and many, such as cranberries, grow in swamps or bogs, but they will also grow in dry, sandy soils or in a garden. They rely on an association between their roots and fungus to gather nutrients; this association enables them to grow in nutrient-poor bogs, swamps, and dry woodlands, but always in acid soil. Lime does not suit them: if you put lime on your lawn, keep it well away from rhododendrons and their relatives.

CRANBERRY BOGS

Cranberries are native plants whose berries were eaten by the native peoples and by explorers and settlers. The name is due to the resemblance of the blossom to the head and bill of Great Blue Herons, still sometimes called "cranes" locally. When Europeans arrived on the Cape, cranberries grew wild in wet places as they do today, particularly in sandy areas where the water level falls below the ground surface in the summer. In the early 1800s Henry Hall, a ship captain, salt maker, and farmer in Dennis, realized that the most productive cranberries were those that received a layer of sand blown in from an adjacent

Fig. 27. Leatherleaf (*Chamaedaphne calyculata*). This member of the heath family may be found around the margins of many bogs and boggy ponds. The progressively smaller leaves on the young shoots is typical of Leatherleaf.

dune. He experimented with transplanting the cranberry vines to specially constructed "cranberry yards" and succeeded in increasing yield sufficiently that others followed his lead. Cranberries rapidly became a cultivated crop; swamps and bogs all over the Cape were drained and engineered for cranberry farming. Today's cranberry bogs are modeled on Hall's plan: a layer of sand above the rich muck of an old bog, surrounded by ditches to control the water level.

Acres of cultivated cranberries fill the channels and kettles of the Cape today, and cranberries are a multimillion dollar business. The water level in the bogs is controlled so that the plants are above water in the growing season but under a protective cover of water or ice in winter. Ice hockey games frequently take place on flooded bogs because the shallow water of the bogs freezes before the ponds. In the fall the cranberry plants go dormant, and the leaves turn cranberry-colored. The leaves keep that color until the new growth appears in the spring. Every few years each bog is "sanded," covered with ½ inch or so of sand. As Captain Hall discovered, this sand encourages new growth of the cranberry plants and discourages weeds. Sometimes the sand is applied on the ice on the frozen bog, which probably also discourages hockey games. Originally, sand was dug from "borrow pits" in the upland immediately surrounding a bog; an old borrow pit is a clue to

Environments

Fig. 28. Large Cranberry (*Vaccinium macrocarpon*). This plant and the similar Small Cranberry (*V. oxycoccus*) still grow and produce fruit in wild bogs. The many varieties of cultivated cranberries are strains of the Large Cranberry.

the proximity of old bogs. Today sand may be trucked in and stock-piled in large heaps near the bogs.

In spring or early summer you may see a bog that is white with frost or ice in the early morning. Although it may look like a disaster, the grower has actually protected the plants by turning on sprinklers when frost threatened the new growth. As the water freezes on the plants, it liberates heat that keeps the blossoms from freezing; the ice melts as soon as the sun comes up and the air warms.

Many bogs now use herbicides and pesticides to control weeds (in a commercial bog Rose Pogonia is a weed) and insects, and those agricultural chemicals sometimes enter the aquatic system of which the cranberry bogs are a part. The chemicals are, by their nature, hard on many plants and animals, but they have helped increase the yield of berries. There is some movement toward organic cranberries and reduced chemical use, which would be advantageous to the rest of the ecosystem.

Raising cranberries is much less labor-intensive than it used to be thanks to sprinklers, harvesters, graders, and sanders. Cape Cod schools are no longer recessed during harvest; a few workers with machines do the work in short order. Cranberries are dry-harvested with a mechanical picker for sale as fresh berries, or wet-harvested for juice and sauce. In the latter process, a harvester that looks like a cross between a Rototiller and a paddle-wheel boat knocks the berries loose from the vines in a flooded bog. The berries, tough things that they are, float to the surface and are corralled and pumped into waiting trucks. Cranberries were once sorted by hand, but most now are sorted in an ingenious device that drops the berries a short distance onto a slanted surface. Those that bounce over a small divider pass; those that don't bounce after several tries probably have some defect and are rejected.

Some wild bogs still exist where the original mixture of wetland plants can be seen—cranberries, sundews, Sphagnum Moss, orchids, and other water-tolerant plants.

CEDAR SWAMPS

Few trees can live in standing water, but we have one kind here on the Cape that can, Atlantic White Cedar. Red Maples can live in very wet areas and survive occasional inundation, and Tupelos grow around the edges of ponds and streams; but where the acidic, coffee-colored water of a swamp stands for much of the year, only Atlantic White Cedar will grow. Atlantic White Cedars are conifers, with tiny scalelike leaves closely clothing the branches, pea-size, faceted cones, and fibrous reddish bark. The trees often grow close together, their roots forming hummocks that rise above the Sphagnum Moss and their branches interlacing thickly overhead. The rot-resistant, lightweight wood of the

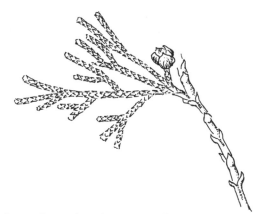

Fig. 29. Atlantic White Cedar (*Chamaecyparis thyoides*). The cedar shingles that typify Cape Cod houses are made from this tree, which still grows in cedar swamps on the Cape as well as south along the coast to Florida.

Atlantic White Cedar spelled doom for many cedar swamps. The trees were avidly cut by European settlers and explorers (Gosnold took some back to England) for ships, shingles, pilings, and posts.

In some cut-over Atlantic White Cedar swamps, it was discovered that additional lumber could be found by "mining" the peat for fallen logs that had been preserved by burial in that acidic, low-oxygen environment. Such mining lowered the level of the peat and reduced the likelihood that cedars would regenerate there; eventually many swamps were drained and converted to cranberry cultivation. Other swamps were apparently managed for a sustained yield or allowed to regrow, as today some cedar swamps have fairly old trees. One cedar swamp in Woods Hole has some Atlantic White Cedar trees that germinated in the 1820s.

The Atlantic White Cedar will grow on dry sites—you could plant one in your yard—but in the wild they cannot compete with other trees that grow in the dry forest; they therefore are restricted to swamps. But Atlantic White Cedar trees can drown if the water level is rapidly raised by blocking the drainage—road building is often responsible. New Atlantic White Cedars will grow in such a swamp only if the seeds find hummocks or logs above water on which to germinate.

During the age of sail, captains planning a long voyage often filled their drinking-water casks with the brown water from cedar swamps. The acidity of the water prevented the growth of microorganisms and preserved the water for long periods. The water reportedly has a distinctive but not unpleasant taste, evidently much better than the green, stinking water that often was the lot of the whaler or deep-sea sailor after months at sea.

Not many other plants can grow in the standing water and dense shade of a mature Atlantic White Cedar swamp, but Sphagnum Moss manages in many places. Ferns can survive around the margins and on hummocks out in the swamp. Old cedars may be hung with *Usnea*, a gray-green lichen sometimes called "Old Man's Beard." Parula Warblers sometimes use *Usnea* for their nests in cedar swamps.

WOODED SWAMPS

Abandoned cranberry bogs and swamps that have filled in are often taken over by Highbush Blueberries, Swamp Azaleas, and Red Maples. Such damp areas are too wet for many plants, but these versatile plants will grow in wet soil as well as on drier hillsides. Swamps also may be home to Skunk Cabbage, the earliest flower to bloom on the Cape. Truthfully, Skunk Cabbage doesn't fit the image created by the word "flower," and because it is pollinated by flies that breed on carrion, it produces a fragrance attractive to those flies—more like, well, carrion than roses. But this interesting flower is the first in the spring at least partly because of its ability to produce and trap heat inside its pointed hoodlike spathe. Spring Peepers often bring wooded swamps to our attention by their loud chorus on early spring evenings. These tiny frogs are rarely seen in spring because they can hide under a bit of bark or a withered leaf and are usually active only at night. In late summer, however, they can sometimes be seen moving about on dry land in daylight, usually not far from where they were heard in the spring.

Unusual Running Water: Streams

Streams are few on the Cape; the porous sand and gravel left by the glacier causes most rain and snowmelt to sink in rather than run off. On the south side of the Mid- and Upper Cape however, almost a dozen small streams (most called rivers) flow in the bottoms of the long, straight valleys whose lower ends are narrow estuaries that dissect the south shore. These valleys were cut after the glacier had melted and as sea level was rising, by the action of springs (see page 19.)

Fig. 30. Swamp Azalea (*Rhododendron viscosum*). Follow your nose to find this attractive tall shrub of moist places; it advertises its June blooms with a wonderful perfume.

Fig. 31. Cranberry bogs like this one occupy the flat bottoms of many spring-sapping valleys on the Cape, often bordering both sides of the stream. The lower ends of many such valleys have been flooded by the sea; the upper ends are dry or contain small streams or wetlands.

Although some of the streams begin at ponds, they are fed mostly by groundwater. Because these valleys cut into the water table, groundwater flows into the streams not only at their heads but also from seeps and springs all along their length.

Some of the springs are obvious because of the iron in the water that stains the rocks and precipitates in soft flakes on the mud. A number of streams are named "Red Brook" for these rusty-red iron stains. This iron has been leached out of the sand by the slightly acidic rainwater as it trickled down to the water table. In some areas there is enough iron that it precipitates as clumps of "bog iron" in the mud of bogs or streams. This low-grade iron ore was mined and smelted here and all along the coast through the time of the Revolutionary War. Large-scale mining of bog iron took place in Wareham, Rochester, and Middleborough; many bogs were converted to cranberry production after the iron was gone. Although it is no longer an industrial resource, bog iron is still forming in these environments.

The streams on the Cape have been much altered from their precolonial conditions and even from the state they were in when Daniel Webster came to the Cape in the early 1800s to fish for the sea-run Trout that made these streams famous. Construction of dams for water-driven mills, conversion of wetlands bordering the streams to cranberry bogs, and clearing for pasture or construction all took their toll on the stream ecosystem, stopping water flow, destroying streamside vegetation, and filling the steams with mud. By the 1970s the famous Trout fishery was almost gone. Since that time some of the streams have been partially restored, a complex and labor-intensive process of creating flow conditions that carry away the mud, and also providing shade and protection along the stream banks. Where the proper conditions exist the fish have returned, as have the insects and other invertebrates that rely on running water.

Other than the Trout, there are few large organisms unique to streams. Most of the obvious plants and animals of streams also inhabit ponds or the surrounding woods.

Water Level

The water level in freshwater wetlands, ponds, streams, and wells is determined by the level of the groundwater. Because all the water pumped from wells or drawn from ponds comes from the same groundwater lenses (see fig. 19), the increasing human demand for water as the population grows may draw down the water table and dry up wetlands. Pumping for public use has lowered the water table in the area of town wells in Hyannis and Yarmouth 5 to 6 feet from the predevelopment levels, in some cases allowing upland vegetation to move into previous wetland zones. Once the vegetation has adjusted to lower water levels, it is hard to imagine that the water level was once higher. As the population grows and water withdrawals increase, the water table will be drawn down farther in zones concentric around major water wells.

NOR ANY DROP TO DRINK: SALTWATER ENVIRONMENTS

Saltwater environments, from estuaries to ocean beaches, have much in common because they share the same ocean. Bays are bordered by the plants that form salt marshes; burrowing creatures that live between high and low tide may occur wherever the bottom has the right proportions of sand and mud; and fish found in the open ocean may also live in estuaries. In addition, many creatures move from one saltwater environment to another at different seasons or stages of their lives, so the divisions that follow are somewhat arbitrary. Think of salt-water environments as a continuum that grades from protected, brackish estuaries through salt marshes and bays to the open ocean, where the seawater is 3 percent salt. See page 77 (Beaches) for the creatures that live in the surf zone.

Salt Marshes

From the land, salt marshes in summer look almost featureless: tall green grass, a glimpse through the grass of the winding tidal creeks,

Fig. 32. Salt marshes grow in the quiet waters of estuaries and protected bays. The zonation of vegetation is characteristic, with Cordgrass along the creeks and the aptly named High-tide Bush growing just above the reach of the salt water.

and maybe a duck or some terns. But out in the marsh there is much more happening than meets the eye of a passerby. Walking in a marsh can be difficult, especially at high tide, and many creatures hide before you are aware of them. In addition walking can damage the marsh. But a small boat lets you move quietly up a tidal creek and see both the environment and its inhabitants up close. Early morning is a good time, but tides will affect where you can go and what the creatures are doing.

Salt marshes form in areas of quiet salt water, protected from ocean waves. Here the *Spartinas*, grasses that grow in salt water, find a foothold and spread by underground runners. Silt and plant debris accumulate among the stems, raising the surface of the marsh. Beneath the surface the accumulating layers of silty plant material compact but, because there is no oxygen, decompose very slowly. Over time this process forms a deposit of saltmarsh peat. The sections of the marsh below high tide can accumulate peat at the rate of 2 or 3 feet per hundred years.

Many salt marshes occupy coastal kettle holes or valleys that contained freshwater marshes or cedar swamps until sea level rose high enough to flood them; others developed after a sand spit or barrier beach formed a protected bay. Fresh water enters marshes from the landward side, from springs or small streams, creating a salt gradient in the marshes—freshest close to the upland, saltiest near the inlet, where sea water comes in with the tide.

The saltiest, wettest areas of the marsh, inundated by salt water at every high tide, are dominated by the tall, sturdy spears of Cordgrass, one of the *Spartinas*. Cordgrass is the pioneer of salt marshes; it colonizes bare mudflats and begins a new marsh. Cordgrass tolerates regular flooding by salt water, but it won't grow where it is always underwater. A wide band of Cordgrass typically grows along the tidal creeks close to the inlet, narrowing inland along the creeks and disappearing altogether on the high marsh where tidal flooding is infrequent. Salt Marsh Hay, another *Spartina*, grows on the high marsh where the Cordgrass cannot live, in areas that are flooded only at the highest tides. Salt Marsh Hay is usually only 1 to 2 feet tall and has fine stalks and leaves, which is why it was used as fodder for livestock; it often lies in flat "cowlicks" on the marsh surface. Once you know to look for them, you'll see bands of 3- to 6-foot Cordgrass marking the windings of the creeks through the marsh, with the shorter, lighter green expanses of Salt Marsh Hay mixed with Spike Grass in between. Cordgrass and Salt Marsh Hay have developed adaptations that allow them to use salt water. The roots of both species selectively take in fresh water and leave salt behind in the marsh muck. These plants also can excrete excess salt; the minute salt crystals can sometimes be seen on the leaves; look closely with a hand lens.

In the high marsh, where fresh water predominates, there may be patches of the dark green Black Grass, which, like many other plants with "grass" in their names, is not a grass but a rush; you can tell by its tubular leaves. At the highest level of the marsh, Marsh Elder, or High-tide Bush, marks areas that are flooded only by moon high-tides. Its presence is an indicator of somewhat higher ground, while the similar Groundsel Tree grows high enough that it is not reached by storm tides.

Where the marsh has been disturbed or the tidal flow has been restricted, the 10-foot plumes of Phragmites (pronounced "frag mite´ ees), or Common Reed, rustle in the wind. Both Phragmites and Cord-grass were cut for thatching in colonial times. Phragmites is an oppor-tunist that takes advantage of the toehold provided by construction or drainage changes that damage the original marsh plants. Phrag-mites grows quickly in the disturbed areas, making such a dense mat of roots that the original marsh plants rarely return.

Some low plants add late summer and fall color among the grasses of the marsh. Several species of *Salicornia*, or Pickleweed, grow in low areas where salt water collects. Their plump stems look a bit like a series of tiny pickles—they even taste like pickles and are eaten, usually in salads. This plant is also called Samphire, and Glasswort; the latter name results from its use in the early 1800s as a source of potash for glass making. The annual Pickleweed turns brilliant red or orange in the fall. Sea Lavender's rosette of basal leaves does not attract attention most of the year. In the late summer, however, Sea Lavender tints the marsh a delicate lavender with its tiny flowers on thin, 2-foot-tall, branching stems. Sea Lavender is related to Statice and, like Statice, holds its color when dry. These days there are so many of us on the Cape that some towns have acted to protect Sea Lavender from pick-ing. It's better to enjoy Sea Lavender on the marsh, and get some Stat-ice from the farmers' market for indoor color.

Salt marshes are as biologically productive per acre as the most productive agricultural fields. In addition to the foregoing plants, primary producers in the marsh include abundant algae and diatoms in the mud and water, and Eelgrass in the tidal creeks. Living off this productivity are a large number of animals. There may be lots to eat, but because of the alternation between flooding by high tide and exposure to sun and drying wind, the salt marsh is a demanding place to live. As a result fewer species live in a salt marsh than in many terrestrial environments. The species that have successfully adapted, however, live in the marsh in large numbers.

The brown Salt Marsh Snails graze on the algae that lives on the surface of the mud and on the leaves and stems of the Cordgrass. These snails breathe air, so they graze their way down the grass to the mud during the falling tide and back up as the tide rises, clustering at the tips of the top leaves during the highest tides. Periwinkles and Mud Snails graze on the algae and detritus in the mud, leaving shallow wandering trails behind them.

Fiddler Crabs can be seen in large numbers on the marsh at low tide on the south and west sides of the Cape. They are not as common in the colder waters on the north and east shores. These nickel-size crabs are named for the way the male waves his oversize claw like an enthusiastic fiddle player. They are not making music; they are trying to attract females and impress or scare off other males. When you first see a group of Fiddler Crabs, you might think you are seeing two different species, because only the males have an enlarged claw. Oddly, some

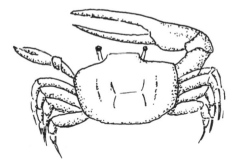

Fig. 33. Sand Fiddler Crab (*Uca pugilator*). Common in sandy salt marshes. The similar *U. pugnax* lives where the bottom is muddier; *U. minax* chooses the fresh borders of salt marshes.

Environments

of the males are lefties and some are righties; they are about evenly split, and neither is more successful. Fiddlers (there are three similar species) find the algae that is their food on the mud and sand grains of the marsh—the females are two-handed eaters; the males can use only their small claw for eating. As they eat they spit out tiny balls of neatly cleaned sand, piling them up outside their burrows along with the larger sand balls from burrow renovation. Every tide, like good room service, cleans up the leavings of the last meal and brings new food right to the door. When they see you, Fiddler Crabs retreat into their burrows. If you freeze they will venture out again, which is why they are often eaten by herons and other hunters that freeze between steps. Apparently these birds pick up the males by the enlarged claw and shake them, breaking off the claw. Then they drop the claw and eat the crab. Females are presumably easier to eat.

Of the other crabs that live in salt marshes, Blue Crabs are the most sought-after. These are the crabs that are served as crab cakes or soft-shell crabs in restaurants around Chesapeake Bay, where they are more common. They retreat to the deep marsh creeks at low tide because they mostly move about by swimming, not walking. The smaller Green Crab, an immigrant from Europe, walks rather than swims. Check out their feet to see the adaptations each species has for its mode of locomotion. In the summer you can sometimes see males of both species carrying and protecting a soft-shell female. The female molts just before mating, and the male protects her from predators and from other males until her new shell hardens.

Many filter feeders also live in the marsh; they eat the floating algae and whatever tiny particles of detritus they can collect from the water. Ribbed Mussels (similar to edible Blue Mussels but not good to eat) burrow in the mud. They are easiest to see at low tide where they burrow in the peat among the Cordgrass roots; gulls have learned to look for them there. Barnacles, which are more closely related to shrimp than to clams or mussels, live wherever they can find something hard to attach to—a log, rock, or shell. Oysters, Soft-shell Clams (called Steamers on the restaurant menu), and Hard Clams (served as Cherry-stones or Littlenecks when young, chopped in chowder or as stuffed Quahogs when they grow large) live in the sandier areas as well as on tide flats beyond the marsh. Other clams live there as well, lots of them, but they are small enough that they are not sought by humans.

Smaller creatures, from birds to Horseshoe Crabs, eat the tiny Gemma Clam in vast numbers. These are the most common clams—as many as 250,000 per square yard—but you will have to look closely because they are less than ⅛ inch across.

Many kinds of fish spend some part of their lives in the food-filled water of the salt marsh. Salt marshes, like other estuarine environments, serve as nursery and feeding area for young fish, including many of our favorites such as Flounders, Bluefish, and Striped Bass that live at sea as adults. Other fish, mostly small ones such as Silversides and Mummichogs, but also the larger Tomcod and White Perch, live in estuaries or salt marshes most of their lives. On a still day if you wade, or sit still in a small boat, you sometimes can see schools of 1- to 4-inch fish feeding in the tidal creeks. Fish of the open water also come to the salt marsh for short periods to feed on the smaller fish and the aquatic plants and animals. Marshes export nutrients on every tide to the estuaries and coastal waters around them. So salt marshes support not only the organisms that live in or visit the marsh but many that live in the nearby coastal waters too—Lobsters and clams and creatures of the open ocean.

Almost three dozen species of birds can be found in salt marshes at some time of the year. Marsh Wrens, American Bitterns, Canada Geese, and Black Ducks nest in the marsh, as do Spotted Sandpipers, which you will see on almost any paddling trip in the marsh from spring to fall. Herons, terns, Kingfishers, and gulls commute to the marshes to feed on the fish, clams, and crabs. Migrating shorebirds

Fig. 34. Gemma Clams (*Gemma gemma*). These clams are extremely abundant and are eaten by many creatures, but they never appear on a menu because they average about ⅛ inch across.

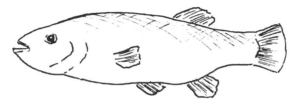

Fig. 35. Mummichog (*Fundulus hetroclitus*). The Mummichog's other name—Mosquito Fish—suggests its feeding habits: it eats insects and insect larvae from the surface of the water.

feed in the marshes each spring and again in late summer and fall as they migrate past us. Northern Harriers (once called Marsh Hawks) nest at the edge of the marsh and hunt over the marshes year-round. They often can be seen, even in winter, flying low, tilting from side to side as they search for the mice, small birds, and insects that are their prey.

Oh, yes . . . the insects. Salt marshes are home to some of our least favorite insects. Mosquitoes, Green-head Flies, Deerflies, and Horseflies are all common around salt marshes. They are food for many birds and other creatures, but they are a nuisance to humans. The ruler-straight ditches you will see in many salt marshes were cut to drain the pools in the high marsh that were home to the Salt Marsh Mosquito. Deep ditches can dry out the marsh and allow the invasion of upland species; current practice apparently calls for shallow ditches with just enough gradient to drain the pools while preventing a complete drying of the high marsh. The large blue boxes on legs in some salt marshes are traps for Green-head Flies, those large flies whose bite feels as though they have teeth. The traps apparently work because the flies are attracted to any large thing standing in the marsh. When cattle were pastured in salt marshes the animals were reportedly beleaguered by the flies. In an odd outgrowth of that fact, some of the traps are baited with "synthetic ox breath" and attract many times as many flies as unbaited boxes.

From a small boat you can see ripples forming in the sand at the bottom of marsh creeks as the current moves over it. Watch it for a few moments and you will see the sand grains moving up the gently sloping side of the ripple and dropping into the lee at the top of the steep side, where they eventually avalanche down the slope. With that observation you can tell the direction of flow of the water that formed ripples in sand even after the tide has gone out, whether on the tidal flats or in a creek. Because this is the same process that moves dry sand, you can tell which way the wind blew that formed dunes and ripples in dry sand too.

Bays and Salt Ponds

The protected saltwater environments on the shores of Cape Cod are quite varied; they range from open bays to enclosed salt ponds with a narrow tidal inlet, and from the muddy, brackish upper reaches of an estuary to the sandy, salty conditions at the mouth. Salt marshes are a part of many bays, so these descriptions also apply there.

Eelgrass forms a crucial part of all these ecosystems. This plant, whose blades can grow several feet long, has adapted to a completely marine life; it puts down its roots, produces flowers (they are hidden in the leaf sheath), and makes seeds entirely underwater. Eelgrass grows in both brackish water and seawater, always below the low-tide level. In very clear water it can grow as deep as 100 feet, but most Eelgrass beds are in the shallow, turbid water of bays and estuaries. Eelgrass can root in sand or even soft mud. Where it grows, it provides the foundation for an entire community; its roots stabilize the

Fig. 36. Eelgrass (*Zostera marina*). You can tell if a bay or estuary still supports Eelgrass beds by looking for its leaves on the beach in fall.

Environments

sediments, and its leaves provide a solid surface for other organisms. Snails, algae, bryozoans, and worms live on the Eelgrass blades, and these, in turn, are food for more mobile creatures. Many fish and shellfish need Eelgrass beds for the survival of their juvenile or larval forms—young Bay Scallops, for example, attach themselves to Eelgrass blades until they grow large enough to live independently; juvenile Herring, Flounders, and, of course, Eels live in the Eelgrass beds, finding food and protection from predators.

Eelgrass beds are much reduced from historical levels and may still be shrinking. In 1930–31 an epidemic wiped out about 90 percent of the Eelgrass on the East Coast; the loss of the Eelgrass caused the collapse of populations of Brant (a smaller cousin of the Canada Goose) and Bay Scallops that depend on it. Some Eelgrass survived in brackish estuaries, and these plants have reseeded the saltier waters. But Eelgrass is suffering from other stresses. Studies done on Waquoit Bay in Falmouth/Mashpee suggest that excess nitrogen is fueling algal population explosions. The algae damages Eelgrass by shading it and even uprooting it. In addition, the immense algae populations can deplete the bay of oxygen. On warm, calm, cloudy days the plants deplete the oxygen in the water through respiration. At other times the decomposition of such large quantities of algae can use up the oxygen in the water. The oxygen depletion can be so severe that it damages the entire ecosystem and kills fish and shellfish in large numbers.

The excess nitrogen entering the bay is from human sources; there is no doubt about that—septic systems, lawn and garden fertilizers, and deposition from the air being the largest contributors. The question of what to do about the problem engenders somewhat more contention, but ultimately, if we are to maintain healthy coastal ecosystems, we must decrease the nitrogen we put into coastal waters by preventing the nitrogen from entering the groundwater in the first place.

In summer the coastal waters are home to many fish, and to the fish eaters. Ospreys dive talons-first on fish and sometimes struggle to get airborne again with fish up to a foot long. Flocks of terns call shrilly to each other as they search for small fish. Often schools of small fish are chased to the surface by predatory large fish, only to find the terns waiting. Terns dive headfirst into schools of small fish like Sand Lance and somehow manage to collect several fish crosswise in their beaks before heading back to the nesting colony to feed their young. Loons and cormorants catch fish underwater. It is hard to see how they do it, but sometimes you can see a cormorant bring a fish to the surface and work (no hands!) to turn the fish around so it can be swallowed headfirst. Gulls eat clams, mussels, and oysters when they can manage to break the shells by dropping them on a rock or parking lot. As garbage dumps have closed and fish processing has decreased, gulls have had to rely again on these natural foods. The gull populations may begin to drop back to precolonial levels in response to these changes.

Summer also brings scenes of humans on shore or in small boats fishing for Bluefish or Striped Bass, especially in moving water. Trawlers drag nets for squid in spring and early summer in Vineyard Sound. Lobstermen haul their traps, each trap marked by a brightly painted float. And children fish off piers for whatever they can catch, usually Scup, Cunner, or Sea Robins.

In winter, except when bays or sounds freeze over, ducks and gulls are busy along the shore. Eiders, scoters, Goldeneyes, buffleheads, Red-breasted Mergansers, and loons dive for the fish and shellfish. During much of the winter Harbor Seals can be seen on rocks along the south side of the Cape; both Gray and Harbor Seals congregate on Monomoy in those months. They have come south to our warmer water for the winter season. Like most visitors they dine on Cape Cod's famous seafood: fish, squid, crabs, shellfish—whatever is fresh, just like the Captain's Plate before it goes into the fryer.

Fig. 37. Male Bufflehead. This small diving duck is a common winter visitor. From October to May it can be seen diving for fish, mollusks, and vegetation in salt ponds and along the coast. The female wears less dramatic plumage—shades of dark brown and gray with a small white cheek patch.

BEACHES

Beaches are among the most dynamic locales on Cape Cod, changing slightly with each wave, each tide, and perhaps drastically with each storm. The beach will look different in February than in July and, though the beach may look about the same every July, the sand you sit on today is not the sand that you sat on last summer.

Between Sea and Land

Beaches are shaped by the ocean waves, but the materials that make beaches come from the land. On Cape Cod the only source of beach materials is erosion of the pile of rocks, sand, and gravel left by the glacier, that is to say Cape Cod itself. Along many of the world's shores rivers bring sand from inland to make beaches. Here on the Cape we have no large rivers to import sand, so the beaches are made entirely of local material eroded from the shore.

Erosion of the glacial deposits that form Cape Cod began when rising sea level allowed waves to break against materials that were previously above their reach. Waves breaking against the land pick up sand and silt and carry them back down into the surf zone. Rocks, and more sand and silt, cascade down the steep bank cut by the waves. In the surf zone the rocks and sand are incessantly tossed and tumbled. Most of the minerals in rock are not very resistant to this treatment and soon break down into tiny silt-size particles. Because silt particles are so small, it takes only a tiny amount of motion to keep them in suspension in the water. So the silt remains suspended in the water and is carried away by currents; eventually it will be deposited in the quiet water of a marsh or offshore in deep water. The sand grains that are left form a beach. Beach sand is so clean and uniform in grain size because of the efficient winnowing that goes on day and night in the surf zone.

Quartz and feldspars are common minerals in the granitic rocks that make up much of New England and, therefore, most of the rocks on the Cape. Beach sand on Cape Cod is made mostly of tough quartz and feldspar grains that remain after the other, softer minerals are worn away to silt. If you look closely at a handful of beach sand (a magnifier helps) you can see that most of the grains are clear or milky, and many have sharp corners. These are quartz grains. Some other quartz grains are stained yellow or brown with rust. You will see also quite a few white, gray, or yellow-white grains. These are feldspars, only a little less hard than quartz. You can see these same minerals in the gray-and-white speckled granitic rocks on the beach. Most of the black minerals that you can see in the rocks are relatively soft; they have been weathered and ground up into silt and washed away from the beach sand.

You may see a few gemlike pink garnet grains or opaque black magnetite (a magnet will pick up the magnetite) in the sand. These minerals are much less common than quartz and feldspar, but they are even tougher, and they are denser than quartz. Because they are so resistant to weathering, these minerals are better represented in the sand than they are in the rocks the sand is made from; occasionally wave conditions will be just right to concentrate these dense minerals and make an area of dark sand. Really fine sand, such as in a dune, may be almost pure quartz. Coarse sand usually has more feldspars and dark minerals and some bits of rock that have not completely broken down.

Waves Shape Beaches

Beaches form first where waves cut into the land, gradually eroding inland from the original shoreline. The land is cut away down to below the base of the waves, leaving a bluff on land and a wave-cut platform to seaward. You can see the shallow area seaward of a beach when large storm waves, feeling the bottom much farther out than the smaller fair-weather waves, break well offshore. Sandy beaches are built on the wave-cut bench where waves, breaking and energetically foaming ashore, have enough energy to carry sand up the slope. The water running back down the slope toward the surf zone has lost some of its energy, so not all the sand carried up the beach is carried back down; some is left behind, forming a beach with the typical gently sloping summer profile.

At places or times where the waves are larger and stronger, such as at headlands or during storms, the waves have enough energy even after they break to keep sand in suspension as they run back down

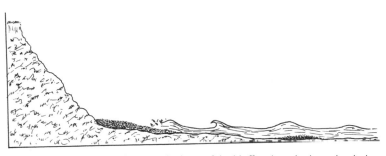

Fig. 38. Storm waves undermine the base of the bluff and erode the upland; the eroded sand from the bluff forms the beach. Beneath that mobile sand is the gently sloping platform that was cut into the fabric of the Cape as sea level rose.

the slope. Under those conditions the sand will be carried off the beach, leaving only rocks and cobbles too large for those waves to carry (and not much fun to walk on barefoot). Because of this sorting by waves, the size of the particles on a beach is a general guide to the average strength of the waves that shaped it; a beach of cobbles and pebbles indicates much more energetic waves than a beach of fine sand. The only exception to this rule is a beach where there is no source of sand, such as where jetties have interrupted the movement of sand. In those areas even small waves can carry away the sand, leaving only the rocks behind.

The beaches of the Cape change with the seasons because storm waves tend to come in fall and winter. These large and energetic waves erode the beach, carrying more sand into deep water than is carried up the beach. So a succession of storms may leave a beach narrow, steep, and rocky: the typical "winter beach." A long period of calm weather with smaller waves, whether in winter or summer, will carry sand back up onto the beach and rebuild the gentle, sandy beach known by summer beachgoers. Some of the sand eroded off the beaches by storm waves may be kept in suspension so long that it is carried far beyond the surf zone. This sand may be deposited in deep water offshore where waves cannot reach it to carry it back up the beach.

Sand does not move just toward and away from the shore, however. Waves that strike the beach at an angle (which most waves do) carry sand along the beach in the surf zone. As a wave breaks, the swash moves sand particles diagonally up the beach. As the backwash drains back into the ocean, it runs straight downhill, carrying sand grains into the surf a bit farther along the beach than they started. This zigzag motion of the sand grains produces a net movement of sand along

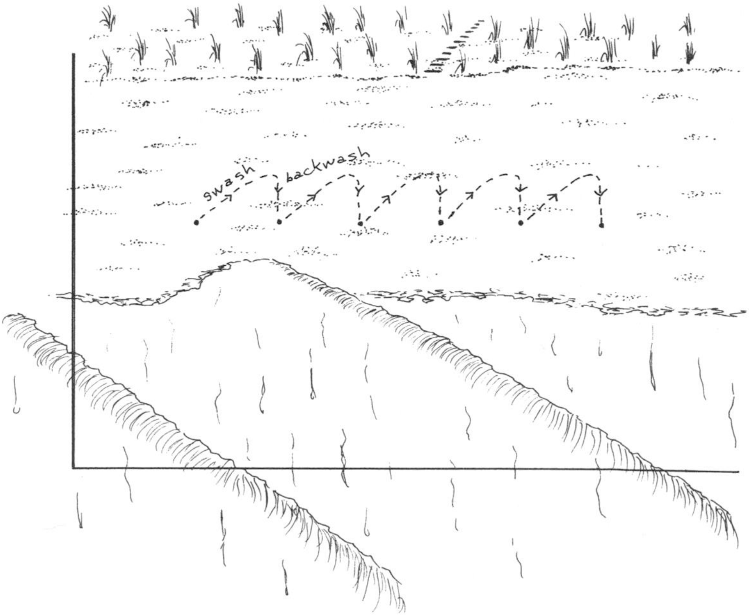

Fig. 39. Sand moves along a beach by the infinite arrivals of waves. Waves carry sand particles up the beach in their foaming edge; the backwash carries them down again. The paths followed by those sand particles are not straight lines up and back down, but rather a sawtooth pattern that results in net alongshore motion.

the beach. In some areas the direction of sand movement reverses seasonally, due to the seasonal change of winds. Along the south shore of the Upper and Mid-Cape, for instance, the general movement of sand is eastward in the summer in response to southwest winds. Occasionally, particularly in winter, the sand will move west in response to northeast storms.

Sand moving along a beach will fill openings in the shore and also will build barrier beaches across shallow water, as you can see at Sandy Neck in Barnstable and Nauset spit in Eastham. These barrier beaches protect the area shoreward, creating calm bays; salt marshes may form in this quiet water. Barrier beaches are the most changeable of beaches because they have water on both sides that is affected by winds and tides. Barrier beaches may be breached in storms from time to time, creating a new inlet to the bay behind.

Large boulders dot the beaches and the surf zone along many miles of shoreline, particularly where the moraines come down to the water, as along Buzzards Bay. Sailors have found that large rocks lurk along the shorelines close beneath the surface of bays and sounds as well. These rocks, brought by the glacier and dumped here as it melted, are too heavy for most waves to move, so they remain after the waves have carried away all the finer sediments that surrounded them. In time the boulders will weather and wear down from the constant battering by sand and stones carried by the waves. That is small consolation to a sailor who has put a new rock on the chart by finding it with a boat.

The upper part of a beach is usually dry and flatter than the sloping lower part. This part of the beach is reached only by the waves on the highest tides of the month, or during storms. The rest of the time this upper beach is the domain of the wind. Wind off the water will move the sand around, creating ripples like those made by waves in shallow water. The faster the wind, the heavier the grains it can carry. The wind also winnows the finer grains out of the sand and carries them away, often forming dunes behind the beach.

Whither the Beach

Because sand is always moving on the beaches and is sometimes carried out into deep water or inland, beaches can exist only where there is a continuing source of sand. On the Cape that source of sand is erosion of the bluffs and headlands. If the upland is not eroded, no new sand will replace the sand that is carried away every day. The beach will erode, and no new sand will arrive—until at last no beach remains.

Beaches, themselves such seemingly defenseless piles of loose sand, defend the land behind them. The offshore bars cause waves to break before reaching the land, and the rush of water up a beach expends energy that would otherwise be spent on the land behind the beach. Beaches are strong by being soft, by absorbing the energy of the waves and by yielding and rearranging themselves in response to the level of the sea and the energy of the waves that break against them. But beaches are made of sand in transit. If the system that supplies sand is interrupted, the beaches, those defenseless defenses, will soon be gone.

Inhabitants and Visitors

Most of the living things on beaches are so small that they are invisible without a microscope, but they are important because they are the base of the food chain. Tiny diatoms, bacteria, and cyanobacteria live in the wet spaces between the grains of sand, close enough to the surface to get some sunlight. They are eaten by protozoans, microscopic single-cell animals that also live among the sand grains. Preying on the protozoans are some barely visible creatures such as nematodes and copepods. These small creatures are the prey of yet larger animals such as the sandpipers that we see searching for food along the water's edge; birds also eat burrowing worms and Gemma Clams, the sesame-seed-size clams that live in the sand by the millions.

Under damp seaweed or around logs on the beach slope you will find Sand Hoppers, or Beach Fleas, tiny amphipods that look somewhat like shrimp and that forage on detritus. You've probably felt them bouncing off your legs as you cross the wrack line; they can jump several feet. You might see their ¼-inch-diameter holes just above the high-tide line. Before the days of off-road vehicles, Beach Tiger Beetles lived their entire lives on the sand of beaches. These days these striking ivory beetles with delicate brown stripes remain only on Martha's Vineyard, though entomologists are working to establish a population on Monomoy Island.

The animals that live in the surf zone cope with the constant motion of the sand by burrowing. Most of these small burrowers are hard to see, but Mole Crabs, inch-long egg-shaped crabs, can be seen if you are quick. They come up out of the sand to feed in each breaking wave, burrowing back into the sand as the wave runs out. A quick grab will sometimes reward you with one to look at up close. Surf clams, as the name suggests, also live in the surf zone, as well as in deeper water. These big (up to 8-inch) clams don't burrow very deep, relying on digging back into the sand quickly if they are excavated by a wave. It is astonishing how quickly clams can disappear into the sand—they extend their foot down into the sand, expand the lower end to anchor it, and pull themselves down to it edgewise. Hermit Crabs live in a wide variety of edge-of-the sea habitats and can be found on many beaches, in whatever cast-off shells they can find.

In the intertidal zone of rocky beaches live a number of snails (if the rocks are large you may have to look under the strands of the yellow-brown rockweed to find them). The Periwinkle (also frequently found in salt marshes) is an inch-long black or grey snail that grazes on algae. If you see a Periwinkle shell traveling along on legs, you know you are not seeing the sedentary snail but rather a Hermit Crab living in an old Periwinkle shell. The brighter-colored Dogwinkle is a bit

Fig. 40. Gull track. On soft mud or sand tracks like these are as common as the gulls themselves.

larger and is predatory, eating mussels and barnacles. Moon Snails (3 inches) and whelks (up to 7 inches) are also predatory. The whelks pry open the shells of clams and oysters; Moon Snails drill neat round holes through the shells of their chosen dinner. Either way the result is the same: the snail eats the clam.

Most other animals at the beach are visitors, like us. Raccoons come for clams, as do gulls—you can sometimes see gulls trying to break clams by dropping them onto the hard beach at low tide. You can expect to see Herring Gulls, Great Black-backed Gulls, and Ring-billed Gulls year-round. In summer Laughing Gulls add their hysterical cackle to the general chatter; in winter they are joined by the small, white-winged Bonaparte's Gulls, and there may be a few Black-legged Kittiwakes among them. Gulls and terns sometimes roost on the beach in large numbers, all facing into the wind, as though waiting for the show to start. Piping Plovers, however, actually raise their young on the bare sand of the upper beach. They lay their eggs in a shallow scrape in the sand, often among scattered tufts of Beach Grass. To nest successfully they need peace and solitude, conditions that are rare on Cape Cod beaches even in May, never mind July when the chicks fledge. Some sections of beaches are closed while these once common birds, now endangered, incubate their eggs and raise their young.

Horseshoe Crabs come in large numbers to more sheltered beaches on a moon high tide in May or June to lay eggs, though a few stay around until mid-July. Most of the seemingly dead Horseshoe Crabs on the summer beach are only the molted exoskeletons—look for the split along the forward margin where the animal wriggled out, leg by leg by leg. Migrating shorebirds such as Sanderlings and Red Knots time their arrival along the coast to coincide with Horseshoe Crab egg laying, taking advantage of the abundant food source to fuel flights farther north or for their own breeding and egg laying.

HORSESHOE CRABS

Horseshoe Crabs are survivors. For at least 350 million years these hard-shelled creatures have plowed along in shallow water, eating worms, clams, and whatever else they could grind up and put into their mouths. And every year they have come to the beaches in large numbers to lay eggs. Horseshoe Crabs do things slowly—walking, egg laying, living (they may live for twenty years)—and they do not reach sexual maturity for at least nine years after hatching. For all those past millions of years, as dinosaurs and other species have come and gone, the habits of Horseshoe Crabs have stood them in good stead. But recently a faster-moving species—us—has collected them in large and increasing numbers for bait and for medical research. Because they reproduce so slowly, and because so many birds and other creatures rely on their eggs for spring food, there is real concern about the potential collapse of the species and the domino effect the crabs' disappearance might have on the ecosystems that have evolved a dependence on them. Regulation may be slowing the harvesting of these creatures sufficiently to allow them to survive, but it may be years before we know.

In late summer and into the fall the beaches are again good places to find migratory shorebirds, eating as fast as they can to fatten up before they take off for grueling flights to wintering sites as far away as Central and South America.

Walking the high-tide line, you might find evidence of creatures that live offshore, including Slipper Shells (often with the velvety "fingers" of the green alga *Codium* attached), Moon Snails, Razor Clams, Jingle Shells, and Scallops, mixed with rockweed, Eelgrass, bird feathers, Sea Lettuce, Jellyfish, molted crab shells, Skate and whelk egg cases, Irish Moss, and, of course, human castoffs, mostly plastic.

Only a few plants have succeeded in adapting to the beach life. Chief among these hardy pioneers is Beach Grass, which sends out underground runners to start new plants, even in the shifting sand of the upper beach or dunes. Of course, it sometimes gets washed away completely, so it rarely grows as thickly on the beach as it does in a somewhat more protected location on a dune. Beach Pea, Sea Rocket, Dusty Miller, and Seaside Goldenrod also sometimes manage to survive for a time on the beach proper, although they, too, live longer and grow better farther from the water, behind a dune.

Until the late 1800s people rarely spent much time on beaches unless they were earning a living there, fishing or scavenging what-

Fig. 41. The high-tide line is often marked by a wavery line of marine castoffs: here, rockweed, Jingle Shell, Skate egg case, Scallop shell, Horseshoe Crab exoskeleton, and *Codium*. Plastic often figures large in this collection.

ever the sea sent ashore. Now beaches are prime real estate, a change that has had a big impact on the plants and animals of the beaches. If we are careful, we can continue to share beaches with them, but certainly there are some summer days when there seems to be no space on the beaches for anything other than ourselves.

Shoreline Hardening

Today many miles of the shoreline of the Cape have been subjected to the various processes probably best described as "hardening" or even "armoring." Bays, estuaries, and harbors are faced with bulkheads or seawalls; headlands and points are armored with revetments of large rocks; channels and inlets are straight and narrow, flanked by jetties; and beaches are broken every few hundred yards by groins running from the dunes to the level of the lowest tide.

All these engineered structures were built to protect something from the natural processes of the sea. In the short term, at least, these structures do work, but always the protection they provide is at the expense of something else. This is because the entire coastal system is connected.

The sand on Cape Cod beaches comes from the erosion of the Cape itself, and is carried along the coast by waves (see fig. 39). Some sand is carried out into deep water during storms whence it cannot return to shore, but the same storms may erode new sand from the bluffs. Thus, in their natural state, beaches are in dynamic equilibrium with the conditions that have created them, rearranging themselves in response to storm waves or rising sea level. But once we began to build on beaches, or on the bluffs that provide sand to them, we became less willing to tolerate the natural movement of the shoreline. So we have begun the losing battle, for even with engineering and repairs, in the face of rising sea level we must always lose . . . either the bluffs or the beaches.

JETTIES AND GROINS

Groins are the most common hardening structures. Groins are low walls, mostly of stone or concrete, set at right angles to the beach. They are designed to catch the sand moving along the beach and make the beach wider. And of course they do this—on the "upstream" side of the groin. Sand moves in its zigzag path along the beach until it is stopped by the groin. Over time, sand builds up against the groin until it has widened the upstream beachfront enough so that sand is carried around the end of the groin. As it is carried around the end, however, some of the sand may be deposited in deeper water offshore; the beach just downstream of the groin gets that much less sand. In addition, the downstream beach will be eroded by the relatively sand-free waves breaking against it.

Jetties protect channels. They work like large groins by intercepting the sand that would otherwise move into the inlet. The biggest jetties on the Cape protect the eastern entrance of the Cape Cod Canal. Unfor-

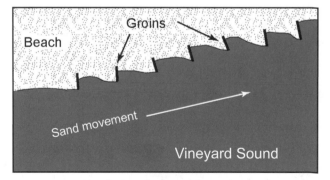

Fig. 42. A Section of Falmouth's south shore. The prevailing westerly winds move sand eastward along this shore, as shown by its buildup on the west side of each groin. Occasionally a northeaster will blow from the east long and hard enough to move the sand back to the west and pile it against the east side of the groins. In either state the beachfront is jagged and irregular.

Environments

tunately, the only way to sufficiently reduce shoaling in a channel is to build jetties out so far that the sand swept around the end of the jetty is carried into deep water. So jetties may prevent shoaling in the channel, but they also result in the narrowing and potential loss of the beaches downstream. This is because the sand that is prevented from moving into the channel also is prevented from moving on to the next beach.

Examples of the effects of groins and jetties on beaches can be seen on most Cape shorelines except those facing the Atlantic in the Cape Cod National Seashore. The characteristic saw-toothed shape of a beach with groins and the difference in width of beaches on either side of even a small set of jetties is obvious on maps and aerial photographs and clear to anyone walking the beach.

SEAWALLS, BULKHEADS, AND REVETMENTS

As more houses, and more expensive ones, have been built near the water's edge or near the edges of bluffs, the owners have begun to worry about the effect of erosion on the land. In general, erosion on the Mid- and Upper Cape is slower than on the Cape's exposed eastern side, where the average erosion rate is 3 feet per year. But even in the more protected waters of the sounds and Buzzards Bay, headlands, beaches, and islands periodically experience the effect of storm-driven waves. These waves can erode more land in a few crashing hours than was eroded in the previous twenty or thirty years. It is an understandable reaction, as you see your front yard disappearing into the sea, to seek a way to protect your house. This desire to protect the land produces bulkheads, seawalls, and revetments, and these structures can protect the land behind them for a while. They do so by reflecting the energy of the waves and resisting, rather than yielding to, the battering of the storm.

Seawalls and revetments protect land at the expense of beaches. The hard shore reflects the energy of the waves; the reflected waves erode nearby beaches both above and below water. Without the protective beach and shallow water, bigger waves can then reach the coast, to batter and eventually undermine the protective structure. In addition, by protecting the land, the hardening of the shore deprives the downstream beaches of new sand. In order to have beaches on the Cape, we must have erosion of the upland. When we prevent that erosion we protect the upland, temporarily, but we lose the beaches. In the long run erosion of the upland will begin again, once the beaches are worn away. Pumping sand onto the beaches from offshore is possible, but it is expensive, temporary, and damaging to the fish and other creatures that live where the sand might be mined. The choice between protecting the land and having beaches is a choice made every year by property owners concerned about their homes or investments, but it is a choice that affects not just themselves but all of us.

This question of shoreline hardening is a difficult one because of the intertwined emotional and economic interests of those of us who live near and depend on the shore. The revetment desired by some to protect an investment or a lighthouse may stop the sand and destroy the beach that is the protection, pleasure, or livelihood of others. The jetties that allow boats to use an inlet may eventually cause the destruction of the very barrier beach that protects the bay.

The movement of sand along a shoreline is the result of natural processes. We can change the movement, but we cannot change the processes.

DUNES

Dunes and beaches are often closely connected, but they work differently. Beaches are the domain of water; the erosion and deposition of sand on a beach is controlled by the ocean and its waves. Dunes are the domain of the wind. Although they have much in common with the dry upper parts of beaches, dunes are worth considering separately.

How Dunes Work

Dunes, like the dry parts of beaches, are made of loose sand grains that are easily moved by the wind. Gentle zephyrs, of course, cannot stir even fine dry sand. But every beachgoer knows that strong winds can pick up sand grains and blow them high enough not only to pepper your sandwich as you recline on your beach chair but to get in your eyes as you run to a less windy spot. Where the wind, bearing its load of sand grains, encounters an obstruction it swirls around the obstruction and slows down. This slower wind can't carry the sand, so a pile of sand develops downwind, in the lee of the obstruction, as you'll see when you go back to find your beach chair. If the wind continues, the pile of sand in the lee of the obstruction can grow high enough that it interrupts the airflow itself, thus collecting more sand and eventually becoming a dune.

Fig. 43. Sand moved by the wind builds up in the lee of any obstacle.

Fig. 44. The avalanches of sand that slide down the leeward side of dunes create a distinctive pattern, as seen here in cross-section. That pattern is preserved in sandstones made of dune sand and can be seen in them, for instance in the cross-bedded sandstones of the American Southwest.

An active dune has one steep face, on the leeward or downwind side, and a gently sloping side to windward. The wind sweeps up this gentle windward side, collecting sand and carrying it onward and upward. At the top of the slope the wind eddies into the lee of the dune and drops its sand. The sand piles up higher and steeper to the point of instability, then slides down the lee face, creating a distinctive sloping layer of sand that flattens toward the bottom. You can see these layers in places where rain or waves have cut through a dune. Ripples, whether made by sand or water, work in the same way.

Entire dunes can actually move (and dune fields can expand) if the wind carries sand downwind long enough. Grain by grain, the sand is cut away from the windward side, carried up to the top, and dropped in the lee. The sand accumulates and avalanches down the lee side, and the dune gradually migrates downwind. This is how thick bands of dunes develop, such as the ones on Sandy Neck and in the Provincelands. Sand blows inland from the beachfront dunes, moves across the flats, and accumulates in the lee of some plant or stone to form a new dune.

Dune sand is typically well sorted, finer-grained, and whiter than beach sand, because the finer grains and less dense minerals are carried more easily by the wind (quartz and feldspar are the lightweight, white minerals in Cape sand). A magnifier will help you see the difference between the sand on a beach and the finer, more homogeneous dune sand winnowed out of that beach. Sand grains in dunes usually have a frosted appearance because they scratch one another as they blow and bounce across the surface.

The dunes on Cape Cod—the miles of 50-foot dunes on Barnstable's Sandy Neck, the vegetation-stabilized dunes at Stage Harbor

Environments

in Chatham, and the really big dunes in the Provincelands—were all built in this same way. Sand blew off the beaches and piled up inland wherever the wind met an obstruction. As long as there is enough sand on beaches and the wind blows from the water to the land, dunes will form and migrate inland. On many Cape Cod beaches today, however, the supply of sand has been cut off or drastically reduced by jetties, groins, or revetments. That, combined with the continuing rise in sea level, means that beaches and dunes are being eroded instead of readjusting by moving a little farther inland. Remember that these dunes were built during a time of rising sea level, so it is not the rising sea level alone that is causing the loss of the dunes.

When Dunes Settle Down

A dune, being just a pile of loose sand created by the wind, will continue to move when the wind blows unless something prevents the sand from being picked up by the wind. Wet or frozen dunes are relatively stable, but dunes may dry or thaw in short order, making the sand available to the wind again. Many dunes on the Cape are thus movable features, but vegetation may slow or actually stop them. The leaves and stems of the plants slow the wind, causing it to drop any sand grains it is carrying and preventing it from picking up new sand from the dune surface. The roots of the plants hold moisture and also physically knit the sand together. When the plants die, the decaying plant matter holds moisture and contributes nutrients, beginning the process of soil formation.

The plant most likely to be found in the harsh dune environment is Beach Grass, which shows none of the finicky nature of lawn grass—it can grow in bare sand. A Beach Grass plant quickly grows underground runners that sprout roots and new bunches of leaves every 6 to 8 inches. Each bunch of leaves is stimulated, not smothered, by the sand that accumulates on and around it. As a result Beach Grass can quickly colonize a patch of bare dune and knit it together with vertical stems and roots and horizontal layers of rhizomes. To cope with the harsh and variable conditions on a dune, the leaves of Beach Grass roll up in hot, dry weather to preserve moisture and open out in damp weather when the plant won't dry out. You can see where this pioneer plant is moving into new areas by following with your eyes the lines of leaves that sprout from the runners. Beach Grass is sometimes planted for the purpose of stabilizing dunes; these plantings usually are recognizable because of their regular rows.

Inhabitants

The few other plants that can tolerate the salty, dry conditions and shifting sand of the beach or a new dune may soon follow the pioneer Beach Grass. Dusty Miller, a garden escapee with fuzzy pale green leaves, must originally have come from some hot, dry clime. The white fuzz shades the surface of the leaf and gives Dusty Miller the protection it needs to survive here. Sea Rocket has adapted to the dry dune with waxy, fleshy leaves that can store water and resist salt. Beach Pea also has somewhat fleshy leaves, and it extracts nitrogen from the air and fixes it in the soil, which helps both it and other plants survive in the bare sand. A bit farther from the water, perhaps on the back of a dune, the dark, gray-green mounds of yellow-flowering Beach Heather (also known locally as Poverty Grass) can be found, along with Beach Plum (it has a deep taproot to reach down to water), Seaside Goldenrod, Beach Rose, and Bayberry (the wax that coats its tiny gray berries is what bayberry candles are made from), all gradually increasing in height away from the strong, salt-laden winds of the ocean.

Surprisingly, a number of fungi live in dunes and bare sand. Most of the time they grow invisibly underground, but in the late summer and fall the fruiting bodies show up aboveground. Most common are the Earthstars, small spherical spore bodies whose outer covering splits to form a star shape in damp weather, but several kinds of mushrooms also are common, especially in dune hollows or places where dunes have buried trees or shrubs.

Relatively few animals live permanently in dunes, mostly insects and spiders that burrow in the sand or live on or in plant stems. The insects that have found ways of living in the harsh dune environment include the Dune Grasshopper and Wolf Spider (they wear protective speckled coloration) and a few flies and wasps.

Protective Dunes

Dune fields are more or less permanent features, made of transitory individual dunes. They are important to the Cape not only because of the unusual habitats they provide, but also because they protect the

Fig. 45. Some plants can establish themselves on active dunes: here, Dusty Miller, Sea Rocket, and Beach Grass, showing the marks in the sand that give it the name "Compass Grass."

land from the large, destructive waves of hurricanes and winter storms. This is one reason that many dunes are protected from foot and vehicle traffic—we protect them because they protect us. Dunes are fragile because they are built of loose sand which, if stripped of vegetation, can blow or wash away in a few hours. For all their toughness in the face of salt spray and winter winds, many of the dune plants are quite sensitive to trampling. Do your best to stay off them.

IDENTIFICATION

TREES AND SHRUBS

The native trees and the common shrubs of Cape Cod are listed here, with notes on the most useful characteristics for identification: leaf shape, blossom, trunk, or autumn leaf color. Some trees are distinctive and can be recognized at a glance; others need closer examination.

The list, like most field guides, groups related plants, and it places the oldest groups at the beginning and the most recently evolved at the end. Relatively few types of trees grow on the Cape, so you can flip through the pages and compare the illustrations and descriptions to the plant you are looking at, or refer to the index to find trees by name.

Conifers

Hemlock (*Tsuga canadensis*) Fig. 46
> Occasional. Native to Northeast, probably introduced to Cape. Needles 0.3 to 0.7 inch, variable in length on each branch. Cones less than 1 inch long, at branch tips.

~

Atlantic White Cedar (*Chamaecyparis thyoides*) Fig. 47
> Locally common but restricted to Atlantic White Cedar swamps. Blue-gray needles flat against the twigs; tips of twigs blunt; cones look like faceted, blue-gray raisins.

~

Red Cedar (*Juniperus virginiana*) Fig. 48
> Common in abandoned fields and along roads. Grows to 40 feet. Needles flattened scales; new growth pointed and prickly; smooth, blue-gray berries.

~

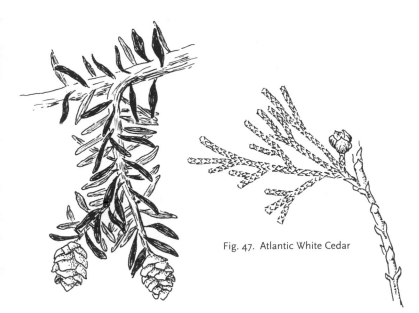

Fig. 47. Atlantic White Cedar

Fig. 46. Hemlock

Fig. 48. Red Cedar

Pines (*Pinus*)
Pine needles grow in bundles of one to five, with a papery wrapping around the base of each bundle. The needle bundle is a cylinder that may be divided—the more needles it is divided into, the finer the needles, and the more acute the needle cross-section. Mentally compare a pie cut into five slices to one cut in half.

Eastern White Pine (*P. strobus*) Fig. 49
Common. Foliage soft and wispy; needles in bundles of five, 5 inches long. Can be a large tree. Cones long and thin, coated with white pitch.

Pitch Pine (*P. rigida*) Fig. 50
Common. Needles in bunches of three, 3 inches long; yellower than White Pine. Many trees small, ragged-looking. Cones rounded; some persist for years, opening only after a fire.

Red Pine (*P. resinosa*)
Planted, not native to Cape. Needles in twos.

Broadleaf Trees and Shrubs

Willows (*Salix*)
Willows are easily identified by the narrow, alternate leaves and the catkins (pussy willows) but are hard to distinguish from each other; many are escapees from cultivation.

Bebb Willow (*S. bebbiana*) Fig. 51
Common near water. Small tree. Leaves broad and blunt for a willow; many are fuzzy on the back. Leaf veins sunken.

Black Willow (*S. nigra*)
Occasional on pond shores. Can be a large tree, though rarely tall. Leaves 3 to 6 inches long, less than ¾ inch wide.

Pussy Willow (*S. discolor*)
Common, often in damp places. Easily identified in early spring when flower buds are much larger than leaf buds or later when the buds have opened into pussy willows.

~

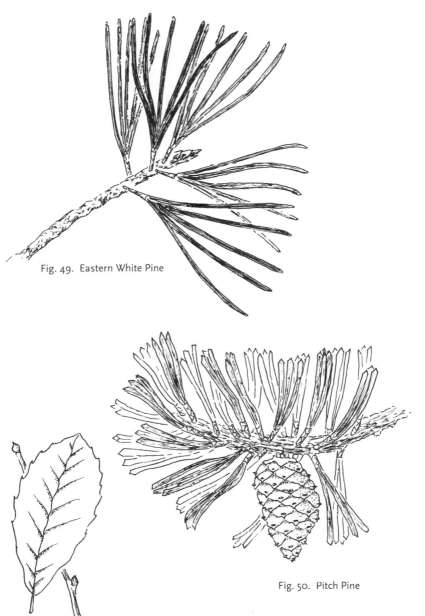

Fig. 49. Eastern White Pine

Fig. 50. Pitch Pine

Fig. 51. Bebb Willow

Trees and Shrubs

99

Poplars (*Populus*) Fig. 52
Quaking Aspen (*P. tremuloides*)
Common. Leaf stems flat, allowing leaves to flutter in slight breeze. Leaves rounded-triangular, with small teeth. Aspens spread by root sprouts; clumps are usually clones.

Big-Toothed Aspen (*P. grandidentata*)
Common. Leaf stems flat. Leaves larger than Quaking Aspen, with large teeth. Bark on old trees furrowed.

~

Wax-myrtles (*Myrica*)
Bayberry (*M. pensylvanica*) Fig. 53
Common. Shrub, 2 to 8 feet tall. Leaves aromatic; gray, waxy berries grow on twigs. Favored food of birds; bayberry candles are made from the wax.

Sweet Gale (*M. gale*) Fig. 54
Common in wetlands. Leaves similar to Bayberry. Small cones at ends of branches, no berries. Fixes nitrogen.

~

Sweet Fern (*Comptonia peregrina*) Fig. 55
Common. Not a fern. Small shrub with leaves lobed like ferns. Foliage fragrant.

~

Hickory (*Carya*) Fig. 56
Leaves pinnately compound with five or seven leaflets, 8 to 12 inches long, turn a distinctive golden yellow in the fall, often with brown spots. Nut 1 to 1½ inches in diameter, with a green husk around a ribbed nutshell.

Mockernut Hickory (*C. tomentosa*)
Locally common. Leaves fragrant when crushed, usually covered on the back with short hairs. In winter terminal bud large and smooth, twigs stout, may be fuzzy. Nut husk thick, does not split to base. Nutshell tough, nut good to eat.

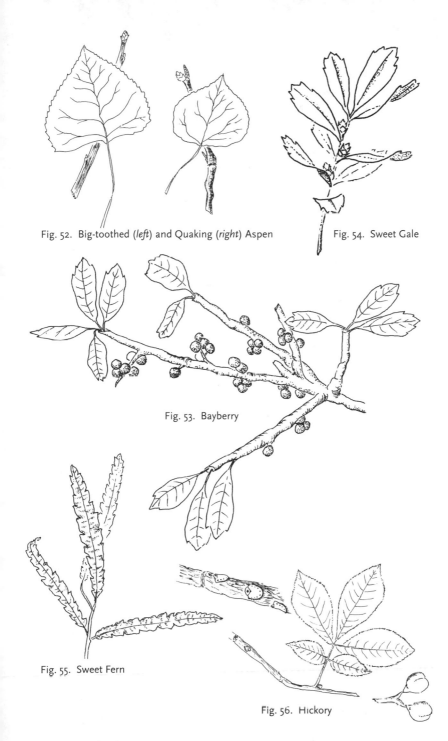

Fig. 52. Big-toothed (*left*) and Quaking (*right*) Aspen

Fig. 54. Sweet Gale

Fig. 53. Bayberry

Fig. 55. Sweet Fern

Fig. 56. Hickory

Trees and Shrubs

Pignut Hickory (*C. glabra*)
> Scattered. A variable species. Leaves smooth on back; terminal bud scales stick out into points; twigs smooth and slender. The husk and nut are often pear-shaped.

~

Hazelnut (*Corylus*)
Beaked Hazel (*C. cornuta*) Fig. 57
> Fairly common. Shrub. Doubly toothed, birchlike leaves. Tiny red flowers. Nuts, usually two back to back, enclosed in hairy husks with a long tube-shaped beak. The small nuts are good but the squirrels harvest them early.

American Hazel (*C. americana*)
> Occasional. Leaves like above but downy on back; twigs hairy. Nut surrounded by leafy bract.

~

American Hop-hornbeam (*Ostrya virginiana*) Fig. 58
> Occasional. Leaves birchlike, bark reddish and shreddy. Seeds grouped, enclosed in puffy pods, remain on tree into winter.

~

American Hornbeam (*Carpinus caroliniana*) Fig. 59
> Occasional in rich woods. Leaves birchlike; twigs very slender; buds small; no catkins in winter. Trunk and branches "muscular," with smooth gray bark. Each small nut enclosed in three-lobed, leafy bract.

~

Birch (*Betula*)
Sweet or Black Birch (*B. lenta*)
> Uncommon, on Upper Cape. Leaves smell strongly of wintergreen when crushed.

Yellow Birch (*B. alleghaniensis*)
> Uncommon, mostly in damp soil. Leaves oval; bark yellowish to bronze, in horizontally peeling strips. Also has wintergreen smell.

Gray Birch (*B. populifolia*) Fig. 60
> Common. White bark with black horizontal lines and black triangles below branch base. Leaves triangular.

Identification

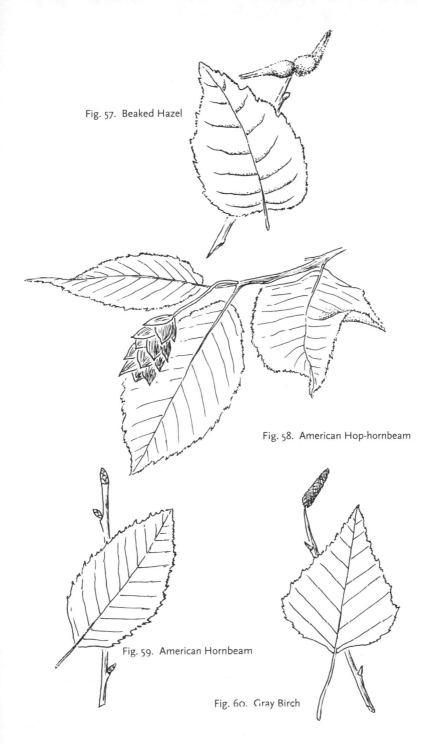

Fig. 57. Beaked Hazel

Fig. 58. American Hop-hornbeam

Fig. 59. American Hornbeam

Fig. 60. Gray Birch

White Birch (*B. papyrifera*)
Occasional. White bark, with horizontally peeling strips. Young trunks and branches bronze. Leaves oval, with rounded base.

~

Alder (*Alnus*)
Near water. Have oval, toothed leaves and ½-inch cones like miniature pinecones. Alders fix nitrogen.

Speckled Alder (*A. rugosa*) Fig. 61
Occasional. Shrub or small tree. Bark speckled.

Common Alder (*A. serrulata*)
Common. Shrub or small tree.

European Alder (*A. glutinosa*)
Locally common. Tree. Leaves rounded, often notched at the tip, gummy when young. Spread from cultivation.

~

Beech (*Fagus*)
American Beech (*F. grandifolia*) Fig. 62
Common but local. May be large tree. Toothed leaves oval, 2½ to 8 inches long; bark grey, smooth; buds long, pointed.

European Beech (*F. sylvatica*) Fig. 63
Occasional. Introduced. Both the copper-colored and typical green-leafed varieties reproduce in the woods. Leaves smaller and less toothed than American Beeches. Beeches may hybridize.

~

American Chestnut (*Castanea dentata*) Fig. 64
Uncommon. Leaves to 8 inches. Adult trees killed by chestnut blight from Europe in early 1900s; some roots still sprout, may grow to 25 feet, rarely reproduce. Recognize in winter as cluster of saplings, some dead, some with smooth, shining, red-brown bark. Sprouts may show bulging longitudinal splits in bark characteristic of blight.

~

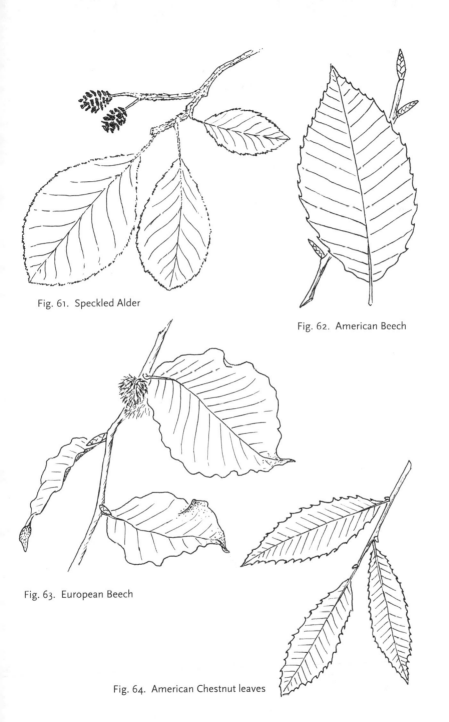

Fig. 61. Speckled Alder

Fig. 62. American Beech

Fig. 63. European Beech

Fig. 64. American Chestnut leaves

Horse Chestnut (*Aesculus hippocastanum*)

An introduced member of the buckeye family, often planted as an ornamental. Five-part compound leaves.

~

Oak (*Quercus*)

Leaves of root sprouts and saplings may be large and unusual; leaves produced after defoliation by caterpillars may be small and uncharacteristic.

White Oak group

Members of the White Oak group have leaves with rounded lobes and acorns that mature in one year.

White Oak (*Q. alba*) Fig. 65

Common. Leaves with long, rounded lobes. Back of leaf often whitish.

Dwarf Chinquapin Oak (*Q. prinoides*) Fig. 66

Occasional in pine barrens, dry woods. Shrub-size. Leaves have three to seven somewhat sharp scallops or teeth.

Post Oak (*Q. stellata*) Fig. 67

Local. A small tree. Leaf lobes squarish. Back of leaves covered with tawny hairs in radiating starlike groups.

~

Black Oak group

Members of the Black Oak group have leaves with bristle-tipped lobes. Acorns mature in two years; thus in autumn they have both large, ripe acorns on last year's growth and tiny (⅛ inch long) new acorns on this year's growth.

Red Oak (*Q. rubra*) Fig. 68

Uncommon and local. Leaves have seven to twelve bristle-tipped lobes. Leaf buds ¼ inch or more, pointed, rounded. Twigs often strongly ridged or fluted.

Scarlet Oak (*Q. coccinea*) Fig. 69

Abundant. Sinuses between lobes very deep, reaching almost to the midrib; fewer lobes than Red Oak. Turns bright red in fall.

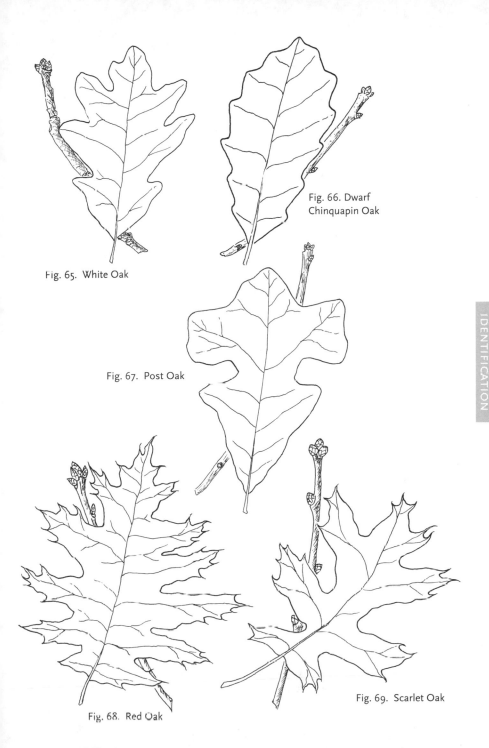

Fig. 65. White Oak

Fig. 66. Dwarf Chinquapin Oak

Fig. 67. Post Oak

Fig. 68. Red Oak

Fig. 69. Scarlet Oak

Trees and Shrubs

Black Oak (*Q. velutina*) Fig. 70
Abundant. Leaves variable; sinuses may be deep or shallow. Leaves velvety on back. Twigs may be downy. Leaf buds ¼ inch or more, five-sided, grayish-downy.

Bear Oak (*Q. ilicifolia*) Fig. 71
Common, often as undergrowth in Pitch Pine woods. Shrub or small tree. Leaves barely lobate. When "scrub oak" refers to a species, this is it; though the phrase often means "short oak."

~

American Elm (*Ulmus americana*) Fig. 72
Native but uncommon; in wet woods. Many grow in towns despite Dutch elm disease. Leaves oval and toothed.

~

Sassafras (*Sassafras albidum*) Fig. 73
Common. Most often seen as a small tree or thicket, but can grow to 40 feet with a thick trunk. Three kinds of leaves: oval, mitten-shaped, and mitten-with-a-thumb-on-each-side. Twigs smooth and shiny green, with spicy fragrance. Leaves turn distinctive yellow-orange in fall.

~

Spicebush (*Lindera benzoin*)
Occasional, in damp woods on Upper Cape. Shrub, to 9 feet. Small yellow flowers, April. Bark fragrant when scraped, similar to Sassafras. Leaves 4 inches, pointed-oval, yellow in fall. Berries red.

~

Witch Hazel (*Hamamelis virginiana*) Fig. 74
Common. A shrub or small tree with small spidery yellow flowers in fall. Leaves have rounded teeth and, with bark, are source of the astringent called "witch hazel."

~

Chokeberry (*Aronia*)
Three species of chokeberry on the Cape differ chiefly in color of small, applelike fruit (red, purple, or black). Leaves similar to apple, somewhat furry beneath.

~

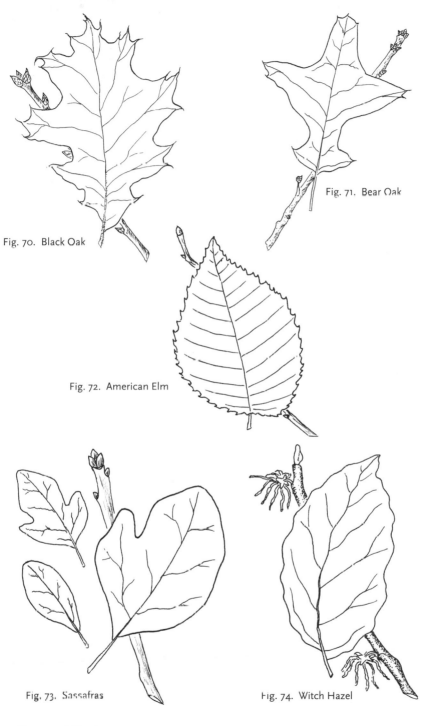

Fig. 70. Black Oak

Fig. 71. Bear Oak

Fig. 72. American Elm

Fig. 73. Sassafras

Fig. 74. Witch Hazel

Shadbush or Serviceberry (*Amelanchier canadensis*) Fig. 75
Common in wet places. Large shrub (to 20+ feet). Small oval leaves;
dark blue or black tasteless fruit. Blooms just as the Herring (sometimes called Shad) begin to run.

~

Hawthorn (*Crataegus*) Fig. 76
Occasional. Small trees. It is easy to tell a hawthorn, but difficult to
distinguish among the twelve species found on the Cape. Leaves
toothed and notched, white flowers followed by small red fruits;
long, extremely sharp thorns.

~

Blackberries and Raspberries (*Rubus*)
Fourteen species of *Rubus* grow wild on the Cape. All have compound, coarsely toothed leaves, prickles or thorns on the stems, and
white or pale pink, roselike flowers. Berries ripen August to September; all are edible, most are delicious (for jam too).

~

Cherry (*Prunus*)
Pointed-oval, toothed leaves. Many show typical cherry bark:
smooth and shiny with short, horizontal pinstripes.

Beach Plum (*P. maritima*) Fig. 77
Common in dunes. Low, thickly branched shrub with somewhat
hairy twigs. Blooms white in May and June. Small purple plums
ripen in late August, good for eating and jelly.

Wild Plum (*P. americana*)
Local in the Sandy Neck dunes.

Pin Cherry (*P. pensylvanica*)
Red fruit, in clusters.

Black Cherry (*P. serotina*) Fig. 78
Common. Can be large tree. Bark on old trees has squarish scales;
inner bark of twigs has bitter taste and smell. Racemes of white
flowers in June. Fruit black. Trees commonly infected with Black
Knot fungus that forms lumps on branches.

~

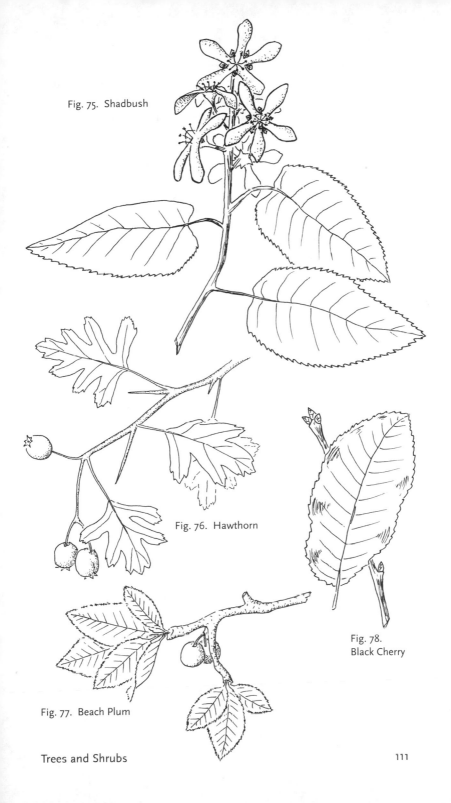

Fig. 75. Shadbush

Fig. 76. Hawthorn

Fig. 78.
Black Cherry

Fig. 77. Beach Plum

Trees and Shrubs

Black Locust (*Robinia pseudoacacia*) Fig. 79
Common. Introduced from the south. Leaves pinnately compound, 8 to 14 inches long. Fragrant white flowers in drooping racemes, followed by 2- to 4-inch-long flat pods, like dried bean pods. Twigs have spines.

~

Sumac (*Rhus*) Fig. 80
Sumacs have pinnately compound leaves and most have upright clusters of red, hairy fruits at the ends of the branches.

Staghorn Sumac (*R. typhina*)
Common. Stems hairy.

Shining Sumac (*R. copallina*)
Occasional. Shrub-size. Leaves winged between leaflets.

Smooth Sumac (*R. glabra*)
Common. Smooth stems.

~

Poison Sumac (*Toxicodendron vernix*)
Locally common along borders of swamps and salt marshes. Shrub or small tree. Leaves with smooth margins. Berries white, smooth. Sap can cause severe skin rashes and allergic reactions.

~

Holly (*Ilex*)
American Holly (*I. opaca*)
Locally common. Leaves evergreen, typical holly shape, yellower than English Holly.

Inkberry (*I. glabra*) Fig. 81
Common. Narrow, shiny leaves with smooth margins, mostly evergreen. Berries black, on short stem in leaf axils.

Winterberry (*I. verticillata*)
Common in damp woods and swamps. Small shrub with 2-inch-long, alternate, oval, slightly toothed, deciduous leaves. Female bushes bear brilliant red-orange berries that last into winter; berries are eaten by birds but are not preferred food.

~

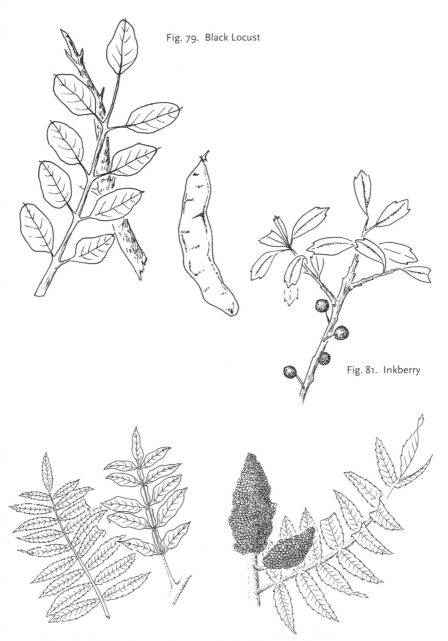

Fig. 79. Black Locust

Fig. 81. Inkberry

Fig. 80. *Left to right*: Smooth Sumac, Shining Sumac, Staghorn Sumac

Trees and Shrubs

Maple (*Acer*)
Red Maple (*A. rubrum*) Fig. 82
   Common, especially in damp woods. Leaves smaller and less deeply
   cleft than most maples. Buds and leaf stems often red. Turns red
   or orange and yellow in fall.

~

Basswood, Linden (*Tilia*)
Basswood (*T. neglecta*)
   On Sandy Neck in Barnstable. Native. Leaves fuzzy on the back.

European Linden (*T. europaea*) Fig. 83
   Occasional. Escaped from cultivation. Most Lindens on the Cape
   are this species, recognizable by the smooth leaves with large tufts
   of hair in the axils of veins at the base of the leaf.

~

Autumn Olive (*Elaeagnus umbellata*)
   Invasive in many areas. Introduced. Small tree. Oblong, pointed
   leaves, silvery or brownish beneath. Long, sharp thorns. Fruits reddish or pink-brown, eaten by birds, which then spread the seed.

~

Tupelo [Sour Gum, Black Gum, Pepperidge, Beetle Bung]
   (*Nyssa sylvatica*) Fig. 84
   Common around water. Medium-size tree with contorted, horizontal branches. Shiny oval leaves turn brilliant scarlet in late summer. Fruit dark blue, usually clustered; favorite food of Catbirds.

~

Dogwood (*Cornus*)
Flowering Dogwood (*C. florida*) Fig. 85
   Occasional in rich woods. Small tree with oval-pointed leaves. Four
   wide, white bracts surround small flowers. Fruit clustered, red;
   favored food of birds. Flowering Dogwoods have been reduced by a
   fungus that spread from the south during the 1980s.

Alternate Leaf Dogwood (*C. alternifolia*)
   Occasional. Shrub or small tree. Leaves like Flowering Dogwood
   but alternate. Clustered small flowers; blue fruits.

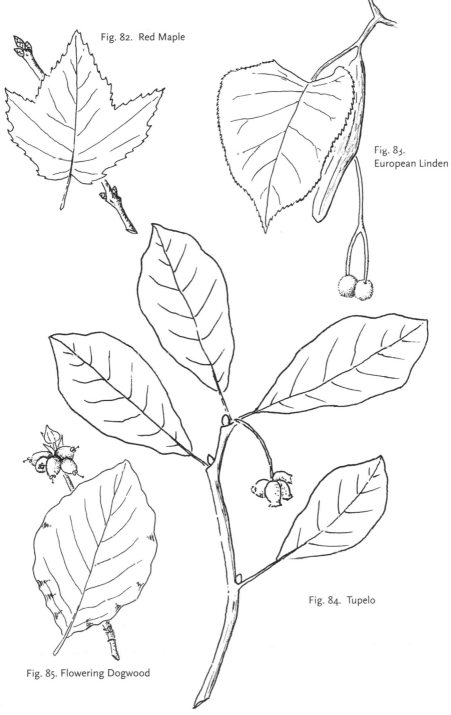

Fig. 82. Red Maple

Fig. 83.
European Linden

Fig. 84. Tupelo

Fig. 85. Flowering Dogwood

Trees and Shrubs

Gray Dogwood or Panicled Dogwood (*C. racemosa*)
Occasional. Small tree or shrub. Small white flowers in elongate or convex clusters. Branches gray.

~

Sweet Pepperbush (*Clethra alnifolia*) Fig. 86
Common, mostly in damp areas. Shrub, 5 to 8 feet. Leaves oval and toothed. Blooms in August—erect spikes of fragrant white flowers. Dry seed spikes with round seed capsules persist through winter.

~

Heath Family

Swamp Azalea (*Rhododendron viscosum*) Fig. 87
Common in damp soil. Shrub, to 6 feet. Pointed-oval leaves, 2 inches long. Fragrant, white, trumpet-shaped flowers in June. Flowers and buds may be hairy and sticky—this keeps the ants away from the nectar.

Sheep Laurel (*Kalmia angustifolia*) Fig. 88
Abundant. Shrub, to 3 feet. Blooms summer; blossoms like Mountain Laurel but bright magenta, ½ inch across. Leaves gray-green, often drooping.

Maleberry (*Lyonia ligustrina*)
Common. Shrub, to 6 feet. Leaves and flowers similar to blueberries. Fruit is tiny, dry, and hard, like peppercorn.

Fetterbush (*Leucothoe racemosa*)
Common in moist thickets. Oval leaves, similar to those of blueberries; racemes of small white flowers; dry fruits with a persisting upright style.

Leatherleaf (*Chamaedaphne calyculata*) Fig. 89
Common in wet areas. Low shrub. Leaves smallest at end of twig; nearly evergreen (may be purple-brown in winter), brownish and fuzzy beneath.

Huckleberries (*Gaylussacia*)
Huckleberries are related to the similar blueberries. Three similar species grow on the Cape. The common one, Black Huckleberry (*G. baccata*), a shrub to 2 feet, was Thoreau's favorite. Huckleberries

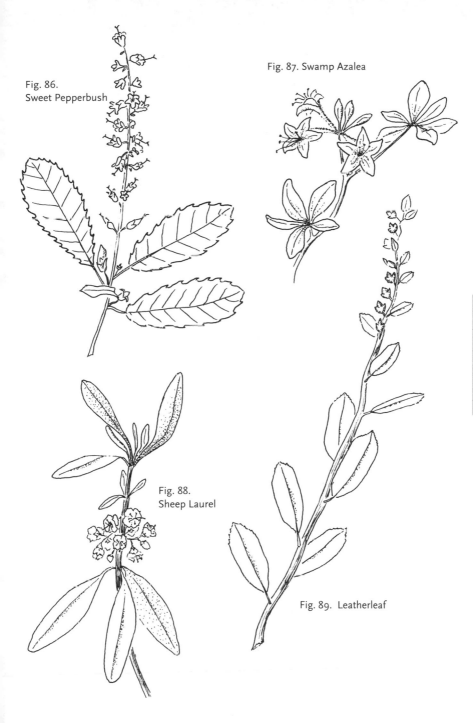

Fig. 86.
Sweet Pepperbush

Fig. 87. Swamp Azalea

Fig. 88.
Sheep Laurel

Fig. 89. Leatherleaf

have sweet, black fruits with 10 seeds each. The leaves are dotted with resin globules on the underside.

Blueberries (*Vaccinium*)
Seven species occur on the Cape. Oval leaves, bell-shaped white or pink flowers and, in winter, red twigs. Highbush Blueberry (*V. corymbosum*) may grow to 8 feet, with multiple twisted trunks, usually in wet areas.

~

Ashes (*Fraxinus*)
Ashes have large, opposite, pinnately compound leaves that color a distinctive yellow-brown tinged with purple in the fall. Seed a single-winged samara.

White Ash (*F. americana*)
Occasional. Can be large tree. Leaves 8 to 12 inches long, usually with seven leaflets.

Red Ash (*F. pennsylvanica*) Fig. 90
Occasional in wet areas. Small tree. Leaves similar to White Ash but smaller. Also called Green Ash.

~

Buttonbush (*Cephalanthus occidentalis*) Fig. 91
Common near water. Shrub, mostly less than 6 feet. Smooth-edged leaves, 4 inches, long oval with pointed tip. Flowers white 1½-inch balls; fruits also round. Summer blooming.

~

Viburnum (*Viburnum*)
Shrubs; small white flowers in clusters; fruits blue or black.

Wild Raisin (*V. nudum*) Fig. 92
Common. Shrub to 6 feet. Flower and fruit on stalks. Fruits ripen from white through pink to blue—all colors can occur together. Leaf margin smooth near base, toothed from midpoint to tip.

Arrowwood (*V. dentatum*) Fig. 93
Common shrub in moist ground. Leaves with coarse teeth.

Maple-leaved Viburnum (*V. acerifolium*)
Upper Cape. Shrub. Leaves like Red Maple, teeth more rounded.

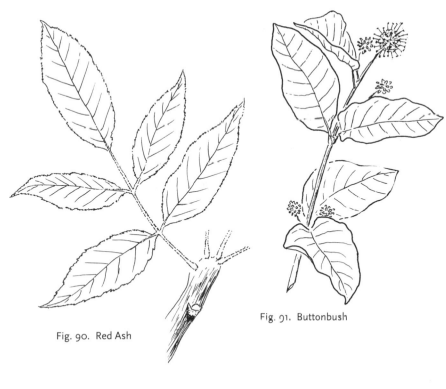

Fig. 90. Red Ash

Fig. 91. Buttonbush

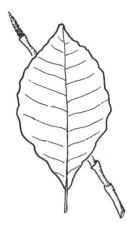

Fig. 92. Wild Raisin

Fig. 93. Arrowwood

COMMON PLANTS, BY ECOSYSTEM

These common plants of Cape Cod are grouped by the environment in which they occur most frequently (note that shrubs are to be found in the Trees and Shrubs section). To identify a plant, look under the heading representing its habitat, or use the index to find plants by name. For flowering plants the time of bloom and flower color are noted.

Woodlands and Wood Edges

Fig. 95. Trailing Arbutus (*Epigaea repens*); April, pink or white.

Fig. 94. Pink Lady's Slipper (*Cypripedium acaule*); May, pinky-purple or white.

Fig. 96. *Left*, Maystar [Starflower] (*Trientalis borealis*); May, white. *Right*, Canada Mayflower (*Maianthemum canadense*); May, white.

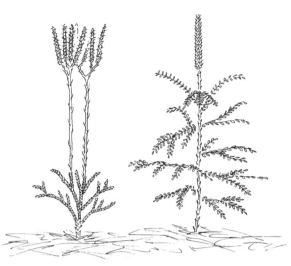

Fig. 97. Club mosses (*Lycopodium* spp.). Other, less common species have trailing, furry-looking stems with occasional upright branches, or flat sprays with toothed edges.

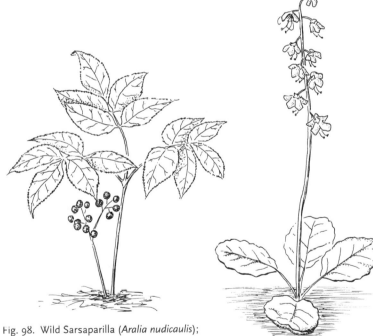

Fig. 98. Wild Sarsaparilla (*Aralia nudicaulis*); summer, white.

Fig. 99. Pyrola (*Pyrola rotundifolia*); July, white.

Fig. 100. *Left*, Wintergreen (*Gaultheria procumbens*); July, white. *Right*, Partridge-berry (*Mitchella repens*); July, white.

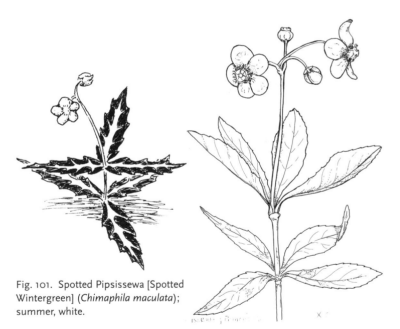

Fig. 101. Spotted Pipsissewa [Spotted Wintergreen] (*Chimaphila maculata*); summer, white.

Fig. 102. Pipsissewa (*Chimaphila umbel-lata*); summer, white. Drawing by Mabel B. Crittenden.

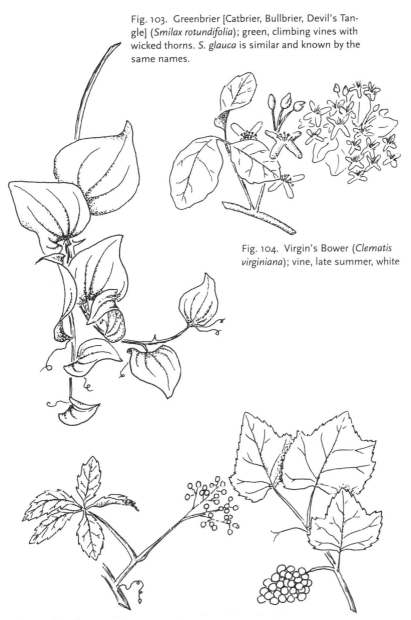

Fig. 103. Greenbrier [Catbrier, Bullbrier, Devil's Tangle] (*Smilax rotundifolia*); green, climbing vines with wicked thorns. *S. glauca* is similar and known by the same names.

Fig. 104. Virgin's Bower (*Clematis virginiana*); vine, late summer, white

Fig. 105. *Left*, Virginia Creeper (*Parthenocissus quinquefolia*); vine, leaves brilliant red in fall. *Right*, Grape (*Vitis* spp.); vine, to 50 feet. *V. labrusca* was progenitor of Concord grape.

Fig. 106. Poison Ivy (*Toxicodendron radicans*); vine or shrub, leaves shiny, in threes, turn red in fall, berries white. "Leaves of three, let it be." The sap of this plant causes an unpleasant skin rash in most people.

Fig. 107. *Left*, Honeysuckle (*Lonicera japonica*); vine or shrub, summer, white or yellow. *Right*, Bittersweet (*Celastrus orbiculatus*); invasive climbing vine, yellow fruits open to reveal bright orange berries.

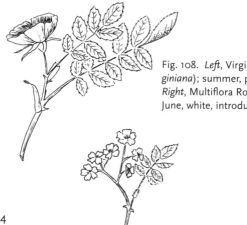

Fig. 108. *Left*, Virginia Rose (*Rosa virginiana*); summer, pink.
Right, Multiflora Rose (*R. multiflora*); June, white, introduced.

Identification

Fig. 109. Butterfly Weed (*Asclepias tuberosa*); summer, orange.

Fig. 110. *Left*, Butter-and-Eggs (*Linaria vulgaris*); summer, yellow with orange throat, introduced. *Right*, Blue Toadflax (*L. canadensis*); summer, blue.

Fig. 111. Bracken Fern (*Pteridium aquilinum*); stalks separated, not in clumps as other ferns. "Fiddlehead" is how frond first appears in spring; it unrolls as it grows.

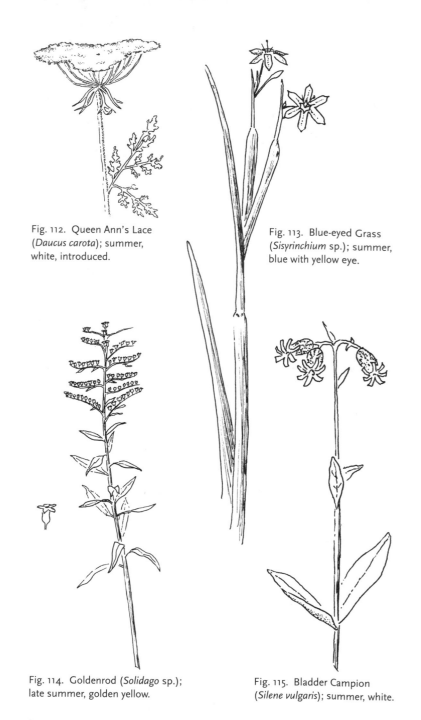

Fig. 112. Queen Ann's Lace
(*Daucus carota*); summer,
white, introduced.

Fig. 113. Blue-eyed Grass
(*Sisyrinchium* sp.); summer,
blue with yellow eye.

Fig. 114. Goldenrod (*Solidago* sp.);
late summer, golden yellow.

Fig. 115. Bladder Campion
(*Silene vulgaris*); summer, white.

Identification

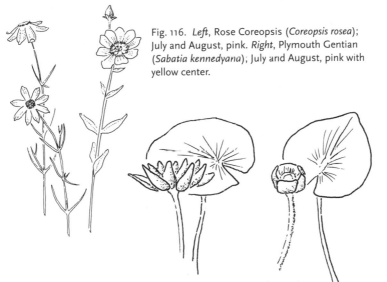

Fig. 116. *Left*, Rose Coreopsis (*Coreopsis rosea*); July and August, pink. *Right*, Plymouth Gentian (*Sabatia kennedyana*); July and August, pink with yellow center.

Fig. 117. *Left*, White Water Lily (*Nymphaea odorata*); summer, white. *Right*, Yellow Pond Lily [Spatter Dock] (*Nuphar lutea*); summer, golden-yellow.

Fig. 118. *Left to right*: Pickerelweed (*Pontederia cordata*); summer, blue or light purple. Bur Reed (*Sparganium americanum*); summer, green. Duckweed (*Lemna minor*).

Fig. 119. *Left*, Blue Flag Iris (*Iris versicolor*); June, light blue. *Right*, Yellow Iris (*I. pseudacorus*); June, yellow, introduced.

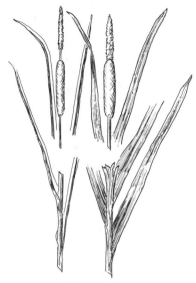

Fig. 120. *Left*, Narrow-leaved Cattail
(*Typha angustifolia*) grows in brackish
water. *Right*, Broad-leaved Cattail
(*T. latifolia*) grows in fresh water.

Fig. 122. Swamp Loosestrife (*Decodon
verticilliata*); July, reddish purple.

Fig. 121. *From the left*: Chair-makers
Rush (*Scirpus americana*), Salt-marsh
Bulrush (*S. maritimus*), and *S. atrovirens*, which, despite the names, are
all sedges; and Soft Rush (*Juncus
effusus*) and Black Rush (*J. gerardi*),
which actually are rushes. The old
mnemonic "Sedges have edges, but
rushes are round" is helpful but not
exhaustive—some common sedges
(including *S. atrovirens*) are almost
round.

Identification

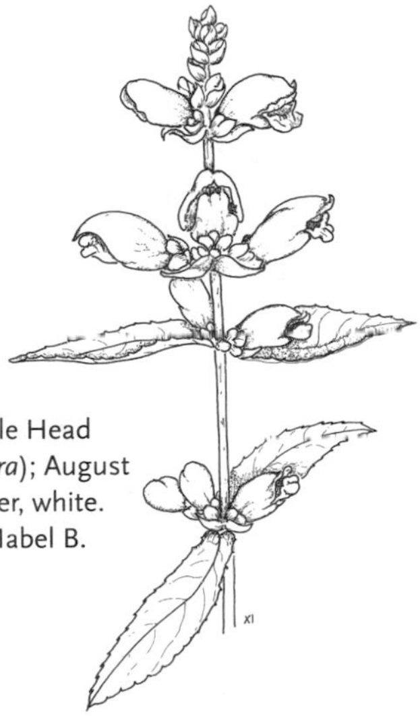

Fig. 124. Turtle Head
(*Chelone glabra*); August
and September, white.
Drawing by Mabel B.
Crittenden.

Fig 123 Cardinal Flower
(*Lobelia cardinalis*); August
and September, red.

Fig. 125. Spotted Joe Pye Weed
(*Eupatorium maculatum*); late
summer, pinky-purple.

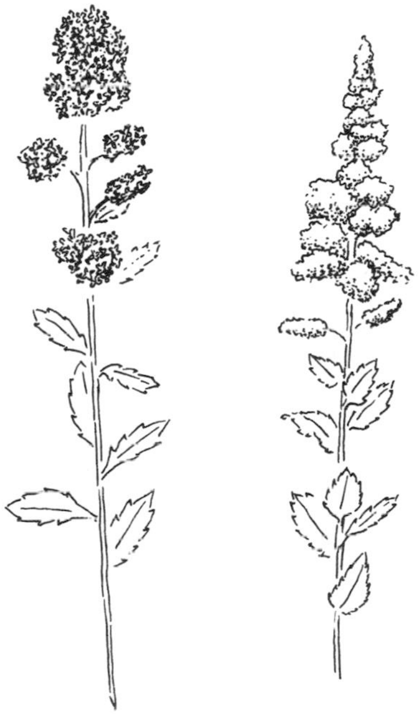

Fig. 126. *Left*, Meadowsweet (*Spiraea
latifolia*); summer, white. *Right*, Steeplebush [Hardhack] (*S. tomentosa*); summer, pink.

IDENTIFICATION

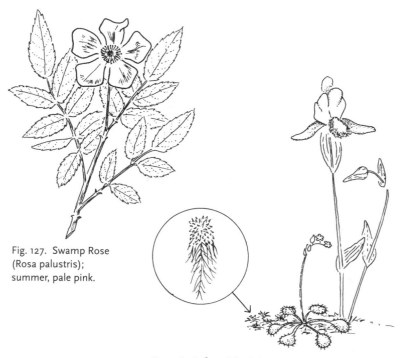

Fig. 127. Swamp Rose (Rosa palustris); summer, pale pink.

Fig. 128. *Left to right*: Sphagnum Moss (*Sphagnum* sp.). Sundew (*Drosera sp.*); summer, white. Rose Pogonia (*Pogonia ophioglossoides*); June, pink.

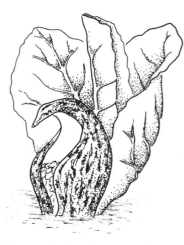

Fig. 129. Skunk Cabbage (*Symplocarpus foetidus*); February and March, reddish-green; leaves to 2 feet.

Fig. 130. Large Cranberry (*Vaccinium macrocarpon*); June, pink or white.

Identification

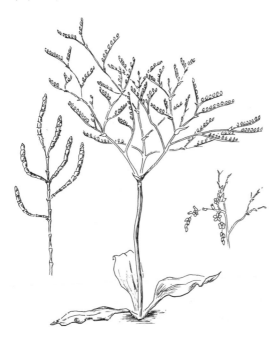

Fig. 132. Spike Grass (*Distichlis spicata*).

Fig. 131. *Left*, Cordgrass (*Spartina alterniflora*). *Right*, Salt Marsh Hay (*S. patens*).

Fig. 133. *Left*, Pickle-weed [Glasswort] (*Salicornia* sp.); annual species turn red-orange in fall. *Right*, Sea Lavender (*Limonium carolini-anum*); late summer, lavender.

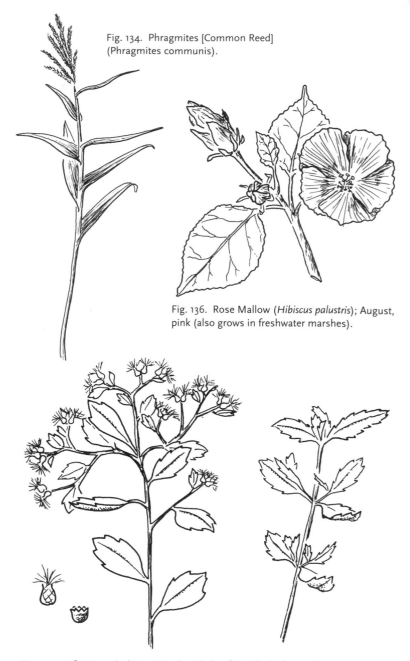

Fig. 134. Phragmites [Common Reed] (Phragmites communis).

Fig. 136. Rose Mallow (*Hibiscus palustris*); August, pink (also grows in freshwater marshes).

Fig. 135. *Left*, Groundsel Tree (*Baccharis halimifolia*); fleshy leaves, late summer, white. *Right*, High-tide Bush [Marsh Elder] (*Iva frutescens*); late summer, greenish white.

Identification

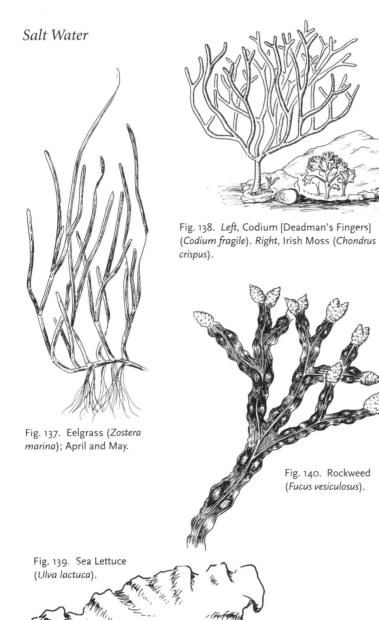

Fig. 138. *Left*, Codium [Deadman's Fingers] (*Codium fragile*). *Right*, Irish Moss (*Chondrus crispus*).

Fig. 137. Eelgrass (*Zostera marina*); April and May.

Fig. 140. Rockweed (*Fucus vesiculosus*).

Fig. 139. Sea Lettuce (*Ulva lactuca*).

Beaches and Dunes

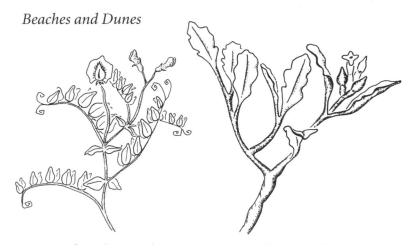

Fig. 141. *Left*, Beach Pea (*Lathyrus japonicus*); summer, blue or purple, peas edible. *Right*, Sea Rocket (*Cakile edentula*); summer, lavender.

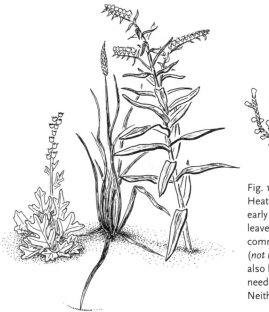

Fig. 143. Poverty Grass [Beach Heather] (*Hudsonia tomentosa*); early summer, bright yellow; leaves fuzzy, scale-like. Less common Golden Heather (*not illustrated*) *H. ericoides*, also blooms yellow, leaves needle-like, not fuzzy. Neither plant is a heather.

Fig. 142. *Left to right*: Dusty Miller (*Artemisia stelleriana*); summer, yellow, introduced. American Beach Grass (*Ammophila breviligulata*). Seaside Goldenrod (*Solidago sempervirens*); late summer, golden yellow.

Identification

Fig. 144. *Left*, Broom Crowberry (*Corema conradii*); April and May, purple. *Right*, Bearberry (*Arctostaphylos uva-ursi*); May and June, white or pinkish.

Fig. 145. Beach Rose [Salt Spray Rose] (*Rosa rugosa*); summer, white or pale to deep pink, introduced.

COMMON, FREQUENTLY SEEN, AND INTERESTING ANIMALS

Freshwater Fish

American Eel (*Anguilla rostrata*) Transparent juveniles, called Glass Eels, swim into streams in summer. Females live in fresh water for 8–20 years before returning to sea to spawn; males live in brackish water.

Northern Pike (*Esox lucius*) Coldwater ponds.

Chain Pickerel (*Esox niger*) Coldwater ponds.

Brown Bullhead [Horned Pout, Catfish] (*Ameiurus nebulosus*) Ponds and streams.

Brook Trout (*Salvelinus fontinalis*) Streams; those that spend time in salt water are called Salters.

Yellow Perch (*Perca flavescens*) Ponds and streams.

Pumpkinseed Sunfish (*Lepomis gibbosus*) Ponds and streams; make circular spawning redds in pond bottoms in summer.

Fig. 146. Pumpkinseed Sunfish

Largemouth Bass (*Micropterus salmoides*) Introduced from South into some ponds.

Smallmouth Bass (*Micropterus dolomieu*) Introduced from Midwest into some ponds.

Brown Trout (*Salmo trutta*) Introduced; stocked in some ponds.

Marine Invertebrates

American Lobster (*Homarus americanus*) Part of the image of summer on Cape Cod; they are green when living.

Blue Crab (*Callinectes sapidus*) Common in estuaries on south side of Cape; to 6 inches; long spine on each side of shell.

Green Crab (*Carcinus maenas*) Live under small rocks; shell to 3 inches, squarish, with five rounded teeth on each side.

Lady Crab (*Ovalipes ocellatus*) Carapace rounded, gray with purple spots; to 2½ inches.

Hermit Crab (*Pagurus* spp.) Shallow salt water; occupy empty snail shells.

Horseshoe Crab (*Limulus polyphemus*) A relative of scorpions, not a crab. Lays eggs on beaches in May and June; lives in muddy bottoms at other times. Molted shells wash up on beaches.

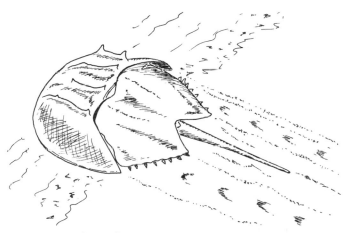

Fig. 147. Horseshoe Crab

Mole Crab [Sand Crab] (*Emerita talpoida*) Carapace oval, egglike, to 1 inch. Swash zone; strains minute food particles from water as waves retreat; burrow in sand.

Fiddler Crab (*Uca* spp.) Carapace to 1½ inch. Salt marshes.

Squid (*Loligo pealei*) To 20 inches; eight arms, two tentacles. Common in the sounds in the spring.

Quahog [Hard Clam] (*Mercenaria mercenaria*) Sandy bottoms; heavy shell, to 5 inches across, gray or white.

Surf Clam (*Spisula solidissima*) Heavy shell, to 7 inches, yellow to brown; frequent prey of gulls.

Soft-shelled Clam [Steamer] (*Mya arenaria*) To 4 inches; shell thin, doesn't quite close.

Razor Clam (*Ensis directus*) Resembles old-fashioned straight-edged razor; shell thin, open at the end; to 7 inches.

Cardium [Cockle] (*Cardium islandicum*) Mostly found on Lower Cape; at southern limit of range on Cape Cod. The two half-shells, when closed together, make a heart shape. To 2 inches; filter feeder.

Gemma Clam (*Gemma gemma*) Tiny (⅛ inch) clam of beaches; favored food of sandpipers.

Eastern Oyster (*Crassostrea virginica*) In bays and estuaries. Shell irregular, attached to hard object.

Bay Scallop (*Argopecten irradians*) Shallow bays and Eelgrass beds; free-swimming; short-lived.

Ribbed Mussel (*Geukensia demissa*) Common; burrow into salt marsh peat.

Periwinkle (*Littorina littorea*) Common; brown or grey shell up to 1 inch, in fat, rounded spiral; grazes on algae.

Dogwinkle (*Nucella lapillus*) Eats barnacles and mussels; colorful 1½-inch spiral shell.

Channeled Whelk (*Busycon canaliculatum*) Predatory; eats clams by prying them open. To 6 inches.

Knobbed Whelk (*Busycon carica*) Similar to Channeled Whelk; larger— to 7 inches, knob on each whorl.

Oyster Drill (*Urosalpinx cinerea*) Predatory; drills neat, round holes in oyster and clam shells. Under 1 inch, high-turreted spiral shell.

Moon Snail (*Lunatia heros*) Drills holes in clams; makes sandy gelatinous "collar" to protect eggs.

Slipper Shells (*Crepidula fornicata*) Cling to rocks, clams, or other Slipper Shells; to 2½ inches.

Jingle Shells (*Anomia simplex*) Thin, ridged, gold, pink, or gray shell; top shell curved, bottom shell flat, with a hole at the hinge. Cling to rocks.

Barnacle (*Balanus balanoides*) Free-swimming larvae settle on hard surface; grow white, truncated-conical shell. Related to shrimp.

Common Starfish (*Asterias forbesi*) In rocky areas; feeds on oysters and mussels.

Saltwater Fish

Alewife [Herring or Sawbelly] (*Alosa pseudoharengus*) Spawn in ponds; fry migrate to salt water in late summer.

Blueback Herring (*Alosa aestivalis*) Life cycle similar to Alewives.

Menhaden (*Brevoortia tyrannus*) Bays and open ocean; large schools; 6 to 12 inches long; caught in large numbers for fertilizer and animal food.

Mummichog (*Fundulus heteroclitus*) Estuaries; 3 to 4 inches; one of several related estuarine minnows.

Silverside (*Menidia* spp.) Flashy silver schooling fish; to 3½ inches; often followed by Bluefish and terns.

Sand Lance (*Ammodytes* spp.) Schools at surface, especially in shallow water. Eel-shaped; to 6 inches. Favored prey of birds and whales.

Bluefish (*Pomatomus salatrix*) Migratory; schooling; predatory; to 30 inches. Favored prey of fishermen; will bite when handled.

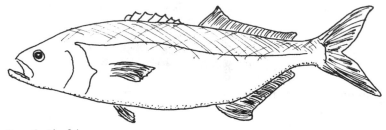

Fig. 148. Bluefish

Striped Bass (*Morone saxatilis*) Longitudinal stripes; to 25 inches; summer and fall. Favored food fish; population crashed in the 1980s, rebounded when fishing curtailed.

White Perch (*Morone americana*) Spawns in fresh water. To 10 inches. Silvery, very scaly, high rounded back.

Tomcod [Frostfish] (*Microgadus tomcod*) Spawns in estuaries and rivers in fall and early winter, near the time of first frost; hence the old common name. A member of the cod family, so has three dorsal fins. To 12 inches.

Scup [Porgy] (*Stenotomus chrysops*) Schooling; to 12 inches; vertical stripe on side; high forehead.

Tautog (*Tautoga onitis*) Eats shellfish. To 18 inches; mottled black, brown, or buff.

Winter Flounder (*Pseudopleuronectes americanus*) In shallow water in winter, summers in deep water; at northern limit of range on Cape Cod. A right-eye flounder; to 15 inches.

Summer Flounder (*Paralichthys dentatus*) Mostly shallow water in summer; at northern limit of range on Cape Cod. A left-eye flounder; to 24 inches.

Little Skate (*Raja erinacea*) to 20 inches. Winter inshore, summer ofshore. Often seen in shallow water. Eggs are deposited in shallow water, each encased in a tough, squarish, dark brown envelope with a tendril at each corner. The empty egg cases are called "Mermaid's Purses" when found on the beach.

Fig. 149. Spotted Salamander

Amphibians

Salamanders

Moderately common but restricted to specific habitats.

Red-spotted Newt (*Notophthalmus viridescens*) Aquatic as larva and adult; immature "eft," all red, in woods.

Red-backed Salamander (*Plethodon cinereus*) In woods under leaf litter, rocks, and logs.

Spotted Salamander (*Ambystoma maculatum*) In woods especially around vernal pools, where they breed.

Frogs and Toads

Apparently less common than formerly, whether because of habitat destruction or some other cause. Only a few species are frequently seen.

Northern Leopard Frog (*Rana pipiens*)

Green Frog (*Rana clamitans*) Around water; when startled says "eeck" before jumping into water.

Bullfrog (*Rana catesbeiana*) Around some ponds; loud, deep voice; to 5 inches.

Wood Frog (*Rana sylvatica*) Common around ponds; voice between a "quack" and a "bark."

Fig. 150. American Toad

Pickerel Frog (*Rana palustris*)

American Toad (*Bufo americanus*) Woods and fields.

Eastern Spadefoot Toad (*Scaphiopus holbrooki*)

Woodhouse's Toad (*Bufo woodhousii*)

Spring Peeper (*Hyla crucifer*) Heard in spring around water; most often seen in fall; 1 inch; brown X on back.

Gray Treefrog (*Hyla versicolor*) Heard in spring, high trill; to 1¾ inch.

Reptiles

Snakes

No poisonous snakes live on the Cape. Of the snakes below, only the Garter Snake is regularly seen.

Black Racer (*Coluber constrictor*) All black; to 4 feet.

Eastern Milk Snake (*Lampropeltis triangulum*) Large reddish-brown spots edged in black on grayish background; to 2½ feet.

Northern Ringneck Snake (*Diadophis punctatus*) Dark gray with yellow belly and neck ring; to 1 foot.

Northern Water Snake (*Nerodia sipedon*) Swims; brown-speckled; to 3 feet. May bite if handled.

Fig. 151. Painted Turtle

Eastern Hognose Snake (*Heterodon platyrhinos*)

Eastern Garter Snake (*Thamnophis sirtalis*) Common; thin yellow stripe down back between rows of black spots.

Turtles

Eastern Box Turtle (*Terrapene carolina*) Meadows and woods; carapace high.

Eastern Painted Turtle (*Chrysemys picta*) Ponds, swamps; often seen basking; yellow and red markings.

Spotted Turtle (*Clemmys guttata*) Uncommon; marshes, swamps.

Snapping Turtle (*Chelydra serpentina*) Ponds; preys on small aquatic animals; shell to 2 feet.

Musk Turtle (*Sternothaerus odoratus*) Not common; swamps or muddy ponds.

Wood Turtle (*Clemmys insculpta*) Not common; in woods.

Diamondback Terrapin (*Malaclemys terrapin*) Marshes with access to sand dunes. Few populations: Wellfleet Bay, Pleasant Bay, Orleans, and Barnstable Great Marshes.

Kemp's Ridley Sea Turtles (*Lepidochelys kempii*) Juveniles may spend time in Cape Cod Bay in summer; in fall may be "stunned" by rapid cooling and wash onto beaches. Occasionally Loggerheads and Green Turtles also wash up.

Fig. 152. Rabbit Track

Terrestrial Mammals

Virginia Opossum (*Didelphis virginiana*) Woods; omnivorous, nocturnal.

Northern Short-tailed Shrew (*Blarina brevicauda*) Common and ubiquitous; eats worms, insects, mice; active day and night. To 4½ inches; dark gray fur, large rounded head, short legs and tail.

Bats

Nine species live on the Cape; significant predators of insects, especially mosquitoes; nocturnal in warm weather, hibernate or migrate in winter; seen as fluttering silhouette at dusk.

Eastern Cottontail (*Sylvilagus floridanus*) Common; woods and fields. Active year-round; bites small twigs off neatly.

Fig. 153. Squirrel Track

Fig. 154. Red Fox Track

Eastern Chipmunk (*Tamias striatus*) Common in rocky woods; eats nuts and seeds; hibernates.

Woodchuck (*Marmota monax*) Common in fields, wood edges. Vegetarian; hibernates.

Red Squirrel (*Tamiasciurus hudsonicus*) Moderately common in woods though distribution spotty. Stores nuts and seeds; active year-round.

Southern Flying Squirrel (*Glaucomys volans*) Rarely seen; nocturnal. Eats seeds, nuts, insects; in winter is active during thaws.

Eastern Gray Squirrel (*Sciurus carolinensis*) Common in woods. Eats nuts and seeds; active year-round; makes globular leaf nest high in tree for winter.

Fig. 155. Raccoon Track

Common Animals

White-footed Mouse (*Peromyscus leucopus*) Common; nocturnal. Active year-round; a host of Lyme disease.

Meadow Vole (*Microtus pennsylvanicus*) Common; makes runways under snow and grass. Active year-round, day and night.

Muskrat (*Ondatra zibethicus*) Common around water; makes domed lodge of cattails in marshes, or lives in burrow in bank. Eats aquatic vegetation; active year-round.

Coyote (*Canis latrans*) Common; omnivorous; active year-round. Arrived on Cape in early 1980s.

Red Fox (*Vulpes vulpes*) Fairly common; omnivorous; mostly nocturnal; active year-round. May be reduced by competition with Coyotes; disease periodically reduces numbers.

Raccoon (*Procyon lotor*) Common; den in hollow tree or under log or building. Omnivorous; active year-round, mostly at night.

Mink (*Mustela vison*) Uncommon; around water. Active year-round, evening to early morning; eats fish, frogs, birds, small mammals.

Striped Skunk (*Mephitis mephitis*) Common. Not striped in common pattern. On the Cape most skunks are almost all white on the back; tail white or gray. Omnivorous; nocturnal; sleeps in winter.

River Otter (*Lutra canadensis*) Moderately common around ponds and streams; most often seen when ponds are frozen. Eats fish, frogs, Eels, turtles; active year-round, day or night.

White-tailed Deer (*Odocoileus virginianus*) Common; active year-round, mainly nocturnal. Browse on vegetation, leaving raggedly torn twigs. A host of Lyme disease.

Marine Mammals

Harbor Seal (*Phoca vitulina*) Winter; often hauls out on beaches or rocks; breeds on Monomoy Island. To 5 feet; has doglike head, large eyes.

Gray Seal (*Halichoerus grypus*) Winter; recently began breeding on Monomoy Island for the first time in one hundred years. To 8 feet; has large horselike head.

Fig. 156. Harbor Seal (left) and Gray Seal (right)

Baleen Whales

Baleen whales eat by straining small fish and floating plants and animals from the water through baleen filters; they frequent the rich waters of Stellwagen and Georges Banks as well as the shallow water east of the Lower Cape.

Minke Whale (*Balaenoptera acutorostrata*) Off Cape Cod in spring and summer. Slender; to 30 feet; pointed snout; has white bands on flippers.

Finback Whale (*Balaenoptera physalus*) Off Cape Cod spring, summer and fall. Flat head; to 80 feet; endangered.

Humpback Whale (*Megaptera novaeangliae*) Off Cape Cod in spring through fall. To 50 feet; long white flippers; endangered.

Northern Right Whale (*Balaena glacialis*) Off Cape Cod in late winter and spring. To 60 feet; slow swimmer; severely endangered.

Toothed Whales

Only two toothed whales occur around Cape Cod.

Pilot Whale [Blackfish] (*Globicephala melaena*) Off Cape Cod in fall; occasionally groups become stranded on Cape Cod Bay beaches. To 20 feet; eat squid; travel in groups. Once extremely common; major source of oil for early settlers.

Atlantic White-sided Dolphin (*Lagenorhynchus acutus*) Off Cape Cod spring and fall. To 8 feet; eat Herring, Sand Lance.

IDENTIFICATION

NATURE
MONTH BY MONTH

Space for your own notes is at the end of each month

JANUARY

Fig. 157. Track of River Otter

✦ This is the coldest month. The ground freezes; cranberry bogs and freshwater ponds usually freeze; bays and sounds sometimes freeze.

✦ Wintering ducks populate the salt ponds. Buffleheads and Goldeneyes feed during the day. Flocks of Scaup and Canvasback sleep all day on the sheltered side of ponds, each with its head beneath its wing but with one eye open and one-half of its brain awake. They switch eyes and sides of the brain from time to time. They dive for small invertebrates in shallow salt water around dawn and dusk.

✦ Eiders, loons, and mergansers dive for food in the bays, often close to shore. Great Cormorants perch on rocks to dry their wings after fishing.

✦ Although January can be snowy, the Cape often gets rain while it is snowing just across the bridges.

✦ River Otters often travel to fish in the salt ponds.

MONTHS

FEBRUARY

Fig. 158. Skunk Cabbage

+ The weather is still cold, but increasing sunlight begins to thaw the ponds.

+ Red-breasted Mergansers hunt in packs, diving and surfacing like a team; they are often attended by hopeful gulls looking for a scrap or an unwary fish.

+ Skunks come out of hibernation during thaws and hunt for food at dawn or dusk.

+ Gray Squirrels are active all winter; they become more active now, racing and chasing about as they court and establish territories.

+ Overwintering Cardinals, Carolina Wrens, and Chickadees look for nesting sites on warm days. Mockingbirds maintain their winter feeding territories.

+ Red-winged Blackbirds return and sing in the marshes.

+ Sap begins to rise in large trees during thaws.

+ Skunk Cabbage blooms about now, in swamps.

+ Red Maple and blueberry buds turn brighter red and begin to swell.

MARCH

Fig. 159. Spring Peeper

+ Migrating Turkey Vultures and Red-tailed Hawks pass through beginning early this month, soon followed by other raptors.

+ Ospreys return from Central and South America or the Caribbean, arriving on the Upper Cape about midmonth and on the Lower Cape by the end of the month.

+ Wintering Great Cormorants leave for the north, replaced by smaller Double-crested Cormorants returning from the south.

+ Daylight and dark are of equal length about the 21st.

+ Grackles and other blackbirds return.

+ Hooded Mergansers, Goldeneyes, Canada Geese, Mallards, and Buffleheads court on the ponds; migratory ones head north.

+ Spring Peepers start their shrill evening chorus.

+ The first shorebirds arrive from the south; the melodic yodeling of the Greater Yellowlegs can be heard over the marshes.

+ Mourning Cloak Butterflies coming out of hibernation are sometimes seen on warm days.

+ Sand builds back onto the beaches as winter winds and storm waves become less frequent.

+ The first Herring "scouts" show up in the streams.

APRIL

Fig. 160. Bracken Fern Fiddlehead

+ Spring Peepers chorus in the evening.

+ The first leaves begin to open, especially in the thickets.

+ Elms, alders, birches, maples, and willows bloom.

+ The first of the Pine and Palm Warblers arrive; sparrows arrive in numbers.

+ Piping Plovers return to potential nesting beaches.

+ Woodland flowers start to bloom, beginning with Trailing Arbutus.

+ The average date of last frost is the 15th.

+ Many ponds turn green or greenish-brown as algae reproduce.

+ The presence of squid in the shallow waters of the sounds is signaled by the trawlers dragging for them.

+ Red Fox and Coyote pups are born.

+ Terns return and fish noisily in bays and salt ponds.

+ Flickers claim their territories by pecking noisily on branches, tree trunks, downspouts, and TV antennas.

+ Tightly coiled fern "fiddleheads" push up through dead leaves. They are one of the earliest vegetable foods available at the end of the "hungry moon."

+ Migratory Striped Bass return to the waters around the Cape following the Herring, but usually preceded by the fishermen.

MONTHS

MAY

Fig. 161. Shadbush

✦ Orioles return just as the flowering fruit trees come into bloom. Watch for them eating the blossoms and listen for their melodious song in tall shade trees.

✦ Humid air from over the Gulf Stream is sometimes blown over cool Cape waters, opening the fog season and ending the bright blue skies of winter.

✦ Horseshoe Crabs lay eggs on beaches at moon high tides.

✦ Wintering seals head north.

✦ Beach Plums, Flowering Dogwoods, and Lady's Slippers bloom.

✦ The peak of the spring songbird migration occurs; many rest and eat, then continue on to the forests of the north.

✦ The Herring (and Shad) runs reach their peak; at about the same time the Shadbush produces its white flowers.

✦ Gulls, terns, and cormorants establish their nesting colonies, mostly on islands. About the end of the month they begin to defend their nests by dive-bombing those who come too close.

✦ The sound of the breeze in the trees changes from a rush to a rustle as the trees come into full leaf.

✦ First Canada Goose goslings hatch.

✦ Female Snapping Turtles lay eggs now through early June. They travel as far as ¼ mile from the pond shore looking for soft soil in which to lay their eggs.

✦ Though mosquitoes are not present in large numbers until sometime in June, you may swat the first ones about now.

✦ Tick season begins in earnest.

✦ Birds continue nest building; the first broods hatch, and the parent birds carry food industriously to their young.

Nature Month by Month

JUNE

Fig. 162. June Bug

+ "June Bugs" gather around lights at night; these large, handsome, harmless beetles sometimes bang against the window screens of lighted rooms.

+ Cranberries and Black Locust trees bloom.

+ Ducklings, goslings, and cygnets follow their parents on training missions around the ponds.

+ Crickets begin to sing at night.

+ Swamp Azalea fills the air with perfume.

+ Fireflies flash in the dusk all this month.

+ Terns fish ceaselessly to feed their young.

+ The longest day of the year is about the 21st, with almost 15½ hours of sunlight.

+ Grasses bloom; pollen covers car windshields.

+ Salt marshes green up.

+ Fog continues.

+ Hurricane season officially begins.

+ Afternoon southwest winds whip up Buzzards Bay and Vineyard Sound.

MONTHS

JULY

Fig. 163. Monarch Butterfly

+ Monarch Butterflies arrive. These are the children or grandchildren of the ones that migrated to Mexico last fall.

+ Green Frogs and Bullfrogs croak around ponds.

+ Bigger Bluefish begin to come inshore on the south side of the Cape.

+ Fog still forms with southerly winds, but its frequency decreases toward the end of the month as the inshore water warms.

+ Parent birds start refusing to feed their large and demanding young, pushing them toward independence; some raise a second brood.

+ Wild blueberries ripen.

+ Butterfly Weed blooms.

+ First southbound shorebirds arrive after nesting in the far north. Most early arrivals are adults.

Nature Month by Month

AUGUST

Fig. 164. Sweet Pepperbush

+ Less fog forms in August than July, though the Lower Cape, especially Chatham, still has plenty.

+ Rose Mallow blooms in the marshes.

+ Blackberries and Beach Plums begin to ripen.

+ Shorebirds continue their migration south; young of the year begin to appear.

+ Seawater temperature reaches its peak about the middle of the month.

+ This is the time of greatest bird abundance: this year's fledglings are added to the adults, before the losses of migration.

+ Seawater is warm enough in southern New England to support hurricanes.

+ Goldenrod and asters begin to bloom; many will bloom until frost. Sea Lavender blooms in the salt marshes.

+ Thunderstorms may bring heavy rain and gusty winds.

+ Sweet Pepperbush blooms just as the first Tupelos and Red Maples turn red.

+ Bayberry berries ripen; these gray-green, wax-covered berries are a favorite food of warblers and other migrating birds.

SEPTEMBER

Fig. 165. Hickory

+ Virginia Creeper and Poison Ivy begin to turn red.

+ Virgin's Bower Clematis blooms; the white flowers are followed by feathery seed heads that persist into fall.

+ Ocean water is still warm enough to support hurricanes.

+ Fog season ends.

+ Warblers from the north woods, wearing their "confusing fall plumage," filter south.

+ Southbound shorebird migration reaches its peak; thousands of birds pass through this month.

+ Ospreys begin to depart for South America and the Caribbean.

+ Red Maples and Tupelo are at their brilliant red peak.

+ Goldenrod and asters are still in bloom.

+ Terns depart for the south.

+ Monarch Butterflies become common as they migrate south; they are often seen on blooming asters and Butterfly Bush.

+ Acorns and hickory nuts ripen, and squirrels scurry about, storing them for winter.

+ Salt marshes turn brown

OCTOBER

Fig. 166. Earthstar

✦ Cranberries ripen, and commercial harvest is in full swing.

✦ Migration of southbound land birds is at its peak: summer birds gradually disappear; White-throated Sparrows, Juncos, Oldsquaws, loons, ciders, and other winter birds arrive.

✦ Gray Squirrels build leaf nests for winter.

✦ Fall rains bring mushrooms poking through forest soil and dune sand. They are the spore-producing bodies of fungi; most of the plant is underground. Squirrels and people harvest mushrooms about now. Earthstars, a kind of puffball, are common on some dunes.

✦ Warm weather lingers. Frost is possible but not certain.

✦ The best fall color usually occurs in the last week of October. Beech, hickory, and oak leaves turn red, golden, or russet; many cling to the trees all winter, thinning to pale shadows by spring.

✦ First northeaster brings blustery winds; its waves erode the sandy summer beaches, beginning the change toward the narrow, rocky winter beach.

✦ Witch Hazel blooms.

✦ Gray and Harbor Seals arrive to spend the winter in our warm waters.

MONTHS

NOVEMBER

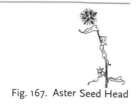

Fig. 167. Aster Seed Head

✦ On still mornings wisps of steam rise from ponds, evidence of the loss of summer's warmth to the cold fall air.

✦ The last asters bloom, then hold their fuzzy seed heads until the seeds are blown away by winter winds.

✦ First frost may not occur until well into November.

✦ Wintering ducks arrive: Buffleheads, scaup, mergansers, and goldeneyes.

✦ Most winds are northerly for the next several months.

✦ First snowfall often occurs early in the month, followed by a few more warm days.

✦ Whales, which have been feeding the shallow waters of Stellwagen Bank and off the "Back Side" of the Cape, begin to leave for the far south.

✦ Leaves fall.

✦ Cranberry leaves turn burgundy color; the bogs are flooded against frost.

✦ Cooling water may "stun" sea turtles migrating south; they may wash up on Cape Cod Bay beaches.

✦ Official end of hurricane season on the 30th.

✦ Holly berries turn red after frost.

Nature Month by Month

DECEMBER

Fig. 168. Club mosses

+ Late-fruiting trees and shrubs begin to look bare after flocks of Cedar Waxwings, Robins, and warblers pass through.

+ Some plants stay green all winter: Sheep Laurel, Wintergreen, Trailing Arbutus, Holly, and club mosses.

+ Great Cormorants and Bonaparte's Gulls arrive from the north.

+ Ponds clear as the algae dies. By mid-December many ponds begin to freeze.

+ More ducks come south: Canvasbacks, Redheads, and Hooded Mergansers.

+ The shortest day is around the 21st: 9 hours and 5 minutes between sunrise and sunset.

+ Orion rises in the east in the evening; stars seem particularly bright in the dry air of winter.

+ The ground may freeze by the end of December.

MONTHS

ABOUT THE SITES

The fifty sites described in the following pages are significant areas of open space that represent the natural environments of Cape Cod. Most are large enough to provide a number of walks or paddles; smaller sites have some particularly attractive aspect. *The Nature of Cape Cod* includes descriptions and drawings of the plants and animals you are most likely to see. But it does not include everything—a guide that you can carry with you without benefit of pack animals cannot be comprehensive. If you want to identify every bird, insect, or shrub, you will also want a field guide on the subject of your special interest.

The Nature of Cape Cod is keyed to quiet, low-speed activities. Although it is possible to see many natural features from a moving car, a powerboat, or a bicycle, both the conveyance and the speed separate you from the experience. You will see, hear, smell, and learn more if you walk or paddle.

On each map, areas of protected land open to the public are shown in white, in contrast with the shaded areas surrounding them. In some areas, especially in the Cape Cod National Seashore on the Lower Cape, the open space encloses some holdings of private land. They are not shown on the maps, but in general the trails avoid them, and they pose no problem to walkers. One historical note about private property along the shoreline: In Massachusetts (and Maine, then part of the Commonwealth), the public trust doctrine—which in all other states provides public access to the shore below the *high-tide line*—was abrogated in 1647 by a Colonial Ordinance that extended private property to the *low-tide line*. Despite the exemption for "fishing and fowling," this law has resulted in more and more areas, especially near expensive housing developments, where the public cannot walk along the beach. Although many property owners permit walkers to pass along their beaches, others enforce their property rights. Such areas tend to be rather heavily signed.

Parking at many of the sites, especially along the shore, is restricted to residents or sticker holders, as noted in the site descriptions, during summer days. Many of those parking areas are open to all, however, in the evenings and early mornings.

Fig. 169. Poison Ivy

Although the various environments of the Cape are generally safe and benign, for those new to the Cape three concerns are worth mentioning. First, Poison Ivy abounds in many woodlands. Remember the old warning: "Shiny leaves of three, let it be."

Second, the Cape has both Dog and Deer Ticks. The latter are the ones that carry Lyme disease; they are small, about the size of a lowercase o; Dog Ticks are the size of an uppercase O. Check yourself carefully if you go bushwhacking; you are less likely to acquire ticks on a wide trail, though it is possible to find ticks anywhere, even in dunes.

Finally, hunting is allowed in many conservation areas. You should be most careful during deer season, usually two weeks beginning the Monday after Thanksgiving. Hunting is not allowed on Sunday in Massachusetts.

Although the site maps are detailed, they do not include every trail or byway. Don't let that stop you from exploring smaller trails, where less human traffic means more to see. Also don't confine yourself to these sites. There are many other areas of interest, some well known, others secret gems, and still others newly acquired through Land Bank purchases. The discussions in this book of the Cape's environments apply equally well to them.

So choose a site, read about the relevant environments (or not—you can always read later), put *The Nature of Cape Cod* in your pack, and head out. Enjoy.

1. Cape Cod Canal
2. Carter-Beal Conservation Area
3. Hog Island and Mashnee Dike
4. Four Ponds Conservation Area
5. Pocasset River and Phinneys Harbor
6. Great Sippewissett Marsh
7. Long Pond and Woodlots Area
8. Beebe Woods and Peterson Farm
9. Crane Wildlife Management Area
10. Coonamessett Pond and River
11. Western Waquoit Bay
12. Quashnet/Moonakis River
13. South Mashpee Pine Barrens
14. Mashpee River Corridor
15. Eastern Waquoit Bay
16. Mashpee and Wakeby Ponds
17. Scusset Beach State Reservation
18. Sandwich Marshes and Old Harbor
19. Maple Swamp Conservation Area
20. Scorton Creek Area
21. Sandy Neck and the Great Marshes
22. West Barnstable Conservation Area
23. Bridge Creek Conservation Area
24. Skunknett Brook Sanctuary
25. Crocker Neck and Popponesset Bay

26. Hathaway Ponds Conservation Area
27. Chase-Garden Creek Area
28. Chapin Beach and New Boston Road
29. West Yarmouth Woodlands and Ponds
30. Swan Pond/Parkers River Corridor
31. Bass River Corridor
32. Quivett Creek and Crowes Pasture
33. Paines Creek/Stony Brook
34. Punkhorn Parklands
35. Nickerson State Park
36. Herring River Area
37. Hawksnest State Park
38. Thompsons Field Area
39. Stage Harbor Area
40. South Beach and Monomoy Island
41. Nauset Beach
42. Little Pleasant Bay Area
43. Nauset Marsh and Fort Hill
44. Plains of Nauset and Nauset Spit
45. Marconi Area
46. Great Island Tombolo
47. Bound Brook to the Great Beach
48. Pamet River and the Great Beach
49. High Head and Head of the Meadow
50. Provincelands

SITES

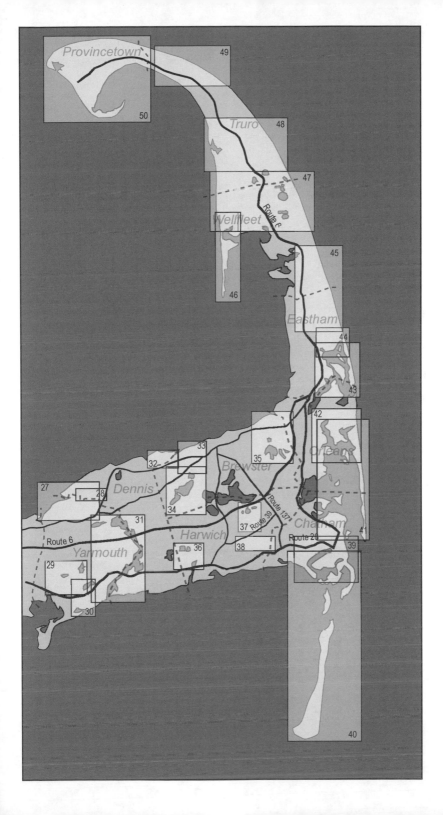

UPPER CAPE SITES

1. CAPE COD CANAL, BOURNE AND SANDWICH

Beaches, Salt Water, Stream, Woodlands

Walking, Birdwatching

PREVIEW

From the bridges across "the widest sea-level canal in the world," as the U.S. Army Corps of Engineers boasts, the Cape Cod Canal and its protecting hills look small and featureless, but much awaits at sea level. See also Scusset Beach State Park (site 17) at the east end of the canal, Hog Island (site 13) at the west end, and Carter-Beal Conservation Area (site 2) just to the north.

ACCESS

Parking and access on the north side are at the Railroad Bridge, Herring Run, and Sagamore Bridge Recreation Areas; on the south side at the Railroad Bridge, Bourne Bridge, Midway Station, and Sandcatcher Recreation Areas, and at scenic overlooks along the roads paralleling the canal.

GEOLOGY

The Cape Cod Canal passes through the rocky Sandwich Moraine, which rises to more than 200 feet above sea level. The canal builders did not have to cut through 200-foot hills, however, because a glacial river did most of the cutting some fifteen thousand years ago. Before the canal, the Herring River flowed down from Great Herring Pond (35 feet above sea level) into the tidal estuary in the wide, east-west valley now occupied by the canal (see site 2). The size of this valley indicates that the glacial river was much larger than today's Herring River.

This glacial river drained a short-lived lake that formed north of the Mid-Cape in what is now Cape Cod Bay as the glacier melted. The water from the melting ice was dammed up between the ice and the Sandwich Moraine. The water in the lake rose until it reached the moraine's lowest point, at Sagamore. There it poured across the moraine, eroding a valley almost to today's sea level and, of course, draining the lake.

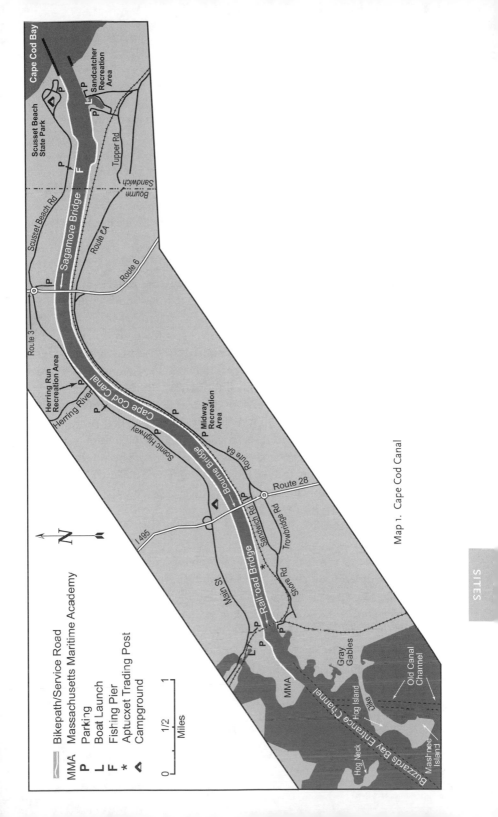

Map 1. Cape Cod Canal

In recent times the construction of the canal changed the shape of the valley, replacing marshes with rushing seawater and cutting through the low divide just east of the Herring Run. If you stand by the Belmont stone at the scenic overlook west of the Herring Run, you can imagine the valley in prehistoric times. Directly below you is the old Herring River Valley; by the 1860 canal survey cranberry bogs had been developed along the river from here west to tidewater. Look east and you can see the edges of the canal cut 50 to 100 feet above the water of the canal. Project the edges of the cut out and down to join about 30 feet above the water, and you are imagining the shape of the divide between the old west-flowing Herring River and the east-flowing Scusset River.

HISTORY

The Pilgrims discovered the route of the future canal soon after settling in Plymouth in 1620. They sailed 16 miles south to the marshy Scusset River and worked their way to its head of navigation. Walking 3 miles west, up the valley of the Scusset River and then over the divide, the Pilgrim explorers encountered the native village of Manomet on the Manomet River (later anglicized to Monument River, now called Herring River) flowing out of Great Herring Pond. They followed the banks of this newfound river down to Buzzards Bay. By 1627 the colonists had built the Aptucxet Trading Post on the south bank of the Monument River to trade with the Dutch from New York.

Although it was possible to walk from Plymouth to Aptucxet before the canal was built, it was much easier to follow the lead of the native peoples and travel by water to the portage between the two rivers. Nevertheless, carrying cargo through the woods over that ridge must have made the idea of an all-water route very appealing—construction of a canal was first proposed that very year, possibly by Miles Standish.

A canal across the Cape was far too big a project for the colony at that time, of course—all the work would have been done with wooden spades by people who had no hands to spare. So vessels trading with the Dutch, and later with the English colonies to the south, sailed the long and hazardous route outside the Cape and its shoals. In 1697 the Massachusetts legislature commissioned a survey for a canal across the isthmus of Cape Cod. The survey found that a canal was feasible, but when it came to raising the money and digging in, the difficulties were insuperable—no canal was built. And so it went for two hundred years—resolutions, surveys, and talk were plentiful, but they produced no canal.

Upper Cape Sites

During the Revolutionary War and the War of 1812 the British navy preyed on shipping in Vineyard and Nantucket Sounds, and goods were portaged once again between the Monument and Scusset Rivers. As the population of the East Coast grew, shipping increased along the coast and so did shipwrecks on the shoals of Cape Cod, each wreck causing someone to bemoan the lack of a canal. But the moaning and surveying continued with no significant results until 1909, when the Boston, Cape Cod, and New York Canal Company began digging the present canal.

They found the difficulties greater than the surveys and even the subsequent failed efforts had suggested. One reason was that ships were bigger in 1909 than in 1697. Another was that the surveys had reported that rocks would not be an obstacle for the canal. As we now know, the route of the canal cuts through the moraine; the moraine has car- and house-size boulders in it like the chips in chocolate-chip cookie dough. Many of these boulders were large enough to stymie all the steam shovels and dredges on the job; in the end they had to be removed by blasting. It took five years, but a canal through swamps, moraine, tidal river, and estuary was dug and was opened to shipping in July 1914.

The Cape Cod Canal turned the Cape into an island. Thoreau, in 1849, came to the Cape on dry land, like the native peoples and Pilgrims who had walked here before him. Once the canal was dug, travel between the Cape and mainland Massachusetts became subject to ferries and drawbridges, and later to the high bridges that put traffic 150 feet above water level. A new phrase entered the local lingo, and "crossing the bridge" became a demarcation as exact as "crossing the Rubicon."

Despite three hundred years of demand for a canal, the new Cape Cod Canal did not get much business. Sailing ships had to be towed, the currents were strong, and the narrow, crooked canal presented many dangers. Frugal captains on coastal schooners preferred to avoid the canal tolls and take their chances with the shoals. With little business, the canal company couldn't even keep the canal dredged. The federal government finally bought the canal in 1928, with an eye on national defense. At that time the Cape Cod Canal was only 120 feet wide and about 20 feet deep, shoaling in many places.

The Corps of Engineers immediately set about widening, deepening, and straightening the canal to allow two-way traffic. It also built the Bourne and Sagamore Bridges to replace the drawbridges, making transit easier for vessels (those with masts shorter than 135 feet, anyway) and vehicles. Today the canal is 480 feet wide, with a controlling depth of 32 feet. It carries two-way traffic day and night, year-round. Strong, reversing currents, up to 5.2 knots (about 6 miles per hour) still cause low-powered vessels to time their passage with the current. But the canal is so convenient that everyone uses it. No toll is charged, a fact that would have gladdened the hearts of the tightfisted New England schooner captains of yore.

The Buzzards Bay end of the canal originally passed east of Mashnee and Hog Islands. The Corps of Engineers dredged a new approach through shallow water west of the islands and used the dredge spoils to build a causeway connecting the islands to Gray Gables. The new channel has reduced shoaling and eliminated two bends in the canal, but it creates an unpleasant situation for small vessels westbound with the current on windy summer afternoons. Where the current meets the prevailing southwest wind in the shallow waters of Buzzards Bay it creates a steep, short chop that can bring low-powered vessels to a pounding standstill. To avoid the worst of this chop, many small craft detour into the more protected old channel once they pass Mashnee Island.

WHAT'S TO SEE AND DO

The Canal Itself
Nowhere else on the Upper Cape can you travel so quickly between such different weather and water conditions as at the Cape Cod Canal. In the summer the dunes and beaches of Cape Cod Bay are sheltered from the prevailing southwest winds. At the west end of the canal the summer afternoon southwest wind funnels up the bay—you can experience for yourself why old-time sailors referred to these winds as "smoky southwesters," but the water is warmer than in Cape Cod Bay. In winter the east end of the canal experiences the battering wind and waves of northeast storms, while the Buzzards Bay side is relatively protected. In severe winters Buzzards Bay may freeze over, and icebreakers keep the western approach to the canal open. The waves in Cape Cod Bay and the currents in the canal itself prevent these waters from freezing solid, though the canal currents sometimes carry ice floes through the land cut.

Passage through the canal by boat gives you a personal experience of the water and weather of the two bays surrounding the Upper Cape. Boats are required to have an engine to transit the canal. Launching ramps are at both ends of the canal—in Sandwich at the East Boat Basin and in Bourne at the Taylor Point Marina.

Canal Service Roads/Bike Paths

Paved service roads run the length of the canal on both sides. They are closed to private vehicles but open for walking and bicycling. The roads are popular year-round, but especially so on summer weekends. The thickets and woods along the path are a good place to find birds, especially in the quiet of early morning. Pieces of clam and mussel shells on the roadway are remnants of the meals of gulls that have found that they can dine by dropping the shells from a height onto the handy pavement, then swooping down to pick the helpless clam from its broken shell.

Special Notes

The Herring River is the site of a significant Herring run. The Herring swim up a fish ladder—dodging Herring Gulls (well, why did you think they were called that?), Red-breasted Mergansers, cormorants, and the official Town of Bourne herring catcher—out of the valley to Great Herring Pond to spawn. A path along the fish ladder provides a good view of the amazing sight of the fish working their way from pool to pool. This fishery is regulated by the Town of Bourne.

In winter diving birds congregate at both ends of the Cape Cod Canal in large numbers. Common and Red-throated Loons, Red-breasted Mergansers, and flocks of Common Eiders can be seen up close. They are busy fishing (or shellfishing in the case of the Eiders) in the swiftly moving current and seem undisturbed by people. In summer Common and Roseate Terns, most of which nest on Bird Island on the west side of Buzzards Bay, dive for small fish. The Sandcatcher Recreation Area (egregiously misnamed, because it is being starved of sand by the canal jetties), with its marshes and thickets and its frontage on the bay and canal, is a good place to see birds in fall and winter.

The Cape Cod Canal is a popular spot for fishing. Year-round, folks perch on the riprap along the canal seeking saltwater fish—Striped Bass, Bluefish, Tautog, Cod, and Herring in spring and summer, Mackerel in summer and fall, and Flounder and Pollack year-round.

2. CARTER-BEAL CONSERVATION AREA, BOURNE
Woodlands, Ponds, Stream
Walking, Birdwatching

PREVIEW

The Carter-Beal area of woods and wetlands runs along the Herring River north of the Cape Cod Canal (see site 1) for almost ½ mile. It is an attractive place, especially for winter walking. The Herring River is a major Herring run; Herring can be seen here almost any time between April and early December. A light boat can be launched into the millpond at the dam, giving access to about ¼ mile of marshy water; Great Herring Pond to the north provides wider waters.

ACCESS

Parking is at the trailhead where Bournedale Road crosses Herring River, and at the ramp on Great Herring Pond.

GEOLOGY

This northern section of the Sandwich Moraine is extremely rough and rocky, with many large boulders. Several kinds of rock occur in the Sandwich Moraine that are not found in the Buzzards Bay Moraine, including black slate, brown sandstone, and black-and-white laminated quartzite. The precipitous 100-foot-high west side of the steep ridge along the river may have been formed directly against ice of the Buzzards Bay lobe of the glacier.

The Herring River is one of the few rivers on the Cape (yes, this *is* part of the Cape) that drains a pond; its headwaters are Great Herring Pond to the north. The river meanders through the almost level valley between the pond and the Carter-Beal tract, heading for the steep 30-foot drop down to sea level at the canal. The wide, gentle valley of the Herring River (including Great and Little Herring Ponds) was probably cut by a meltwater stream when the glacier was just to the north. It may have been dammed by the Cape Cod Bay lobe for a

Upper Cape Sites

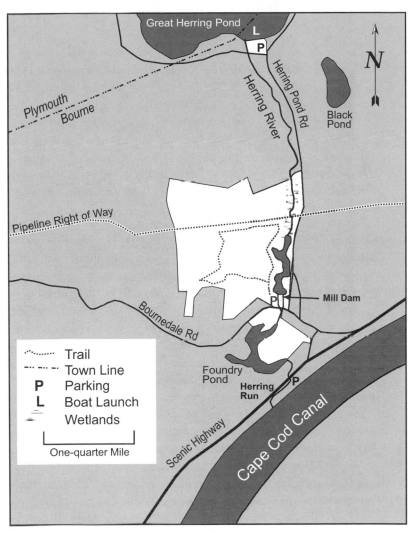

Map 2. Carter-Beal Conservation Area

time. Eventually the meltwater stream cut through the dam of ice and rock, creating the opening through which the Herring River now runs.

HISTORY

The ancient village the native peoples called Manomet was situated along the Herring River. They were apparently decimated by European diseases soon after settlers arrived; by the 1690s their property had mostly been transferred to the colonists.

The 30-foot drop from the upper valley to sea level made the Herring River a natural candidate for damming for water power. This was one of Sandwich's industrial centers until fossil fuel took over (Bourne was part of Sandwich until 1884). A dam built here at Carter-Beal in 1695 was the first on the Herring River—it appears to have been rebuilt since. The dam provided power for a gristmill; a fishway was built to preserve the valuable Herring run, perhaps the very one of hand-hewn granite that still exists along the western edge of the park. A dam was built in the 1830s to serve an iron foundry south of Bournedale Road, forming Foundry Pond.

WHAT'S TO SEE AND DO

Walking

A 1½-mile loop trail begins at the mill dam, on the west side of the river. It is a pretty good pull to the top of the ridge to the west, but generally the walking is easy. The trail along the river (probably once a cart track to the mill) is shaded by large White Pines and oaks and carpeted with Wintergreen. In the fall and winter the thickets here can be a good place to see foraging warblers and other small birds. The river itself is bordered by wet ground where Sphagnum Moss forms sodden hummocks, and red Cardinal Flower and purple Joe Pye Weed bloom in summer. Much of this wet area was cranberry bog by 1860. The bogs are now abandoned, and the cranberries are being shaded out by 30-foot Red Maples and pines that have grown since irrigation ceased.

From the top of the ridge at the cleared pipeline right-of-way you can glimpse Buzzards Bay to the southwest and get a clear idea of how very rough and irregular this part of the moraine is. As you walk the ridge, note the impressively steep slope on the west side that marks the location of the Buzzards Bay glacial lobe at one moment in time. This moraine ridge was pushed up against the ice of the Buzzards Bay lobe by an advance of the Cape Cod Bay lobe.

Launch a Small Boat and Go Paddling

The millpond is a small but pleasantly winding pool with interestingly wooded or marshy shores and lots of birds and Herring. You won't get much exercise, but you'll see a great deal.

Check Out the Herring

This is the next-to-last step in the long route followed by the Herring to their spawning grounds. From the ocean the Herring swim into the canal, up the fishway at the Herring Run Recreation Area, under the multilane road along the canal, up another section of fishway, through Foundry Pond, up a very steep cascading fishway, under Bournedale Road, up the fishway here at Carter-Beal with its hand-cut granite walls, through the millpond and the swampy Herring River to Great Herring Pond—it is a grueling journey, and watching the fish swim it adds to one's amazement. In the summer the adult Herring work their way back down to the sea, followed later by the fry. See the Cape Cod Canal (site 1) for more about the Herring run.

SITES

3. HOG ISLAND AND MASHNEE DIKE, BOURNE

Salt Water, Beaches, Dunes, Woodlands
Walking, Birdwatching, Paddling

PREVIEW

High, wooded Hog Island is connected to the Cape by man-made Mashnee Dike. The dike now looks almost natural, with wide beaches and dunes covered with tough pioneer plants. From the island there are vistas across the canal and the upper end of Buzzards Bay. (See site 1 for more about the Cape Cod Canal.)

ACCESS

Visiting Hog Island requires a bit more dedication than most sites in this book. Hog Island is part of the canal property administered by the Corps of Engineers. It is open to the public, but there is a catch: no parking. You can get to Hog Island by small boat from the town landing at Phinney's Harbor or by walking or biking from somewhere that you can leave a car. The closest official parking area is the Cape Cod Canal Tidal Flats Recreation Area off Shore Road, near the south end of the railroad bridge (see map 1).

GEOLOGY

Hog Island is a pile of rock and sand deposited in a hole or indentation in the southern edge of the glacial ice. The glacier subsequently advanced over the island, smoothing it into its streamlined shape. Great Neck and Hog Neck in Wareham, just across the canal, look similar and were built in the same way.

HISTORY

Mashnee Island and Hog Island were, indeed, originally islands. When the Corps of Engineers dug a new approach channel to the Cape Cod Canal west of these islands, they placed the dredge spoils here to build Mashnee Dike. The dike crosses the old channel about halfway between the mainland and Hog Island. Rock bases for defunct navigation lights along the old channel still stand, one north of the dike and two

180   Upper Cape Sites

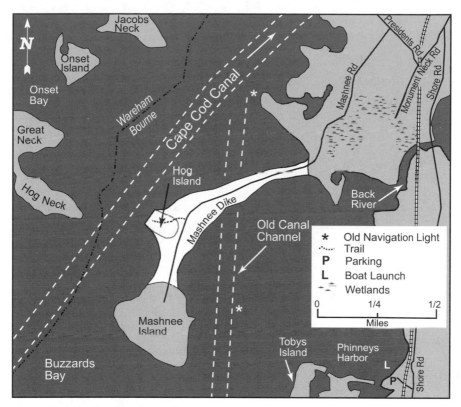

Map 3. Hog Island and Mashnee Dike

to the south. Mashnee Island was the site of saltworks beginning early in the 1790s. The site took advantage of the undiluted seawater and the unfettered sweep of the wind in Buzzards Bay; the latter turned windmills that pumped salt water to the solar evaporators. The saltworks were destroyed more than once by those same unfettered winds during storms. The south side of the island is now heavily armored with a revetment of large boulders constructed in an attempt to protect the houses that have replaced the saltworks in recent years.

Hog Island and Hog Neck were named for their use by the colonists. Domestic animals were turned loose to forage on islands or on peninsulas that could be easily fenced. One of the advantages of such an arrangement was that the animals were somewhat protected from wolves and other predators. In the early 1700s a proposal was discussed to build a "good board fence" across the isthmus of the Cape at

Bournedale to keep out the wolves from the forests to the north. The proposal came to nothing, but it reminds us how much things have changed in three hundred years.

WHAT'S TO SEE AND DO

Mashnee Dike
Saying that Mashnee Dike was made from dredge spoils suggests a dreary place of mud that smells like the bottom of the bay. Not so today, though it may have been so when the dike was built. Today's dike is fringed with wide white beaches and tide flats and covered with small dunes. Except for its unnatural shape it looks like any other vegetated sand spit. Beach Grass, Reindeer Moss, Poverty Grass, and other tough pioneer plants flourish here, anchoring the sand. Fishermen often fish here, especially on the north side of the dike, where the strong current is close to shore and they can hope for Bluefish and Striped Bass. The road on the dike is littered with broken shells, the remnants of gulls' dinners. Here, however, most are oyster shells instead of the more common clams and mussels.

Hog Island
A sand road leads to the abandoned navigation light on the north end of Hog Island, overlooking the canal. Though only 30 feet above sea level, this spot commands views of Onset and Buttermilk Bays, Stony Point Dike, and Great Neck in Wareham, and on west across Buzzards Bay toward Marion. The mature oak forest on the island contrasts strongly with the surrounding sandy flats. Large oaks, by Cape Cod standards anyway, stand tall and spread wide; it looks quite different from most Cape woods. You can walk along the beach on the canal side of the island for a good view of the canal currents and shipping. The steep northern bluff was created when that end of the island was cut away to make room for the new canal channel. In the bluff you can see the mix of sand, boulders, silt, and rocks of all sizes that characterizes moraine deposits. Note how brown the bluff is compared with the sandy beach—the silt that colors the bluff has been washed away from the beach.

Birds
This is a good place for birdwatching, especially in fall and winter. The tide flats and nascent salt marshes harbor shorebirds, and the

eddies north of Hog Island often have Common Eiders, Red-breasted Mergansers, and other wintering ducks in significant numbers. The woods and thickets provide food and resting sites to small birds. Both Snowy and Short-eared Owls are sometimes seen here.

As you head for the dike from the mainland, you pass the apparently landlocked salt marshes of Back River. On foot or on a bike you can ignore the No Parking signs and take a look for marsh birds. To paddle Back River, see the Pocasset River (site 5).

4. FOUR PONDS CONSERVATION AREA AND TOWN FOREST, BOURNE

Ponds, Freshwater Marshes, Stream, Woodlands
Walking, Birdwatching

PREVIEW

Wooded uplands, marshes, and ponds make Four Ponds a varied and interesting area. The ponds are artificial, created in the 1800s by damming a small stream to control the flow of water for local industry. Miles of trails encircle the ponds and cut through the woods of the Town Forest to the north. West of County Road the stream enters the Pocasset River marshes, which you can explore by small boat (see site 5).

ACCESS

The main entrance and parking are on the north side of Barlows Landing Road about 500 yards east of County Road. Another trailhead is off Valley Bars Road.

GEOLOGY

In Bourne, Route 28 runs along the west side of the Buzzards Bay Moraine; between Route 28 and the bay is a large area of outwash from the Cape Cod Bay lobe of the glacier. This ice lobe overtopped the northern end of the Buzzards Bay Moraine after the Buzzards Bay lobe had melted back away from the moraine. The sediment-charged meltwater streams from the ice front ran south into the space between the Buzzards Bay ice and its moraine, depositing a fan of gravel and sand southward along the front of the Buzzards Bay lobe, and covering this area with a thick layer of outwash. The grain size of this outwash is largest at the head of the fan in Monument Beach and becomes finer to the south. Some hills of boulder-laden moraine stick up through the outwash; many depressions testify to the later collapse of buried ice blocks.

After the Cape Cod Bay lobe of the glacier melted, the Pocasset River Valley was cut into the outwash, probably by surface runoff. The valley, like Red Brook and several others in this area, runs south-

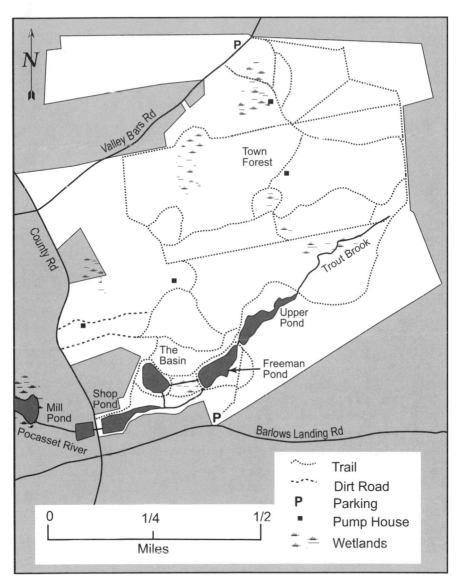

Map 4. Four Ponds Conservation Area and Bourne Town Forest

west, down the sloping surface of the outwash. As sea level rose to its current level, the stream (fed mostly by groundwater) backed up, and freshwater marshes formed in the bottom of the valley, setting the stage for the creation of ponds when European settlers wanted water power.

Site 4: Four Ponds Area

HISTORY

In 1776 Jesse Barlow got permission from the town of Sandwich (Bourne was a part of Sandwich until 1884) to move County Road so that he could build a dam, millpond, and gristmill on the Pocasset River. That millpond still exists just west of County Road. More extensive damming occurred upstream on what was called Trout Brook, where Shop Pond, the Basin, Freeman Pond, and Upper Pond were created with a series of dams and dikes, probably when the iron foundry was built at Shop Pond in 1822.

WHAT'S TO SEE AND DO

Walk around the Ponds

From the entrance on Barlow's Landing Road the main trail leads down the steep side of the stream valley to the string of ponds for which the area was named. Trails encircle the Basin and Freeman Pond, partly on the tops of the dikes that created them. The borrow pits in the valley sides were presumably dug to get sand and gravel to build the dams. Skunk Cabbage grows profusely in the wet areas beside the paths, along with ferns, Swamp Azalea, and Red Maples.

The water in the ponds is clear, not dyed brown by bogs, and the sandy bottom is easily visible. These ponds are home to numerous Painted Turtles that bask on logs in summer, at least one pair of Swans, and lots of Pickerel Frogs. Spring Peepers, who chorus on early spring evenings, are more likely to be seen in late summer. They are brown and less than an inch long; they are almost invisible among dead leaves until they hop. Look for the dark brown X across their shoulders for positive identification.

Walk in the Forest

The welter of mapped trails through this oak-pine forest is a mixture of old woods roads, dirt service roads for the Bourne Water Department, and walking trails. The Bourne Conservation Commission has marked three trails with colored tags, but you'll have to keep a sharp eye out, as the marked trail often turns off the main track. A map at the entrance to the area lists the Town Forest long trail as "difficult." It is something over 3 miles and has some small hills, but at ordinary walking speed it is about an hour's walk. On this trail you will cross the stream valley twice and pass a number of bogs and swamps.

The woods here are quite variable. In some areas the trees are exclusively Pitch Pine and small Bear Oaks; in other areas there is somewhat more variety, including White Pines and other oaks but only a few hickory, aspen, or birch. Both the patchiness of the woods and the limited variety are probably due to fire. There are records of many fires in the area, beginning with the extensive "White Fire" in 1800. It began near the Pocasset Iron Foundry at Shop Pond where a Mr. White was burning wood to make charcoal; the fire got away from him and burned for days. The understory likewise has a limited range of species, mostly low blueberry and huckleberry; Highbush Blueberries in some swampy areas produce good berries. Wild Raisin, one of the viburnums, makes a striking sight in late summer with its bunches of white, pink, purple, and blue-black berries. Several different club mosses grow here in profuse colonies. They are especially visible in the winter.

5. POCASSET RIVER AND PHINNEY'S HARBOR, BOURNE

Salt Water, Salt Marshes
Paddling, Birdwatching

PREVIEW

The boat-filled estuary of the Pocasset River gives way upstream to a salt marsh with winding tidal creeks. Out beyond the jetties at the river mouth your small boat can take you to see the interesting shores to the north including Back River, Hog Island, and Mashnee Dike (see site 3).

ACCESS

For the Pocasset River, parking is at the Town of Bourne Pocasset River Marina west of Shore Road and on the east side of the road near the Conservation Land sign, where you can carry your boat down a path east of the bridge if you can't launch at the marina. There is access to salt water at the west end of Valley Bars Road (Bourne beach sticker only in summer) and at Phinney's Harbor Town Marina at Eamons Road.

GEOLOGY

The Pocasset River is the lower end of a drowned stream valley. It was inundated by salt water as sea level rose toward its current height about a thousand years ago. Here you are west of the Buzzards Bay Moraine in an area of outwash that came from the Cape Cod Bay lobe of the glacier. Just upstream of the railroad bridge is a steep, sandy bluff where outwash materials are exposed. The salt marshes began to develop when the sea reached them, but these low areas probably had freshwater marshes before that time. This valley may have originally drained into Pocasset Harbor just to the south around the point. That outlet was probably blocked by sand that moved alongshore as the sea rose to its present level, forcing the lower section of the river into its unusual northwest orientation.

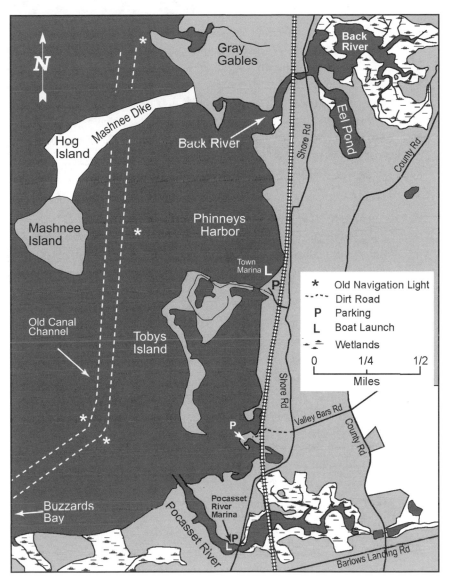

Map 5. Pocasset River and Phinney's Harbor

HISTORY

The stream draining into the Pocasset River was dammed in 1776 to provide water power for a gristmill. In 1822 an iron foundry was established farther upstream. It operated until the late 1880s, processing local bog iron until better ore became available. The upper part of the stream was once called Trout Brook; it may have supported a sea-run Trout fishery like the Quashnet and Mashpee Rivers (see Quashnet/ Moonakis and Mashpee Rivers, sites 12 and 14) and probably Herring as well. Those fisheries presumably disappeared here with the building of the dams, as there are no fishways.

WHAT'S TO SEE AND DO

Explore the River and Marshes by Boat

Seaward of Shore Road the estuary has been dredged to accommodate boats that draw 6 feet. This section of the river couldn't be more different from the salt marsh upstream. Scores of boats fill the docks and moorings between banks lined with closely packed houses and cottages.

Upstream of the road bridge you see no one, and the few houses are barely visible. The water is wide but thinly spread (at the lowest tides even kayaks run aground). The constrictions formed by the highway and railroad embankments have slowed the water enough to cause silting, and there is not enough current to keep a deep channel open. Beyond the railroad trestle the sounds of traffic crossing the bridge are replaced by the wind in the Cordgrass and the cries of the Kingfishers that nest in the high sandy bank.

Below midtide a sandbar is exposed in the middle of the river. In summer and fall yellowlegs, Semipalmated Plovers, and various smaller shorebirds forage industriously here, seemingly unfazed by the quiet approach of a paddler. The herons that fish along the edges of the marsh creeks take a dimmer view of intruders, squawking as they fly off. From the nesting pole the Ospreys, too, may comment on your presence, though it seems unlikely that they feel threatened. The cormorants drying their wings on the midchannel islands rarely say anything; they just fly when approached.

The river narrows upstream, ramifying into various twisting channels between banks of peat topped with Cordgrass and Salt Marsh Hay. The tide range here is only about 3 feet, so you are never far below the surface. At the higher levels of the marsh the banks are riddled with the burrows of Fiddler Crabs who retreat en masse from the water's edge on your approach. If you hold very still they will return, each male holding his oversize claw in front of him like a boxing glove.

This marsh is cut by the straight, narrow ditches dug to drain the pools where saltwater mosquitoes breed. Fresh water enters the marsh at the head of tidewater from the string of ponds upstream, which you can explore on foot in the Four Ponds Conservation Area (see site 4).

The combination of fresh water, upland, and salt marsh attracts a great variety of birds. In addition to the herons and shorebirds, many birds nest on the uplands but forage for food in the marsh.

Paddle outside the River

Though this area can sometimes be too rough for small craft, on a calm day the area around private Tobys Island makes attractive paddling; you can paddle close along shore and take it all in. Shorebirds, terns, cormorants, herons, schools of Bluefish, big homes on the island, and ships traversing the Cape Cod Canal provide lots to look at. The canal originally ran between Mashnee Island and Tobys Island. The dredged channel still exists; it runs south from the middle of Mashnee Dike to the fixed light northwest of the Pocasset River jetties. From there the it runs southwest to join the channel in the center of the bay. You can see low, sandy Mashnee Dike north of Phinney's Harbor. It, too, is an interesting destination by boat or on foot (see site 3). The shore of the bay presents many surprising inlets and grassy flats. Small boats can pass under the Tobys Island bridge (if the tide is very low you'll have to portage across a tide flat) and thus circumnavigate Tobys Island. From here you can also paddle under the railroad and Route 28A bridges into Back River, a tidal stream that feeds a secluded salt marsh. Enough Bay Scallops still live in the Eelgrass beds around Tobys Island to attract the occasional scalloper.

6. GREAT SIPPEWISSETT MARSH AND CHAPOQUOIT BEACH, FALMOUTH

Beaches, Dunes, Salt Marshes

Walking, Paddling, Birdwatching

PREVIEW

Chapoquoit Beach is part of the barrier beach that extends south from Chapoquoit Island. The beach and dunes protect the Great Sippewissett Marsh and its rich ecosystem from the waves of Buzzards Bay.

ACCESS

Parking and access are at the Chapoquoit Beach parking lot; in summer parking is by Falmouth beach sticker only. Access to the marsh (and thence the beach) is via a dirt road beginning behind the West Falmouth Post Office on West Falmouth Highway. You can launch a boat at the town landing off Old Dock Road in West Falmouth Harbor. The public part of Black Beach is accessible only by boat or via the marsh, because a stretch of private beach intervenes.

GEOLOGY

Great Sippewissett Marsh lies in a long, narrow depression between the Buzzards Bay Moraine and some outlying hills of moraine that project into Buzzards Bay. The outliers of moraine were formed at the ragged front of the glacier when it had melted back away from the Buzzards Bay Moraine. Wings Neck and Scraggy Neck to the north, Chapoquoit and Little Island here at West Falmouth, and the shoals off Quissett Harbor to the south were formed where rocks and sand piled up in crevasses and holes between ice blocks. That means that this shoreline is a negative image of the shape of the ice front at a stage in the retreat of the glacier. Ice occupied the areas between the necks of land, creating the low areas now occupied by West Falmouth Harbor and both Great and Little Sippewissett Marshes.

SITES

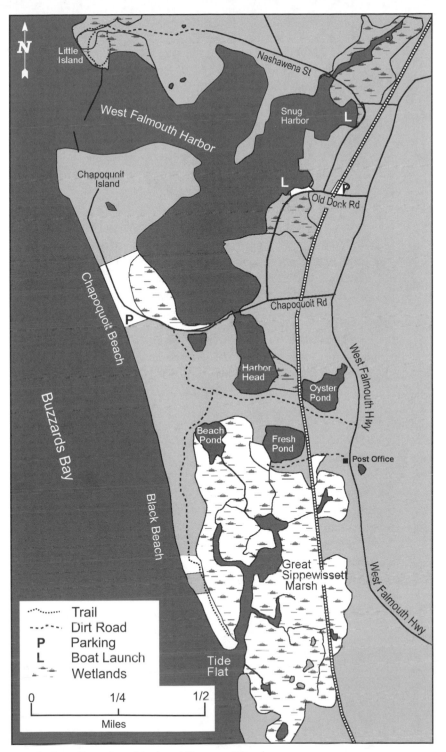

Map 6. Great Sippewissett Marsh and Chapoquoit Beach

About six thousand years ago the sea rose high enough to invade Buzzards Bay, and waves began to erode the outlying moraine deposits. The eroded sand and gravel formed offshore bars that moved east toward today's shoreline as the sea rose, reaching approximately their current position less than a thousand years ago. The low areas between the moraine and the outliers developed freshwater marshes and swamps because the groundwater along the shore rose as sea level rose. Salt water flooded the area of the present Sippewissett salt marshes about three thousand years ago, killing the Atlantic White Cedars and other freshwater plants. Salt marsh plants have since built up the peat that now fills the basin. Salt marsh originally extended farther west, under what is now beach or shallow bay waters. As sea level, rose the line between marsh and wave-battered shoreline retreated landward; the seaward edge of the marsh was first buried under advancing dunes and then excavated and exposed by wave action on the beach.

HISTORY

Chapoquoit Island was known as Hog Island until it was developed for summer places in the 1890s. The older name reflected the island's previous use as safe pasture for livestock. Salt Marsh Hay was cut on the marshes for animal fodder until at least the 1890s.

WHAT'S TO SEE AND DO

The Beaches

Chapoquoit and Black Beaches are rather narrow, rocky beaches, backed by eroding dunes. In contrast to many beaches, these tend to be a bit wider and sandier in winter than in summer, because they are mostly protected from the northeast winter storms, but strong southwest summer winds bring energetic waves almost every afternoon.

The effect of human activity on beaches can be seen all along this shore. On days of strong southwest winds the waves erode the beaches and deposit the sand in offshore bars and sand flats. On gentler days the sand comes back to the beach, farther along the shore. The groins that make out from the shore stop the alongshore movement of sand and create the saw-toothed pattern so visible to beach walkers. Sand accumulates on the "upstream" side of each groin, sometimes up to the top of the groin and seaward of its end. On the downstream side water extends high up the beach because the sand has eroded and no new sand has replaced it.

Some houses that were built on the dunes now sit behind armored revetments and eroded beach. These strongholds are now to seaward of the land on either side; they have been preserved at the expense of their neighbors. No sand from the armored part of the dune has nourished the beach, allowing the beach to erode even faster. With rising sea level the dunes and beach will continue to retreat. The houses with armored revetments will likely last the longest, but their revetments will also succumb to the waves as the shoreline responds naturally to rising sea level.

On the north side of the creek that drains the marsh you can see the foundation of a house that once sat on the dunes where there is now only sand flat. What is destroying them is lack of sand at a time when sea level is rising. Both to the north and the south the bluffs that once supplied sand to this beach/dune system are armored, preventing erosion of the upland and reducing the supply of sand. Under these conditions waves will continue to eat away at the beach and dunes, and will eventually breach them. When that happens, the marsh will be exposed to waves and the whole picture here will change.

The Great Sippewissett Marsh

This is one of the most-studied salt marshes in the world. Because of its proximity to the research institutions in Woods Hole, this is where textbook examples come from. Here you will find Cordgrass and Salt Marsh Hay, Fiddler Crabs, salt marsh snails, small fish, herons, shorebirds, and all the other occupants of rich salt marshes.

The tidal creeks are best explored by small boat. In summer and fall shorebirds foraging in the mud for worms and crustaceans will often let a small boat approach. On the south side of the mouth of the tidal creek you can see some large areas where beach sand has been washed by storm waves onto the surface of the marsh. A layer of peat, created in the salt marsh when sea level was lower, is being eroded away along the bank of the creek. These are signs of the continued rise in sea level.

Explore West Falmouth Harbor

This lovely harbor has much of interest: on the cultural side, boats at their moorings and historic summer houses; on the natural side, the many nooks and coves of the harbor itself, the salt marshes behind Chapoquoit Beach and inside the breakwater, and the views of the high hills of the moraine and Buzzards Bay.

7. LONG POND AND THE WOODLOTS CONSERVATION AREA, FALMOUTH

Woodlands, Ponds, Freshwater Swamps, Bogs, Vernal Pools
Walking, Cross-country Skiing

PREVIEW

Long Pond, Falmouth's drinking water reservoir, is surrounded by almost 1,000 acres of conservation land. Grews Pond is open to swimming and canoeing. The waters of Long Pond are off-limits, but the walking is excellent on the network of trails that circle the pond and connect to a 6-mile trail that runs north along the moraine.

ACCESS

Parking is in Goodwill Park, off either Gifford Street or Route 28; near the Falmouth Conservation Lands sign on Service Road north of Brick Kiln Road, and in the Falmouth Technology Park. Fire Tower Road (gravel) runs through the conservation land near the top of 207-foot Falmouth Hill.

GEOLOGY

The Woodlots Conservation Area is located entirely on the moraine and thus has hilly, rocky, irregular terrain. Long Pond lies across the boundary between the moraine and the outwash plain. The northern and western sides of the pond are rimmed with large boulders and steep slopes. The southeastern part of Long Pond and all of Grews Pond lie in the outwash plain. Here the land is flatter, and many bogs and small ponds border the trail. Long Pond is one of the deepest ponds on the Upper Cape: its greatest depth is 76 feet—66 feet below sea level. Long Pond is a kettle hole, formed by the melting of a large swath of buried ice, perhaps deepened by glacial runoff.

HISTORY

The east-west property boundaries in the Woodlots area are remnants of the narrow strips of land into which woodlot areas on the moraines were often divided.

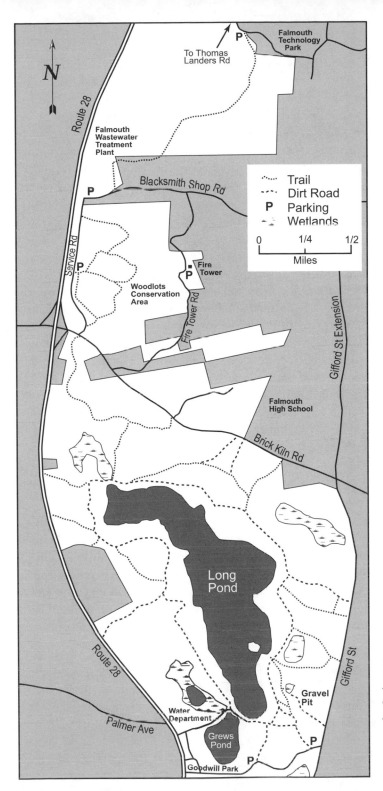

Map 7.
Long Pond and
the Woodlots
Conservation
Area

Goodwill Park was given to Falmouth in 1894 by Joseph Fay, the first of the "summer people" in Woods Hole. Much of the rest of the Long Pond area was given to the town by his children. When Mr. Fay began acquiring land here in 1850 this area was pasture, but he was determined to restore the woods. Perhaps his Johnny Appleseed–style tree planting accounts for the variety of trees around Grews Pond and along the southern end of Long Pond. Hickory, Hop-Hornbeam, birch, and beech trees are much more common here than elsewhere nearby. The evergreen leaves of many American Hollies brighten the winter woods, and rhododendrons flourish in several areas.

WHAT'S TO SEE AND DO

Walk around Long Pond

The 3-mile circuit of Long Pond is unusually varied and attractive. The hill beside the Falmouth pumping station is the edge of the moraine; a similar but somewhat less obvious slope marks the same transition at the northeast corner of the pond. On the moraine, knots of large boulders stick out of the ground, some of which were quarried for building stone. The even-age stands of White Pines or spruce were all planted. A Red Maple swamp at the northwest corner of the pond marks the point where a trail leads off to the north, climbing up the slopes above the pond. It crosses Brick Kiln Road and connects with the trails in the Woodlots and Kettleholes Conservation Areas to the north.

The slopes above the northern end of the pond are steep, dropping precipitously from the 150-foot-high hills to the north. The land around the southeast side of the pond is level outwash except for the bogs east of the trail. The small island shown on the map is a peninsula at usual water levels. During very wet years it becomes an island again.

Sphagnum Bog

East of Long Pond is a Sphagnum bog—a dense, wet mat of Sphagnum surrounded by water-tolerant members of the heath family including blueberries and Swamp Azalea. Insectivorous Round-leaf Sundews grow in the Sphagnum, tinting the surface red.

Vernal Pools

In the old gravel pit just north of the Gifford Street entrance to Goodwill Park a number of vernal pools develop in the spring. The easiest way to find them is to follow the chorus of the Spring Peepers past the piles of sand, rocks, and asphalt that were dumped here in the cleanup of the ruined Shining Sea Bike Path after Hurricane Bob. You will find moisture-loving plants as well as the typical amphibians that take advantage of the fish-free water of these pools to breed.

Woodlots Conservation Area

The loop trails in these tranquil woods are marked by colored signs placed by The 300 Committee, Falmouth's land trust. This area was woodlots and cleared pastures into the nineteenth century, as you can tell by the stone walls and the youth of the trees. The ages of various parts of the woods differ, and they provide clues to the uses and times of abandonment of these areas. Many of the oaks, Black Locusts, and Red Maples have multiple stems, the result of new sprouts growing from stumps after trees were cut.

The terrain here along the west-sloping top of the moraine is completely disorganized. This is no disparagement but refers to the lumpy knob-and-kettle topography with no streams organizing precipitation into stream drainages. Rain and melting snow sink right into the porous sand and gravel of the moraine. Most of the trails skirt small knobs and swales, but one swings down into a deep, silent depression called Pine Bowl whose bottom is about 50 feet lower than the surrounding ridges.

The trail continues to the north all the way to Route 151, after crossing Blacksmith Shop Road and passing the Falmouth wastewater facility with its spray infiltration system, but it is only a narrow corridor.

Stonecutting

Look for the evidence of stone-cutting: flat surfaces on boulders where blocks of stone were removed. West Falmouth was known for its pink granite—President John F. Kennedy's grave in Arlington National Cemetery is paved with this stone. It would be easy to think that there was a hill of that granite in West Falmouth. But like all the rocks on the Cape, the rocks of pink granite were brought by the glacier and dropped wherever they were as the glacier melted. There may be an unusually high proportion of pink granite on the West Falmouth hills, or the locals may have preferentially cut pink granite boulders when they found that it was desirable. Quarries like the ones in Quincy, where stone was cut from bedrock, do not exist on Cape Cod, because there is no bedrock exposed here anywhere.

8. BEEBE WOODS AND PETERSON FARM, FALMOUTH

Woodlands, Grasslands, Ponds, Freshwater Marshes
Walking, Cross-country Skiing, Birdwatching

PREVIEW

For much of the past three hundred years the pastures and "mowing" of today's Beebe Woods commanded wide views over Buzzards Bay and Vineyard Sound, but today the trees are so thick that those views are obscured, even in winter. Foot trails and old carriage roads wind past ponds and wetlands through these quiet woods and farm fields.

ACCESS

Parking is at the end of Highfield Drive; off Ter Heun Drive; and at Peterson Farm off Woods Hole Road. Parking for Ice House Pond is at the site of the old ice house on Sippewissett Road, but the only access from there into Beebe Woods or the farm is by crossing the pond. Footpaths enter the woods at a number of points.

GEOLOGY

Beebe Woods lies across the broad top of the Buzzards Bay Moraine. As you go west on Depot or Ter Heun Avenues you cross from the flat outwash plain onto the hilly moraine just as you cross the railroad tracks. The moraine has irregular terrain of bouldery hills and swales. Peterson Farm lies in one of those swales; although the hills around the fields are rocky, there are no rocks in the fields, and few rock walls. The original farmers chose an area with rich, rock-free soil. This fine-grained soil washed and blew in after the glacier melted but before vegetation anchored the surface of the hills. Reportedly, good soils like this existed in many areas of the Cape but were eroded after the forests were cut.

HISTORY

Beebe Woods was the center of the estate owned by the Beebe family of Boston from the 1870s to the 1930s. Prior to that time the land was used

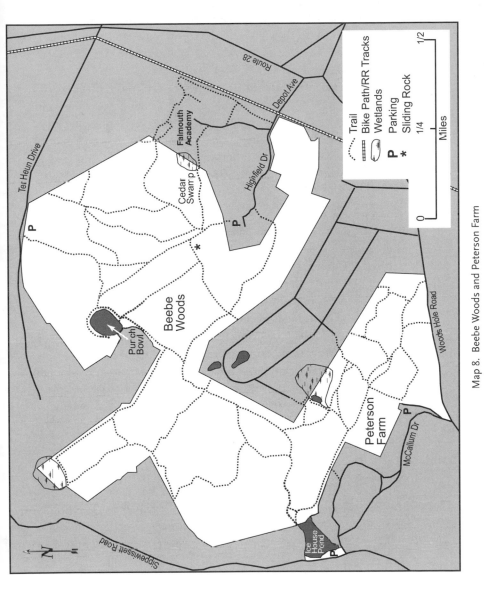

Map 8. Beebe Woods and Peterson Farm

as woodlots and pasture. A photo of Falmouth from the top of the
Beebes' Highfield Hall taken in 1896 shows woods on the slope of the
hill below the house, though other areas that are now wooded were
bare. The Beebe family put their mark on Beebe Woods. They had the
roads and rock walls built or rebuilt, quarrying some stone on-site.

Look for the cut-stone walls that carry the carriage roads across swales. Young European Beeches can be found today among the native American Beeches in the woods. They are seedlings of the planted parent trees around Highfield.

Peterson Farm was owned by the Weeks family as far back as the 1660s. The flat fields were farmed, and lumber and firewood were cut on the slopes. By the 1850s most of the land between Woods Hole Road and Ice House Pond was fields and pasture. The Peterson family farmed it from the 1930s until the 1990s.

WHAT'S TO SEE AND DO

Go for a Walk

There are many walks in this large area, but a particularly nice 3-mile walk is from the parking lot at Highfield to Ice House Pond and back through Peterson Farm. This walk takes you from the top of the moraine down its gently sloping west side, through some of the less-frequented parts of the woods to the pond, then back along the wood margins and open fields of the farm. The small pond with its adjacent marsh at the farm was created by the earthen dam built to provide water before the advent of town water.

A gentle loop of about 1¼ miles leads to the Punch Bowl from Highfield. Fanciful names given by the Beebes have replaced many of the matter-of-fact Cape Cod names; the Punch Bowl was originally called Deep Pond. Local legend held that it was "bottomless" until a naturalist lugged a boat to the pond and found it no more than 13 feet deep. The trail to the Punch Bowl drops almost 60 feet down the steep slopes above the pond. This would be "Deep Pond" indeed if the water rose that high, but a valley to the northwest would drain water into Little Sippewissett Marsh if the pond rose more than 10 feet. The peat-brown water in the pond is usually still because of the protection of the hills. When the Swamp Azalea is in bloom its heady fragrance fills the valley. Red Maples, Tupelos, and Highbush Blueberries turn brilliant red in late summer and illuminate the pond doubly—once on shore and again in the reflections. In midsummer Painted Turtles sun on logs, and dragonflies snatch mosquitoes from the air above the water. This is a favorite local swimming spot. Barking, joyous shouts, and vigorous splashing often banish the warier pond creatures on warm summer afternoons.

Upper Cape Sites

Stone Walls

On any walk in Beebe Woods you will come across stone walls. You might expect them to bound fields; they seem incongruous deep in the woods. In fact these walls *were* built in open fields; they probably kept sheep or cows out of the hay fields or separated one farmer's land from another's. The trees have grown back since farming ended here.

The boulders in the woods are characteristic of moraine deposits. The "Sliding Rock" is one of the larger boulders and certainly the best known—it was a stop on a driving tour suggested by the Falmouth Board of Trade and Industry in 1896. You'll find it on the west side of the trail to the Punch Bowl about ¼ mile west of the Punch Bowl sign. The slanting surface of this 10-foot-high block of granite seems much too rough for sliding; perhaps the sliding was in winter. This rock was originally larger; big blocks of stone have been quarried here. You can see lines of ½-inch-diameter holes made by hand drills. Many other boulders in the woods bear evidence of quarrying; stones cut in this way can be seen in old foundations all over Falmouth.

Look at the Forest and the Trees

The top of the moraine is a rather surprising place to find a swamp, but swamp there is, 40 or 50 feet higher than the surfaces of the nearest ponds. This swamp, which straddles the boundary between Beebe Woods and Falmouth Academy, has standing water all year, even in dry spells, and is populated with Atlantic White Cedars, Red Maples, Swamp Azalea, Highbush Blueberries, and ferns. Although no cranberries grow here now, this swamp may once have been a cultivated cranberry bog; the oldest cedars date back only to 1911. This wetland is perched high above the water table because the bottom of the swale is sealed with glacial clay. The clay was washed into the bottom of the swale, where the tiny particles clogged the open spaces among the sand grains. Today the swale holds the water that seeps down from the higher land to the northwest. Spring Peepers chorus here on early spring evenings.

One of the few surviving American Chestnut trees on the Cape grows just east of this swamp, on Falmouth Academy property, less than 30 yards north of the trail. Its multiple small trunks show that it is a root sprout. The older trunks are infected by the blight that killed the original tree, but new stems continue to grow. Research suggests

SITES

that the blight may be slowed or stopped by packing the cankers with a slurry of forest soil; wrappings of burlap or plastic keep the soil in place.

Many parts of Beebe Woods have burned in the last hundred years, and a big fire swept the woods in October 1947, a dry time all across New England. In four days fire burned from Sippewissett Road across the hill almost to the railroad tracks (now the bike path). The area around Highfield Hall was protected by fire hoses, and a few other areas escaped. You can estimate the extent of the fire by noting the size of the trees in various parts of the woods.

Much of this land was woodlot when the Beebes acquired it; wood for lumber and firewood had probably been cut here from the time Falmouth was settled. The Beebes probably also had wood cut here to supply the needs of the houses and the farm as late as the 1930s. As a result of this wood cutting, double-trunked trees, especially oaks and maples, are to be found throughout the woods. You can determine how long ago a tree was cut if you can estimate how old the multiple trunks are that sprouted from the cut stump. Many of these trees are obviously quite young, but a few seem to have survived the fires and may record wood cutting in the 1800s.

On the east side of the woods, in areas that escaped the fires in the 1940s, there are many patches of Black Locust trees. Although locust makes good firewood, it has another virtue: it is extremely resistant to rot. Locust is often used in places where it will be in contact with the soil, such as fence posts. The Village Green in Falmouth, just to the east, is surrounded by a fence of large locust posts. As Black Locust sprouts vigorously when cut, the repeated harvesting of posts has resulted in areas where it is the only species of tree.

Birds
In fall and winter flocks of Chickadees forage noisily in the trees; look for the quieter Titmice, White-breasted Nuthatches, Brown Creepers, and Downy Woodpeckers that often travel with them. In summer warblers and tanagers nest in the thickets, Bluebirds are sometimes seen along the wood margins, and Ospreys nest on the antenna on the hilltop. Peterson Farm, with a wide variety of habitats, shelters many different kinds of birds and is a good spot for birdwatching, especially during spring and fall.

Special Notes

Trailing Arbutus blooms on steep banks in early April, followed in May by Pink Lady's Slippers, which are common here despite three hundred years of tree cutting and grazing. Look (or sniff) for the fragrant blossoms of Swamp Azalea in June. In winter the red berries of Wintergreen come out from beneath its evergreen—"winter-green," right?—leaves.

Peterson Farm continues to have some agricultural use. A flock of sheep lives here, watched over by a large Llama and other caretakers, human and canine.

SITES

9. CRANE WILDLIFE MANAGEMENT AREA, FAL-MOUTH

Woodlands, Grasslands, Ponds
Walking, Cross-country Skiing

PREVIEW

More than 1,800 acres of woodlands and grasslands threaded through by old woods roads and miles of footpaths make the Crane Wildlife Management Area an unusual and interesting site. It is managed by the Massachusetts Department of Fish and Wildlife for upland game birds—Pheasant and Quail are stocked, and hunted during fall hunting season—but other open-country species take advantage of the environment. Besides the grasslands there is a pond, extensive pine barrens, and rugged moraine hills. This area is adjacent to the Coonamessett Reservation and Coonamessett Pond (see site 10).

ACCESS

The main parking area is just west of the powerline crossing on Route 151; other small parking areas are at trailheads along 151 and on Sandwich Road. Parking for the section south of Route 151 is off Hayway Road.

GEOLOGY

Most of the Crane area is on the smooth, gently sloping surface of the outwash plain, but the rugged, bouldery western part, striped with narrow woodlots, is on the Buzzards Bay Moraine. This area is quite high; the outwash plain is above 100 feet, sloping up to the high moraine, which rises steeply to over 200 feet. The steep east side of this section of the moraine resulted from a re-advance of the glacial ice that pushed forward both the moraine and the outwash that had been deposited beyond it. This is one of the few places where you can see a good stretch of the moraine/outwash contact. The moraine ridge continues to the north; about 3 miles north of here Pine Hill rises to the dizzying height of 306 feet, the highest elevation on the Cape.

Upper Cape Sites

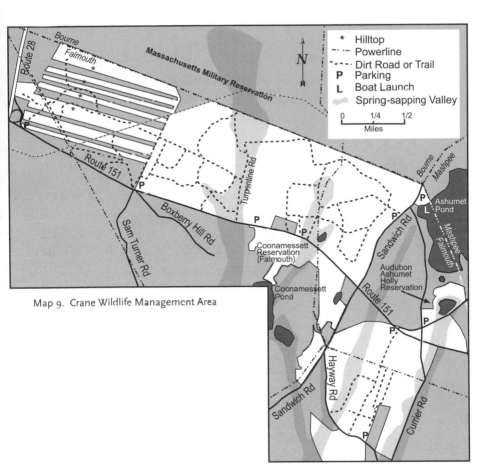

Map 9. Crane Wildlife Management Area

The upper ends of a number of spring-sapping valleys cut the out-wash plain here. Their floors are as much as 40 feet below the surface of the plain, but the valleys are mostly dry because the water table is 10 to 20 feet below that, as shown by the 45-foot elevation of the surface of nearby Ashumet Pond.

Although there are no large rocks in the outwash, the sandy out-wash deposits contain many smaller rocks. A layer of polished and faceted ventifacts is exposed in a number of the roads.

HISTORY

Turpentine Road, which runs north into the Massachusetts Military Reservation, is in the bottom of the largest of the spring-sapping valleys. Both turpentine and pine tar (which was used extensively on ships) were distilled from the resinous Pitch Pine trees of the pine barrens on the Cape. There may have been turpentine or tar kilns somewhere along Turpentine Road to take advantage of this extensive area of Pitch Pines.

WHAT'S TO SEE AND DO

Go for a Walk, Long or Short
The map only begins to hint at the routes open to you: mowed paths, old roads, footpaths, open fields—options are everywhere, and nowhere near all of them are on the map. Any walk will present you with constant choices. For an introduction to the grasslands and spring-sapping valleys, try a loop including Turpentine Road and the small, unnamed pond, which is somewhere between 1½ and 2½ miles, depending on the paths you take.

A good first walk in the young woods of the moraine hills is a round trip from the parking area close to Route 28 to one or more of the hilltops on the high moraine ridge, where there are views through the trees out over Buzzards Bay. Here again you have multitudinous trails to choose from. The irregular moraine terrain is studded with boulders, only a few of which show signs of stonecutting; apparently the rough country made these rocks less attractive than the ones on gentler slopes. The trees, however, do show signs of cutting. The woodlots here were apparently cut quite recently, probably into the mid-1900s.

Explore the Grasslands
The Crane area is notable for its large areas of grassland. Because grassland plants can be quickly overwhelmed by trees and shrubs, grasslands persist only where the woody species are suppressed. Natural suppressers include fire and grazing. Here the wildlife managers use brush mowers and chain saws in lieu of grazers to keep fields open. In addition to Pheasants and Quail, the open fields attract sparrows, Eastern Bluebirds, Bobolinks, even Upland Sandpipers. The most abundant grassland plants are of course grasses, but look also for the flowering plants, including the lovely orange-flowered Butterfly Weed in summer.

Explore the Spring-sapping Valleys

The spring-sapping valleys contrast with the dry woods and open fields around them. The only pond in the area occupies a deep kettle hole in one of these valleys. It is surrounded by water-loving shrubs, including Swamp Azalea, Highbush Blueberry, Sweet Pepperbush, and Leatherleaf, and the arching stems of Swamp Loosestrife fill the shallow water. This pond exists because the kettle hole is deep enough to intersect groundwater. Because it is deep and shadowed by trees, it freezes early and stays frozen late in the spring.

Outside the kettle hole these valleys are somewhat damper than the woods around them and have richer soil, both of which contribute to the wider variety of plants to be found here: Pyrola, Sheep Laurel, Red Maple, and American Holly.

10. COONAMESSETT POND AND COONAMESSETT RIVER CORRIDOR, FALMOUTH

Streams, Cranberry Bogs, Ponds, Woodlands
Walking, Paddling, Birdwatching

PREVIEW

The 158-acre Coonamessett Pond is at the headwaters of the Coonamessett River, which flows south through a narrow valley filled with cranberry bogs to the estuary of Great Pond. From one end to the other there are interesting places to walk or paddle.

ACCESS

Pond access is off Hatchville Road at the Matthew Souza Memorial Conservation Access (sand road and beach launching area) and at the Coonamessett Reservation off Boxberry Hill Road (path at the eastern edge of the site along the golf course leads down the bank to the beach). For the river, parking is beside the bogs off John Parker Road south of Sandwich Road (you can launch a boat into the bog pond here too) and off Hatchville Road near the water treatment facility. Access to Great Pond is on the south side of Route 28, where you can carry a light boat to the water, and at a small town landing off Harrington Street a mile south of Route 28.

GEOLOGY

Coonamessett Pond is one of the larger kettle holes on the Cape. It is the negative impression of a great chunk of stranded glacial ice that was buried beneath the sand and gravel of the outwash plain some fifteen thousand years ago. The sandy material that buried the ice can be seen in bluffs around the pond. The Coonamessett River lies in one of the spring-sapping valleys that cut the outwash plain. This valley was cut before the Coonamessett Pond ice block melted, as you can see from the fact that the valley crosses the pond and continues to the north. When the ice finally melted, the collapse of the sand and gravel

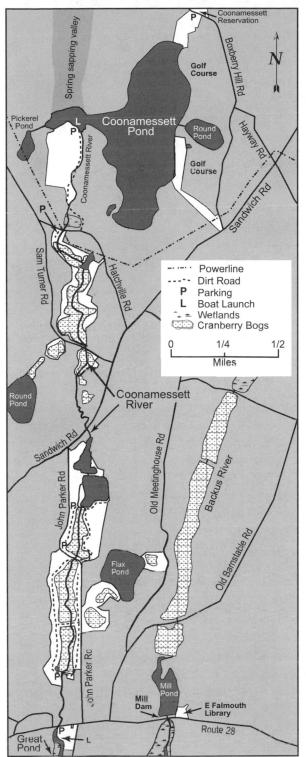

Map 10.
Coonamessett Pond and
Coonamessett River Corridor

above it interrupted the valley. Most of the water in the Coonamessett River comes from groundwater. In wet seasons water also flows into the river from the pond, but you need only compare the significant river that flows into the estuary at Great Pond with the dry bed or small trickle at the pond to recognize that most of the water enters the river below the pond.

WHAT'S TO SEE AND DO

Enjoy the Pond
The swimming is nice, and Coonamessett Pond is a good place for paddling or sailing a small sailboat. People fish here for Bass and Yellow Perch. Look for families of Mallards in the summer and also for shells of freshwater clams that may have been the meal of a Raccoon, Muskrat, or Otter.

Paddle into Pickerel Pond
To find the narrow stream that connects to Pickerel Pond, work your way along the bank of arching Swamp Loosestrife at the west end of Coonamessett Pond. In the stream you enter another world. Trees and shrubs overhang the stream, and ferns and flowering plants crowd close to put their roots in the water. When water levels are low, you can estimate the high water level by the height of the many small roots on the stems that the plants had put out to take advantage of high water.

In 100 yards the stream opens into Pickerel Pond, yet another world. In summer this shallow pond is covered with the circular leaves and the white and yellow blossoms of water lilies, and is rimmed with the purple flowers of Pickerelweed. The air buzzes with dragonflies and damselflies; Grackles and Red-winged Blackbirds cluck in the cattails. The vegetation growing out into the water is Buttonbush, which has fragrant 1½-inch balls of flowers in July. In the shallows the male Sunfish clear away the brown plants and organic debris in summer to create circular spawning redds, which they guard assiduously. The sandy redds stand out white against the dark weedy bottom. If you paddle up carefully, you can watch the fish patrolling.

Explore the River and the Cranberry Bogs
The Coonamessett River, a Herring run, begins beside the beach at the Souza Conservation Area, where it is controlled by a small weir. In dry seasons the upper part of the river may be dry (this segment of

the river is an artificial ditch). You can see the river at many points along its course and can launch a small boat into the stream on the south side of Route 28 just east of the bridge. At high tide you can paddle a short way upstream from the launch point, but most of the time you will only be able to go downstream toward Great Pond. The first mile is a gradually widening estuary fringed with a narrow ribbon of salt marshes backed with woods. Downstream the river opens out into Great Pond. Most of the shoreline is developed but is still very beautiful, particularly in the fall. The beaches along the west side of the pond are public.

The cranberry bogs along the river were developed a long time ago, as can be seen from the shapes that conform to the natural channel, with the river running through them. New bogs are rectilinear for efficiency, and separated from rivers. The bogs are encircled by dirt roads that make for good walking. These bogs belong to the town of Falmouth and have been leased to a farmer. In 1997 and 1998 the river water in the bogs was found to be contaminated by the toxin EDB emanating from the Masachusetts Military Reservation to the north. Although the berries did not contain toxic chemicals, they were destroyed. This same plume caused the closure of the Town of Falmouth Coonamessett water well; the treatment plant just south of Hatchville Road is using charcoal to remove contaminants. This problem reminds us of the wide-spreading effects of contamination of our groundwater.

In June the cranberries bloom, in summer the bogs may be flooded for a short time to reduce insects, and in September or October they may be flooded again for harvest. At times when there isn't much human activity on the bogs, there is lots of bird life. Ospreys fish for Herring in the river, Swans nest here and forage for submersed vegetation, Kingfishers and herons hunt along the ditches, and many insect-eating birds patrol above the bogs. Around the bogs you can see the many borrow pits where sand is extracted for bog maintenance, flanked by the remnants of both upland and streamside vegetation: Bear Oak, Swamp Azalea, Sweet Pepperbush, White and Scarlet Oaks, and Tupelo. The small earthen dam that impounds the river water for irrigation forms a pond that is a likely place for ducks, herons, and other waterbirds. The short trails around it give interesting views, and it is an appealing place for a small boat.

11. WESTERN WAQUOIT BAY, FALMOUTH

Salt Water, Salt Marshes, Beaches, Woodlands
Walking, Paddling, Birdwatching

PREVIEW

Waquoit Bay is the largest estuary on the south shore of Cape Cod. Although much of its shoreline is densely developed, and more than a thousand boats tie up here in summer, important open space remains, including 330-acre Washburn Island, a part of the Waquoit Bay National Estuarine Research Reserve (WBNERR—pronounced "Web´ ner"). Washburn is mostly wooded and is laced with trails. South Cape Beach and the Mashpee side of the bay are covered in the Eastern Waquoit Bay section (see site 15). The Quashnet/Moonakis River (see site 12) flows into Waquoit Bay.

ACCESS

White's Landing on the west bank of the Childs River, off Route 28, has a boat ramp and a large parking area. The town landing off Seapit Road has little parking. WBNERR headquarters on Route 28 has a visitor center and a nature trail. Washburn Island can be reached only by boat; contact WBNERR for information about camping.

GEOLOGY

The upland surrounding Waquoit Bay is flat, fine-grained sandy out-wash plain except for small areas of rocky ice-contact deposits that rise a little higher. Waquoit Bay, which is less than 8 feet deep, probably was not a kettle hole. More likely it developed where the four spring-sapping valleys that enter the bay coalesced at their mouths.

Freshwater swamps or marshes developed in some of the valleys by about 4,000 years ago. The sea was beginning to creep into Vineyard Sound by then, but Waquoit Bay was still some 25 feet above sea level. The sea finally reached the area about 2,300 years ago; it eroded the headlands until the main barrier beach closed across the mouth of Waquoit Bay about 1,200 years ago. An inlet (or outlet) must have

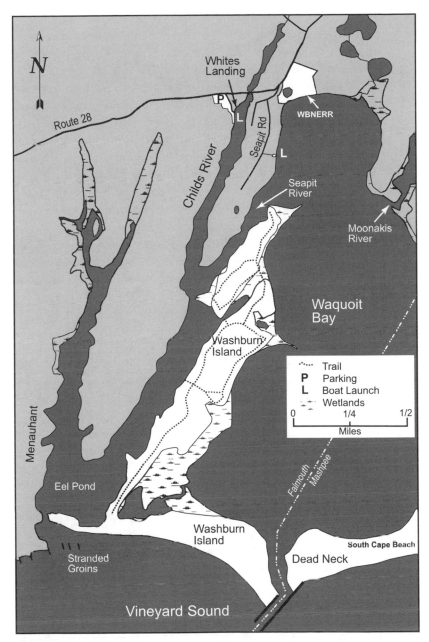

Map 11. Western Waquoit Bay

existed, at least at times. Natural inlets tend to migrate along the beach, and this one was not an exception. Now the inlet is immobilized and armored with a long jetty, and the channel across the bay is dredged to allow access for boats drawing up to 6 feet.

The eastern section of the barrier beach is attached to the end of Great Neck in Mashpee; it is called Dead Neck, like a number of other long, bare sand spits on the Cape.

The western section of the beach was breached by Hurricane Bob in 1991. This western section of the barrier beach is a striking example of the effect of shore hardening on the mobile sandbanks that make up our barrier beaches. Most of the movement of sand along this shore is from west to east, in response to prevailing westerly winds. That means that the source of sand to the spit that grew across the mouth of Eel Pond is the now-developed shoreline from Nobska Point in Woods Hole to Falmouth Heights and Menauhant. These shores are armored with revetments and groins to prevent erosion of the upland. No erosion of the upland means no new sand for the beach. As a result the western spit, like most of the beaches to the west, has eroded. Here the beach has retreated landward more than 100 yards, a retreat made visible by the row of groins offshore—they were originally built on the beach. The Waquoit Bay jetties have also affected this area, preventing sand from moving west from Dead Neck in winter.

WHAT'S TO SEE AND DO

Washburn Island
Although Washburn Island looks like wilderness, that has not always been the case. In fact, it has not always been an island. Before jetties and groins were built along the shore, the western section of the barrier beach periodically closed Eel Pond completely, connecting Washburn to Menauhant.

Native peoples apparently visited Washburn; but there is no sign of permanent habitation. By the 1850s there were several farms on the island. They were replaced in the 1920s with a large summer house that was not rebuilt when it burned down. The Great Hurricane of 1938 breached the spit, but the U.S. Army filled it in and used the island as a training site during World War II. The channel at Menauhant is now dredged and has jetties to keep it open. The state acquired Washburn Island for open space in 1983.

A network of trails gives access to most of the island. The primitive campsites are open to the public by reservation; an island manager is in residence in the summer.

Go Boating
Launch a small boat at White's Landing and paddle north under the Route 28 bridge and up the Childs River. In only ½ mile you are stopped by a road embankment, but it is a pleasant place when the bay is too rough. Here there are fewer houses than in the lower parts of the estuary, and few boats. Pine/oak woods cover most of the upland, but huge Tupelos lean over the water at the upper end. In the late summer their brilliant red leaves make a striking picture against the dark water. Water-loving birds are common here. Narrow-leaved Cattails at the upper end of the river suggest that this is the top of tidewater.

Tour the bay and the barrier beaches by boat from either of the town landings. A good deal of the bay is shoal, so this is a good place for paddling or rowing. Some sections of the barrier beach are accessible only by boat.

Special Notes
Endangered Piping Plovers and Roseate Terns nest on the Waquoit Bay barrier beach. Signs indicate nesting season, and some sections of the beach may be closed in early summer. Be careful not to disturb the birds.

Waquoit Bay is divided between Falmouth and Mashpee. The two towns are trying to manage the bay cooperatively, especially the shellfish, but many difficult issues remain, chiefly related to the intensity of the human use of the bay and its watershed.

The bay has a serious eutrophication problem. Every summer a smothering layer of filamentous algae develops near the bottom over much of the bay; blobs of algae tear loose and float on the surface. This massive growth of algae is fueled by nitrogen in the wastewater from the hundreds of houses in the watershed. The thick algae shades out Eelgrass, reduces habitat for fish and shellfish, and can use up the oxygen in the water and cause the death of fish and other animals. Physically removing the algae improves conditions for Eelgrass and the creatures that depend on it, but such removal is not practical for large areas and deals with the symptom, not the cause. The only long-term solution is to prevent this excess nitrogen from reaching the bay, chiefly by removing it from household sewage effluent before it enters the groundwater.

12. QUASHNET/MOONAKIS RIVER, MASHPEE AND FALMOUTH

Streams, Ponds, Woodlands, Salt Water
Walking, Paddling

PREVIEW

Here is an opportunity to explore a spring-sapping valley from its upper reaches on the outwash plain all the way down to salt water. Due to a ditch dug to bring water to cranberry bogs, Johns Pond is now part of the Quashnet/Moonakis River system. From the cranberry bogs the river runs over an old mill dam, through woods and salt marsh to Waquoit Bay. Despite the two names, this is one river. (For more on Waquoit Bay, see sites 11 and 15.)

ACCESS

For the Johns Pond area, park at the end of Back Road at the Mashpee Town Beach (Mashpee sticker parking only in summer), off a bog road, or near Moody Pond. For the section of river between Route 151 and Route 28, park off Martin Road or at the Whiting Road entrance off Route 28. For the tidal portion of the river, park at the Margaret Doutt Moonakis River Reserve off Moonakis River Road south of Route 28 in Falmouth.

GEOLOGY

Johns Pond is a kettle hole formed by the melting of a block of buried glacial ice. The Quashnet/Moonakis River, just to the east, lies in a spring-sapping valley that continues north of the pond. The southern portion of this valley was flooded by seawater as the sea approached its current level about a thousand years ago, creating the Moonakis River estuary.

Most of the fresh water in the Quashnet/Moonakis enters the river from springs and groundwater seeps along its length. Originally the headwaters of the Quashnet River were in a bog in the Quashnet Valley just south of Route 151—there was no surface water connection

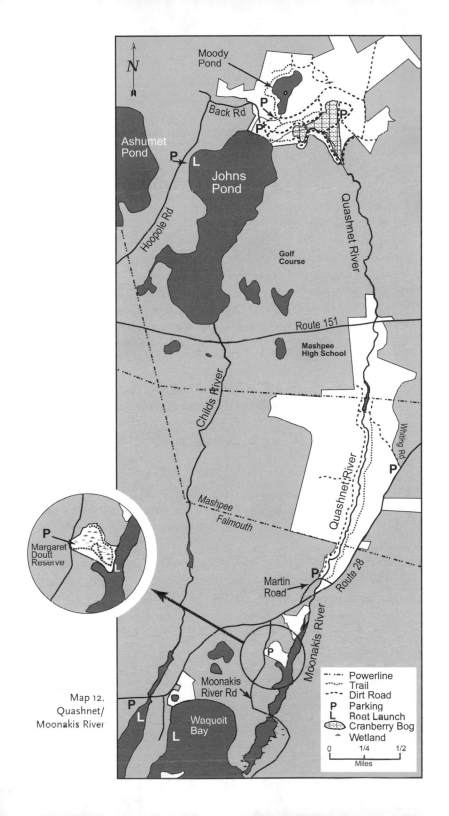

Moody
Pond

Back Rd

Ashumet
Pond

P L

Johns
Pond

Hoopole Rd

Quashnet River

Golf
Course

Route 151

Mashpee
High School

Childs River

Quashnet River

Whiting Rd

P

Mashpee
Falmouth

P
Margaret
Doutt
Reserve

L

Martin
Road

P

Route 28

Moonakis River

P

Moonakis
River Rd

Map 12.
Quashnet/
Moonakis River

P
L

L

Waquoit
Bay

Powerline
Trail
Dirt Road
P   Parking
L   Boat Launch
     Cranberry Bog
     Wetland

0   1/4   1/2

Miles

between Johns Pond and the Quashnet River. The ditch at the east end of the Mashpee Town Beach was dug to carry water from Johns Pond to the cranberry bogs in the upper Quashnet Valley. It has made the upper part the the Quashnet a permanent stream.

The nearby Childs River shows the relationship between kettle hole ponds and the spring-sapping valleys here. The Childs River valley runs south from Johns Pond to Waquoit. If you follow the trend of that valley northward across Johns Pond, you will see that the valley holds Moody Pond and extends north well into the Massachusetts Military Reservation—the valley is broken by Johns Pond. This implies that when the valley was cut this pond did not exist. At that time a large block of ice was still buried here beneath the outwash plain. When the ice melted, the collapse cut off the upper part of the valley from the lower part. Similarly, the valley of the Quashnet was probably cut before the pond basin formed. This explains why the Quashnet River did not originally drain Johns Pond—the pond did not exist when the valley was cut.

HISTORY

The Quashnet was a noted fishing stream as early as such things were noted. The most famous fish were the sea-run Brook Trout; Herring and Eels were numerous here too. But the stream eventually also caught the interest of the locals for its potential to provide water power. In 1832 a dam was built just north of the present Route 28; the dam has been breached but still stands, capped by Martin Road. The dam and its millpond provided water power for a gristmill. In 1860 the addition of a shingle mill (a special-purpose sawmill) caused the dam to be enlarged. The expanded dam turned the entire Quashnet Valley upstream into a pond, effectively ending the fishery above the dam and greatly reducing it downstream by destroying the spawning grounds. After the mills burned in 1894, the dam was opened and the millpond was drawn down. Over the next few years the valley was ditched and diked to create cranberry bogs, and the river silted in. Many bogs were abandoned soon after they were flooded by salt water during Hurricane Carol in 1954. Since then the abandoned bogs have reverted to Red Maple swamps.

Despite the years of alteration, the Quashnet River is once again home to significant numbers of sea-run Brook Trout thanks to the work of volunteers and state purchase of part of the valley. About 1¼ miles of the Quashnet River north of Route 28 have been restored to Trout-quality conditions (catch and release only). The Quashnet is also a Herring run (both Alewives and Blueback Herring), and American Eels, Striped Bass, White Perch, and White Suckers can be found here.

In 1725 Falmouth annexed the village of Waquoit and the lower reaches of the Quashnet from Mashpee. The section of the river in Falmouth is called the Moonakis River—a name that may have reflected (or obscured?) that land taking.

WHAT'S TO SEE AND DO

Visit the Conservation Area at the North End of Johns Pond

Miles of trails and old roads wind through the woods; access roads encircle the many cranberry bogs. Some of the cranberry bogs have been abandoned and are reverting to a greater variety of water-tolerant plants. Others are still worked; they demonstrate the effort, chemistry, and energy that has greatly increased berry production from these native plants. Oak, hickory, Sassafras, Red Maple, and pines are the most common trees in the woods; a few scattered Flowering Dogwoods are lovely in spring, and the abundant Tupelos provide fall color. Moody Pond, with its little island, is a place for a quiet paddle in a small boat. Johns Pond has a state landing off Hoopole Road; the pond is often busy with powerboats in the summer.

Walk the Quashnet River between Routes 151 and 28

A 1½-mile loop walk takes you from the Whiting Road parking area to the small northern mill dam and back; it's a 2½-mile loop from Martin Road. Some of the flow deflectors along the river built to improve conditions for Trout are still visible, but most of the river looks completely natural. Old woods roads and some trails let you walk both along the river and on the upland along the edge of the valley. Here there are quite a few large, branching, old White Pines that must have grown in an open field. These large trees are surrounded by a forest of smaller ones that grew up together later. There is always a surprising amount of water in the river, even in dry seasons, coming from both visible springs and invisible groundwater seepage. Some of the springs are obvious because of the red iron stains on the gravel and sand. There are remnants of bogs along the river in several areas, making walking damp but providing close-up views of Sphagnum Moss.

Explore the Margaret Doutt Moonakis River Reserve

The old bog road into the reserve begins near the Conservation Land sign. The upland areas of the preserve are mostly wooded with oaks, Sassafras, Black Cherry, Red Maple, and Pitch Pines. Bearberry and Reindeer Moss grow under the trees, an indication of the low level of nutrients in the sandy soil. Wintergreen and Pipsissewa grow nearby, but in somewhat richer soil. Along the steep banks of the river are Tupelos and Red Maples above some small fringing salt marshes with tiny beaches. This is a nice picnic spot in summer and a good place to look for wintering ducks.

Several trails lead into and around the cranberry bog. It is being overgrown by grasses, Pitch Pines, Highbush Blueberries, and various wetland plants, but lots of cranberry vines remain. The fact that they are thriving reminds us that the Large Cranberry is a native plant that grew successfully on the Cape long before people started cultivating it.

Paddle the Moonakis River from the Doutt Reserve

It is only a two- or three-minute walk down the dirt road to the bank of the Moonakis River, where you can launch a light canoe or kayak. You can explore the brackish marshes upstream almost to Route 28, but only on high tide—the river gets shallow at lower tides. Like other estuaries along the south shore of Cape Cod, the Moonakis River was deeper before the arrival of the European settlers. Their land-use practices, including tree clearing, plowing, and pasturing livestock, resulted in significant soil erosion. That soil washed down the streams and was deposited in the estuaries, where much of it still resides. In addition, the construction of dams and cranberry bogs contributed sediment to the estuary; after all that, it is a wonder that the water is deep enough for paddling today.

Downstream you can pass under the bridge at Metoxit Road and paddle out of the river into Waquoit Bay: South Cape Beach, Washburn Island—the world is your oyster. On summer afternoons when the wind is blowing strongly from the southwest, the open bay can get a bit rough.

Just below the bridge on the east side of the river is a tiny island of upland in the salt marsh. From your boat you can see the characteristic progression of plants from salt water to upland. Cordgrass grows in the edge of the water with the peat at its roots full of mussels. Above the Cordgrass is a narrow ring of finer Salt Marsh Hay, followed by a ring of High-tide Bush mixed with grasses. Above this is a narrow band of Bayberry and blueberries; the center of the islet is crowned with small Pitch Pines and oaks, and once, on the highest branch, a Great Blue Heron.

13. SOUTH MASHPEE PINE BARRENS, MASHPEE
Woodlands, Atlantic White Cedar Swamps
Walking, Cross-country Skiing

PREVIEW
The words "pine barrens" may suggest desolate, monotonous country; not so. The South Mashpee pine barrens are not tropical rain forest, of course, but the plants that have adapted to the dry, sandy soil or the Atlantic White Cedar swamps provide much interest; they contrast with the more varied woods along the Mashpee River. Miles of old woods roads provide flat, sandy walking and, in season, cross-country skiing.

ACCESS
Park at the intersection of DeGrasse and Red Brook Roads for access to Great Hay Road; park on the west side of Great Neck Road opposite Old Dock Lane for access via Holland Mill Road. The pine barrens lie between the Mashpee River (site 14) and Eastern Waquoit Bay (site 15). Some of the trails connect from one parcel to another.

GEOLOGY
This area is at the extreme southern edge of the outwash plain. The surface is made of fine-grained sand that was carried miles from the melting glacier by meltwater streams. The rocks and gravel were left behind farther north, closer to where all this material melted out of the ice. The flat or undulating surface of the land slopes gently south. Because this area is close to the shoreline where groundwater comes to the surface, the water table is so shallow that even slight swales form wetlands. There is one surprise, however: higher land rises south of Red Brook Road, with the highest elevations to the south. This local reversal of the regional slope is due to a lump of gravelly sand deposited in a hole or indentation in the ice; it is now mostly occupied by a golf course. The front of the ice apparently lingered here long enough to shed this pile of unsorted rock and sand before melting

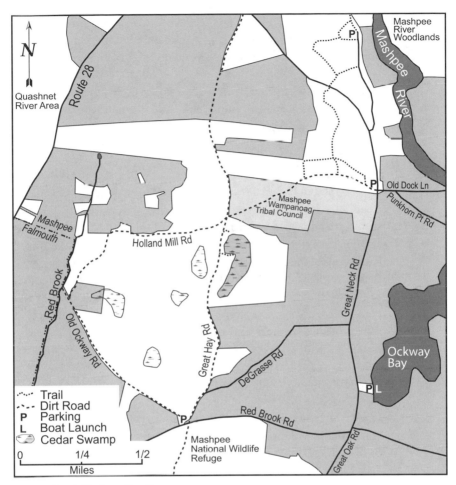

Map 13. South Mashpee Pine Barrens

back to the north. See Eastern Waquoit Bay (site 15) for more on these ice-contact deposits.

HISTORY

The land around the Mashpee River was the home of the ancestors of the contemporary Wampanoag people. The tribal council owns a strip of land running between Great Neck Road South and Great Hay Road, south of Holland Mill Road. This land is sacred to the Wampanoag, but they permit others to cross it. A large fire burned the area between

Route 28, Red Brook Road, and Great Neck Road in the 1930s, the most recent of the many fires that have shaped the environment of the pine barrens. Plants that can survive frequent fires, or that grow in wetlands, have become dominant here.

Great Hay Road (sand) runs 6 miles from a point north of Mashpee Pond to the salt marshes around Jehu Pond. Its name comes from the access it provided to the salt marshes for haying.

WHAT'S TO SEE AND DO

Go for a Walk

A good introduction to the area is the 2¼-mile loop via Great Hay Road, Holland Mill Road, and Old Ockway Road. Pitch Pine has sprouted and seeded here since the fires of the 1930s, creating a typical pine barren that contrasts strongly with the older forest of mixed hardwoods along the river. Although Pitch Pine is the dominant tree, there are others: A few Black Oaks and White Oaks were large enough to survive the fires, and around the edges of swamps and other wet places there are some large White Pines and a few Red Maples that were protected by the moisture. The understory is largely shrub-size Bear Oaks, with some Dwarf Chinquapin Oak and lots of huckleberry, blueberry, and Bracken Fern.

The old woods roads are soft sand, good for finding the tracks of Deer, Fox, and Raccoon. The short pine trees provide relatively little shade, and the area is hot and dry in summer. The edges of the roads are bordered with hearty growths of Bearberry, a plant that can outcompete most others in sterile sand and full sun. Patches of gray Reindeer Moss, a lichen, have colonized bare spots in the sandy soil. Lichens produce their own food so do not need rich soil, but they do help to produce the soil needed by other plants. Unless fire clears the area again, soil will build up, and other plants will eventually get a foothold.

Check Out the Cedar Swamp

There are five Atlantic White Cedar swamps along Great Hay Road, where dark, moist shade contrasts with the dry woods around them. Most are not easily accessible, but the one on the east side of Great Hay Road just south of the intersection with Holland Mill Road has two short access trails. Here you may find, in addition to the Cedars, a number of water-loving plants, mostly members of the heath family:

Highbush Blueberry, Swamp Azalea, Sheep Laurel, Leatherleaf, and Sweet Pepperbush. Sphagnum Moss grows in the ale-brown water, and you may even see some of the small sundew plants that supplement photosynthesis by trapping insects.

14. MASHPEE RIVER CORRIDOR, MASHPEE

Woodlands, Streams, Salt Marshes
Walking, Paddling

PREVIEW

Miles of trails and old roads give access to the deep woods and the marshes along the Mashpee River; paddling the river brings another perspective. This area is so large and varied that even in busy August you can feel as though you have slipped into a quieter and less populous century. Here there is conservation land along much of the watershed, from the headwater ponds to the sea. (See site 16 for Mashpee/ Wakeby Pond, the river's headwaters, and site 25 for Crocker Neck/ Popponesset Bay and the estuary of the river.) This site is also contiguous with the South Mashpee Pine Barrens (site 13).

ACCESS

Parking and trail access for the conservation lands south of Route 28 is off Quinaquisset Avenue, also off Mashpee Neck Road almost to the town landing, and off River Road on the west side of the river. For the section north of Route 28 there are parking areas for the Lopez and Fitch properties on the west side of Meetinghouse Road, and for the Mashpee River Reservation at Ashers Path. Boats can be launched at the Mashpee town landings at the end of Mashpee Neck Road, at Punkhorn Point, and off Great Neck Road at Ockway Bay (see map 13).

GEOLOGY

The Mashpee River lies in the glacial outwash plain. Here the plain is quite wide, extending from the edge of the moraine in Sandwich to the shoreline at Popponesset. The river begins in the middle of the plain, where the meltwater streams deposited sand and fine gravel. This sandy soil is porous, and rain sinks in rapidly, making the upland away from the river a rather dry environment. South of Route 28 the river lies in a spring-sapping valley cut into the outwash plain, but the mile-long section of the Mashpee River Valley north of Route 28

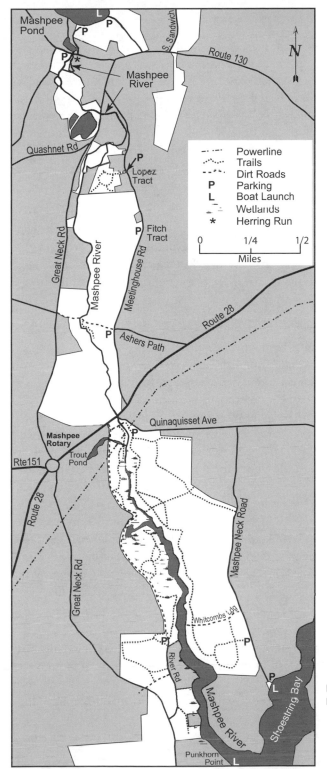

Map 14
Mashpee River Corridor

is rather unusual for the Cape. Here the valley is remarkably narrow, deep, and steep-sided; the curves of the valley match the curves of the river. These characteristics are typical of down-cutting rivers and are unlike groundwater rivers in spring-sapping valleys. It seems likely that outflow from Mashpee Pond found the head of the spring-sapping valley and cut the upper section as it eroded upstream. The lower end of the valley has been flooded by rising sea level to form the estuary at the mouth of the river; tidewater reaches two-thirds of the way to Route 28.

HISTORY

This area was the heart of the territory of the ancestors of the contemporary Wampanoag people. They lived along the river and bays in summer and moved to more sheltered locations in winter. Through gifts and state and local purchases a significant section of the river is now preserved as open space.

WHAT'S TO SEE AND DO

Walk along the River South of Route 28

The large tract of rich woodland on both sides of the river is laced with trails, some named and marked. A pleasant 1-mile introduction is the loop walk from the southern parking area on Mashpee Neck Road to the river and back via old Whitcomb's Landing Road.

The trails wind through woods of White Pine and mixed oaks, with a few beech, hickory, Sassafras, and birch. There are many unusually large trees here; the woods must have been undisturbed for a hundred years or more. Spring wildflowers, Wintergreen, ferns, and blueberries form the understory. Many Red Maples and Tupelos grow along the water, creating wonderful late summer and fall color. Migrating songbirds are often found here in fall and early winter, foraging for insects or eating the abundant berries of Tupelo, Poison Ivy, and Bayberry. The trails sometimes take you through the quiet shade of the deep woods, sometimes bring you out to wide views across the marsh and river.

Explore the River Canyon North of Route 28

The Mashpee River Reservation and the Fitch and Lopez conservation properties feature mature, open forest, mostly of large White Pines, with some large White Oaks, American Hollies, and American Beech trees. Wintergreen, Trailing Arbutus, and Pipsissewa bloom here in spring and early summer. Loops of trail have been cleared in the Lopez and Fitch properties; a woods road and footpaths lead to the river from Ashers Path. The river here flows through a beautiful and surprisingly deep, narrow valley, 30 to 40 feet below the level of the outwash plain. Despite the visual isolation you can hear evidence of the proximity of modern life: Great Neck Road, often very busy, runs along the western edge of the river valley, and the local dogs seem to have a telegraph system, passing the walker from dog to dog.

Paddle the River

The mouth of the Mashpee River is set about with houses and docks, busy with boats, and in summer often covered with floating mats of algae that result from the intense local development. The conservation area at Punkhorn Point and uninhabited Gooseberry Island give a hint of what waits just around the bend to the north, where the river flows through conservation lands for almost a mile and a half.

The lower section of the river is bordered with salt marshes that gradually give way upstream to banks of Narrow-leaved Cattail. At midtide or higher you can take a small boat up the river almost to Route 28, where the river runs strongly down to meet the rising tide. Here the river is narrow and shaded by Tupelo, Red Maple, and oaks above banks of Sweet Gale, rushes, and, in late summer, brilliant red Cardinal Flower, white Turtle Head, large umbels of purple Joe Pye Weed, and swaths of blue Forget-me-nots. The river water is clear, so you can see the iron-stained sediments beneath you. Be careful about stepping out of your boat—the bottom is a loose, water-filled mixture of algae, mud, and decaying vegetation and is softer than it looks.

In spring and summer, Ospreys soar over the water looking for fish. Harriers and Red-tailed Hawks patrol the marshes and meadows, and Sharp-shinned Hawks scout the woods for small birds. Kingfishers chatter as they swoop over the river, but Great Blue Herons and the smaller Green Herons stalk silently in the shallows or perch stock-still on streamside branches. Canada Geese and Mallards probably nest along the river. Wintering ducks often include Buffleheads, Goldeneyes, and Red-breasted Mergansers.

The Mashpee River still has sea-run Trout. This is also a Herring run. You'll have to look carefully to see these well-camouflaged fish in the lower part of the river, but they are easy to see at the fish ladder near Mashpee/Wakeby Pond (site 16).

SITES

15. EASTERN WAQUOIT BAY, MASHPEE
Salt Water, Salt Marshes, Beaches,
Freshwater Swamps and Bogs, Woodlands
Walking, Paddling

PREVIEW
On the east side of Waquoit Bay the Mashpee National Wildlife Refuge
and South Cape Beach State Park include more than 1,000 acres of
woodlands, old cranberry bogs, Atlantic White Cedar swamps, salt
marshes, dunes, and barrier beach, all threaded through with trails and
old cartways. Hamblin and Jehu Ponds and their connecting tidal creeks
invite exploration by small boat. This site is contiguous with the South
Mashpee Pine Barrens (site 13) and Western Waquoit Bay (site 11).

ACCESS
Access is via Great Neck Road (which becomes Great Oak Road) off
the Mashpee Rotary (see map 14), with parking at South Cape Beach
State Park (fee in summer), Mashpee Town Beach (Mashpee parking
sticker in summer), Jehu Pond Conservation Area on Great Oak Road,
near Wills Work Road, and at the corner of DeGrasse and Red Brook
Roads. Boats can be launched at the Mashpee town landing on Great
River, and kayaks or light canoes can be put into the water at the
Seconsett Island Causeway (parking for one or two cars).

GEOLOGY
As its name suggests, Great Neck is a large peninsula; it lies between
Waquoit and Popponesset Bays. The high land of Great Neck separates
the western group of spring-sapping valleys that run south from the
eastern ones that run southeast. This neck consists mostly of a large
upland area of mixed rock, sand, and silt deposited directly from the
ice. Because this unsorted material includes both silt and rocks, Great
Neck is more resistant to erosion than the sandy outwash around it.
It also stands higher than the outwash and slopes north from bluffs at
the shore down almost to sea level north of Abigail's Brook. The south-

Upper Cape Sites

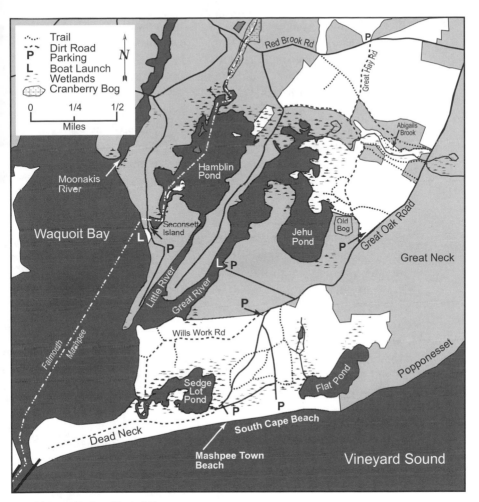

Map 15. Eastern Waquoit Bay

ern section of Great Hay Road runs on the surface of this ice-contact deposit. Here you can see ventifacts—faceted stones that were sand-blasted by the winds after the glacier melted, before vegetation anchored the sand. These stones, recognizable by a distinctive sheen and low-angle pyramidal shape, were formed in many areas, but most are hidden today by forest duff and vegetation.

South Cape Beach is the eastern section of the large barrier beach complex that closes off the mouth of Waquoit Bay. Before summer visitors focused our attention on the beach, this area was known as Dead

Neck—a common name for sand spits hereabouts. The sand that formed Dead Neck came mostly from the southeast-facing side of Great Neck. This headland is vulnerable to erosion from both east and west. Winter storm waves from the east feed sand to Dead Neck; waves from the southwest carry sand east to Popponesset Spit (see Crocker Neck, site 25). As Great Neck has been developed, the headland has been armored with revetments. Hardening of the shoreline along Popponesset Beach has already decreased the supply of sand to Popponesset Spit and caused that spit to retreat; more general armoring of Great Neck is starving South Cape Beach of sand as well.

HISTORY

Back when cartways were major transportation arteries, Great Hay Road was an important thoroughfare. It runs on the surface of the ice-contact deposits and outwash from the marshes around Waquoit Bay all the way north (with some minor interruptions in the vicinity of Route 28) to what is now the Massachusetts Military Reservation. Great Hay Road was used for carting Salt Marsh Hay inland to farmsteads and probably also for woodcutting and all the other foraging and gathering operations of a rural economy. The cartway probably followed a footpath established by the native peoples.

The abandoned cranberry bogs near Jehu Pond have probably not been worked for twenty years or so, judging by the size of the trees in them.

WHAT'S TO SEE AND DO

Walk in the Jehu Pond Conservation Area

A 2-mile loop via the southern section of Great Hay Road and around Abigail's Brook is a good introduction to the woods, salt marsh, cranberry bogs, and Atlantic White Cedar swamps in this varied area. The upland forests, developed on the moderately rich soil of the ice-contact deposits, are a mixture of all the oaks, White and Pitch Pine (including some large, wide-branched White Pines that grew in the open), Red Maple, Tupelo, Sassafras, Black Cherry, and a few pioneer American Beech. Large Swamp Azaleas and Highbush Blueberries grow near the wetlands, and Trailing Arbutus covers trailside banks.

There are lovely views across the marshes toward Jehu Pond and Great River from a number of places along Great Hay Road and the loop trail to the west. Look for ducks in winter and herons and other waterbirds in summer.

Paddle the Salt Ponds and Rivers

From the town landing on Great River you can paddle into Sedge Lot, Hamblin, and Jehu Ponds. Sedge Lot Pond is the least developed and has the lowest excess nitrogen levels of these salt ponds, so it is used as a comparison in studies of the effect of excess nitrogen on estuaries. You can also follow Great River into Waquoit Bay and explore Washburn Island, the head of Waquoit Bay, and the marshes behind Dead Neck. Who knows how far you could go if the wind is calm—all salt water is connected.

Walk on Dead Neck

Of course this barrier beach is far from dead—the name may refer to the bare sand. The dunes and marshes are not as large as those that make up Sandy Neck (site 21) or Nauset Beach (site 41), but they are quite lovely. An abandoned road leads west from the paved road past a boardwalk to the beach and continues about a mile to the jettied Waquoit Bay entrance channel. The low vegetation of Bayberry and Beach Plum, Red Cedar, Beach Grass, and Poverty Grass recall the sandy reaches of the Lower Cape. Gulls, ducks, and other waterbirds can be seen on Sedge Lot Pond and in the marshes along the way. In winter sparrows and other migrating songbirds forage in the Red Cedars, Poison Ivy, and Bayberries.

In summer the beach is home to a large nesting colony of Least Terns; be especially careful on the upper beach, and note the warning signs. Piping Plovers, an endangered species, also nest here on the mid-beach. Sometimes their nests are surrounded with fencing to protect the eggs and hatchlings. WBNERR (see site 11), which administers South Cape Beach, has a volunteer Plover patrol in nesting season. Its goal is to protect the nesting adults and increase the numbers of fledglings from Dead Neck.

Walk Wills Work Road

Wills Work Road leads through typical pine barrens landscape to small beaches on the shore of Waquoit Bay. The sweeping views across the marsh around Sedge Lot Pond are subtly colored by the plant zonation from salt water to upland. A number of foot trails lead from the road to the shore and the marshes. In summer Ospreys use the nesting platforms and may be seen fishing in the nearby salt ponds; in winter Buffleheads and other saltwater ducks do the fishing.

SITES

16. MASHPEE AND WAKEBY PONDS, MASHPEE AND SANDWICH

Ponds, Woodlands

Walking, Paddling, Sailing

PREVIEW

Although there are two names, Mashpee and Wakeby Ponds are one body of water: Conaumet Neck almost, but not quite, separates these rather different ponds. This is a great place to explore by boat—lots of water and three islands. Two large, contiguous conservation areas provide 2½ miles of shoreline, walking trails, cranberry bogs, a small pond, and deep woods. The Mashpee River (see site 14) flows out of the south end of Mashpee Pond at Attaquin Park.

ACCESS

You can launch a boat into Mashpee Pond at the state ramp off Route 130 just east of Attaquin Park. The Lowell Holly Reservation, off South Sandwich Road, charges a fee for parking close to the pond during the summer, but the area is accessible for walking all year from free parking at a trailhead just north of the summer entrance. The adjoining Ryder Conservation Area has parking at the beach in the summer by Sandwich beach sticker only, but trailhead parking is available at the northern entrance off Cotuit Road. Parking at Attaquin Park is by Mashpee resident sticker in summer.

GEOLOGY

The ponds are mostly on outwash plain, though some of the gravelly hills around the pond shore may have been deposited directly from the ice. Except for these hills, the land is flat or gently rolling and made of sand and gravel; there are few large rocks like those found on the moraine. These two ponds, like most Cape ponds, are kettle holes. Their shapes roughly indicate the shapes of the blocks of glacial ice that were buried in the outwash as the rest of the glacier melted away. Wakeby Pond (the irregular, northern one) is of medium depth—

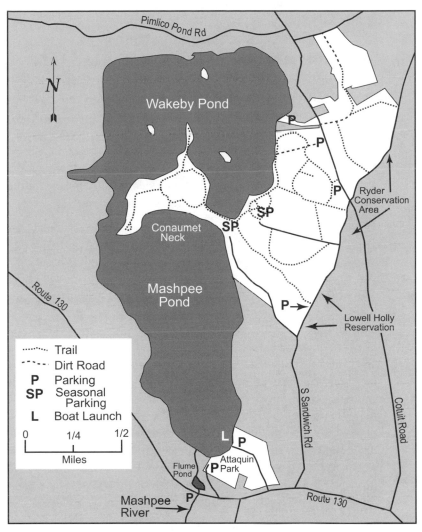

Map 16. Mashpee and Wakeby Ponds

mostly less than 35 feet deep. It has the three small islands, formed of sand and gravel that accumulated in cracks or holes in the ice. Mashpee Pond, on the other hand, is the deepest pond on the Upper Cape: most of it is more than 40 feet deep, and its deepest point is 87 feet deep—more than 30 feet below sea level. Conaumet Neck shows that a large gap developed between the blocks of ice that formed the basins of the two ponds. Sand and gravel filled this space and now stands much higher than the sand that collected on top of the ice blocks and collapsed when the ice melted.

WHAT'S TO SEE AND DO

Go Boating
This is the second-biggest freshwater area on the Cape, and it attracts lots of motorboats for fishing and high-speed activities (the speed limit in the daytime is 45 mph). But the ponds are big enough that there is still space for lower-speed craft except perhaps on the busiest hot summer weekends. As on most lakes the breeze tends to be fluky and gusty, sometimes making sailing a challenge. You can land on the islands and on the south side of Conaumet Neck.

Lowell Holly Reservation
This conservation area occupies Conaumet Neck as well as a goodly section of woods between the neck and South Sandwich Road. The trail from the winter entrance to the pond traverses the upland portion of the reserve through deep woods of large oak, hickory, and pines. It is pleasant to find unmanicured woods, with many big trees and standing snags that provide homes to woodpeckers and Flickers. The trails on Conaumet Neck pass through dry forests, damp woods, and even a Red Maple swamp. On these pondside trails you will find many of the same trees as on the uplands, with the addition of American Beech, Tupelo, Sweet Birch, Witch Hazel, and American Holly. Many of these trees are quite large, probably indicating the richness of the soil rather than great age. The Mountain Laurels, rhododendrons, and some of the Hollies were planted by Abbott Lowell (for whom the site is named), a former president of Harvard who gave this land to the Trustees of Reservations in 1943.

Ryder Conservation Area
In summer the access road to the parking for the Sandwich Town Beach is busy, but in winter the entire area belongs to walkers. The trails pass through quiet woods full of mature American Holly trees and unusually large oak, Yellow Birch, and American Beech trees but, oddly, no hickories. The trails wind around abandoned cranberry bogs and along the pond shore. This is a particularly nice place for a walk in fall or winter, when the green leaves of the Holly, Wintergreen, and club mosses stand out against the dead leaves of the oaks; and the tall

trees break the wind. This area is hillier than elsewhere around the pond, perhaps reflecting the collapse of sediments deposited on and around the blocks of ice. The Ryder Conservation Area also includes a parcel of dry forest east of Cotuit Road.

Wildlife
The Mashpee River flows out of the pond at the weir at Attaquin Park. During April and May you can watch the Herring make their way up the fish ladders a few hundred yards south at Route 130 (parking on the west side of the road) and then come to Attaquin Park and watch them move out into the pond at the culmination of their 6-mile journey from Vineyard Sound—through Popponesset Bay into the estuary of the Mashpee River, up the river, under Route 28, up another stretch of river, under Great Neck Road North, up the fish ladder, under Route 130, through Flume Pond, and finally into Mashpee/Wakeby Pond, 55 feet above sea level. The Herring come here to spawn; they must be reproducing successfully, as the population still exists, but once in the pond they are pretty much invisible. Invisible to us, that is; fish-eating birds such as Ospreys, Kingfishers, and cormorants apparently can see them well enough. Attracted by this rich food source, these birds are a common sight in spring, summer, and fall. These are two-story ponds, meaning that the warm surface waters are underlain by cooler deep waters; such ponds have both warm-water fish—Bass and Pickerel, for example—and cool-water fish such as Trout.

In many places along the shores of the ponds empty Freshwater Clam shells gape in the shallow water. Although they are large—up to 6 inches—the shells are very thin. Freshwater ponds here contain little calcium for shell formation; compare these lightweight shells with the heavy shells of saltwater clams such as Quahogs.

17. SCUSSET BEACH STATE RESERVATION, SANDWICH

Beaches, Dunes, Salt Marshes, Woodlands
Walking, Birdwatching

PREVIEW
Scusset Beach is one of the widest beaches on Cape Cod. Yes, this is Cape Cod. It is part of the town of Sandwich, the oldest town on the Cape. In addition to the extensive beach, there is a fishing pier, trails through the woods and marshes, a view out over Cape Cod Bay, and access to the canal service road for walking.

ACCESS
Scusset Beach is on the north side of Cape Cod Canal. Follow Scusset Beach Road from the Sagamore Rotary (map 1). There are a number of parking areas. An entrance fee is charged in summer.

GEOLOGY
Sagamore Hill is a 75-foot pile of moraine material deposited in a hole or indentation in the ragged, melting edge of the glacier. It stands above fresh and salt marshes that are protected by a barrier beach. This beach was formed and is maintained by sand that moves south from the bluffs of Sagamore Highlands to the north. This stretch of coast is exposed to the powerful waves generated by winter northeasters.

HISTORY
The road, campground, and parking area are built on marsh filled in by dredging for the Cape Cod Canal, which borders the park on the south. The winding, marshy Scusset River, which was a thoroughfare for native peoples and European settlers, has been replaced with the wide and swiftly flowing tidewater of the Cape Cod Canal (see site 1).

   At the end of the year 2000 a project was undertaken at Scusset to restore some saltwater flow to the marshes north of the canal, in the area where the Scusset River once flowed. The culverts under Scusset

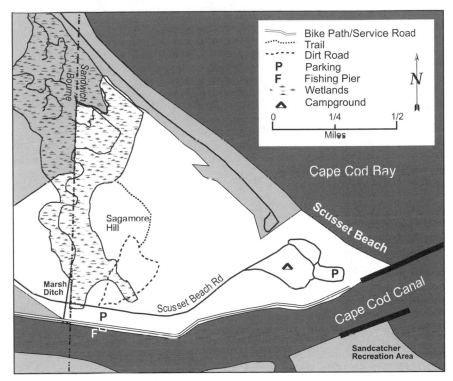

Map 17. Scusset Beach State Reservation

Beach Road and the canal service road were greatly enlarged and fitted with weirs to control the water, and the small connecting ditch was widened to 12 feet. A particular concern was the Phragmites that had taken over the marshes, replacing the more varied salt marsh flora. It will be interesting to look for the effects of this circulation change.

WHAT'S TO SEE AND DO

The Beach

Scusset Beach, on Cape Cod Bay, is indeed one of the widest beaches on the Cape. Though it was always large, this beach has grown wider since the construction of the canal and its enormous jetties. This is because waves carry sand southward from the bluffs and drop it where they are stopped by the northern jetty. Sand blown inland from the beach has built dunes over the dredge spoils and the pre-canal marshes. On the south side of the canal the beach, starved for sand, has eroded. Before the canal and its jetties were built, the beaches to the north and south of the canal were one beach, broken only by the small and mobile mouth of the Scusset River. This is a very clear demonstration of the effect of interrupting the flow of sand along a beach. South of the canal the beach is mostly cobbles, because the sand that would have been on the beach has been trapped behind the northern canal jetty or carried out into deep water in Cape Cod Bay.

Fishing

Fishing is a big activity at Scusset. The fishing pier and the breakwater and canal banks often are liberally dotted with anglers of all ages, fishing for Striped Bass, Scup, Bluefish, and whatever else is biting.

Walk to Sagamore Hill

A nice 1½-mile loop walk goes north from the parking lot at the fishing pier to Sagamore Hill. The hill provides a wide view over the marshes and the east entrance of the canal. The walk follows Artillery Road, a dirt road that is mostly raised above the level of the wet woods, passing through a forest of Red Maple, hickory, Pitch Pine, oaks, and large Tupelo. The remains of a gun emplacement can be seen on the top of the hill; presumably the road was built to serve that site. A number of paths and woods roads lead off the main trail toward thickets and the marsh, where a wide variety of plants, both common and uncommon, are found: ferns, Sweet Pepperbush, Trout Lily, Swamp Azalea, and Rhodora in the damp woods and Bearberry, Poverty Grass, blueberries, and Asters in the open spaces among the Pitch Pines. The marshes have been cut off from the sea by roads and the canal. Now they are mostly fresh or brackish water and have been taken over by Phragmites; they harbor much less life than the thickets, but some boggy spots have cranberries and sundews. Salt marsh plants may eventually grow here again if the newly enlarged culverts provide enough circulation.

Birds

This is a well-known spot for watching birds, especially in the fall and winter. The thickets, marshes, and woods host flocks of small songbirds during migrations. Golden-crowned Kinglets, Song Sparrows, Yellow-rumped Warblers, Chickadees, and Titmice fill the woods in winter with their high thin "tzeets" and "chips," and the grasslands provide forage for wintering Horned Larks, Song Sparrows, and Snow

Buntings. Hawks can often be seen cruising above the marsh or the barrier beach beyond.

In summer much of Scusset is the domain of *Homo sapiens*. Only a few creatures (gulls, for instance) can tolerate proximity to large numbers of humans; most retreat to the thickets and marshes or are active only at night.

18. SANDWICH MARSHES, OLD HARBOR CREEK, AND TOWN BEACH, SANDWICH

Beaches, Salt Marshes, Salt Water

Walking, Paddling, Birdwatching

PREVIEW

A boardwalk gives access to the spectacular beach and marsh area northeast of Sandwich village. There is good walking on the beach, on the boardwalk, and along Mill Creek. A small boat can take you to large areas of marsh along the winding tidal creeks.

ACCESS

Take Jarves Street north off Route 6A at the traffic light. At the end go left on Factory Street, and follow the road to the parking area at the end of Boardwalk Road. Small boats may be launched down a gravel slope into Mill Creek. More parking is at the end of Town Neck Road.

GEOLOGY

This area lies between the high hills of the Sandwich Moraine to the south and Cape Cod Bay to the north. The low upland on which Sandwich Center and Boardwalk Road are built is composed of lake deposits—well-sorted, fine-grained silts, gravels, and sands deposited in the short-lived lake that occupied what is now Cape Cod Bay. This lake formed once the glacier had melted back far enough to expose a basin between the moraine and the ice front. The glacier continued to release sand, gravel, and other rock debris into the still waters of the lake, forming deltas and lake deposits. The lake soon emptied, cutting part of the valley now occupied by the Cape Cod Canal as it drained.

When the sea reached these uplands some four to five thousand years ago, the ocean waves broke against the seaward ends of the delta deposits, eroding them and depositing the resulting sand and silt in low areas between the headlands. As soon as the currents began to build a sand spit eastward from Town Neck, the Sandwich uplands

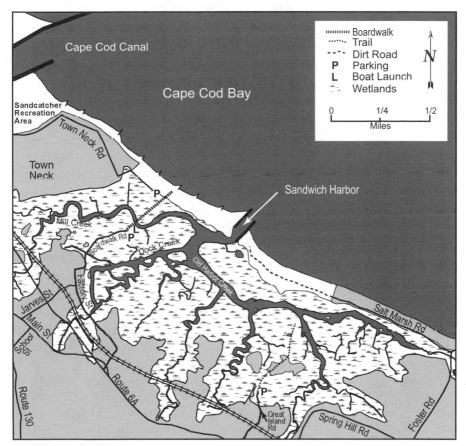

Map 18. Sandwich Marshes, Old Harbor Creek, and Town Beach

were protected, and the water behind the sand spit began to fill in. By
about three to four thousand years ago the water was shallow enough
that *Spartina* could grow and create a salt marsh. The Barnstable Great
Marshes also began about this time; they are protected behind Sandy
Neck, whose dunes are visible about 6 miles to the east.

HISTORY

Sandwich, incorporated in 1639, is the oldest town on Cape Cod. Its
inhabitants were mostly engaged in farming and fishing until the early
1800s, when glassmaking became a local industry. Factory Street was
named for the glass factory that sat between the road and the water of

Dock Creek. The straight banks and right angle in the creek reflect the abandoned working waterfront where small vessels were loaded with Sandwich glass until 1888. The local resource that drew the factory was not the beach sand (sand for glassmaking must be pure quartz) but wood from nearby forests, for firing the kilns. A brick kiln had been built in the late 1700s at the end of Town Neck to take advantage of clay that had been deposited in the temporary glacial lake. The boardwalk was first built in 1875 from the end of the long, narrow peninsula of upland, now followed by the road, that stretches out to Mill Creek. It provided access for "fishing and fowling" along the shore.

WHAT'S TO SEE AND DO

Explore the Marsh and the Shore
The walk across the boardwalk carries you into a world of color, brilliant or subtle depending on the weather and season. From the elevation of the boardwalk you can see the bands of Cordgrass marking the marsh creeks and the patches of *Salicornia* in the salty spots on the marsh flats. In fall the *Salicornia* turns orange and then brilliant red, matching the Tupelos and Red Maples along the rim of upland to the south. From the boardwalk just south of the dunes, you can walk east along the bank of Mill Creek toward the jetties and thence to the beach. Tread lightly and in single file on the marsh.

The beach between the boardwalk and the Cape Cod Canal is rocky, but it was not always so. Before the construction of the canal the wide sand beach at Scusset extended southeast all the way to Sandy Neck. Wave-generated currents have always brought sand south from the white bluffs at Sagamore and Manomet. That's how the beaches and spits of Town Neck and Sandy Neck were formed. But the canal and its jetties interrupted that flow of sand, forcing it to stop north of the jetties, or directing it out into deep water in Cape Cod Bay. So an unintended consequence of the construction of the Cape Cod Canal is the reduction of the beaches south of the canal to narrow, rocky strips. Each of the small groins along the beach shows the same effect—sand is piled up on the northwest side of the groin; south of each one the beach is lower, narrower, and rockier. You can walk along the beach all the way to the south jetty of the canal; see the Cape Cod Canal (site 1) and Scusset Beach (site 17).

Paddle the Marshes

A small boat gives you access to about 8 miles of marsh creeks including wide, salty Old Harbor Creek and the winding, almost fresh, upper reaches of its tributaries. At high tide you float high among the grasses and can look abroad at the marsh and the hills beyond. At lower water you'll find solitude between the banks of peat. A quiet paddler will find something new around each bend. You may see the remains of old wharves along some creeks as well as the straight, narrow ditches that drained the salt ponds on the marsh to reduce the saltwater mosquito population. Birds are abundant on the marshes, especially during spring and fall shorebird migrations.

Mill Creek, named for the Dexter Grist Mill upstream in the center of Sandwich (worth a visit) is a Herring run. Fresh water from the water table to the north supports freshwater vegetation along the upper reaches of the creek.

19. MAPLE SWAMP CONSERVATION AREA, SANDWICH

Woodlands, Freshwater Swamps, Vernal Pools
Hiking, Views

PREVIEW

Some maple swamps do occupy deep kettle holes at the Maple Swamp Conservation Area, but the 800+ acres also include high hilltops, dry woods, vernal pools, miles of trails, a view across Cape Cod Bay, and rugged hills.

ACCESS

Parking is in the lot off Service Road, between exits 3 and 4 of Route 6.

GEOLOGY

This is the Sandwich Moraine, consisting of the rocky hills bulldozed up by a re-advance of the glacier and capped by rocks and sand deposited directly from the ice as it subsequently melted. Irregular topography of deep hollows and high hills is typical of moraine landscapes, but this area is extraordinarily rough, with steep 100-foot slopes between ridges and hollows. The rugged section of the moraine between Mill Road and Maple Swamp Road resulted from the collapse of moraine deposits that had been piled up on remnant blocks of ice. When the glacier re-advanced, it bulldozed up not only the sand and rock in front of it but also the ice of the ragged glacial front. The resulting mixture of ice and rock debris set up the conditions for irregular collapse when the buried ice blocks finally melted.

The Sandwich Moraine has fewer and smaller boulders than the Buzzards Bay Moraine, and some rock types occur here that are not found there—the lobes of the glacier flowed south over different areas and thus collected different kinds of rocks. The dominant rock type in both moraines is granite, but there is much more sandstone and volcanic rock in the Sandwich Moraine, and an unusual black-and-

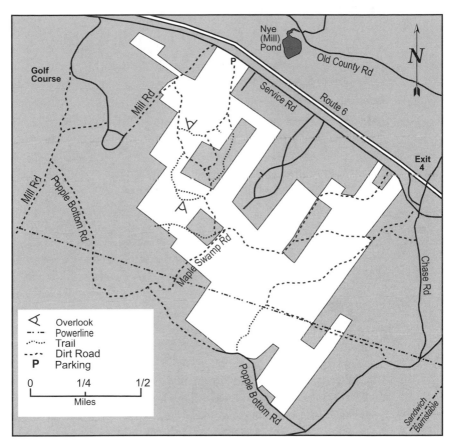

Map 19. Maple Swamp Conservation Area

white laminated quartzite is found on Cape Cod only in materials derived from the Cape Cod Bay lobe.

HISTORY

Henry David Thoreau, in the journal of his 1857 visit to the Cape, noted that there was a band of trees 3 miles wide that extended 30 miles east from Sandwich. That wooded land would have included this area. It was apparently used as woodlots, not pasture. The trees here at Maple Swamp are fairly young, probably only fifty to one hundred years old; perhaps these woods were cut wholesale for firewood for the Sandwich glass factory.

Mill Road was an old cartway that probably followed an even older footpath. It was used by farmers in the southern part of Sandwich to reach the Nye mill just north of the present Route 6.

WHAT'S TO SEE AND DO

Walk to the Scenic Overlooks

Many days' worth of trails exist in this area, but a nice introductory walk is the loop from the parking area to the two scenic overlooks and back. This 2-mile walk might take you about an hour, depending on how much time you spend admiring the views. The walk has some steep hills, but it is all on good trails or old cart roads. It takes you past several of the deepest kettle holes and to the tops of two ridges where the views are maintained by some selective tree cutting. The northern overlook provides a view across Scorton Creek (see site 20) and the east end of Scorton Neck to Provincetown. On a clear day the large white water tank in Provincetown can be seen with the naked eye, but it usually requires binoculars to pick out the nearby gray stone of the Pilgrim Monument (see map, site 50). The southern vista point overlooks a stretch of Sandwich Moraine in the direction of Spectacle Pond, but the 150-foot moraine ridges to the south hide the wide outwash plain and Vineyard Sound beyond.

Short spur trails along the way lead down into deep kettle holes. Some are filled with Red Maple or Highbush Blueberry swamps; others are dry except for late winter and early spring, when they hold vernal pools.

Few species of trees grow here. The most common trees, as almost everywhere, are the oaks, with some Pitch Pine and White Pine mixed in. Scattered among them are a few American Beeches, some American Holly and hickories, and some Red Maples in the wet places. A couple of unusual low evergreen plants grow here: Partridgeberry and Pipsissewa occur along the sides of the cart road north of the junction with Maple Swamp Road.

Explore the Moraine on the Powerline Right-of-Way

The high-tension powerline running down Cape from the generating plant at the Cape Cod Canal crosses the southern section of Maple Swamp; a number of the trails intersect the cleared strip beneath the wires. Walking a mile or so of the right-of-way will give you a clearer sense of the irregular moraine landscape than exploring by trail or old road. Both roads and trails chose the easiest routes, even if they were longer, detouring around deep kettles and taking gentle diagonals across steep slopes. The powerline right-of-way does not do that. It is a straight-line random sample, cutting across whatever is on its route. The clearing beneath the wires lays the terrain bare and allows you to see both the shape of the land and the material it is made of. The latter is quite a rare opportunity in this heavily vegetated area. Low plants that can survive the periodic mowing that keeps the trees down flourish here. Insects and other animals take advantage of the concentration of sun-loving plants beneath the powerlines. You may see butterflies and birds that you don't see in the woods.

Take a Long Hike

The main trail connects to Mill Road, the old cartway that led from South Sandwich over the moraine to the Nye mills on County Road. By following Popple Bottom Road and Maple Swamp Road (and the powerline if you like), you can see most of the conservation area in a 5-mile walk.

20. SCORTON CREEK AREA, SANDWICH

Salt Marshes, Salt Water, Woodlands

Walking, Paddling, Birdwatching

PREVIEW

Scorton Creek and its tributaries run for more than 5 miles through the salt marshes between Scorton Neck and the low uplands to the south; the twisting tidal creeks invite exploration by small boat. Some of the upland areas around the marsh are thickly settled, but three wooded peninsulas are conservation land; they have attractive walking trails with occasional marsh views.

ACCESS

Light boats can be launched into Scorton Creek at the trailhead parking at the old State Game Farm. Parking for the Murkwood Trail is across Route 6A at the East Sandwich Fire Station. For Talbot's Point Conservation Area, watch for the sign on Old County Road; cross the railroad tracks into the parking area.

GEOLOGY

This area of marshes and low land lies between Cape Cod Bay and the hills of the Sandwich Moraine. The peninsulas of upland extending into the marsh from the south are gently sloping sand and silt deposited in the bottom of the glacial lake that briefly occupied the area as the glacier was melting. The higher land of Scorton Neck is a delta deposited by streams of meltwater running south into the lake from the glacier. This delta contains coarse gravel and some cobbles, indicating that the front of the glacier was close. The lake lasted only a short time; it soon drained by cutting its way down through the soft moraine deposits at Scusset (see site 17) and near Bass River (see site 31). The bare lakebeds here were deeply eroded by runoff and spring sapping before vegetation stabilized the surfaces and rising sea level allowed marshes to grow around them.

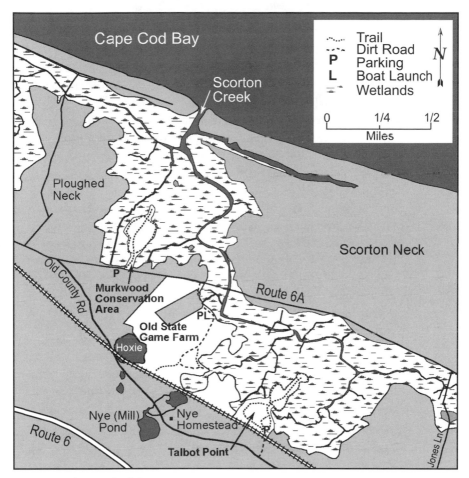

Map 20. Scorton Creek Area

Scorton Creek receives a great deal of groundwater from the high land of the Sandwich Moraine—look for running springs and abundant freshwater plants such as Red Maple, cattails, and Skunk Cabbage at the edges of the upland. The area now occupied by salt marsh was first inundated by the sea between 3,500 and 4,000 years ago, the same time as the Barnstable Great Marshes just to the east (see site 21).

HISTORY
The relatively level, fertile, and rock-free former lakebeds between the moraine and the marshes provided good farmland that attracted early

settlers. By 1667 there were eleven farms along Old County Road here. Old County Road was the main road at the time—the road cuts, bridges, and fills that were necessary to build Route 6A in this area were beyond the capacity, and needs, of the times. The many springs of good water, the marshes for pasture, and the potential for water power were additional attractions.

Benjamin Nye built a dam and gristmill at Nye Pond before 1669 and later added a fulling mill to prepare woolen cloth for use. The Nye house on County Road near Talbot Point is now a museum that details this history. Despite today's woods, all this area was cleared and farmed, as the name "Ploughed Neck" indicates. Little evidence of fields remains (hardly any rock walls were built out here on the rockless lakebeds), but abandoned cranberry bogs can be recognized by the ditches and dikes and nearby borrow pits. The vegetation we see here today is a mosaic of what was planted, what was left untouched, and what has returned since the farms were abandoned. The woods are still in the early stages of succession; tree species have not had time to spread and even out the patchy distribution resulting from chance seedlings as trees colonized abandoned fields.

WHAT'S TO SEE AND DO

Here is an opportunity to explore the entire width of the historic, intensively used land between the foot of the Sandwich Moraine and the beaches on Cape Cod Bay. Location, exposure, soil, groundwater, tides, and human activity all helped shape the landscape we see today.

Explore the Marshes by Boat

There is no better way to meet the marsh than by boat. You can get much closer to the denizens of the marsh than you can afoot; by boat you can reach places you can not even see in any other way.

Because of the tremendous flow of fresh water into the marshes at the foot of the uplands, you can take a boat into the highest reaches of the marsh, where the water is almost fresh, even at low tide. The tidal range is 9 feet, so this trip is quite different at high and low tides. At low tide you'll find yourself in a mini–Grand Canyon of peat; you'll focus on the small creatures of the peat and those that fly or swim. At high tide the close-up views are submerged, and you have wide vistas across the marsh from the dunes to the moraine. In early summer Canada Geese raise their young here, as do Osprey, Grackles, and Red-winged Blackbirds. Shorebirds are common during migrations.

At first glance this area seems quite untouched by the human hand, but a second look reveals everywhere the effects of the long years of human activity. The circles of posts in the high marsh are the remains of the staddles that were used to dry Salt Marsh Hay. The straight ditches were cut to drain the pools in the marsh where the saltwater mosquitoes breed. Draining those pools changed the food web of the marsh, though the changes may not be obvious. Even if you close your eyes, you are aware of the population on the Cape: Route 6A can be heard if the wind is northerly, Route 6 can be heard almost all the time because of the high speed of the cars, and trains periodically pass on the tracks at the head of the marsh. For all that, this is a remarkably quiet and isolated place. If you take the time to watch, you'll see many of nature's soap operas starring the birds, crabs, and even fish.

Walk the Murkwood Conservation Area

This area, a peninsula in the marsh, rises only about 10 feet above sea level and lies opposite the mouth of Scorton Creek. This proximity to seawater might make you expect salt-pruned, stunted trees and a wide transition zone from marsh to upland, but that is not the case. The northern end of the peninsula supports tall White Pines and Tupelos; a few steps take you from the shade of the trees to the sun and wind of the marshes. The upland here is separated from the tidal water of the creek by several hundred yards of high marsh and a small marsh island; these, along with the barrier beach and Scorton Neck to the northeast, protect this area from the effects of the wind off the water. Although it is clear that storm tides reach into the high marsh—the wrack line a few yards from the trees contains Eelgrass and Mermaids' Purses (otherwise known as Skate egg cases)—the strong flow of fresh water into the high marsh probably prevents salt water from reaching the tree roots even during storm tides.

The peninsula of Murkwood is just under ½ mile long. An old cartway runs down its center to the marshes, probably dating from the time this area was farmed and Salt Marsh Hay was harvested from the marsh. Both the road and the trails along the marsh are flat and easy walking, though in a couple of places the footing can be wet. A brisk walk around the entire loop takes less than an hour, but there is much to be seen on a slower perambulation.

There is a grove of good-size Sassafras at the southern junction of the cartway with the perimeter trails. In the winter the Sassafras some-

SITES

what resemble the large Tupelos that are more common here, but note the "herringbone" pattern of the bark and the greenish twigs with large buds. Tupelos have bark with an alligatorlike pattern of square plates and short, horizontal branches with many stiff twigs. Several short spur trails lead off the main trail toward the salt marshes. Look for marsh birds here at high tide, and note the numerous large Tupelos along the edges of the upland across the marsh on Ploughed Neck.

About halfway along the east side of the peninsula is an abandoned cranberry bog. You can recognize it by the straight ditches and nearby sand pit, even though Red Maples now dominate. The Red Maple swamp along Route 6A between the fire station and the Murkwood sign is also abandoned cranberry bog.

Walk Talbot Point Conservation Area

This narrow peninsula is more than 20 feet above sea level—noticeably higher than Murkwood. As at Murkwood there is an old cartway down the center with trails branching off to the perimeter. A circuit of the peninsula takes less than forty-five minutes—it is about a mile—but do stop to smell the Swamp Azalea or Sweet Pepperbush.

Freshwater springs flow into the salt marsh along the base of the upland bank where the groundwater, floating on salt water, comes to the surface. Here, freshwater plants flourish even though at first glance the whole area looks like salt marsh: Red Maples, Skunk Cabbage, cattails, and Sweet Pepperbush delineate the area of fresh water.

The large White Pines on the highest land were almost certainly planted, as were the spruces and probably the rhododendrons. Sheep Laurel, Trailing Arbutus, and Spotted Pipsissewa bloom in spring and summer among the oaks, pines, and American Holly.

Explore the Old State Game Farm

This was part of the Nye homestead (now a museum) across the rail-road tracks. From the 1930s to the 1990s game birds were raised here for hunting. It is now administered by the Thornton Burgess Society, which plans to use it for environmental education. In the meantime the old roads through the woods and fields provide pleasant walking and good birdwatching. The Thornton Burgess Society's Greenbrier Nature Center, just to the west on Route 6A, provides nature trails and programs at the former home of this prolific author of the Old Mother Westwind stories.

Upper Cape Sites

MID-CAPE SITES

21. SANDY NECK AND BARNSTABLE GREAT MARSHES, BARNSTABLE

Beaches, Dunes, Salt Marshes, Salt Water, Freshwater Marshes
Walking, Paddling, Birdwatching

PREVIEW

Sandy Neck is a 6-mile barrier beach that protects Barnstable Harbor and the Barnstable Great Marshes. With beach, dunes, the open waters of the harbor, the marsh, and the tidal creeks, this area provides almost unlimited possibilities for exploration. A number of houses on private property exist on Sandy Neck. They are concentrated along the edge of the marsh and in the tightly packed "village" at the lighthouse.

ACCESS

Parking is at the town parking lot at the end of Sandy Neck Road (off Route 6A about 3 miles west of Route 149). Parking during summer is by resident sticker or daily fee. You can launch a boat at the state ramp at Blish Point at the end of Commerce Street.

GEOLOGY

Scorton Neck, just to the west, is the origin and anchor of Sandy Neck. A hill of rocky sand, Scorton Neck is part of a delta deposited in the lake that occupied Cape Cod Bay as the glacier melted. After the lake drained, the former deltas were left high and dry until the sea reached them five to six thousand years ago. As sea level rose, the ocean waves eroded the soft delta deposits. The wave-cut bluffs at the end of Calves Pasture Point were cut before Sandy Neck began to grow some four to five thousand years ago.

Ocean waves also built Sandy Neck. Along this section of Cape Cod Bay the net movement of sand is toward the east. As waves eroded the highlands of Manomet and Sagamore north of the canal, and Scorton Neck, sand was liberated to form beaches. The wind-driven waves moved the sand south along the shore until it eddied out in the lee of

258   Mid-Cape Sites

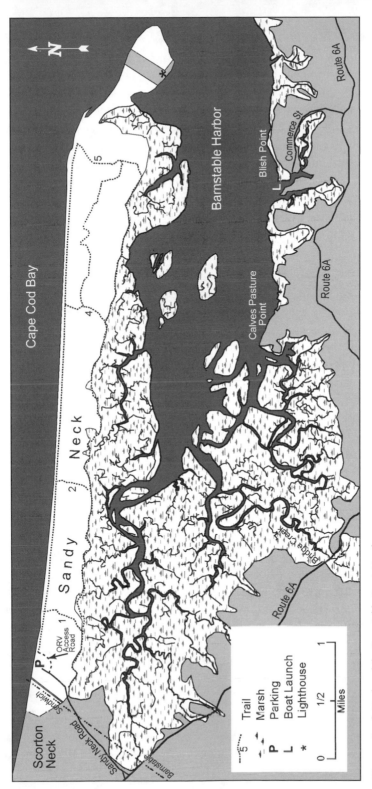

Map 21. Sandy Neck and the Barnstable Great Marshes

headlands like Sagamore Hill and Scorton Neck. In each of these areas sand accumulated and built eastward, creating beaches and sand spits.

Once Sandy Neck began to form it protected the uplands to the south. In the quiet water behind the barrier beach, silt accumulated and built tide flats. About 3,700 years ago Cordgrass took root on the flats, beginning the Barnstable Great Marshes. As sea level rose toward its present level, the sand spit continued to grow eastward, protecting more shoreline and creating more quiet water. The extensive marshes we see today were created by an expansion of salt marsh plants in both directions—out onto the tidal flats as silt accumulated and landward as sea level rose.

HISTORY
European settlers acquired Sandy Neck from the native peoples in the 1640s. No one lived on Sandy Neck; it was used for grazing, wood-cutting, hunting, and the many foraging and gathering activities of a rural economy. At first the settlers let their livestock graze on Sandy Neck; before long the damage they did to the dunes caused the animals to be restricted to the marshes, where Salt Marsh Hay and thatching materials were also cut. Fishing and hunting continued on Sandy Neck itself, as they do today. And woodcutting continued, sometimes on a semi-industrial scale for shoreline industries such as trying out whale oil and boiling seawater to make salt.

Evidence of human use of Sandy Neck appears from time to time in the "blowouts" in the dunes. Archaeologists have found eight- to ten-thousand-year-old campsites and artifacts of native peoples. Large timbers with rusting bolts and spikes (wrecked ships? tryworks?), bits of iron, shotgun shells, rusting steel beer cans, and shiny aluminum ones attest to historic and continued use. Even now, when much of the use of the dunes is of the "take only pictures, leave only footprints" type, those footprints form trails across the dunes that can have a lasting impact on the area.

Barnstable Harbor must have been a busy port in the nineteenth century, busy enough to require the construction of a lighthouse on the end of Sandy Neck in 1827. It was replaced in 1857 by the tower and keeper's house that still stand, though the light was retired as an aid to navigation in 1931 as road transportation took over from coastal ships.

Mid-Cape Sites

The Beach

The 6 miles of Sandy Neck Beach are indeed sandy, though patches of rounded pebbles and small cobbles are always present near the water—more just after storms, fewer after days of calm weather. The particular mix of rocks collected by the Cape Cod Bay lobe of the glacier as it came south distinguishes its deposits from those of the other glacial lobes. Characteristic rock types here include deep red granites, gray and black volcanic rocks, brown sandstone, and laminated black-and-white quartzite.

Walkers should be aware that vehicles are permitted on the beach east of the ORV access road.

The beach and the dunes that back it are eroding with each big storm. This erosion is due to the accelerated rise of sea level and perhaps to the reduction in the supply of sand due to the jetties of the Cape Cod Canal. Those jetties stop the sand and deflect some of it out into Cape Cod Bay. Although some of that sand may eventually be carried on to the beaches south of the canal, much of it is deposited in deep water from which it can not continue to the beaches to the southeast. A continuing supply of sand is necessary for Sandy Neck to survive.

The Marsh

If these lovely marshes look just like the examples in textbooks, it is because this is one of the places where the information in those textbooks was collected. Barnstable Great Marshes have been intensively studied; they have been cored, the cores have been dated, and the plants and animals have been inventoried, counted, and analyzed. Much of what we know about how marshes respond to rising sea level was learned in the Barnstable Great Marshes.

A remnant population of the Diamondback Terrapin still lives in these marshes. This 15- to 20-inch turtle was common on Cape Cod until commercial hunters nearly wiped it out in the late 1800s. Diamondbacks are at the northern edge of their range on Cape Cod—they are somewhat more common in the South. The female Diamondbacks lay their eggs in a warm, south-facing sand slope above the marshes in June and July. Just the right spot is crucial because the temperature of the nest determines the sex of the hatchlings. The eggs

SITES

hatch in September or October, and the hatchlings quickly scramble for the safety of the marsh.

A small boat is the best way to explore the marsh except when the channels are hidden under cakes of ice; you can follow the miles of tidal creeks without causing great alarm among the inhabitants or any damage to the marsh. Here you will find all the variety of salt marsh creatures, from the snails that graze on the mud to the Osprey that soar overhead. High and low tide give different opportunities both to you and to the creatures that live here. Crabs and the myriad burrowers and crawlers are easier to see at low tide; high tide may bring the foraging fish from open water, and allow you to work up into the high marsh channels.

The average tidal range in Barnstable Harbor is 9 feet. Deep water at high tide gives way at low tide to muddy tide flats; deep-draft vessels are confined to the dredged channel. During cold winters ice floes that form in the open water of the harbor can be driven across the marsh by the wind, plowing up or cutting off the plants; the ice plowing may have a significant effect on plant distribution. At low tide these cakes of ice lie jumbled on the marsh surface, creating an Arctic scene.

The Dunes

Between the miles of beach and the acres of marsh lies a band of dunes, some as much as 80 feet tall. Closest to the beach is an irregular line of primary dunes, dunes made by sand blowing right off the beach. It is windy on these dunes much of the time, especially on the bay side, and the surface is blasted by sand and salt spray, but a few plants eke out a living. On the more protected south side of the dunes Seaside Goldenrod, Beach Rose, Bayberry, and Beach Plum grow more thickly.

Behind this first set of dunes are irregular low areas that are sheltered from the winds by the primary dunes. These swales intersect groundwater, creating surprising freshwater marshes. These wetlands can feature cattails, cranberries, even orchids, in addition to more vigorous specimens of the dune plants and a few small trees.

Farther downwind, beyond these low areas, rises another set of dunes. These secondary dunes are formed by sand that is winnowed out of the beachfront dunes, and the sand therefore is even finer than that of the primary dunes. These dunes are slowly extending themselves out over the woods and marshes to the south.

On the south side of these secondary dunes hardwood and pine trees, perhaps descended from the original woods, overlook the marshes. Sandy Neck was certainly more heavily wooded than it is today, but we will never know the details. The trees in the forests that huddle on the south side of the dunes are "pruned" by salt spray that is blown from Cape Cod Bay by winter northeasters and the strong northwest winds that often follow them. As a result of this ongoing damage to the treetops, the trees are short; most do not reach the height of the protective dunes to windward of them. They have something of the look of mountaintop trees, with short, twisted trunks and stunted branches.

Walks

You can walk nearly the whole length of Sandy Neck on either the beach side or the marsh side. Four trails cross the dunes and allow you to make a loop walk of whatever length you like. The marshside trail is close to high-tide level and is sometimes underwater, but you can always pick your way around through the brush. Occasional inholdings of private property exist on Sandy Neck; most are too small to show on the map, but by staying on the trail around buildings you will be on public open space.

The shortest walk, via Trail 1, is about 1½ miles and is a good introduction. The loop via Trail 2 is about 4½ miles, and via Trail 4 is about 9 miles (there is no Trail 3). Connecting Trail 4 and Trail 5 is a trail that lets you see some of the younger dunes. Walking the entire length of Sandy Neck and back is something over 13 miles. In planning your trip remember that much of the walking will be slow going on soft sand.

Birds

Sandy Neck is a well-known place to see seabirds during northeasters. The strong onshore wind brings birds such as Razorbills, jaegers, and storm-petrels right along the beach. Even in calmer weather you can sometimes see Gannets plunge-diving offshore, and a variety of sea ducks, gulls, hawks, and migratory shorebirds is often present. Peregrine Falcons and owls are regularly seen here in winter.

22. WEST BARNSTABLE CONSERVATION AREA, BARNSTABLE

Woodlands

Hiking, Cross-country Skiing

PREVIEW

The forested 1,100-acre West Barnstable site is one of the larger conservation areas on the Cape. About two-thirds of it is on the rough terrain of the moraine; the southwestern third occupies gently sloping outwash. More than 15 miles of trails and old dirt roads provide lots of opportunities for hiking—choose the roads for mostly level walking, the trails for lots of up and down. Note the Barnstable shooting range in the northwest part of the area.

ACCESS

Park off Service Road just west of Route 149 under the powerlines, off Popple Bottom Road just west of Route 149, or off Race Lane near the Sandwich town line.

GEOLOGY

The Sandwich Moraine here at the western edge of Barnstable is narrower and lower than it is to the west, and it becomes narrower and lower yet to the east. Although rocks and small boulders dot the moraine surface and there are many steep hills and hollows, this area is neither as rough nor as rocky as the moraine in Sandwich. None of the hollows is deep enough to intersect the water table, so there are no marshes or ponds in these dry woods.

The south face of the moraine is quite steep both east and west of Farmersville Road, showing the "push ridges" formed when the ice bulldozed up the sand and gravel beyond it. Farmersville Road itself takes advantage of a valley filled with gently sloping outwash to climb up onto the moraine—the valley runs ½ mile north from Popple Bottom Road to beyond the powerline right-of-way. When the front of the glacier was forming the moraine here, a meltwater stream apparently

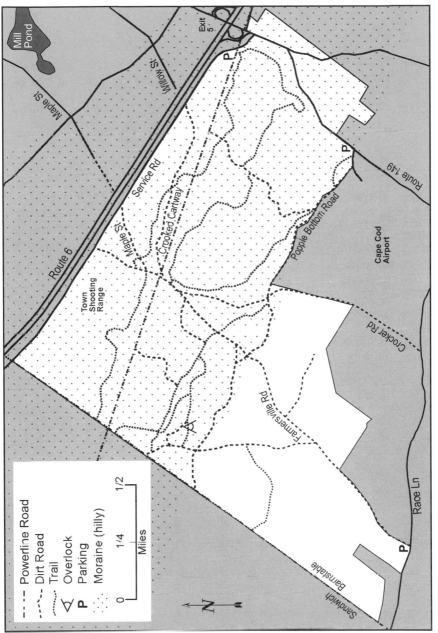

Map 22. West Barnstable Conservation Area

cut through the rocky ridge in front of the ice and deposited a fan of outwash. Popple Bottom Road runs on the flat surface of the outwash plain along the southern edge of the moraine except close to Route 149, where it is on the gentle fringe of the moraine. The "popple" in the road name is a local word for poplars, formally called aspens, which grow here on the low land, known as a "bottom."

HISTORY

Farmersville Road and Crooked Cartway are old roads, probably dating from colonial times. On flat land they run straight, but on the moraine they wander to take advantage of easier slopes and ridges between kettle holes. Modern roads, which are built with a larger tax base and heavy machinery, tend to head straight for their goals, crossing kettle holes with fill and cutting through hills (compare Crooked Cartway with Route 6). As you walk these rocky old roads, you can picture a farmer with a horse and cart slowly bumping up and over the hills with a load of grain for the mill at Mill Pond, now cut off by Route 6, or perhaps wool or wood to sell to a ship in Barnstable Harbor.

Note that there are no rock walls here, despite the availability of rocks. According to Henry David Thoreau, in the 1850s this area was woods. No rock walls were built because the area was woodlot, not farm.

WHAT'S TO SEE AND DO

Hike in the Woods

Woods are what there is. This isn't the forest primeval, of course, but this large area of unbroken woods can give you a sense of what this country looked like before Europeans arrived. One way that this area resembles the woods of yore is that there are few obvious landmarks. In the hilly woods on the moraine, with no ponds or fields, one stretch of woods looks much like another. It is easy to get confused about where you are at first, with the plethora of intersecting trails. But you can't get very lost—the powerline right-of-way is a useful guide, as is the steep southern face of the moraine west of Farmersville Road. And the area is bounded by roads on all sides.

A nice 3-mile hike begins at the Race Lane trailhead and goes north to a scenic overlook on the steep ridge north of Popple Bottom Road, and back. The hike begins in the dry, sandy Pitch Pine and oak woods of the outwash. As you go north up the gradual slope of the outwash plain, the woods gradually become richer, and you begin to see American Holly, Sheep Laurel, and Red Maples. A short, steep climb takes you up the southern side of the moraine to the overlook at 200 feet elevation. From the overlook you can see Mystic Lake in the foreground and Nantucket Sound beyond Osterville (where the two water towers stand close together) in the far distance.

For a somewhat longer hike, walk Popple Bottom Road from the Route 149 parking area to the lookout and back, a round trip of about 4 miles. Popple Bottom Road heads north from the pavement a few hundred yards west of the parking area. The trail that goes north from the parking area joins Popple Bottom Road in ¼ mile, after passing through a lovely stand of large American Hollies and White Pines.

Special Notes
Periodic mowings prevent the powerline right-of-way from reverting to woods. The land looks ragged and bare the first year after the machines have been through, but sun-loving plants such as grasses and blueberries soon make a comeback. Hawks often hunt here. The clearing exposes the rough, rocky nature of the moraine. Without the cover of the trees, the area looks strikingly irregular.

On the average, the boulders here are smaller than on the Buzzards Bay Moraine. A collection of rocks from the moraine will contain many types that are found only rarely in the outwash and virtually never on the beaches: soft brown sandstones, shiny, mica-rich slate, pale volcanic rocks. Rocks of these types mostly were broken up and worn into sand and silt in the rough-and-tumble of the meltwater streams that created the outwash plains. Any that did survive to the far reaches of the outwash were rapidly ground up in the surf as sea level rose; their components make up the silt in the salt marshes and the sand on the beaches.

You might want to notice, coming or going, that the open fields of the Cape Cod Airport are an excellent place to see some of the grassland birds that are becoming unusual on the Cape as trees take over. Bobwhites, Meadowlarks, Whip-poor-wills, and Field Sparrows frequent the area in summer, as do the Kestrels, owls, and hawks that prey on them. During spring migration hawks can often be seen riding the thermals above the southern edge of the moraine.

23. BRIDGE CREEK CONSERVATION AREA, BARNSTABLE

Woodlands, Freshwater Swamps and Bogs, Salt Marshes
Walking, Birdwatching

PREVIEW

The 250-acre Bridge Creek site is an interesting mixture of upland woods, wooded swamps, abandoned fields and cranberry bogs, and fresh- and saltwater marshes. The walking is good on trails and old cartways; some damp places have boardwalks, others are squishy. The compensation for your wet feet is that all the plants that like wet feet themselves grow in abundance. You can explore the lower reaches of Bridge Creek by boat from the marshes behind Sandy Neck (see site 21).

ACCESS

You can park by the kiosk in the northeast corner of the lot behind the West Barnstable Fire Station on the east side of Route 149, north of Route 6, and on the north side of Church Street near the Jenkins Wildlife Sanctuary sign.

GEOLOGY

This site runs from the northern foot of the Sandwich Moraine down into the Barnstable Great Marshes. The southern edge of the site, on the fringe of the moraine, is rocky; many large rocks are exposed in the woods, and more were collected and piled to build the rock walls that divided old farm fields. Some of these rocks show the fluting and polish created by blowing sand before vegetation stabilized the surface. The lower land to the north is made of the sandy and silty lakebeds deposited in the lake that briefly occupied Cape Cod Bay when the glacier had melted back a few miles. The surface of the upland is quite smooth, sloping gently down to the north. The marsh loop trail, by

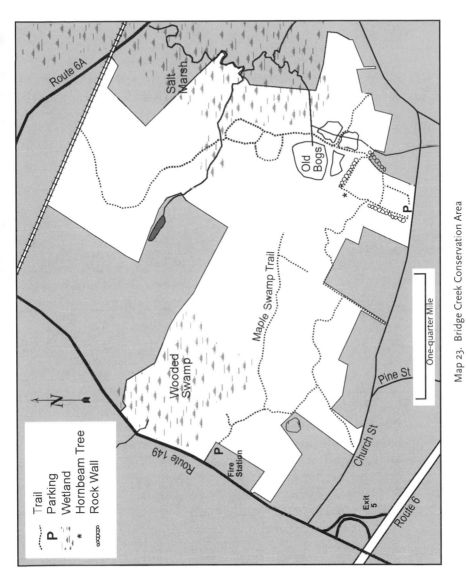

Map 23. Bridge Creek Conservation Area

contrast, is quite irregular due to the erosion and spring sapping that cut the surface before it was stabilized by vegetation. But the steepest slopes are the man-made cut-banks left in borrow pits that were dug to get sand for the old cranberry bogs and to build the cartways across the swamps and marshes.

HISTORY

The upland area centered on the Jenkins Wildlife Sanctuary (at the parking area on Church Street) was an old farmstead. Note the impressive stone walls, the plantings of Mountain Laurel and rhododendrons (look for blooms in May and June) and the built-up cartway between the abandoned cranberry bogs. Where the cartway crosses the stream at the east edge of the farm take a look at the unusual stone culvert; it was probably built several hundred years ago, when manufactured culverts were not available but stone was free to the farmer.

WHAT'S TO SEE AND DO

Go Walking

It's a pleasant 3-mile walk from the fire station to the marsh loop and back. The main trail meanders through the woods of oaks, pines, Black Locust, and American Holly, jogging to avoid wetlands or follow old property lines. The rock walls, fence-line trees, and plant distribution are clues to the history of land use here. You'll be able to unravel some of the story.

The trail to the marsh loop follows an old farm road down the slope toward the marshes, then across the man-made cartway between the abandoned cranberry bogs (a few cranberry vines still survive) to the island of wooded upland surrounded by swamp and marsh. Several benches offer views across the marsh. Look for the spring coming out from the bank practically beneath the trail on the northern edge of the loop. It is interesting to try to spot where the fresh water and salt water meet in the marsh. On the rocky upland of the marsh loop some hickory trees grow; they are unusual on the upland to the west. Perhaps the forest was not completely cleared on this marsh island, or perhaps these trees merely reflect where nuts were buried by a squirrel.

The ¼-mile trail that crosses the stream into the northern section of the conservation area leads to a different environment of old farm fields reverting to woods. These thickets and grasslands make a striking contrast with both the older upland forest and the wet woods. Here too you can read something of the land-use history in the landscape. Look for the rock walls and think about which parcels were abandoned first. In the bare, sandy patches you can see some Poverty Grass, a plant more common on dunes than in the woods.

If you want to explore, and are willing to risk wet feet, try the Maple Swamp Trail. This low trail crosses three small streams, and in wet seasons can become a stream itself in spots. The path is open and obvious at the western end but a bit sketchy and overgrown toward the eastern end. Orange painted blazes on trees may help to locate the foot trails and old cartways that connect up the slope to the main trail. This area is full of wetland plants of all sorts, from Sphagnum Moss to Highbush Blueberries. There are many shallow pools, some with very clear water, others stained brown by the tannin from the bogs. Club mosses thickly carpet the ground in some areas—look for at least five different species, an unusually wide variety.

Special Notes

Skunk Cabbage grows abundantly in the wet areas—look for it wherever you see Sphagnum Moss. In February and early March the spotted Skunk Cabbage blossoms poke up through the mud or moss, even in the middle of the trail; these strange flowers are well camouflaged and may be hard to see until you adjust to looking for their spotted, pointed hoods. By the end of March the stalked, cabbagelike leaves have unrolled, and the plants look less alien.

One of the few American Hornbeam trees on the Cape can be seen here. Although this is a native tree, it is not common, and it never grows very large. The most distinctive characteristic is the "muscular"-looking trunk. Hornbeams apparently prefer this sort of rich, wet soil. If you want to check it out, its location is marked on the map.

24. SKUNKNETT BROOK SANCTUARY, BARNSTABLE

Ponds, Bogs, Streams, Marshes, Woodlands
Walking, Cross-country Skiing, Birdwatching

PREVIEW

The Skunknett Brook area, a Massachusetts Audubon Society sanctuary, is indeed a fine place for birds, and for birdwatchers. Trails and old woods roads lead through woods to the brook, abandoned cranberry bogs, old millponds, and marshes and wet woods along the stream. In this thickly-settled area Skunknett Brook is an island of natural sounds and of natural quiet.

ACCESS

Parking is at the trailhead on the north side of Bumps River Road just east of the junction with Pond Street.

GEOLOGY

Here we are far out on the flat outwash plain, where the land is made mostly of sand, with a small amount of gravel. The low-gradient glacial meltwater streams did not have the energy to transport heavy rocks, so there are none here much bigger than a walnut. The larger rocks got left behind on the moraine—you can find them on the hills in the vicinity of Route 6. Here, where the land-use practices of the past stripped away the soil, the surface of the ground is littered with those small stones, especially in the old road. Some polished and faceted ventifacts can be found among them, giving evidence of the strong winds at the end of the glacial era, and the sand-blasting effect of the sand it drove before it.

Bumps River and its western tributary, Skunknett Brook, lie in spring-sapping valleys that cut as deeply as 40 feet into the outwash plain and drain groundwater into the estuaries of the south coast. Although the stream valley is deep, the steepest bluffs along its edge are

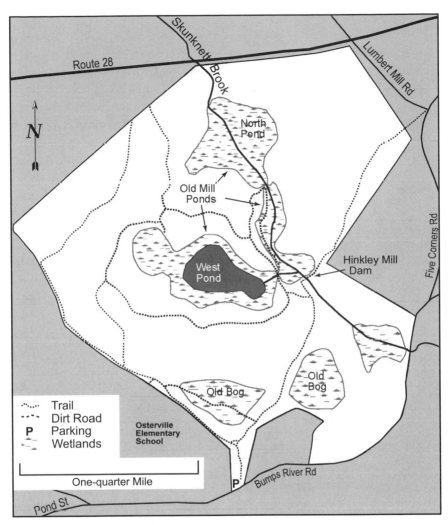

Map 24. Skunknett Brook Sanctuary

in old borrow pits, where earth was dug to build the mill dams and sand was mined to maintain the now-abandoned cranberry bogs. Even though the groundwater gradient is low here, the stream is large because the valley cuts deeply into the water table.

HISTORY

This large stream was an attractive source of water power to the settlers in the area. By at least 1880 Skunknett Brook was dammed to provide water power for a mill. The old gravel road to the brook from the parking area once crossed the stream on that dam. This mill was only one of the many mills in this immediate area, a testament both to the amount of water available here, as well as to the value of its power to the locals. The dam backed water up in the valley, forming a millpond still shown on many maps, though the dam has been breached.

The lovely wide band of marshes along the brook has recovered since the millpond was drained. The dams that created the former West and North Ponds have also been breached. You'll be able to find them because the abutments were not removed. Atlantic White Cedar swamps apparently once occupied much of this low, wide valley and bordered the brook all along its length. When the water level is low you can see the remains of cedar stumps in West Pond. This demonstrates why the wood from these trees was, and is, particularly valuable—it is extremely resistant to rot. Quite a few Atlantic White Cedar trees still live along Skunknett Brook. Most are small, but they have a venerable appearance enhanced by the beard-like gray-green strands of the *Usnea* lichen called "Old Man's Beard."

WHAT'S TO SEE AND DO

Walking

This is a good place for walking in almost any weather that you would care to go walking in, particularly when it is too windy for fields or beaches. Old woods roads make for easy walking through the woods and around the abandoned cranberry bogs. Footpaths join the roads and lead to many of the nicest spots. It is possible to hop across the outlet of West Pond when the water level is low.

The 1½-mile loop walk around West Pond leads past the old bogs, through oak/pine woods, and along the marshes in the stream valley; it is a pleasant introduction to the site. Follow the spur trails to North Pond and the northern edge of the preserve for interesting additions to the walk.

Birds

The varied habitats attract a wide variety and large numbers of birds. Watch for Osprey, Kingfishers, ducks and herons in the marshes and ponds. In the thickets you can expect some songbirds almost any time of year; they may be teeming during spring and fall migrations. The large patch of big White Pines northwest of West Pond is a good place to look and listen for owls.

25. CROCKER NECK CONSERVATION AREA AND POPPONESSET BAY, BARNSTABLE AND MASHPEE

Salt Water, Salt Marshes, Freshwater Marshes, Woodlands
Walking, Paddling

PREVIEW
Though small, Crocker Neck Conservation Area is quite varied: it encompasses upland, freshwater and saltwater wetlands, and a small beach on Popponesset Bay. Despite the houses all around, the preserve is quiet. Popponesset and Shoestring Bays are busy with boats, especially in summer, but some attractive destinations beckon the paddler.

ACCESS
Parking is off Santuit Road at the Conservation Area sign and on the dirt road called "the Lane" on the way to the beach. Small boats can be launched at the Barnstable "Way to Water" opposite the Crocker Neck sign or off the beach at the end of the Lane.

GEOLOGY
Crocker Neck is on the southern reaches of the outwash plain. The land is made of fine sand, with no large rocks and little gravel. The larger material was deposited to the north, closer to where it melted out of the ice. The land surface is fairly smooth, interrupted only by spring-sapping valleys and wave-cut bluffs. Shoestring Bay cuts northeast right across the north-south spring-sapping valleys of Santuit River and Quaker Run. The lower ends of these valleys are now occupied by Rushy Marsh and Fuller's Marsh, respectively. Quaker Run has been obscured by a golf course, but it is identifiable by the strip of cranberry bogs at Quinaquisset Avenue. Shoestring Bay was formed later than the spring-sapping valleys (the valleys could not have cut across if it had been there); it was probably formed by the melting of some buried ice. When the ice melted and the overlying sediments col-

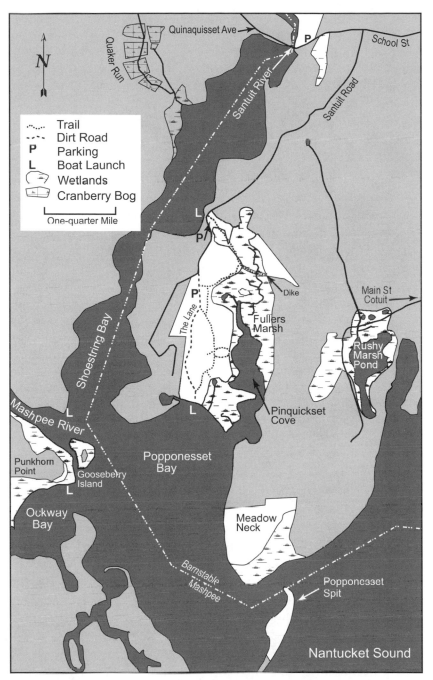

Map 25. Crocker Neck Conservation Area and Popponesset Bay

lapsed, the streams in the spring-sapping valleys would have run into this valley, abandoning their former channels and taking a shortcut to the sea.

HISTORY

The dike across Fuller's Marsh was built to create a cranberry bog, now abandoned. The bog has been taken over by Phragmites, with Tupelo, Red Maple, Inkberry, and other woody plants; no cranberry plants remain.

WHAT'S TO SEE AND DO

Paddle the Bays

With a small boat you can explore Popponesset Bay, Shoestring Bay, and even the Mashpee River (see site 14). You can paddle about ¼ mile up the Santuit River above the bridge, explore Pinquickset Cove and Fuller's Marsh, cross to Meadow Neck, and paddle out to Popponesset Spit. The spit, a narrow barrier beach extending eastward from Great Neck in Mashpee, protects the bay from the larger waves of Nantucket Sound. The eastern end is a bird sanctuary managed by the Massachusetts Audubon Society and may be closed to humans during the bird-nesting season. Popponesset Spit once protected Meadow Neck as well as the bay; it extended farther northeast, to the area of Rushy Marsh Pond, but has eroded and retreated significantly. It is being deprived of sand by the armoring of the bluffs to the west and is becoming more vulnerable to breaching by storm waves. When that happens, Popponesset Bay will become a different place.

This whole estuary system is receiving an excess of nitrogen, mostly from septic systems and lawn and garden fertilizer used in its watershed. In summer the tidal portions of the Mashpee and Santuit Rivers and all of Popponesset Bay have floating mats of filamentous algae that grow in response to that nitrogen. These algal mats have been shown in Waquoit Bay (see Waquoit Bay, sites 11 and 15) to damage Eelgrass and reduce the populations of many fish and shellfish species. The same thing has happened here. The mats of algae wash up on the beach in the fall in place of the Eelgrass of yore. With the disappearance of Eelgrass, the creatures that depend on it, such as Bay Scallops and Brant, have also disappeared. As in other coastal ponds, the only long-term solution is to reduce the amount of nitrogen entering the bay, chiefly by the use of nitrogen-removing sewage treatment systems, though individuals can help by reducing or eliminating lawn fertilizer, especially on areas immediately adjacent to the water.

Watch the Birds

With such a wide variety of habitats this is a good place to see birds of many different feathers. In late summer and fall migrating shorebirds feed on the tide flats and along the marshes. Gulls and ducks feed in the marsh and the bay, hawks hunt over the marshes, and small songbirds forage through the thickets. The occupied Osprey nesting platform on an island of upland in Fuller's Marsh is most easily visible from the dike across the marsh.

Take a Walk

The trail makes several loops, all of them flat and easy walking. The woods are quite varied, and you pass quickly from one habitat to another. In some areas the only tree is Pitch Pine, evidence of fire. In other areas the woods include all the common oaks and many Black Cherry trees. Take the side trails to look over the bog and the marsh. At the edge of the marsh you can see the plant zonation that results from the plants' varying tolerance of salt: from the water toward the land the plants are Cordgrass, Salt Marsh Hay, Spike Grass, and High-tide Bush.

Variation in soil richness also affects plant distribution; that effect is quite clear in this area. Bearberry will grow in bare, loose sand, while viburnums grow most often in damper and richer soil at the edge of a marsh. In spring Pink Lady's Slippers bloom among the trees.

The Hovey parcel, just north of School Street, borders the Santuit River and its marshes for more than ¼ mile. This attractive property was one of the early acquisitions using funds from the Land Bank. The woods, marshes, and shoreline are well worth exploring.

SITES

26. HATHAWAY PONDS CONSERVATION AREA, BARNSTABLE

Woodlands, Ponds
Walking, Paddling

PREVIEW

The Hathaway Ponds area lies like an island of woods and ponds in a sea of developed land between Route 6 and urban Hyannis. Its swimming beach can be busy on warm weekends. Easy trails encircle the northern pond and climb up the gentle southern flank of the moraine.

ACCESS

Entrance and parking (Barnstable beach sticker or daily fee in summer) off Phinneys Lane north of Route 132.

GEOLOGY

North Hathaway Pond lies across the contact between the Sandwich Moraine and the outwash plain. The northwestern half of the pond, with its steep, rocky shore, is in the moraine. The southeastern half, with gentle slopes and sandy beaches, is in the outwash. The pond itself is the negative impression of a block of glacial ice that was buried in the outwash as the glacier melted back across the Cape from the islands. As the glacier re-advanced and bulldozed the moraine against and around it, the block of ice was buried more deeply. The pond is 57 feet deep—the bottom is 24 feet below sea level—so this was a good-size chunk of ice. Many boulders are strewn about on the typically irregular moraine landscape, lying where they melted out of the ice and were exposed by erosion. The flatter outwash plain has no boulders but is composed of coarse-grained materials—rocks as well as gravel and coarse sand—because it was deposited close to the front of the ice. The finer materials were carried off to the south by the meltwater.

The water level in these ponds fluctuates with the level of the water table; it can rise or fall several feet from year to year or season to sea-

Mid-Cape Sites

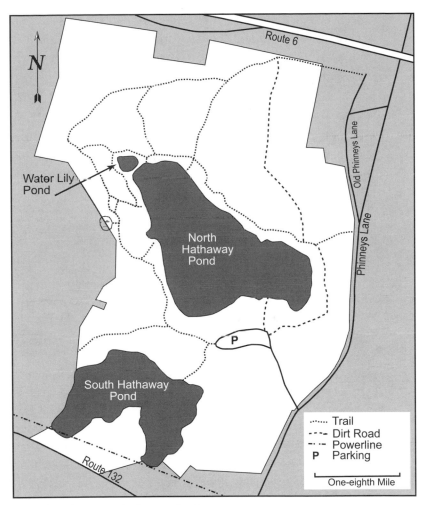

Map 26. Hathaway Ponds Conservation Area

son, depending on precipitation and the pumping of water from nearby town wells. The gentle slope of the pond shore in the outwash means that large areas are covered or uncovered with a change in pond level of only a foot or two.

HISTORY

The young trees across the entire area and the foundation of a house on the bluff overlooking the west side of the pond suggest that this area was treeless not long ago. The house has been abandoned long enough for a 30-foot Red Maple to grow inside the old foundation, but it was not a colonial house: the foundation was built of poured concrete, a technology that probably arrived no earlier than the 1900s. Note the wide variety of introduced plants around the foundation, including Black Locust trees, Day Lilies, and Daffodils.

WHAT'S TO SEE AND DO

Visit South Hathaway Pond

This pond, the less visited of the two, is more likely to have a flock of ducks or a Great Blue Heron in its shallows. Many downed trees north of the pond were felled by southerly winds blasting across the water during Hurricane Bob in 1991. Pussy Willows have taken advantage of the sun and water along the pond shore; look for their large, gray, fuzzy flower buds in February or early March.

Walk the Nature Trail

The nature trail around North Hathaway Pond is a bit over a mile, with a little up and down. Numbered posts refer to an interpretive guide available at Barnstable Town Hall, but all the topics of the nature trail are covered in this book.

Special Notes

Water Lily Pond at the north end of Hathaway Pond was formed by a barrier beach made of sand eroded from the shore and built across a shallow, narrow arm of the pond by waves. When water level is high the barrier beach is barely exposed, but the water can be several feet lower, exposing a wide bar. The bottom of the shallow pool is thick with organic material, and Sphagnum Moss grows around the water, suggesting that it will not be long before it becomes a bog. In summer the pool is filled with White Water Lilies and Pickerelweed and dozens of Green Frogs that say "eeek" as they jump into the shallow water. Sundews grow on the exposed sandbar, and Rose Coreopsis blooms all around the pool. Highbush Blueberry and Fetterbush, members of the heath family, grow thickly along the water in many places.

The woods in this area have remarkably few plant species—the richer soil of the moraine often supports more variety. The trees are almost all Pitch Pine and oaks; a few Red Maple and Gray Birches grow here, but many common trees such as hickory and Tupelo are missing. The same is true of the low plants. Bearberry, Sheep Laurel, and Trailing Arbutus are here but no Wintergreen, Swamp Azalea, or club mosses. This site seems to have experienced many of the land-use practices that have created pine barrens on the outwash plains in many areas: repeated fires or complete clearing and plowing that led to the loss of soil.

27. CHASE GARDEN CREEK AND CALLERY-DARLING CONSERVATION AREA, YARMOUTH

Salt Marshes, Freshwater Marshes, Woodlands
Paddling, Walking

PREVIEW

At the outlet of Chase Garden Creek, some 300 acres of upland and salt marshes form the shore of Cape Cod Bay. You can visit the marshes on the boardwalk, or you can explore them more widely by boat. In the Callery-Darling Conservation Area south of the creek, 2½ miles of trail wind through the woods and around old bogs and abandoned fields, providing variety and views. Sandy Neck is adjacent to the west (see site 21), and Chapin Beach and the New Boston Road Conservation Areas are adjacent to the east (see site 28).

ACCESS

Trailhead parking is on the west side of Homer's Dock Road and off Almshouse Road near its intersection with Center Street. Parking for Gray's Beach, the boardwalk, and the Chase Garden Creek launching ramp is at the end of Center Street. A foot trail enters the area from Ancient Way beside the cemetery.

GEOLOGY

In Sandwich and Barnstable to the west, the moraine ridge stands at almost 300 feet. In Yarmouth its highest point, German Hill, reaches only 130 feet, barely 80 feet above the outwash. Here at Callery-Darling we are north of both moraine and outwash, on the sand and gravel that was deposited in the Cape Cod Bay lake as the glacier melted. Today fresh water seeps from the uplands into the marshes, but less of it than in similar areas in Sandwich. Yarmouth, at the far eastern end of the Sagamore groundwater lens, has fewer and smaller shoreline springs than towns farther west.

Fringing the low upland are salt marshes that form the Cape Cod Bay shore of Yarmouth. No line of barrier beach separates these

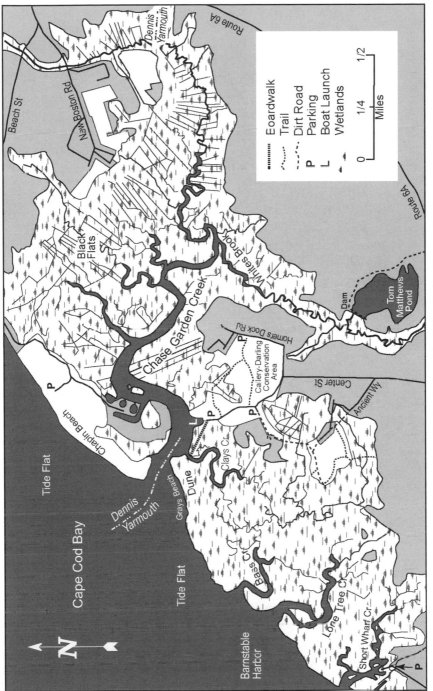

Map 27. Chase Garden Creek and the Calery-Darling Conservation Area

marshes from the sea, and at first glance they seem unprotected, exposed to the waves of the open bay. But it is not so: Sandy Neck to the west, Nobscusset Point to the east, and the extensive tide flats to the north provide good protection, allowing the salt marshes to thrive. The tide flats are the underwater extension of Sandy Neck. Sand from the west moves east with the wind-driven currents along the Barnstable shore; it eventually reaches the end of Sandy Neck and moves on to form the tide flats. Sand also moves west from Nobscusset Point on northeasterly winds and has also accumulated in this deep indentation in the coast.

HISTORY

The old cranberry bogs along Center Street were created by diking off the upper reaches of the salt marshes. The bogs have been abandoned, and no cranberry vines remain; some in freshwater areas have been replaced by Highbush Blueberries that grow well here without human intervention, while other areas with more tidal action have reverted to salt marsh.

Though the upland area between Center Street and Homer's Dock Road was farmed, no rock walls cut through the woods to mark the edges of abandoned fields. The farmers must have marked their bounds with fences—there are not enough rocks in this rich lake-bottom soil to build walls. So they did not have to clear the rocks before plowing, but they must have had to fetch rock for foundations from the moraine to the south.

WHAT'S TO SEE AND DO

Paddle Chase Garden Creek

Chase Garden Creek's extensive marshes occupy the same deep indentation in the Cape Cod Bay shoreline as the Barnstable Great Marshes. The marshes in both areas probably began to form at about the same time, at least 3,700 years ago, when sea level was about 20 feet lower than today. Chase Garden Creek itself is unusually wide for a long distance upstream. This wide channel was cut by the strong currents generated, day and night, year-round, as the tides rise and fall 9 feet over the large area of the marsh. The water, moving fastest on the outside of the bends, undercuts the bank, eventually cutting deep enough that a block of peat collapses into the creek. This process continues today, widening the creek, leaving fresh vertical cut-banks, and creating lumps of peat in the water that look like alligators dozing under the banks.

This marsh is unusually sandy. The sandy tide flats offshore provide a constant supply of sand; some is carried into the marsh by every flood tide. Here it is deposited in sandbars, some in the slow water off the points, more in midchannel islands, leaving deepwater channels along both sides. You can paddle against the current without much trouble here. If you go up the creek at midtide or lower, you will soon learn a great deal about how sand is moved and deposited in channels—it's a fascinating study. This is also a good place to watch rip ples form.

The sandbars and islands are likely places to see shorebirds, and very handy for stretching your legs without wading in the mud. Two Osprey nesting platforms have been placed in the marsh; they are scenes of constant activity from April through September. Few Fiddler Crabs live here, despite what appears to be ideal habitat; this is the northern edge of their range, and the Cape Cod Bay waters are just enough colder than the waters on the south side of the Cape to constrain the population.

The big tidal range here on the north side of the Cape means that the marsh looks quite different at high and low tide. It is fun to explore here at both extremes. The channel is deep enough for canoes and kayaks well up into the marsh even at low tide. Note how the water grows greener and greener as you go upstream. This is because the water high in the creek is not replaced with every tide, so it spends more time in the marsh, becoming warmer, and growing more algae, with each daylight hour.

Downstream from the landing you soon find yourself paddling across the tide flats. On the Dennis side the beach and tide flats are open to vehicles, somewhat reducing the sense of wilderness. The water gets quite shallow at low tide, but because of the exposed tide flats to the north there is no sea, so you can paddle in only a few inches of water. The channel is deeper on the Dennis side. In summer thousands of Common Terns roost on the small low-tide beaches. Many nest on the long, low dune just west of the mouth of the creek. They will make their displeasure clear if you get too close. If you stay in your boat, you probably won't be dive-bombed.

Don't forget the side streams: White's Brook is navigable almost to the dam that created Tom Matthew's Pond, Clays Creek begins near the boardwalk, and Lone Tree and Bass Creeks reach into the marsh from the northwest. Even the small tributaries provide interesting paddling.

Walk the Boardwalk

The boardwalk gives those without a boat a view of the marsh, creek, and shore. From this elevation you can see the taller Cordgrass bands tracing the winding tidal creeks. These creeks allow life-giving salt water to reach deep into the marsh on every tide. Life-giving for the marsh, at any rate; upland plants do not do well if inundated by salt water, so the tides favor salt-tolerant plants. You can also easily spot the long, straight ditches that were cut to drain the saltwater pools in the high marsh where saltwater mosquitoes bred.

From the boardwalk you can see that the dunes at Chapin Beach across Chase Garden Creek are almost as high as the land behind you. Sand that blows off the tide flats on northerly winds builds these impressive dunes. Between two dune masses is an area of salt marsh where storm waves have repeatedly broken through the dunes. To the west, looking like a sandy island, is the eastern end of Sandy Neck, with its decommissioned lighthouse and colony of old summer cottages. In between are the channel into Barnstable Harbor, the wide Dennis tide flats (open to vehicles), and the sand dune at the mouth of Chase Garden Creek.

Explore the Uplands

Two and a half miles of trails and old farm roads lead through the woods and around the edges of this peninsula, with many short spurs to the marsh. The trail is in two loops: the one east of Center Street is a little under a mile; the one to the west is a little over a mile. Each is a pleasant amble through the woods with opportunities for birdwatching in the thickets and at the marsh overlooks.

The vegetation varies from thickets of Highbush Blueberry and Bayberry in old cranberry bogs to seriously impenetrable patches of Red Cedars 18 inches apart in old farm fields to open woods of pine, oak, and cherry. Some of the patchiness of the woods is evidence of land-use history; some is due to the accidents of seed distribution as the trees grew up after farming ceased.

Special Notes

Rather few species of trees grow here compared with similar woods elsewhere—no hickory, beech, Sassafras, or White Pines—but this was once a more varied woodland. We know that because American Chestnut trees grow here—or what pass for Chestnut trees today—a clump of 25-foot root sprouts, some dead, others still growing and producing their long, toothed leaves. Several of these survivor trees grow close to the trail on the western loop. Because Chestnuts need reasonably rich soil, they suggest that this area may once have supported a forest of mixed hardwoods.

The lack of common woodland plants such as Trailing Arbutus, club mosses, Wintergreen, and Spotted Pipsissewa is evidence of the history of the land; plowing presumably wiped them out.

28. CHAPIN BEACH AND THE NEW BOSTON ROAD CONSERVATION AREAS, DENNIS

Salt Marshes, Woodlands, Beach and Tidal Flats, Dunes
Walking, Birdwatching

PREVIEW

Chapin Beach is a sand spit and dune complex that protects the marshes of Chase Garden Creek (see map, site 27). The beautiful beach overlooks a tide flat about 1½ mile wide at low tide (vehicles are allowed on the beach and tide flats). The upland conservation areas off New Boston Road are heavily wooded and interesting; old woods roads provide good walking and occasional access to the Chase Garden Creek marshes. For paddling Chase Garden Creek see site 27.

ACCESS

Parking for the beach is at the end of Beach Street. Parking for the New Boston Road Conservation Areas is the next left after Hall Street, on the south side of New Boston Road.

GEOLOGY

Chapin Beach is building west from the high land in Dennis—all the bluffs west of Nobscusset Point feed sand this direction. The valley now occupied by the marshes of Chase Garden Creek was a bay when the sea first reached this area some three thousand years ago. The protection provided by the sand spit allowed salt marshes to grow in the quiet water.

The wide V in the southwest side of the spit is floored with storm overwash deposits. The dunes have built across the opening, thanks to the continuous supply of sand from the tide flats, but a big storm at high tide might well cut through again. Despite the tide flats, the bay side of the dunes shows the near-vertical cuts of recent erosion. As sea level rises, the waves will continue to cut into the dunes. In the natural state the dunes will build farther landward, and the shore will

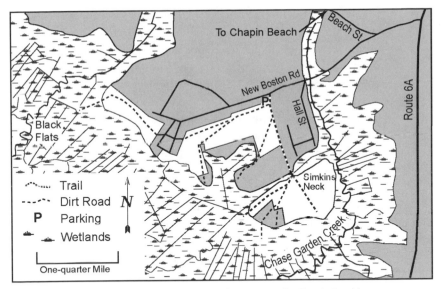

Map 28. New Boston Road Conservation Areas (see map 27 for Chapin Beach)

readjust to the new sea level. This area may be allowed to do that because little is built on the dunes. Not far to the east, however, many houses perch on the eroding dunes, houses that will be lost when the dune moves out from under them.

Several large "blowouts" cut the dunes. These low spots are places where the prevailing southwesterly wind has carried sand away, grain by grain. Blowouts begin where something, whether it is a footprint or wave action, removes the stabilizing vegetation and allows an eddy of wind to cut into the dune.

WHAT'S TO SEE AND DO

Explore Chapin Beach and Tide Flats

As you walk on the beach, look for the chunks of asphalt among the rocks. At first you might not notice them—they are so common and widespread that you might take them for natural rocks. But a closer look will reveal that they are pieces of broken-up pavement. They got here in February 1978 when the old beach parking lot was undermined and the broken pieces were carried along the shore by the waves. The distribution of these pieces of asphalt is a demonstration of the westward movement of sediment along this shore. Almost no asphalt is found east of the beach access road, but many large pieces litter the shore immediately to the west. As you walk farther west the pieces become fewer and smaller, evidence not only of the direction of the sediment transport but of the rarity of waves from the northeast that are large enough to move anything much bigger than gravel.

At low tide the flats extend out about 1½ miles. You can walk out a long way, though channels between the bars can be deep enough to require swimming (you may want to be particularly mindful of this when the tide is rising). On the tide flats you can watch ripple marks forming, and see the result all across the flats. Find a stream with a few inches of water running in it and watch as the current carries sand grains up the low-angle upstream side of the ripple and then drops them into the lee on the steep downstream side. If you watch long enough, you'll see a small avalanche of sand slide down the downstream face and spread out on the flat. Ripples (and dunes) are formed by wind in the same way, but you can watch the process in a runnel without getting your ears full of sand. If you miss the demonstration, do not despair. The evidence is all around you, and another demonstration is scheduled every twelve hours.

Clams, especially the Soft-shell variety, live in abundance on the tide flats. Many shorebirds stop off here in spring and fall, but Oystercatchers, small sandpipers, and yellowlegs can be seen much of the year.

Explore the Conservation Areas off New Boston Road

Here there are three not-quite-contiguous conservation areas. You can walk from one to another by crossing a street or walking on a well-established path between houses. There are no loop trips, but there are pleasures in walking a trail both ways and seeing how different it looks from the new perspective.

All the tracts are heavily wooded; freshwater wetlands and the upper reaches of the salt marshes along Chase Garden Creek are visible through the trees. Simkins Neck actually is an island of upland in the marshes, connected by a short causeway. Cranberry bogs, now abandoned, once occupied the low area crossed by the causeway and also fringed Simkins Neck. Other old bogs occupy kettle holes in the property to the west. The trail paralleling New Boston Road in this area is particularly attractive for the many magnificent large oaks, mostly Black Oak and White Oak, and even some large specimens of the unusual Post Oak. Large Pitch Pines also grow here. These large trees are wide-spreading, indicating that they grew in the open, without competition for sunlight. They are now surrounded by their many progeny, which all grew up together and thus have a tall, narrow profile, with few or no lower branches. Ferns, Skunk Cabbage, Swamp Azalea, Sweet Pepperbush, and Highbush Blueberries grow abundantly at the edges of the upland, where fresh water seeps out and allows a wide band of freshwater plants at the edge of the salt marshes.

Birds

The beach and tide flats host many terns and shorebirds, especially in fall and spring migrations. The deep woods, thickets, and wetlands are good spots to find warblers, orioles, and other forest birds, and swallows, herons, hawks, Kingfishers, and Ospreys may all be seen over the marshes.

29. WEST YARMOUTH WOODLANDS AND PONDS

Ponds, Woodlands, Freshwater Wetlands
Hiking, Birdwatching

PREVIEW

Long walks and variety are the attractions in this wide area of West Yarmouth's woodlands and wetlands. Footpaths connect old woods and bog roads with Water Department well roads, providing pleasant walking and many options for routes. Ponds, bogs, and swamps fill the many swales with lovely views and interesting plants and birds. Much of this area feels quite remote, especially if you have come here from the hurly-burly of a busy summer day on Route 28. Each season has its own attractions, and this is a place to visit year-round. This area is contiguous with the Swan Pond site to the south (see site 30).

ACCESS

Parking is on the east side of Higgins Crowell Road at the trailhead; at Little Sandy Pond Recreation Area on the north side of Buck Island Road (Yarmouth beach sticker in summer); at the Syrjala Conservation Area where Plashes Brook crosses Winslow Gray Road, and off West Yarmouth Road at the entrance to the cranberry bogs.

GEOLOGY

This area is near the middle of the narrow Mid-Cape outwash plain. The outwash here is mostly sand and gravel, with more gravel close to the moraine to the north and more sand to the south. There are some shallow ponds but few deep kettle hole ponds.

During the waning of the glacier, the lake that formed in what is now Cape Cod Bay rose high enough that it overflowed and cut its way through the eastern end of the Sandwich moraine between Prospect and German Hills, just west of exit 8 on Route 6 (see Bass River map, site 31). As the lake drained, the water ran south across the outwash plain, creating the channels in which Town Brook on the west, and Plashes Brook and Parkers River on the east, now lie. The streams

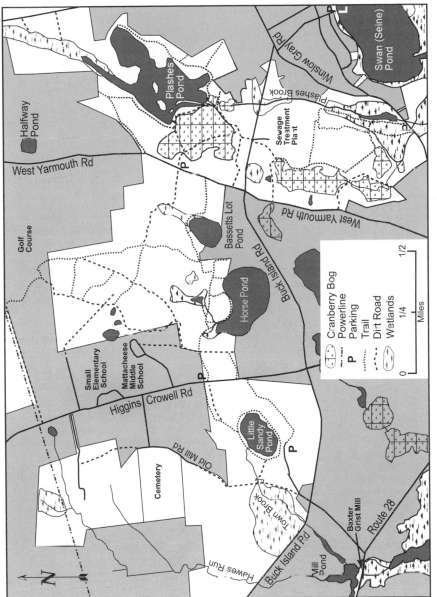

Map 29. West Yarmouth Woodlands and Ponds

draining the lake also deposited sand and gravel across the outwash, making West Yarmouth one of the smoothest, flattest areas on the Cape. The old channels are only a little lower than the surrounding land, but those few feet are enough that groundwater seeps to the surface here, creating the brooks and wetlands. Many of the original wetlands are now cranberry bogs. Parkers River below Swan Pond, the lower part of this ancient drainage, has been flooded by seawater; see site 30 (Swan Pond).

HISTORY

The Plashes Brook watershed would be unrecognizable to its original inhabitants and to the early colonists. From headwaters to mouth, this area has been altered to make use of the water and the low valley it occupies. Plashes Brook was dammed sometime after 1922 (a map made that year shows the brook and the two small ponds that are now covered by the waters of Plashes Pond). The pond was created to provide water for the extensive cranberry bogs just downstream, and was probably built at the same time that the original wetlands were converted for cranberry cultivation.

Mill Pond, on Town Brook southwest of Little Sandy Pond, is the site of the historic Baxter Grist Mill. It too took advantage of the water in this shallow valley, though the gradient of the valley is so low that two dams were necessary to impound enough water to power the mill.

The Town of Yarmouth is making use of the water in the area by situating their water-supply wells here. Pumping has drawn down the water table in the area immediately surrounding the wells and may reduce the amount of water in the lower part of the drainage, especially in dry years. South of the water-supply area is the Yarmouth Wastewater Treatment Plant, where treated wastewater is disposed of by spray irrigation. The groundwater flow here is southward, so the treatment plant is down-gradient from the wells.

WHAT'S TO SEE AND DO

Go Hiking

This large area with its many flat or gentle trails is big enough for many hours of hiking, and nice spots along the way make this a place you'll want to come back to. A pleasant 1½-mile walk takes you from Higgins Crowell Road along the shore of Horse Pond to Bassetts Lot Pond and back through the woods, with a side trip to the bog. Odd little loops of trail leave and rejoin the main trail—it looks like the trail was once more sinuous, and shortcuts have developed.

Another nice walk is the 2-mile trip from the trailhead at Syrjala to Plashes Pond and back, through the wet woods and along the bog roads. This walk gives a close-up view of both natural swamps and the intensively cultivated commercial cranberry bogs. Boardwalks cross the dampest spots in the Red Maple and Highbush Blueberry swamps, where Sphagnum Moss forms hummocks around every tree stump. It is interesting to note that although this wetland is about 1½ mile from Nantucket Sound, it is less than 10 feet above sea level.

Check Out the Bogs and Ponds
The ponds and bogs are good places to look for migrating ducks spring and fall, and the thickets around them may have warblers in spring and fall.

Horse Pond is shallow with a gently sloping bottom, so a small drop in water level exposes a great deal of territory; conversely, a small rise covers a lot of bottom. The north and northwest sides of the pond are edged with concentric rings of cranberry (a beautiful red in winter), Sweet Gale, Leatherleaf (look for the smaller and smaller leaves on the topmost twigs, interspersed with white flowers in April), Tupelo, and Red Maple, which provide a striking early fall show of color. In late summer, when water levels are low, this sandy apron is tinged with pink by the flowers of Rose Coreopsis, Virginia Meadow Beauty, and Plymouth Gentian, and the red leaves of sundews. The cranberry plants produce berries in many years and sometimes bear heavily.

Just north of Horse Pond is a boggy pond carpeted with Sphagnum Moss and ringed with the same bands of water-loving plants as Horse Pond. In early spring Wood Frogs make their surprising call—it sounds like a cross between a bark and a quack. Evidently the water level in this area used to be higher, because the bogs are surrounded by Red Maples a few feet above the cranberries. If those areas had always been dry, they would have an understory of huckleberries and other usual low plants. Instead they are bare, which may reflect increases in water pumped for the Town of Yarmouth or the variation of rainfall from year to year.

Bassetts Lot Pond is more secluded, though you can see houses here too. Look for the interesting Red Maple swamp on the north side of the pond.

Little Sandy Pond is at the edge of a busy recreation area with picnic area and ball fields. The trail around the pond connects with a trail that goes west through the woods to Old Mill Road, and east across Higgins Crowell Road to the trails around Horse Pond. Old Mill Road was the access road to the Baxter Grist Mill on Town Creek, just north of Route 28.

The eastern arm of the trail in the Syrjala Conservation Area runs along the shallow, vegetation-choked pond created where Plashes Brook is dammed by the embankment of Winslow Gray Road. In spring Wood Frogs and Spring Peepers call here as soon as afternoon shadows reach the water. Mallards and other waterbirds may nest in the thick Sweet Gale and Swamp Loosestrife around its shores, and White Water Lilies reach the surface from the marshy pond bottom. The pond never was much deeper than it is today; as it fills with leaves and dead vegetation, it will gradually become a bog.

Although Plashes Brook is nominally a Herring run, it is hard to imagine even the most determined Herring getting up the step into the concrete ditch that carries the stream across the Syrjala parking area. And even if any did get past this barrier, there is no fish ladder from the stream in the cranberry bogs into Plashes Pond.

Plashes Pond was created by the large earthen dam that separates it from the bogs at its southern end. The map outline of the pond suggests damming even without seeing it on the ground: a long arm extends up the old streambed, an unnatural shape for Cape Cod ponds but very characteristic of dammed-up streams. When you stand on the dam, it may be hard to visualize the free-flowing stream, but if the water is low you can see the old stumps in the pond, the remnants of streamside woods or cedar swamps. At the southwest corner of the pond is an artificial outlet built to deliver water to the western section of the bogs. When the water is low you can see the piles of spoils along the ditch that leads from deeper water to the pump house.

The carefully engineered cranberry bogs were built in the old streamside bogs and Atlantic White Cedar swamps. The cedars are all gone in the cranberry bogs, of course, but some survive along the east side of the bogs south of Buck Island Road and on one of the islands in Plashes Pond. Cranberry bogs were often made from cut-over cedar swamps by removing the stumps and spreading a layer of sand on top of the swamp muck. The wet woods of the Syrjala Conservation Area are cut by ditches; apparently some of this area was once cranberry bog too.

It is possible to put a light boat into Plashes Pond and explore the shallow nooks and crannies of its many bays and islands. Park at the bog road entrance and carry your boat to the pond. It is only a two- or three-minute walk, though you can't see the pond until you get there.

30. SWAN POND AND THE PARKERS RIVER CORRIDOR, YARMOUTH

Salt Water, Salt Marshes, Dunes, Beaches
Paddling, Walking, Birdwatching

PREVIEW
Salt marshes, salt ponds, and tidal creeks are the focus of the Swan Pond and Parkers River area, with a wide beach and dunes on Nantucket Sound for good measure. This site is contiguous with the West Yarmouth woodlands and ponds (site 29).

ACCESS
At Swan Pond park at the end of Meadowbrook Road for the boardwalk into the marsh. Launch a small boat at the ramp at the end of Lake Street just to the west. Seagull Beach has parking by beach sticker or fee only in the summer; small boats may be launched into Parkers River from the east end of the parking lot or into Lewis Pond just west of the beach entrance.

GEOLOGY
Parkers River lies in the lower end of the shallow channel that formed as the glacial lake in Cape Cod Bay drained. Freshwater marshes probably began developing in this channel soon after it formed. Salt water entered Lewis Pond between 3,500 and 4,000 years ago; as sea level approached its current level, salt water reached higher up the valley until Swan Pond became tidal.

HISTORY
Until recently, Swan Pond was called Seine Pond. The name change reflects the change from a self-sufficient rural economy to one dominated by tourism and second homes. The European Mute Swans of the current name have been breeding on the Cape only since the 1960s; they congregate in protected salt water like this in winter, sometimes in large groups. But Swan Pond was once most notable for the seines that were used to catch fish that came up the river. This is a Herring

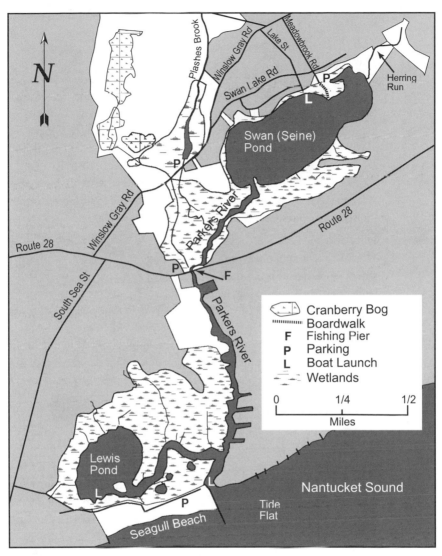

Map 30. Swan Pond and the Parkers River Corridor

run, so Herring may have been among the sought-after prey; the nets may also have caught larger fish that eat Herring, such as Bluefish or Striped Bass. A fish ladder in the northeast corner of the pond still allows Herring to continue their migration upstream to the fresh water of Long Pond.

WHAT'S TO SEE AND DO

Visit the Swan Pond Boardwalk

This is a good place to watch waterbirds, including those swans. The dead trees out in the marsh along the boardwalk are Red Cedars, trees that often colonize the edges of freshwater marshes as the marshes fill with dead vegetation and become dry land. All around the pond there is evidence of rising sea level: dead trees near the water, eroding peat, and plants of the high marsh in the water. The cedars, which obviously once grew well here, have been killed by salt inundation. Rising sea level may have allowed a storm to bring in an exceptionally high tide. Water-tolerant plants along the boardwalk, including Red Maple, Inkberry, and Pussy Willow, suggest freshwater seeps.

Paddle Swan Pond and Parkers River

The north side of Swan Pond is densely populated, but the south side, which is bordered by abandoned cranberry bogs and conservation land, is quite wild-looking. The marshes along the river are home to large numbers of birds in summer, the usual Red-winged Blackbirds and Canada Geese but also Green Herons and Willets.

The strong current in the river reverses with the tide, so you will get a good workout paddling either downstream or back upstream to the pond, but you can always stem the tide, and there are side creeks where you can stop and enjoy the view while you rest.

A small windmill sits on the point at the west end of the pond, powering a bubbler placed by the Department of Natural Resources to aerate the pond. Aeration offsets some of the deleterious effects of the excess nutrients entering the pond from the septic systems of the houses in the watershed. Those nutrients result in algae blooms—great floating mats of algae that form both on the bottom and on the surface. In the past there have been fish kills on warm, windless, cloudy days when the algae used up the oxygen in the water. The mats of algae also produce unwelcome smells as they rot in late summer. Aeration ameliorates both those symptoms by providing additional oxygen, but it does not solve the basic problem of too much nitrogen in the water. Removing the algae mats for garden compost would help, but the only real solution is to reduce the nitrogen going into the groundwater by limiting fertilizers and using nitrogen-removing toilets or sewage systems. Unfortunately, "we have met the enemy and they is us."

Explore Lower Parkers River and Lewis Pond

From either launch site you can paddle through Lewis Pond and the tidal creeks that drain into Parkers River from the surrounding marshes. Houses and roads overlook the marsh at many points, but that does not seem to deter the birds that nest, find food, and roost here at various times of the year. Great Blue Herons, Snowy Egrets, and Green Herons are common in spring and fall; gulls hunt shellfish year-round; and large numbers of migratory shorebirds rest and refuel on the marsh and the tide flats at low tides in spring and fall—Greater Yellowlegs are particularly common. In the marshes you'll see evidence of the ceaseless human war on insects—blue, four-legged boxes trap Green Head Flies, and ditches that drain the breeding places of the saltwater mosquitoes cut straight across the marsh.

Visit Seagull Beach

The width of Seagull Beach is partly due to the effect of the Parkers River jetty—notice how much farther seaward the beach extends here than on the opposite (east) side of the channel. Sand moves mostly east here; the sand that would have been carried to the eastern side of the channel is trapped west of the jetty, creating a wide beach here and narrow, sand-starved beaches to the east.

This popular area shows the complex interactions between people and the shoreline. Not only has the width of the beach been affected by our activity, but our comings and goings have flattened the dunes. The dune just seaward of the bathhouse is man-made, presumably to protect the structure after a natural dune was destroyed. The artificial dune is brownish sand, a great contrast to the wind-winnowed, white sand of the natural dunes. The beach is mechanically groomed to remove the windrows of Eelgrass that accumulate in late summer; the material thus collected is dumped in the dunes. Beach Grass has been planted on both the artificial and the natural dunes, and Beach Rose, Beach Plum, Bayberry, and Seaside Goldenrod are growing in some less-disturbed areas.

Seagull Beach often lives up to its name, with flocks of gulls roosting whenever the press of humankind is not too great. It is relatively easy to get close enough to get a good look at the birds and sort out the Ring-billed Gulls from the Herring, Laughing, and Great Black-backed Gulls.

31. BASS RIVER CORRIDOR, DENNIS AND YARMOUTH

Salt Water, Beaches, Dunes, Woodlands, Bogs
Birdwatching, Paddling, Walking

PREVIEW

Bass River is a 6-mile saltwater inlet that cuts across the Mid-Cape from Nantucket Sound to within 2 miles of Cape Cod Bay. Although there are many interesting natural sites (and sights) here, this is not wilderness—Bass River is crossed by the bridges for Routes 6 and 28, Highbank Road, and the railroad; the shores are heavily developed; and the water is busy with boats in the summer, especially below the Route 28 bridge. Nevertheless, many areas invite walks or exploration by small boat.

ACCESS

On the Dennis side access is at West Dennis Beach; Horsefoot Cove on the north side of Route 28; and, for the Indian Lands Conservation Area, the north parking lot at Town Hall on Main Street just north of Highbank Road. In Yarmouth you can get to Bass River at Bass River Beach, at Wilbur Park on the south side of Highbank Road, and at "Crab Creek" (also known as Weir Creek) off North Dennis Road. Both towns have town landings along the river.

GEOLOGY

Most of this area is on the outwash plain that slopes gently toward Nantucket Sound. The outwash is sand and gravel, with some small cobbles, especially in the northern part of the area, near the moraine. Bass River south of Route 6 probably began life as a spring-sapping valley; it was extended and reshaped by runoff and by the action of the tides once it was inundated by the sea. The upper ends of spring-sapping valleys are visible on the both the Dennis and the Yarmouth sides of Bass River. Labans Pond in the Bass River Golf Club lies in one such valley; the others trend more or less parallel—keep an eye out for them.

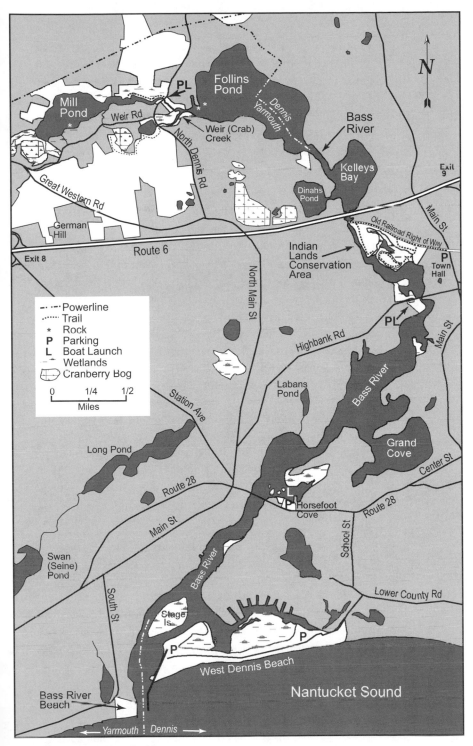

Map 31. Bass River Corridor

Follins Pond and Kelley's Bay are kettle hole ponds formed by buried blocks of ice that were close enough together that the collapse of the overlying sediments left only an easily eroded ridge between them. The hill on the south side of Follins Pond is the easternmost exposure of the Sandwich Moraine. Here the moraine is quite low, but it still shows the characteristic irregular topography of small hills and depressions dotted with boulders.

HISTORY

Bass River was a favored site for both the native peoples and the colonists who displaced them. The Indian Lands Conservation Area was the last area set aside for the native peoples in Yarmouth (Dennis was part of Yarmouth until 1793). Both town centers are close to the river, attesting to its importance for both resources and transportation.

When Thoreau came to the Cape in the 1850s, he walked from the train station in Yarmouthport to Harwich via German Hill and crossed Bass River at "Lower Bridge," where Route 28 crosses today. Thoreau noted paying the toll in his journal. Here he would have seen the hundreds of saltworks in South Yarmouth, occupying many acres of waterfront and extending well inland, across Main Street almost to Long Pond. Saltworks also stood on the Dennis shore, but in smaller numbers.

Mill Pond was created by damming the stream that ran into Follins Pond. The dam has since been expanded to carry North Dennis Road, and fitted with a culvert that allows water to run both directions. Mill Pond is now tidal and brackish; it probably was well above sea level when the dam was built. Certainly, everything points to a recent rise in pond water level—this may be a place where we can see evidence for the 1- to 2-foot rise in sea level since the Cape was colonized.

WHAT'S TO SEE AND DO

Explore West Dennis Beach

This large barrier beach and dune complex closes off the mouth of Bass River except for the narrow channel on the Yarmouth side, kept open by dredging. Offshore is a large sand flat. The low-tide depth between the Bass River breakwater offshore and the jetty at the mouth of the river is about 2 feet—it may look like open water, but only shallow-draft boats can use it. The shoal apparently has a good growth of Eelgrass, which attracts Brant. These small cousins of Canada Geese were once quite common but became an unusual sight with the loss of Eelgrass in the bays. Also on this shoal are several fish traps: mazes of poles strung with nets so arranged that the fish go in easily but can't get out. The fishermen remove the trapped fish with smaller nets.

The low dunes at the west end of the beach support thickets of Beach Rose, Beach Plum, Beach Grass, Beach Pea, and Poverty Grass. As these various plants bloom, they tinge the buff of the dunes with pink, white, yellow, or purple. This is a good place to see quite a variety of birds, from Double-crested Cormorants to Horned Larks and migrating shorebirds.

You can launch a light boat into Bass River here and explore Stage Island, the marshes, and on up the river.

Horsefoot Cove

This is a small island of coastal bank and salt marsh in the midst of the development along Route 28. It is amusing to imagine this noisy, busy shore two hundred years ago—vegetation like the remnant Bear Oak, Bayberry, and Poverty Grass around you extended along the shore, backed by a few houses and sheds, interrupted only by a wharf or some fish flakes. Four hundred years ago there might have been trees to the edge of the marsh and perhaps an encampment of native peoples. And it would have been quiet, except for the calls of the birds and an occasional voice.

Indian Lands Conservation Area

These 46 acres of quiet marsh and woodlands can be reached by a five-minute walk along the sandy railroad right-of-way from Dennis Town Hall, or from a small boat in the river. The woods are mostly Pitch Pine and oak, with limited undergrowth of blueberries and Bearberry, a few young planted White Pines, and numerous Pink Lady's Slipper orchids. Both of the embayments of salt marsh were once enclosed by dikes and cultivated as cranberry bogs. The dike at the head of the southern inlet still blocks water flow, but no cranberries remain. The other dikes have been breached, though not completely removed, and the salt marsh is recovering. This is a good area for birdwatching; you can see wintering ducks on the river, herons and egrets in the marshes, and small songbirds in the thickets.

Paddle Crab Creek, Mill Pond, and Follins Pond

The tidal stream between Mill Pond and Follins Pond is officially called Weir Creek, named for the fish traps once used here. It is now known locally as Crab Creek, and many folks, especially families, often fish here for Blue Crabs, using the chicken-neck-on-a-string technique that relies on the crabs' unwillingness to let go once they get their claws on something good. No license needed, but there are restrictions on size, and no egg-bearing females may be taken. Contact the Yarmouth Natural Resource Department for information.

You can put a light boat in the water and paddle upstream to Mill Pond, or downstream to the salt marshes and Follins Pond. At Mill Pond, most of the north side and west end is conservation land, but even on the south side the houses are few and well back from the water; and the area feels isolated. Few sounds from the outside world penetrate here except when the wind is northwest and the approach to the Hyannis Airport is overhead. Mostly you hear the breeze and the waves, punctuated by the calls of Ospreys and Kingfishers, and the softer clucking of Canada Geese and Mallards that also nest here. Groundwater drains into the pond through old cranberry bogs and some more-natural wetlands along the pond shore. The south side of the pond is rocky; some boulders stand out in the water, making small islands along the shore. These rocks are evidence that here we are on the northern fringes of the moraine, where large rocks melted directly out of the ice.

The pond shore shows signs of a relatively recent rise in water level. Note the many dead trees, some recent, others ancient ghosts, around the pond margins and even out in the water—they drowned as sea level rose, backing water up Bass River and even here, 6 miles from Nantucket Sound. Many shoreline trees have blown down, lifting the layer of peat in which the roots grew. The roots certainly developed above the reach of salt water, so they are further evidence that pond level has risen. Banks of Narrow-leaved Cattails, which prefer brackish water, grow along Weir Creek and around the lower parts of the pond, evidence that fresh and salt water are mixing here, which is easily confirmed by taste.

Downstream of North Dennis Road (the streambed is rocky, but portaging is easy) the plants of brackish water give way immediately to salt marshes. Here Green Herons and Muskrats go about their secretive lives; a quiet approach in a small boat may let you get close enough to watch them. Out in Follins Pond you are once again in the modern age, with powerboats, trophy houses, and large docks replacing the cattails and Cordgrass. The southern and western sides of Follins Pond are moraine, so watch for rocks just underwater. The eastern side is a surprisingly steep 60-foot bank in outwash—its sandy, rock-free character is clear, even from a distance.

SITES

32. QUIVETT CREEK AND THE CROWES PASTURE CONSERVATION AREA, DENNIS AND BREWSTER

Salt Marshes, Dunes, Beaches, Woodlands, Grasslands
Walking, Paddling

PREVIEW

Woods, fields, beach, dunes, bogs, salt marsh, tidal creeks, an island of upland in the marsh—the Quivett Creek area has some of everything. Old farm roads and footpaths let you explore the woods and fields of Crowes Pasture. The marsh is a lovely paddle. The Dennis side of the beach is open to vehicles, so in beach-buggy season it can be busy. Most of the time, however, this area is quiet and feels like the time when there was "less noise and more green." The Paines Creek/Stony Brook area is to the east; see site 33.

ACCESS

The entrance to the Crowes Pasture Conservation Area is at the end of South Street, which, oddly, heads north from Route 6A, almost a mile east of Route 134. Drive in (VERY slowly) on the rough dirt road (in wet weather beware of the deep puddles) and park in one of the designated areas. The Wings Island trailhead is beside the Cape Cod Museum of Natural History (CCMNH) on Route 6A. You can launch a light boat into Quivett Creek near the parking area at Crowes Pasture.

GEOLOGY

Wings Island and Quivett Neck are lake delta deposits—hills of mixed sand and rock deposited into the short-lived Cape Cod Bay lake. These deltas were created close to the ice by meltwater running south from the front of the glacier. After the lake drained, freshwater marshes probably grew in the valley of Quivett Creek until it was inundated by the rising sea some three to four thousand years ago. Since that time salt marshes have taken over the valley, replacing both the freshwater plants and the open water of the estuary.

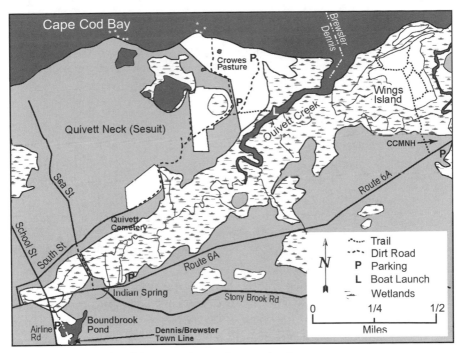

Map 32. Quivett Creek and the Crowes Pasture Conservation Area

HISTORY

CCMNH archeological investigations on Wings Island have found evidence of habitation by native peoples beginning nine to ten thousand years ago.

Quivett Neck was settled in 1637. The many old houses along Sea Street recall the time when the village of Sesuit, then called Suit, was supported by shipbuilding and trading. The beach at the end of Sea Street was the site of a wharf, fish flakes, and all the sheds and storehouses that go with them. Crowes Pasture Conservation Area at the end of the neck was farmland. Although the farm fields and pastures were abandoned and allowed to revert to woods and thickets when farming ended here, rock walls, old cart roads, and farm and garden plants give some idea of the shape of the farm. About 15 acres of the encroaching woods were mowed in the late winter of 2000, and again in winter 2001, to restore some of the open fields.

Quivett marsh was partly open water in historical times: Wings Island was an island in the 1650s when the Wing family lived there. You now can walk dry-shod to Wings Island except at the highest tides, but the Wings rowed from the mainland to the island. They apparently lived on the island to escape the persecution they suffered because, as Quakers, they refused to help pay the salary of the local minister. In the 1850s Wings Island was the site of a large solar saltworks.

WHAT'S TO SEE AND DO

Crowes Pasture

The cartways and footpaths, some from farming days and some from modern activities including hunting, to judge by the number of shotgun shell cartridges lying about, lead all through the woods. The woods are quite varied—areas of pure Pitch Pine and Bear Oak sit next to patches of larger oaks, aspen, willow, Shadbush, and Black Cherry. In late April and early May the Shadbush blooms; the white flowers look like foam against the bare trees.

The round bog just west of the cleared fields now supports mostly Highbush Blueberries, but the encircling ditches suggest that cranberries were once grown here. The old bog is a reminder that it was not far from here that Captain Henry Hall first grew cranberries in a specially prepared bog, an experiment that led to the commercial cultivation of this native plant.

Over time the cleared fields may provide habitat for the plants and animals that rely on open fields: the grasses and wildflowers, Meadowlarks and Bobwhites, Meadow Voles and Cottontail Rabbits, and the hawks, Red Foxes, and Coyotes that prey on them. It will be interesting to watch that evolution.

Wings Island

This is a lovely walk, across the salt marsh (check the tides before you go), through the woodland groves, and out to the dunes and beach (see map 33). Surprisingly, Wings Island has a wider variety of trees than Crowes Pasture, and many of them are unusually large. Hickory, Sassafras, and Tupelo grow here, none of which exist on Crowes Pasture across the creek. Usually islands have fewer species than the mainland because each species is represented by only a few individuals; if those few are wiped out, the difficulty of migration from the mainland may preclude their reestablishment. Wings Island must have reverted to forest long before Crowes Pasture, giving it time to develop a more mature woods; or perhaps it was never completely cleared, so there was a more varied seed bank.

Beach and Dunes

The big sky and far horizons visible from the beach and the dunes are a bit of a shock when you come out from the shady woods. To the east is the shoreline from Brewster north to Wellfleet. On a clear day you can see the dark pencil-shape of the Pilgrim Monument in Province-town, 18 miles north, apparently sticking up out of the water (see map, site 50). Sometimes the white water tank near it stands out more clearly than the gray stone monument, depending on the visibility and the color of the sky. The top of the monument is 348 feet above sea level; the land on which the monument sits is only 50 feet above sea level, so it is not surprising that you can see the monument from a greater distance than you can see the land.

The eroding bluffs between Quivett Neck and Nobscusset Point to the east provide some sand to this beach and to the tide flats out in Cape Cod Bay. Sand probably moves both east and west along this shore—east at times of northwest winds, and west during northeast-ers. At Crowes Pasture you are at the western end of the extensive Brewster tide flats; they continue east and north to Wellfleet Harbor. The lower part of the bluff above the beach here is gravelly glacial lake deposits; the upper section is up to 6 feet of sand dunes. In some places you can see a darker layer partway up the dune deposit, recording the establishment of some plants on the surface for a time, before they were buried by additional dunes.

The foot-thick layer of eroding salt marsh peat on the Crowes Pas-ture beach below the bluffs is clear evidence of the rise in sea level and the erosion of the coast. The salt marsh would not have devel-oped here on the open shore; it grew when sea level was lower and the sandbars to the north protected the marshes. As sea level rose, the bars provided less and less protection, especially from storm waves. The marsh has eroded until only these small remnants remain. *Spar-tina* still grows in this peat, forming mini–salt marshes all along the shore, marshes that were apparently much larger even as late as the 1860s, when a large fish trap was located in the shallow water offshore.

The dunes here are active, fed by sand blown off the tide flats during northeasters. The trees struggle to keep up with the sand; some of the plants that look like shrubs may be rooted 6 feet down, with only the top branches surviving. These trees also face a constant battle with salt. Strong winds from the north—both northeasters and the hard northwest winds that follow them, especially if they come at high tide—carry salt spray far inland. The salt kills the leaf buds at the ends of the twigs and, over time, causes the death of any twig that reaches above the general level of the plants or dunes windward of it. If you stand on the beach to the east and look west, you can see the streamlined shape of the treetops created by the salt and wind "pruning."

Paddle Quivett Creek

The easiest place to launch a light boat is at the end of the old farm road behind the Conservation Area sign at the Crowes Pasture parking area. The road is a bit dim in places, but go straight ahead from its obvious part at the sign, pass between the concrete posts in the clump of trees, and you'll reach the edge of the marsh in a two-minute walk. You can also carry a light boat to the creek at the south end of the old Sea Street causeway, though the creek here is narrow, and shallow at low tide. The creek is the dividing line between Brewster and Dennis, and the old Town Line sign still stands incongruously at the bridge in the middle of the marsh. The road was abandoned because it was often flooded by storm tides unable to pass through the small opening beneath this low dike.

The Quivett Creek marshes are particularly quiet and lovely. Near the mouth the creek is wide, but the upper parts are narrower and very sinuous. Some of the horseshoe bends are so tight that only a few feet of marsh separates the upstream and downstream bends. The bends of the channel allow you to travel against the current rather easily as there are eddies behind every point. The marsh hosts many birds, varying by season. In spring you may see Grackles and Canada Geese nesting; in summer Ospreys call from the nesting platform, while Red-winged Blackbirds and Song Sparrows forage among the Cordgrass stems; and in late summer and fall Great Blue Herons and Crows congregate to feed.

In the upper parts of the marsh where the Cordgrass along the banks is unusually tall (and where it is joined by Freshwater Cordgrass, an even taller *Spartina*) you may see evidence of the work of Muskrats:

Mid-Cape Sites

neatly clipped grass stems and the lodges they make from them. But the creatures themselves are so wary that it is quite unusual to see one.

Herring

Quivett Creek is a Herring run, and Herring may be seen here as they make their way up the creek headed for Boundbrook Pond. A pleasant Brewster conservation area on the south side of Route 6A just east of Airline Road gives access to the pond and to the upper portion of Quivett Creek where it runs in a rock-lined fishway, crossed by a number of small bridges.

33. PAINES CREEK/STONY BROOK AND LOWER MILL POND, BREWSTER

Salt Marshes, Streams, Ponds, Woodlands

Walking, Paddling, Birdwatching

PREVIEW

The short, steep drainage of Paines Creek/Stony Brook drops from the 25-foot elevation of Lower Mill Pond to the sea-level marshes in about a mile. This is one of the most active, and certainly the most famous, Herring runs on the Cape, portrayed in detail in John Hay's *The Run.* Walking is pleasant, and you can explore the marshes and the millpond by small boat. For Quivett Creek see site 32.

ACCESS

For Stony Brook and the upper reaches of the Paines Creek marshes, park at the Cape Cod Museum of Natural History's south lot (CCMNH on the map). There is a town landing at Paines Creek where you can put a small boat in the water (parking by Brewster sticker in summer). Parking for the upper reaches of Stony Brook and the Herring run is at the gristmill on Setucket Road; a light boat could be carried to Lower Mill Pond here, but launching is easier at the town landing off Run Hill Road at Upper Mill Pond. This pond connects via the Narrows to Lower Mill Pond (see Punkhorn Parklands, site 34).

GEOLOGY

Here in Brewster the low eastern end of the moraine is buried beneath the outwash plain, but rocky ice-contact material deposited directly from the ice lies to the north of the buried moraine. Scargo Hill to the west is made of that rocky material, as is the area on the north side of Lower Mill Pond and west along Setucket Road. The deep valley occupied by Stony Brook was probably cut by runoff down the steep northern side of the ridge of ice-contact deposits. That erosion exposed many large boulders in the stream valley.

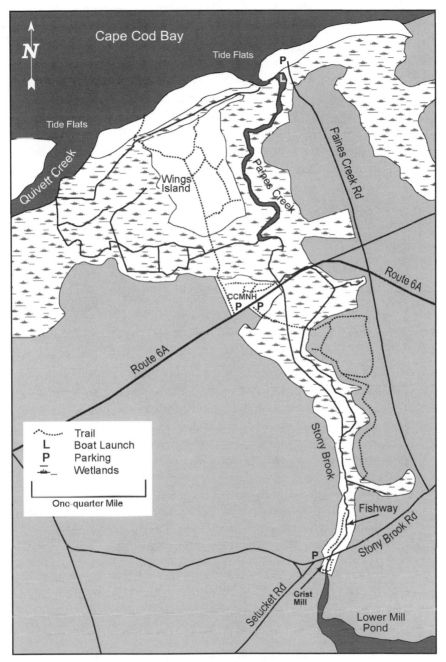

Map 33. Paines Creek/Stony Brook and Lower Mill Pond

HISTORY

This was a busy industrial and agricultural center, beginning in 1663 when the first gristmill was built on Stony Brook. A fishway around the dam must have been built at the same time, or the Herring run would not have survived the damming of the stream. A fulling mill (to clean, tighten, and shrink woven wool cloth) was built a few years later. By the early 1800s a woolen mill was built here too, beginning a factory village that grew up along the stream. Although the buildings are mostly gone and the area has grown back to trees, there is evidence of past uses in the extensive engineering along the stream and the many introduced trees and food plants. The present gristmill was built in 1873 on the foundation of the former fulling mill. The tiny mill building reminds us how much the scale of buildings has grown—even the smallest house built today is several times its size.

The marshes along Stony Brook south of Route 6A, which now look wild and untouched, were cultivated as cranberry bogs through the 1960s. Saltworks existed in the 1860s on both sides of Route 6A in the area of the Cape Cod Museum of Natural History, and on Wings Island.

WHAT'S TO SEE AND DO

Paines Creek

The beach is narrow at high tide but more than a mile wide at low tide. This is a good place to see shorebirds; Brant are common in winter, and seabirds driven inshore by northeasters can be seen during or after the storm. You can put a small boat in the water here and explore the marshes upstream toward Wings Island. The Paines Creek marsh is narrow, but the creek has lots of freshwater flow, allowing a somewhat different mix of vegetation than in the larger, but saltier, Quivett Creek marshes. In very cold weather ice accumulates all along this shore, damping the waves and making a dramatic prospect. You can get another view of these marshes from the trails on Wings Island.

Stony Brook

The Cape Cod Museum of Natural History's parking lot on the south side of Route 6A is about where one of the saltworks was located. Small windmills were used to pump salt water into solar evaporating troughs. It is interesting to speculate why the saltworks was built here, where a large freshwater stream enters the marsh. Perhaps salt water was pumped into the evaporators only on flood tides; before the construction of the Route 6A causeway this area would have been more tidal. There is no sign of the saltworks today; apparently the thrifty locals disassembled it to build the mill at Stony Brook.

The trail south of Route 6A crosses the two branches of Stony Brook on bridges and winds up the east side of the valley. The eastern branch of the brook was created by the ditching that served the now-abandoned cranberry bogs. Take a side trip to the pleasant grove of American Beeches overlooking the brook. Beech trees are common on the Upper Cape, especially on the hills of the moraine, but they become less so Down Cape, where the forests were completely cleared and topsoil was lost. You can walk almost ½ mile up the creek, although the trail gets more overgrown upstream.

The Cape Cod Museum of Natural History offers excellent exhibits, a library, and an outstanding bookstore.

Paddle Lower Mill Pond

This lovely pond (see map 34) looks like something out of the Old Mother Westwind stories, with Tupelos (beautiful in late summer) and beeches drooping over the water and Painted Turtles sunning themselves on the many rocks along the shore. Before the mill dam was built, the long, narrow lower end of the pond was a stream in a narrow valley, like the stream north of Setucket Road. The dam flooded the valley, raising the water level 8 or 9 feet. As the dam was built more than three hundred years ago, the stream and the vegetation have completely adjusted to the engineered water level and obscured the change. The clearest evidence of the raised water level (other than the dam itself, of course) is the delta that the stream from Upper Mill Pond has built out into Lower Mill Pond. This peninsula of vegetation-choked wetland has grown as the stream dropped the sand and silt it was carrying where it hit the still water of the dammed-up pond, creating a delta centered on the stream.

The Herring that come up Stony Brook spawn here and in the upper ponds. The adults can be seen in the spring, and the schools of fingerlings are visible in late summer before they return to the sea. They are especially easy to see at The Narrows between the two Mill Ponds. Many creatures congregate in and around the ponds to eat the Herring. In the spring you may see Ospreys and gulls; in the summer Green Herons, Black-crowned Night-Herons, and large Snapping Turtles.

34. PUNKHORN PARKLANDS, BREWSTER

Woodlands, Ponds, Freshwater Environments
Hiking, Paddling

PREVIEW

More than 830 acres of woods, fields, and wetlands lie in the area between Seymour, Walker's, and Upper Mill Ponds. The woods and fields are crisscrossed with cartways, gravel roads, and footpaths, providing many days of hiking. The ponds themselves are particularly attractive for paddling as only low-power motors are allowed. In winter the ponds are good places to see flocks of ducks. Stony Brook/ Paines Creek is contiguous to the north (see site 33).

ACCESS

The parking area off Run Hill Road is convenient to the town landing and central for walking. You can park under the powerline for the northern Calf Field area. As there are some private inholdings in the parklands many of the roads are open to vehicles, so it is possible to drive to many areas. In addition to the town landing at Run Hill Road you can put a boat in the water at Walker's Pond, off Slough Road.

GEOLOGY

Punkhorn Parklands is at the northern edge of the outwash plain. The area is gently sloping or slightly rolling, made of sand and small gravel, and dotted with kettle hole ponds including Seymour Pond, which is 38 feet deep, and Upper Mill Pond, which is about 30 feet deep. Walker's and Lower Mill Ponds are shallow. Around the Mill Ponds are numerous large boulders, making it clear that this part of the Harwich outwash plain includes ice-contact deposits at or close to the surface. Many boulders have been exposed by erosion on the steep slopes of the kettle holes.

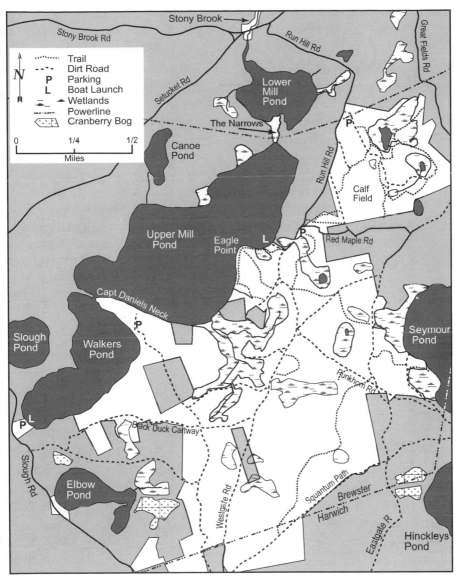

Map 34. Punkhorn Parklands

HISTORY

An archeological investigation on the south shore of Upper Mill Pond
has found evidence of at least seasonal occupation by native peoples as
early as nine to ten thousand years ago.

WHAT'S TO SEE AND DO

Paddle the Ponds

The south sides of Upper Mill Pond and Walker's Pond are in the Punkhorn Parklands, so despite the houses and docks along some shores there is ample quiet pond shoreline. You can land on Captain Daniels Neck between the two ponds and explore the interesting boggy land there. Note the large Tupelos along the shores, which turn glorious red in late summer.

Lower Mill Pond, which you can reach via The Narrows, was created by the Stony Brook mill dam (see site 33). When you pass through this overgrown stream, you will find yourself on close personal terms with Swamp Loosestrife, Bog Hemp (although it looks like Stinging Nettle it doesn't sting), Buttonbush, and Swamp Rose. Floating downstream is easy; coming back you may find it more effective to walk, towing your boat (the water is shallow and the footing solid). When you stand up you can see over the vegetation, and it becomes clear that The Narrows is a delta formed where the outlet stream from Upper Mill Pond flows into the dammed-up waters of Lower Mill Pond. If you do this in late summer you may see Herring fingerlings, schooling up for their trip to the sea, fleeing your feet.

The shores of all these ponds are steep, rising 25 or 30 feet above the pond in many areas. Such steep slopes are characteristic of kettle ponds, suggesting the nearly vertical ice faces against which the sand, gravel, and rocks shed by the melting glacier were piled.

Go for a Walk, Long or Short

The Eagle Point Trail is a ¾-mile loop. The number of different habitats in this short distance is amazing—old cranberry bog, dry woods, rich woods, shrub swamps, and pondside wetlands. In May and June look for blooming Shadbush and Lady's Slippers in the richer, less disturbed areas. In summer you'll find Swamp Azalea, Sweet Pepperbush, Steeplebush, and fruiting Highbush Blueberries. The view from Eagle Point, more than 50 feet above the pond, is worth the walk.

The 3-mile round-trip from Run Hill Road to Seymour Pond via the Cape Cod Pathways trail and back via Punkhorn Road traverses more uniform woods of Pitch Pine and oak, with a rich understory of blueberry and huckleberry bushes. The trail is marked with the Cape Cod Pathways silver arrow on a blue circle. This marker is nailed to trees at trail junctions; look sharp because the trail does not always follow the most obvious path.

Along the way the trail passes just north of a large quaking bog. The mat of Sphagnum Moss and cranberries has mostly filled a shallow pond, with Leatherleaf and Swamp Loosestrife around the edges.

These woods are quite young. It was not long ago that the trees took over this area from pasture: the largest trees are the pioneer Pitch Pines. White and Black Oaks are beginning to overtop the aging Pitch Pines, and hardwood trees are the majority of the seedlings in the understory. Many of the oaks have multiple trunks, evidence that they were cut once and sprouted again from the stumps. This sight is common on the Cape, as firewood and fence posts were cut in the woods long after large-scale grazing was discontinued.

The Calf Field Trail is a 2-mile loop from the entrance off Run Hill Road just north of Red Maple Road. This trail is also marked with Cape Cod Pathway arrows, but there are many other trails that leave and rejoin the official route that also make good walking. This section of the park is much hillier, with the irregular topography that you would expect on a moraine. The rocky soil and the many large boulders make these ice-contact deposits look very different from the outwash plain just to the south. Sandblasted ventifacts are visible in the rocky soil of the old roads in several places.

The rocks of this area were apparently an important resource into the 1900s. Look around for the evidence—holes in the ground, up to 15 feet deep and as much as 30 feet in diameter, with a few sharp-edged chunks of granite lying nearby. Rock was quarried here, but not in the way that it was cut by the farmers and fishermen of the early days with hand tools alone (see page 14). Here, rock was broken into manageable-size pieces by drilling a deep, 2 inch diameter hole, packing it with explosives, and shattering the boulder.

The Calf Field area has a much wider variety of trees and other plants than the rest of the Punkhorn Parklands, probably due to the richer soil of the ice-contact deposits, lighter use that did not destroy the soil, and the earlier end of agricultural uses on this rougher terrain. Look for the beech trees shading the paths as well as the Lady's Slipper orchids, club mosses, Beaked Hazel, Sheep Laurel, and viburnums, which do not grow in such numbers elsewhere in the Punkhorn.

35. NICKERSON STATE PARK, BREWSTER

Ponds, Woodlands, Bogs, Salt Marshes, Beaches, Dunes
Walking, Paddling

PREVIEW

The well-known Nickerson State Park has more than 400 campsites, miles of paved trails, and many sandy beaches on freshwater ponds. As a result it can be crowded in summer. Outside the high season, however, all those attractions beckon, along with unpaved trails, marshes, bogs, woods, and a beach on Cape Cod Bay.

ACCESS

The entrance to Nickerson State Park is on Route 6A about 1 mile west of the Orleans town line. There is no charge for day use; parking is located throughout the park. The Cape Cod Rail Trail runs through the park, so you can also get here by bicycle.

GEOLOGY

Most of the park lies on the outwash plain, which slopes down gently to the south. The surface may be outwash, but it is clear that moraine and ice-contact deposits lie just beneath. Large boulders and cobbles lie along the shores of the ponds in many places; these deep ponds penetrate the outwash and expose the bouldery deposits below. The ponds are kettle holes, many of them very deep. The 100-foot-high bluff on the west side of Cliff Pond does not stop at the waterline; it continues down 40 feet at the same angle, then flattens somewhat and drops down to the deepest part of the pond—88 feet, 62 feet below sea level. Flax Pond is 75 feet deep, and even Little Cliff Pond is more than 30 feet deep. The bluffs around the ponds, and even the rocky shorelines, contain many rocks sandblasted into low-angle pyramids by the strong winds carrying loose sand at the surface after the glacier melted. Buried under soil that accumulated for thousands of years, they have been exposed again by soil erosion resulting from wood-cutting and agriculture.

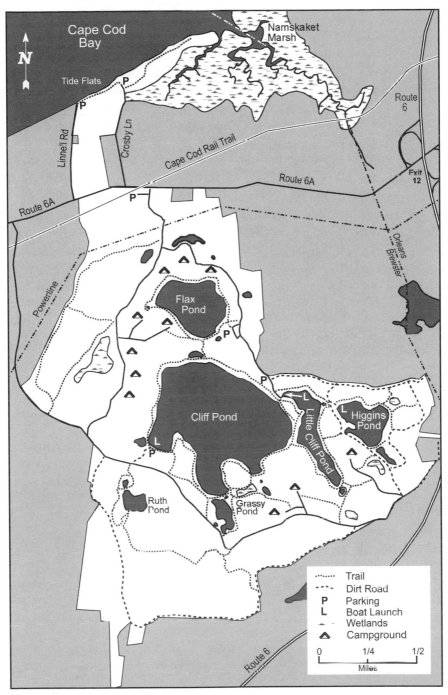

Map 35. Nickerson State Park

These ponds were once even more irregular than they are today. Cliff Pond originally included Little Cliff Pond and Grassy Pond, as well as the ponds and bogs behind the beaches in the many coves. The sandy barrier beaches built out across the former inlets and cut the small bodies of water off from the deeper water of the large pond. The beach-building processes that shape ocean beaches have been at work here also. The waves never get as large as on the ocean beaches, of course, but they have been big enough to create the wide wave-cut bench on which the sandy beaches sit, and to build the sandy barriers between the ponds.

North of the powerline the land is made up of sediments deposited in the Cape Cod Bay lake. This surface slopes sown toward the north and is made of finer, less rocky material than the area to the south.

WHAT'S TO SEE AND DO

Explore the Ponds

The ponds at Nickerson Park, like most Cape ponds, are fed by groundwater and so reflect the level of the water table. In wet seasons, principally spring, and wet years, the water level in the ponds can be high, so that the waves cut into the base of the bluffs. In dry seasons water level typically falls 2 to 4 feet, exposing a wide, gently sloping wave-cut bench. In late summer this exposed shoreline is available for walking and is also home to a beautiful collection of mostly pink wildflowers: Rose Coreopsis, Plymouth Gentian, Virginia Meadow Beauty, Boneset (white), and goldenrods. There is also a trail around each pond just above the high-water mark in the edge of the woods, which lets you walk around the ponds at times of high water. The walk around Cliff Pond is about 3 miles; even nicer is the 1½-mile walk around smaller and less-visited Little Cliff Pond. As you walk, you might note the variation from sandy to rocky to peaty soil, and notice which plants favor which soil. It seems surprising at first glance that Tupelos and other water-tolerant plants do not grow along the high-water line. This is probably due to the fluctuating water level; the rise and fall is enough that the trees would either drown or dry completely at some season.

Walking

These woods apparently have quite a varied history. The patches of even-age White Pines were planted by the Civilian Conservation Corps soon after the land was donated to the state, so they are now more than seventy years old. In other areas there are relatively few planted trees but many multitrunked oaks and maples, suggesting that firewood or lumber was cut here until the early 1900s. Yet other areas have exclusively Bear Oaks and Pitch Pines, which give evidence of the dry, sandy environment and the history of fire. Red Squirrels are quite common here; in many ways they are like the Gray Squirrels, but they are much noisier. Often they seem to resent your intrusion into their territory, and they will chatter and scold until you move on.

The walk to Ruth Pond and back is less than a mile through lovely woods and around a bog. The pond is wonderfully clear—you can watch Painted Turtles, Green Frogs, and Bluegills underwater. This pond is frequented by herons that take advantage of that clear water to make a meal from one of the above.

Visit the Beach, Dunes, and Tide Flats

Low tide exposes the famous Brewster tide flats, which are interesting, beautiful, and provide good walking. Be aware of the state of the tide, because some of the outer sandbars are separated from the beach by deep channels. From the beach you can often see the gray stone tower of the Pilgrim Monument, 15 miles away to the northwest, sticking up from a barely visible sliver of sand that is Provincetown (see map, site 50). Sometimes the white water tower west of the monument is easier to see, depending on how clear or hazy the sky is. Closer to hand, Great Island in Wellfleet (see site 46) is to the north, standing high above the barrier beaches that connect it to the mainland. If you walk east along the beach at low tide you will reach the mouth of the Namskaket Marsh. This marsh seems unprotected from the waves off the bay, but the tide flats provide good protection except at the highest tides. Shorebirds are common here, especially in spring and fall; on the marsh you can often hear the heart-lifting yodel of Greater Yellowlegs (yes, you can recognize these sandpipers by the long, yellow legs).

36. HERRING RIVER AREA, HARWICH

Salt Marshes, Ponds, Woodlands
Paddling, Walking

PREVIEW

Here, not far from the commotion of Route 28, is a quiet preserve of woods, tidal creeks, marshes, and ponds, extensive enough that it feels almost like wilderness. The Herring River meanders through the marshes, taking more than 4 river miles to cover 1 straight-line mile; it is marvelous. You can explore the reservoirs by small boat or on the encircling trails through the woods, and the dirt roads and footbridge increase your range. Whether you are on foot or afloat, this area provides days of delightful exploration.

ACCESS

Parking is off Depot Road south of Great Western Road, off Bell's Neck Road between the reservoirs, and at both ends of the North Road footbridge. Trailhead parking for Coys Brook Woodlands is the gravel road immediately south of the water tank on Lothrop Avenue. Or you can get to this area by bicycle via the Cape Cod Rail Trail. Boats can be launched into West Reservoir at Bell's Neck Road and into the Herring River at the town ramp on the south side of Route 28, at the North Road footbridge, and below the dam on West Reservoir.

GEOLOGY

This area is on the sandy outwash plain that slopes gently southward from elevations of just over 100 feet in central Brewster. The surface of the outwash plain is somewhat irregular, with many small closed depressions and swales. The reservoirs, however, are not kettle holes; they are shallow man-made lakes created by building dikes across sections of salt marsh. West Reservoir is 7 feet above sea level. The surrounding uplands rise to a high point of 30 feet, but the marshes and Herring River lie at sea level, despite being more than a mile from Nantucket Sound.

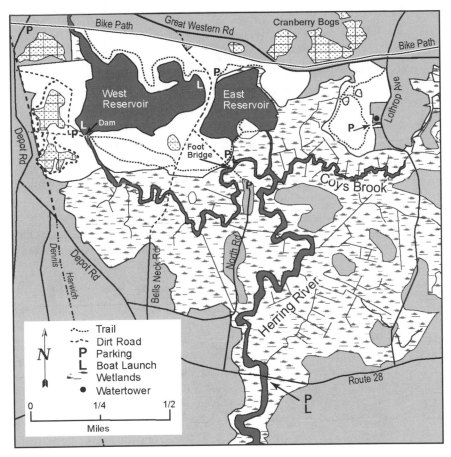

Map 36. Herring River Area

The lower section of the Herring River Valley runs southwest, parallel to the group of spring-sapping valleys between Dennis and Chatham. The Herring River probably has the same origin as these valleys, but the evidence is buried beneath the salt marshes.

HISTORY

The reservoirs and the associated cranberry bogs are probably the product of the late nineteenth or early twentieth century, when large-scale conversions of wetlands to agriculture were fairly common. The shallow East Reservoir may originally have been intended as a cranberry bog like the abandoned bogs north of Coys Brook Woodlands.

The dikes still surround the low area, but the weir is broken, so it is flooded with salt water on every tide.

WHAT'S TO SEE AND DO

Paddle the Herring River
The many possible launch points, long stretches of river, and varied environments make this a particularly attractive paddle. For a long but low-exertion trip, launch at the town landing south of Route 28, ride the tidal flood up the Herring River and Coys Brook, and go back down with the ebb. You can always paddle against the current here, so there are many other possible itineraries—choose your own.

At high tide you can paddle into East Reservoir over the broken weir, but it prevents passage much below midtide. Phragmites has taken over all the banks, so there actually is more to see here from the land at low tide, when shorebirds forage in the mud.

The wide, deep reaches of both the river and the brook allow travel, except just below the dam, at any stage of the tide. Each stage has its own pleasures and points of interest. At high tide you float high enough to see over the banks and grasses to the wide marsh view, and you can paddle up ditches and minor tributaries that are dry at low tide. At lower tides the denizens of the marsh are more visible to the paddler, from the Blue Crabs and minnows in the water to the Fiddler Crabs, herons, and sandpipers along the banks. At low tide you can also see the remains of human constructions, some beneath a foot or more of peat. They may be landing stages, hay staddles, fish traps, or weirs; take a look and see if you can figure them out.

Both the Herring River and Coys Brook are quite fresh in their upper reaches, as evidenced by the freshwater vegetation—deep banks of Narrow-leaved Cattails, lots of sedges, and trees at the edge of the marsh. This fresh water seeps out of the uplands and through the marsh into the channel, letting these plants grow in places that appear at first glance to be salt marsh.

There is evidence of rising sea level here in the marshes. In many areas, particularly near the Bell's Neck Road bridge, Red Cedars that once successfully grew at the edge of the marsh are now just gray skeletons. High in the marsh, at Coys Brook and around some of the islands, you can see at low tide the stumps of long-dead trees sticking up through the thin layer of peat. The name "brook" on this tidal creek suggests that when the name was given its upper reaches may not have been tidal. Even today the vegetation of cattails and sedges here shows that copious fresh water enters the marsh. Sea level continues to rise, apparently at a more rapid pace than a century ago; so we can expect the trend toward salt marsh vegetation to continue.

Each of the islands and peninsulas of upland in the marsh has its own history, both natural and human. Each invites investigation. Oak stumps and sprouts indicate that these woods once had large trees.

Paddle West Reservoir

This is a body of fresh water created by the dam at the southwest corner and the Bell's Neck Road dike. Most of the pond is less than 6 feet deep, and tree stumps up to 18 inches in diameter rise above the surface. Other stumps lurk below the surface—they may have been cut before the area was flooded. These stumps, still intact after years of immersion, are Atlantic White Cedars, and they still release cedar fragrance when fresh wood is exposed. Some stumps are host to their own island ecosystem—birds probably brought in the seeds of blueberries and Black Cherry; Sweet Gale seeds may have floated from the plants at the edge of the pond. The stumps are localized, mostly at the eastern end and around the edges of the pond; before the construction of the dam the Herring River apparently was bordered by cedar swamps. There is a younger generation of dead trees here too. These are Red Cedars that must have seeded into the area after the Atlantic White Cedars were cut. They apparently were killed when the dam was raised to its current level.

This is a lovely place to explore at leisure; the deep banks of Swamp Loosestrife (this is the native plant, not the invasive introduced Purple Loosestrife) have created many quiet bays and passages. In warm weather you will see dozens of Painted Turtles sunning themselves on logs, though unless you are stealthy a splash as they escape may be your only indication of their presence. Snapping Turtles are common here too, some of them up to 2 feet in diameter; they encourage you to stay in your boat. The secluded bays also harbor a wide variety of birds from European Mute Swans (they breed here) and gulls to herons and even elusive Wood Ducks.

Atlantic White Cedars still grow around the edge of the pond, particularly at the northeast corner, but the most common tree at the water's edge is Tupelo. In late summer, when the leaves begin to turn and the berries ripen, you can often hear Catbirds meowing from amid the red leaves. Other lovely water-loving plants around the pond include the August-blooming Rose Mallow, quantities of Sweet Pepperbush, Swamp Azalea, and even some less common flowers such as Turtlehead and Cardinal Flower.

At the southwest corner of the pond is the dam and fish ladder. You can easily portage a light boat around the dam, but at low tide there is very little water below the dam.

The Herring that swim up through the marshes and climb the fish ladder into the pond continue up the Herring River for another 2 miles, passing under several roads including Route 6, to spawn in Hinkleys Pond to the north on the Brewster town line.

Walk around the Reservoirs

Trails almost completely encircle both the reservoirs, making excursions in various places to cranberry bogs and the marshes (you can't cross the breached outlet of East Reservoir). A circuit of these trails, including the North Road footbridge and the bogs on the west side of West Reservoir, is a pleasant 2- to 3-mile walk, depending on how many side trips you take. The woods are mostly oak and Pitch Pine, with a thick understory of Poison Ivy, Sheep Laurel, blueberry, huckleberry, and Greenbrier. Tupelos grow in the damp spots and all along the pond shores, turning glorious reds in late summer. Close to the ponds, Sweet Pepperbush, Swamp Azalea, Swamp Rose, and Inkberry join the understory, making it difficult to reach the water except on paths. In a number of areas the trail skirts steep-sided borrow pits where sand and gravel were dug to create the dikes or to maintain cranberry bogs.

East Reservoir often has a variety of shorebirds during low tides in the spring and fall. They are most easily seen from the island of upland on the south side.

Walk in Coys Brook Woodland

This area of upland adjoins the marshes along Coys Brook. You can walk the trails in these pleasant woods in under an hour, catching glimpses of the marsh and the uplands on the other side of the river through the trees. The area is pockmarked with small closed depressions that contain wooded swamps or abandoned cranberry bogs. One of these has a drainage ditch crossed by a bridge. Note the rusty red water, evidence that iron is precipitating. The trail passes along a number of steep-sided borrow pits. Such pits are a clue that cranberry bogs once existed here; the northern section of the property is a segment of the salt marsh that was diked to create cranberry bogs, which are also abandoned.

37. HAWKSNEST STATE PARK, HARWICH

Ponds, Bogs, Woodlands
Walking, Birdwatching

PREVIEW
Hawksnest State Park, a gem of undeveloped woods and ponds, is well worth a visit in any season. The ponds and their surrounding rim of flowering plants are particularly interesting and beautiful in late summer.

ACCESS
Park off Spruce Street west of Route 137, or along Hawksnest Road.

GEOLOGY
Hawksnest is on the northernmost portion of the outwash plain, an area that was deposited very close to the ice front. The soil is coarse sand and gravel with many rocks up to about softball size, but no large boulders. The many polished and faceted ventifacts show the effects of the blasting winds off the nearby glacier. These stones are most easily seen in the roads, but they certainly exist beneath the soil across much of the area.

Hawksnest Pond is a kettle hole, like Long Pond and the other much larger ponds to the north. Olivers Pond to the east, and the string of ponds to the west, are also kettle holes. This irregular line of ponds probably represents the ragged edge of the melting glacier at one moment in time. That ragged edge consisted of detached and semidetached ice blocks. Cracks and crevasses around these ice blocks filled with the sand and gravel released by the melting ice to the north, eventually burying the blocks of ice completely.

The blocks that formed Olivers and Black Ponds were smaller and thinner than the one that formed Hawksnest Pond, so the resulting ponds are quite shallow. They have filled in with leaves and other decaying plant material to the point that Water Lilies and Pickerelweed

SITES

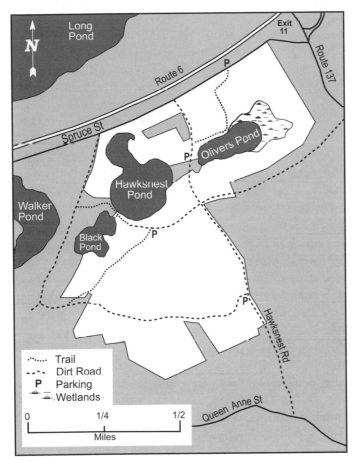

Map 37. Hawksnest State Park

can grow nearly across them. These two ponds are well on their way to becoming bogs.

WHAT'S TO SEE AND DO

Explore the Ponds

The ponds at this site are beautiful, different from one another, and full of interest. A pleasant walk of about 2 miles is from Spruce Street to Black Pond and back via the trail along Olivers Pond. In some weather it is possible to drive right in to Hawksnest Pond, but then you miss Olivers Pond. Olivers Pond is shallow, with a gently sloping bottom in most areas. In late summer, when water level is at its lowest for the year, the sandy shores turn pink and purple with the flowers of Rose Coreopsis, Plymouth Gentian, and Virginia Meadow Beauty, against a reddish mat of sundews. Often you can see the empty exoskeletons of the insects that the sundews have digested, still clinging to the sticky hairs of the leaves. Out in the water are the velvety white, eraser-size knobs of Pipewort, along with the more common White Water Lilies and Pickerelweed. Cranberries grow among the Leatherleaf along the high-water mark. The borrow pits along the north shore of the pond suggest that the boggy area beyond the barrier beach at the east end of the pond may once have been cultivated for cranberries, but if so it was so long ago that other evidence is obscured.

Hawksnest Pond is a rare example of an undeveloped coastal plain pond. This must have been what many of the ponds on the Cape were like before there were so many of us here. The shoreline vegetation is interrupted in only one place and the water is clear, providing a good view of fish many feet below you. The sandy pond margin still supports Rose Coreopsis and Virginia Meadow Beauty except right at the swimming beach. Black Pond is separated from Hawksnest Pond by a barrier beach covered with Highbush Blueberries and Sweet Pepperbush—walk west along the south side of Hawksnest until you see it. This shallow pond is filled with water plants; it won't be long before it becomes a bog. It is a good place to look for Wood Ducks, Kingfishers, and other waterbirds, as well as to admire the luxuriant wetland vegetation.

Walk the Woods

From the road south of Hawksnest Pond you can take a 2-mile loop on old dirt roads south into the wooded heart of the park and back via Hawksnest Road. This area was a typical pine barren of Pitch Pine and Bear Oak until recently but is making the transition to a mixed pine/hardwood forest. The pioneer Pitch Pines are the oldest trees, and some are quite large. But they now are being overtopped by the White Oaks, followed closely by the Black and Scarlet Oaks. Sassafras trees are mostly skinny saplings no more than 20 feet high, and beech and hickory are very young seedlings, scarcely 5 feet tall. If the woods are undisturbed for another fifty years, the newly arrived species will grow into trees, and other trees such as birch, cherry, ash, and Hop-hornbeam may seed into the area, creating a mature mixed woods. Actually the transition might have happened long ago if it hadn't been for the repeated cutting of the hardwood trees. Bearing evidence of that cutting, probably most recently for firewood, are the multitrunked oaks, which grew from the stumps left after the trees were cut. The pioneer Bear Oak and Dwarf Chinquapin Oak are being shaded out; they remain only along the edges of the road and in other dry openings.

38. THOMPSON'S FIELD AREA, HARWICH AND CHATHAM

Grasslands, Woodlands

Walking, Birdwatching

PREVIEW

Flat trails and old roads provide easy and interesting walking in Thompson's Field. The attraction here is the variety—damp woods and dry woods, thickets, pine barrens, and old fields in various stages of reversion to woods—all easily accessible. The varied habitats attract a variety of birds. The 57-acre Thompson's Field parcel abuts several hundred acres of attractive wooded land administered by the Harwich and Chatham Water Departments, providing a large and quiet island of green.

ACCESS

Park at the trailhead off Route 39 or off Chatham Road. You can also get here by bicycle on the Harwich Bike Trail.

GEOLOGY

Here we are on the outwash plain; the surface is sand and gravel deposited by meltwater streams running south toward the sea from the front of the melting glacier. These low-energy streams did not carry big rocks; hardly any are larger than a baseball. On the surface, faceted and polished ventifacts can be found most easily in the parking area off Route 39 where the soil has been eroded and vehicles have disturbed the vegetation. During the fifteen thousand years or so that have passed since these rocks were formed, plants grew and decayed, and dust was trapped in the vegetation, covering the sandblasted layer of stones with soil. But when the trees were cut, beginning in the 1600s, the soil began to erode, eventually exposing the bare sand and rocks, including the ventifacts, again in many places.

Two spring-sapping valleys have their heads in this area. They intersect the water table, so are damper than the surrounding country;

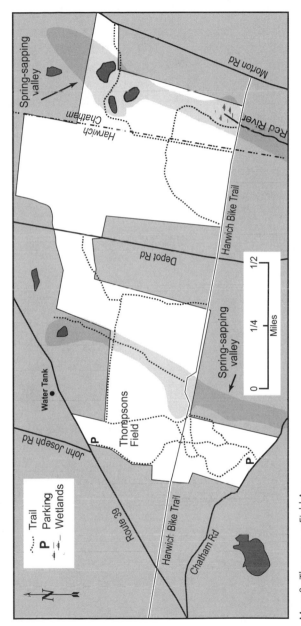

Map 38. Thompsons Field Area

the Red River begins in the eastern one. The Chatham and Yarmouth Water Departments are taking advantage of the proximity of the water table to the surface; they have located several municipal water wells here.

HISTORY

This area was farmed, probably into the early 1900s, at least south of the bike trail. Here there is soil, fields just beginning to sprout shrubs and trees, and various farm and garden plants including apple trees and asparagus. Along the bike trail (formerly railroad tracks) the trees are older but almost exclusively Pitch Pine and Bear Oak, possibly evidence that this strip burned from time to time until the trains stopped running; fires in many areas were set by sparks from trains.

WHAT'S TO SEE AND DO

Go for a Walk

The varied environments provide constantly changing views and invite return trips. As in many well-used areas of open space, there are many informal trails, some of which come and go in the space of a year. It is impossible to put them all on the map, but following some of those "less traveled by" will lead you to attractive areas not reached by the more formal trails.

South of the bike trail some of the fields are mowed, perhaps to stop the reversion to trees, though one area is used by model airplane fans. Flowers grow in profusion, many planted by a garden club. Look for the lovely orange Butterfly Weed as well as Butter-and-Eggs, Common Milkweed, and Queen Anne's Lace. Although these fields are no longer used as pasture or mowed for hay, they can help you imagine the Cape's agricultural past, when working farms were one of the most important elements of the economy. If you watch for the farm and garden plants, you may be able to reconstruct at least the most recent layout of the farm. The thickets and open sandy or grassy patches are likely places to see Bobwhites and other open-land birds as well as small songbirds during spring and fall migrations. Some unusually large, lichen-covered Bear Oaks just south of the bike trail attract Chickadees, Downy Woodpeckers, and nuthatches.

The woods north of the bike trail and east of the fields contrast with the open fields and the Pitch Pines and Bear Oaks surrounding them. These are also not old woods but here the variety of trees is greater. The Black, Scarlet, and White Oaks are overtopping the Pitch Pines, and Sassafras, Big-toothed Aspen, Shadbush, and viburnums are starting to grow beneath the pines, especially in the richer and damper ground in the spring-sapping valleys. But many of the common trees such as Gray Birch, American Beech, and hickory are not found here.

You can make a number of 1½- to 2½-mile loop trips by choosing one or another of the trails through the fields and connecting to the woods trails via the paved bike trail.

LOWER CAPE SITES

SITES

39. STAGE HARBOR AREA, CHATHAM

Salt Water, Salt Marshes, Beach, Dunes, Cedar Swamp
Walking, Paddling, Birdwatching

PREVIEW

There is some question about whether the Stage Harbor area is water surrounded by land or land surrounded by water. Whatever the answer, whether you are walking or paddling, this varied area provides much to explore beyond the busy fishing and shopping village. For South Beach and Monomoy Island, see site 40; for Nauset Beach see site 41.

ACCESS

Trailhead parking for Morris Island and the eastern part of Harding Beach is at the Monomoy National Wildlife Refuge (MNWR) headquarters off Morris Island Road. The main western section of Harding Beach can be reached from the parking area at the end of Harding Beach Road—resident sticker or fee in summer. Trailhead and parking for the Atlantic White Cedar swamp are on the north side of Honeysuckle Lane, off Stage Harbor Road. You can launch a boat at the town landings at Barn Hill Road, Vineyard Avenue, and Bridge Street, or carry it from the Morris Island causeway.

GEOLOGY

The complicated interfingering of land and water in this part of Chatham is due to its creation close to the edge of the South Channel lobe of the glacier. Here, outwash from the more distant Cape Cod Bay lobe to the north was deposited on and around the ice of the South Channel lobe, which added its rocks and sand to the deposit. When all the ice finally melted, it left an irregular surface, pitted with large kettle holes. Many of the kettle holes were inundated by the sea beginning about 3,500 years ago. The straight, northeast-trending section of Oyster Pond River is a spring-sapping valley, probably cut at the

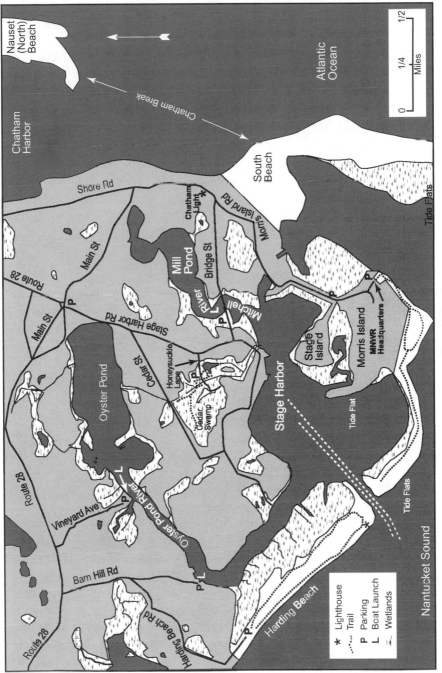

Map 39. Stage Harbor Area

same time as the Red River and other parallel valleys to the west into Dennis (see Thompson's Field, site 38).

Once the sea returned, ocean waves cut into the glacial sediments and transported the eroded sand, building barrier beaches along the coast. These barrier beaches, including Harding Beach, Nauset Beach, South Beach, and Monomoy Island, now protect the old wave-cut bluffs on Morris Island and beneath Chatham Light.

HISTORY

In 1987 Nauset Beach, the barrier beach that protects Chatham Harbor, was overwashed and breached opposite the Chatham Light. For more on this story see South Beach and Monomoy Island (site 40).

Morris Island has been an island, but it also has been a part of the mainland, depending on the state of the Nauset Beach/Monomoy erosion cycle (see site 40). Today Morris Island is connected to the mainland by an artificial dike built in the 1960s to protect Stage Harbor and provide access to the island at all states of the tide. At the same time the channel into Stage Harbor was cut through the Harding barrier beach. A channel had existed in that location in the 1800s, marked by the lighthouse, but as the barrier beach extended eastward the channel moved also; it had become long and circuitous. This project moved it back to the west and fixed it in place with jetties. The dike that connects the amputated eastern section of Harding Beach to Morris Island was constructed as part of the same project. Today sand dunes and natural vegetation make both dikes at Morris Island look natural at first glance.

WHAT'S TO SEE AND DO

Paddle the Protected Waters

From the town landings the waters of Stage Harbor, Oyster Pond, Mitchell River, Mill Pond, and the area inside South Beach are all open to you. The current runs strongly in Oyster Pond River, Mitchell River, and the Stage Harbor channel, though you can paddle against it. There is also a great deal of boat traffic, particularly around midtide, but the fast boats stick pretty much to the buoyed channel (channels are buoyed Red on the Right when Returning); stay outside it except to cut across. Chatham is sometimes called the "fog factory" for the rest of the Cape; fog can come in suddenly, so be aware of the weather. You can land on the eastern part of Harding Beach and on South Beach.

The salt marsh along the inside of Harding Beach has many mud-flats and small channels where shorebirds feed at low tide and Common Eiders dive for Ribbed Mussels and other shellfish. Salt water comes in on every tide, but the only source of fresh water is rain. As a result none of the brackish-water plants common in many salt marshes grows here; saltwater plants extend to the shore. Stage Harbor has productive clam flats, and oysters grow here too. Their shells can be found on the beach, along with the more common clams, Slipper Shells, and Jingle Shells.

Walk Harding Beach

From the beach parking lot it is a lovely mile walk to the Stage Harbor channel. The lighthouse and keeper's house are now private property; the navigation light is shown from a less picturesque metal tower. The parking lots have replaced the dunes and Beach Grass for some distance, but most of the barrier beach is relatively unaffected by the press of humanity that throngs the sand in summer. The movement of sand along this beach is mostly to the east, especially since South Beach connected to the mainland and provided protection from the southeast. The active dunes and wide tide flats testify to the large quantity of sand that comes to this area, giving the beach a rather different look from the sand-starved beaches to the west. But sand is mobile, as evidenced by the breaching of Nauset Beach in 1987 (see South Beach, site 40), and the situation here could change rapidly, as it has before, with a major storm.

The dunes are stable enough to support patches of Bayberry, Beach Rose, and Pitch Pines as well as the faster-growing Beach Grass, Beach Pea, and Seaside Goldenrod. The beach, backed by the dunes and fringed with salt marsh, is a good place to see a wide variety of birds, especially during fall migration.

Visible in the shallow water offshore is a fish trap, an arrangement of tall poles from which nets are hung to guide the fish into a dead end from which they can be easily collected. Farther to the southeast are the dunes, low trees, and shrubs of North and South Monomoy Islands.

Walk the MNWR Morris Island Trail and the
Eastern Section of Harding Beach

The interpretive trail at the MNWR headquarters leads through the woods on the bluff to a stairway down to the beach and on to salt marsh, dunes, and tide flats at the southwest corner of the island. This bluff eroded significantly after the Chatham break, and the trail along the beach is submerged at high tide; check the tides before taking this walk. The bluff is now armored with a revetment of large stones, so the shoreline regime may change yet again in response to this new factor in the system. You can walk beyond the interpretive trail to the dike and the eastern part of Harding Beach. The dunes here appear younger than the ones to the west; there are fewer shrubs and more loose, active sand, but the vegetation is otherwise very much like that across the channel. Due to the interruption of the sand movement by the dredged channel, the ocean side of these dunes has eroded back quite a distance since the channel was cut through the beach.

Birdwatching is good here. Watch for shorebirds, especially during spring and fall migrations. You might expect to see Greater Yellowlegs, Semi-palmated and Black-bellied Plovers, Oystercatchers, Short-billed Dowitchers, Whimbrels, and all sorts of small sandpipers. In the fall terns use the beaches of the MNWR as staging grounds for their southbound migration; they may be seen in large groups, roosting or fishing; they usually leave sometime in September. Herons and Egrets also are particularly common in the fall. The area is famous for the wintering Common Eiders that often rest on the water in huge flocks. Scoters, Mergansers, and other sea ducks also spend the winter in the area and are easily seen. The thickets of the MNWR headquarters can attract hundreds of migrating songbirds, in fall as the birds prepare to migrate south, and in spring when this is the first land they encounter after a long flight over water.

Explore the Old Cedar Swamp and Bog
This quiet area practically in the center of Chatham is worth exploring for a glimpse of the rural past. This must once have been a significant Atlantic White Cedar swamp. Not only is it memorialized in the name of Cedar Street, but the remaining Cedars are imposing trees whose trunks are up to 20 inches in diameter. The trees of this swamp must once have been a source of wood for shingles, buckets, and posts —enough for all of Chatham. However, the old swamp has been drained by ditches that cut the peat and penetrate into the sand below, so the ex-swamp is no longer wet enough to favor the growth of Atlantic White Cedar—there is only one small patch of young trees. This must have happened a long time ago, for the Red Maples, Black

Cherries, and oaks that are outcompeting the Cedars are themselves large. Some large, low-branched Red Maples were probably the first to grow after the Cedars were cut, for they have the silhouette of trees that grew in the open with no competition for sunlight.

On the south side of Honeysuckle Lane is wet meadow, shallow pond, and bog, with some short trails. How far you can go depends on how wet the season is. The trees, thickets, pond, and fields of this area are a likely place to see a variety of migrating birds in spring and fall.

40. SOUTH BEACH AND MONOMOY ISLAND, CHATHAM

Salt Marsh, Salt Water, Beach, Dunes, Freshwater Environments
Walking, Paddling, Birdwatching

PREVIEW

South Beach is a 3-mile barrier beach, connected to Chatham just below the lighthouse. It is part of the river of sand that runs south along the ocean side of the Cape from Truro to Nantucket Sound. Monomoy Island (now two islands) is the southern extension of the river of sand. These constantly changing barrier beaches are extraordinary places, comprising several thousand acres of open space, full of the wildlife that our numbers have driven off many other parts of the shore. Monomoy is a National Wildlife Refuge, and most of it is a designated Wilderness Area. This area is adjacent to Stage Harbor (site 39) and Nauset Beach (site 41).

ACCESS

Parking at the Chatham Lighthouse overlook is limited to one-half hour. For a longer visit park in one of the commercial lots with a beach shuttle or use one of the town lots—the closest are behind Town Hall off Main Street and behind Chatham Elementary School—and walk fifteen minutes to the lighthouse. A number of ferry services will take you to South Beach or North Monomoy by boat. To get to South Monomoy you need your own boat, or you can join one of the tours sponsored by the Wellfleet Bay Audubon Sanctuary or the Cape Cod Museum of Natural History. If you take your own boat, remember that Chatham has been called the "fog factory" for the rest of the Cape. You can launch a light boat from the Morris Island causeway. See Stage Harbor (site 39) for more details on town landings.

GEOLOGY

South Beach is a remnant of the cut-off tip of Nauset Beach, and its story is that of its much larger parent. Nauset Beach (sometimes called North Beach in Chatham) has been building south from Nauset

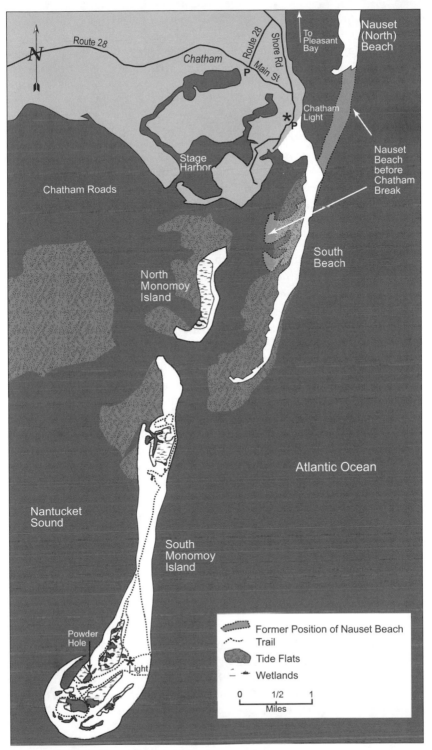

Map 40. South Beach and Monomoy Island

Heights in Orleans for some six thousand years. It is made of the sand eroded from the bluffs to the north, carried south along the shore by the wind-driven waves.

The barrier beach has a cyclical history of growth and breaching, as evidenced by both written and geological records. It grows south several hundred feet every year, forcing tidal waters to travel farther and farther to get into Pleasant Bay through the narrow channel behind the spit here at Chatham. Eventually (and the average appears to be about every 140 years), the distance around becomes so great that a disparity develops between the water levels inside and outside the bay. In some northeaster or hurricane the waves flatten the dunes at a vulnerable spot and wash across the spit. When low tide comes outside, the redoubled waters of the bay pour out through the overwashed area and cut through the spit, creating a new inlet. This happened most recently here in 1989.

Over the next twenty years or so the southern, cut-off section of the spit migrates south and west, and may attach to the mainland as South Beach has now done. As that happens, the southern end of Nauset Beach starts building south again, causing the inlet to migrate southward, and the cycle repeats.

Monomoy's history is similar, though apparently somewhat less regular, depending as it does on the Nauset Beach cycle as well as the local wind and waves. When Nauset Beach is breached the section south of the break migrates south and west, connecting to the mainland at Morris Island. It adds its sand to Monomoy Island, often reconnecting it also to the mainland and filling in the breaks to make one long island. Monomoy will continue to exist only as long as sand streams southward, because sand is constantly being eroded from the eastern edge both by waves that carry it south and by winds that carry it west.

The southern end of Monomoy, however, is growing south as well as both east and west. Here the waves that have carried sand south along the beach bend around the end of the spit and deposit sand in the form of a J. Dunes develop along the backbone of the spit, creating a higher and somewhat more permanent landform. Eventually, the interior of the J fills in, often leaving shallow ponds surrounded by the higher dunes that mark the old beach. The lighthouse on South Monomoy testifies to Monomoy's continuing growth—it was built in

1823 on the dunes at the southern end of the island, but the island has built a mile southward and almost ½ mile seaward since that time.

The southernmost part of the river of sand is the area of shoals between Monomoy and Nantucket. Here the sand is arranged and rearranged by strong tidal currents and storm waves. The sand is carried west into Nantucket Sound on the flood current to form Handkerchief Shoal and east on the ebb to Stone Horse Shoal and Great Round Shoal.

HISTORY

It was a northeaster in 1987 that breached the barrier beach that protected Chatham Harbor just opposite Chatham Light. Since that time the original narrow opening has widened to over a mile, and the cutoff section of the beach has migrated southwest to attach to the mainland. This was not the first time that a new inlet allowed ocean waves to batter Chatham's shoreline, but this time the bluffs and dunes along the harbor were completely built-up with hotels, large summer homes, and small cottages. The development along the harbor turned the natural, and expectable, processes of a barrier beach into a human drama and an item on the evening news.

Monomoy was inhabited, at least seasonally, during much of the past three hundred years. The access to fishing made it worthwhile for people to live there. A tavern operated at Wreck Cove (now called Powder Hole) as early as 1711, and the taverners probably lived nearby. A seasonal fishing village existed through the mid-1800s, when the present shallow pond was a fairly deep harbor. The lighthouse was built in 1823, and the Lifesaving Service had a number of stations on Monomoy until the mid-1900s. With the development of powerboats the fishermen moved ashore, as did the Coast Guard. The area became a National Wildlife Refuge in 1944 (it was a bombing range during World War II, which may have made it a less effective refuge at times) and was designated a Wilderness Area in 1970. Monomoy was separated from Chatham most recently in 1958; the blizzard of February 1978 cut Monomoy in two.

WHAT'S TO SEE AND DO

Walk South Beach
The beach directly below the Chatham Lighthouse is often crowded, but if you walk for ten or fifteen minutes south you find yourself shar-

ing this 3-mile beach with only a few surf fisherman and a scattering of walkers or birdwatchers. This is part of the Cape Cod National Seashore. The beach is often impassable at the highest tides—the waves wash up the steep beach face and erode the dunes, leaving nowhere to walk—so time your exploration to a lower tide. Numerous clam diggers take advantage of the low tide to work the wide flats to the west.

The charm of some places is their variety, the different environments that you see in a day's walk. Not South Beach. South Beach is magnificent in its simplicity and uniformity—sand, Beach Grass, waves, wind. But from day to day, season to season, the conditions can change far more than in most places. One day may be "thick-a-fog," so that a scream a few feet ahead may be the first warning that Great Black-backed Gulls are roosting in your path. Another day may be as clear, blue, and calm as the travel posters imply, making you feel that you could easily walk, not just to the end of the beach, but on across that narrow gutter and down Monomoy, maybe on to Nantucket. Northeasters bring snow or rain, and Gannets diving afterward in the clearing weather. There are the shorebird migrations, the Horseshoe Crabs, the layers of salt marsh peat in the beachfront, the Gray Seals harmonizing on the sand bars. . . . Really, you have to see for yourself. There are no trails, but do try to stay off the dunes to protect the Beach Grass that stabilizes them.

Beginning in midsummer and continuing into late fall, Monomoy Island is an important stopover on the southward migration of hundreds of thousands of shorebirds. At high tide they are forced into narrow bands of dry land above the water; at low tide they spread out across the flats to feed. They are stoking themselves up for the next long leg of their migration. As this is a famous spot, you may also see small flocks of birdwatchers, all facing in the same direction, just like the roosting birds.

The bay side of South Beach, where the shorebirds feed on the flats can be as different from the ocean side as the parking lot is from the beach. Go see.

Visit North Monomoy
This small remnant of the northern section of Monomoy Island can be reached by paddling in fair weather, or one of the commercial ferry services will take you there. It is protected from easterly storms by

South Beach, so is now changing less rapidly than before the Chatham break. It is a major nesting area for gulls and terns.

Visit South Monomoy

An excursion to South Monomoy is even more dependent upon the weather than one to South Beach or North Monomoy. It is an 8-mile boat trip, and fog, wind and waves can all hinder your progress. If you can arrange a trip, plan to spend some time and get a sense of this outermost place.

The southern part of Monomoy has been dry land long enough to develop a wider variety of plants and environments than South Beach. Here you'll find not only beaches, dunes, and tide flats but salt marshes, shrub thickets (beware of the Poison Ivy), and freshwater ponds and marshes. The island is a major nesting area for gulls, terns, herons, and Piping Plovers, as well as a stopover point for both shorebirds and land birds. Some areas may be closed to humans during the nesting season. Even approaching the nesting colonies will disturb the birds. Stay clear of them as much as possible, both for their sake (when the terns are dive-bombing you, their chicks and eggs are unprotected and fall prey to Great Black-backed Gulls and other predators) and for yours.

The island is home to White-tailed Deer, Muskrats, and Coyote, though only the deer are likely to be seen by a visitor.

Seals

Seals come south to winter in our balmy clime; they are often seen fishing close to shore in the tide rips or lounging about on sandbars at low tide, looking like giant, furry slugs. Seals had been extirpated in southern New England by about 1900. Harbor Seals recovered fastest once they were protected and have been common here for many years. These smallish seals have pointed, doglike heads; many people succumb to the impulse to bark at them in greeting. Gray Seals have returned only recently—pups were raised here successfully in 1989, for the first time in about one hundred years. Gray Seals are larger than Harbor Seals, up to 8 feet. Their rectangular, horselike heads do not elicit the barking behavior from humans, though we do tend to congregate to hear them sing—it is the Gray Seals that "hum" while resting on the beaches.

41. NAUSET BEACH, ORLEANS AND CHATHAM
Beaches, Dunes, Marshes, Salt Water
Birdwatching, Walking, Hiking

PREVIEW
Nauset Beach is much more than beach. This 6-mile spit, which runs south from Nauset Heights, has high, vegetated dunes, fringing salt marsh, and several islands of wooded upland. It is a glorious place in fine weather, a fascinating one in any weather. Walkers should be aware that vehicles are permitted on the beach and the road behind the dunes. The traffic can be heavy (by the standards of open space, at least) in summer, but it drops off quickly to the south. This site adjoins Little Pleasant Bay to the north (see site 42) and Chatham and South Beach to the south (see sites 39 and 40).

ACCESS
Parking and beach access are at the Orleans Town Beach (sticker or fee in summer) at the end of Beach Road. You can also reach this area by boat from Little Pleasant Bay and from the northern part of Chatham.

GEOLOGY
Nauset Beach is part of the river of sand that moves south along the ocean side of the Cape from the eroding sea cliffs to the north in Truro, Wellfleet, and Eastham. Nauset Beach began to form some six thousand years ago as the rising ocean eroded the glacial deposits and waves carried sand south along the shore. The sand collected down-drift of headlands like Nauset Heights and built southward, as it continues to do today, but the cliffs were some 2 to 3 miles to seaward when the spit began to form. As the sea rose, the cliffs were eroded, and the barrier beach was doubtless overwashed many times. Overwashing carried sand landward, moving the barrier beach westward in line with the bluffs as they eroded.

The southern end of Nauset Beach builds south by several hundred feet a year, gradually increasing the distance tidewater must travel from the open ocean to the upper reaches of Little Pleasant Bay. About

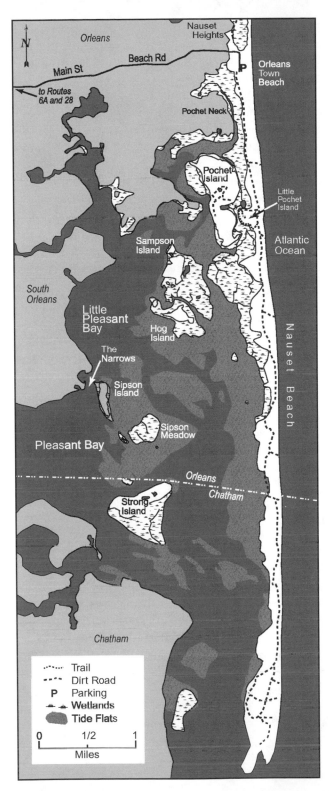

Map 41.
Nauset Beach

every 140 years the distance becomes so great that the tides in Pleasant Bay get out of sync with the ocean tides. If a storm flattens the dunes when the tide on the bay side is higher than outside, the resulting drainage of storm water across the beach can cut down below low tide and create a new inlet. This has been going on for as long as Nauset Beach and Pleasant Bay have existed. For the story of the most recent break, see South Beach (site 40).

Nauset Heights, Pochet, and Little Pochet Islands are made of rocky ice-contact deposits shed to the west from the South Channel lobe of the glacier. They contain boulders up to 20 feet in diameter as well as sand and gravel. The mix of rocks deposited from the South Channel lobe is quite different from that deposited from the Cape Cod Bay lobe just to the west, and different again from the rocks brought by the Buzzards Bay lobe. Here there is much less granite, and more slate and dark volcanic rocks. You can see the difference not only in the rocks on the hillsides but also in the rocks on the beach, where solid or striped rocks in colors of blue-gray, black, green, and red far outnumber the speckled granitic rocks typical of the Mid- and Upper Cape.

HISTORY

One of the string of twelve lifesaving stations along the east side of Cape Cod from Race Point to Monomoy was on Nauset Beach several miles south of the Orleans Town Beach parking lot. It was built about 1870 and was manned until World War II. Local folks built hunting and fishing camps on Nauset Beach for many years before summer cottages were built there. When the Cape Cod National Seashore was created in the 1960s, many of the existing camps were grandfathered. Some remain; others have been carried away by storms.

WHAT'S TO SEE AND DO

Walk the Beach

An 8-mile beach provides lots of scope for walking. Double that, because the beach buggy road runs the length of Nauset Beach on the bay side, behind the dunes. At ten points along the beach, roads cross from the bay side to the ocean side, allowing you to make a loop of whatever length you like. The walking is easier on the beach except during the highest tides, because you can walk on the wet sand; the soft, sandy road is heavy going in many places. The only advantage to the soft sand is that it is a wonderful library of tracks made by those who have walked before you, from Crows and Red Foxes to beetles and mice.

On the beach side you can watch the fishing boats offshore, the people fishing the surf, the sandpipers and gulls, and, of course, the waves. When the waves are small you can see them depositing sand on the beach: each retreating wave leaves a thin layer of sand up the shore, rimmed with slightly coarser grains. The random run-up of succeeding waves makes an intricate pattern. At times of northeasters or when distant storms send large swells ashore, the entire beach seems to shake with the force of each roaring wave. Where the waves have cut into a dune, notice the layers of sand recording the work of past winds, just as layers of sand on the back sides of the dunes reflect yesterday's wind and today's. As you walk the beach, notice the tremendous variety of rocks, many more types than on the beaches of the Mid- and Upper Cape.

Explore the Bay Side of the Beach

On the Pleasant Bay side you will find a different world. Here dunes and dune blowouts, Beach Grass, Beach Rose, Seaside Goldenrod, and Poverty Grass weave a tapestry of endlessly varied colors and patterns. The gulls of the ocean beach rarely venture here, but Harriers, Kestrels, and the occasional Peregrine Falcon search out the mice and migrating warblers in the grasses and thickets, and ducks and shorebirds feed in the marshes. From the top of the roads across the dunes you have a good view over Little Pleasant Bay and Hog and Sampson Islands as well as south to Chatham. (See site 42 for paddling Little Pleasant Bay.)

Pochet and Little Pochet Islands were first hills and then, when the ocean surrounded them, islands in the bay. Now they are islands in the salt marsh, connected to each other and the mainland by the barrier beach, separated only by a small tidal creek. Pochet Island is private but is sparsely inhabited, and the sign says "You are welcome" to walk on the island. Little Pochet (uninhabited, also private, but also open to walkers) has an old road to the top, now overgrown with Pitch Pine and Black Cherry trees and thickets of viburnum, Bayberry, Poison Ivy, and Red Cedar. You can also walk all the way around Little Pochet on deer trails at the edge of the marsh. Both islands are likely places to see migrating land birds in the thickets, especially in the fall. The views are right nice too.

SITES

42. LITTLE PLEASANT BAY AREA, ORLEANS

Salt Water, Salt Marsh, Woodlands, Bog
Paddling, Walking

PREVIEW

The upper end of Pleasant Bay contains inviting coves, saltwater creeks, and inlets as well as two uninhabited wooded islands and vast expanses of salt marsh, all easily reached by small boat. Ashore there are two small but attractive upland conservation areas with short trails, long beaches, and wide views across the bay. This area is contiguous with Nauset Beach (site 41).

ACCESS

The town landing at Pah Wah Pond is at the end of Portanimicut Road. Pah Wah Point Conservation Area is close by boat, but by car you have to go around to Namequoit Road—pass Pah Wah Pond and the Private Property Beyond Town Park sign. Kent's Point is at the end of Frostfish Road off Monument Road. There are additional town landings at River Road, Barley Neck Road, and Sparrowhawk Road.

GEOLOGY

Pleasant Bay and Little Pleasant Bay, like Nauset Marsh (site 43), are the impression of a westerly bulge of the South Channel lobe of the glacier. The rocky, gravelly sand that forms Nauset Heights, Pochet Islands, and Sampson and Hog Islands was shed into holes or indentations in the ice front. At the same time the Cape Cod Bay lobe of the glacier (to the northwest) was shedding outwash southward across the area, covering some stagnant ice and creating the surface of the land from Orleans west into Brewster and south into Chatham. The two lobes of the glacier carried very different mixes of rocks, so by counting rock types it is possible to determine which lobe deposited any given area, and even where outwash from the two lobes mingled.

Sometime after the main body of the glacier melted away, the ice occupying Pleasant Bay melted also, leaving an indentation in the east

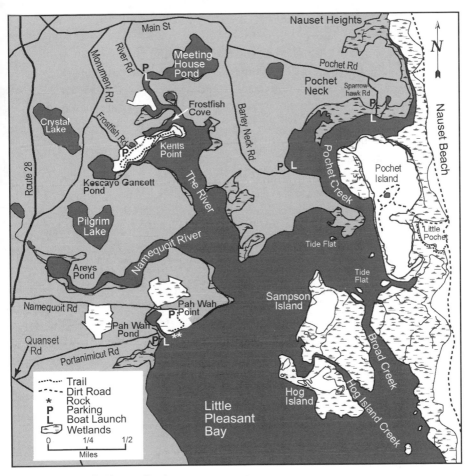

Map 42. Little Pleasant Bay Area

side of the newly exposed glacial deposits. About six thousand years ago the rising sea level reached the glacial deposits, and waves began to erode the new shoreline. The headlands in Eastham and Wellfleet to the north have eroded back somewhere between 1 and 3 miles since that time. The sand, and there was a lot of it, that was eroded from the now-vanished bluffs moved south along this part of the coast. It built the spits and barrier beaches that now characterize this area and, in a pattern that endures today, continued south to form Monomoy Island and the shoals to the south. Here, Nauset Beach gradually built south from the headland of Nauset Heights, forming a protective barrier beach across the indentation that is now Pleasant Bay. This ended the wave erosion of the 40-foot-high bluffs on Pochet Neck, Barley Neck, and Pah Wah Point; sand and silt accumulated and salt marsh grew at their feet. Since that time Pleasant Bay has become shallower—mud has settled in the salt marshes, and sand has blown and washed in from the beach and dunes. Pleasant Bay is now no more than 15 feet deep, shallower than Crystal Lake just to the west, which extends about 30 feet below sea level.

Pah Wah Pond is a kettle hole, one of the many in this area that have been flooded by salt water as sea level rose. These former freshwater bodies, like Arey's and Kescayo Gansett Ponds, are now connected to the bay by narrow rivers through which swift tidal currents run.

WHAT'S TO SEE AND DO

Walk in the Woods at Pah Wah Point
This is a small but attractive area, with large oaks, salt marsh around Pah Wah Pond, and a beach on Little Pleasant Bay. You can walk all the trails in half an hour, but there is much to see if you linger. The marshes are easily accessible, and the beach is interesting. The overlook provides wide views across the bay: Sampson and Hog Islands in the middle of the bay, Pochet Island against Nauset Beach, and the highlands of Chatham in the distance to the south.

The trees here are surprisingly large—we expect stunted trees near the ocean. That is true in some places, where windblown salt prunes the new growth, but this area is more protected. Some of the Scarlet Oaks are almost 2 feet in diameter, and many White Pines seem almost large enough to make masts for square-rigged ships. This area escaped the fate of much of the Lower Cape, where clearing and farming depleted and eroded the soil to the point that only Pitch Pines could reestablish themselves. Here the woods flourish. In fact, just up Namequoit Road is an American Chestnut tree, an unusual sight on this part of the Cape. If you want to see it, look on the north side of the road just west of Heritage Drive. Although this is one of the bigger Chestnuts around, it is not a big tree, just a clump of root sprouts to 6 inches in diameter, some showing the canker of chestnut blight. It appears that here, as in other rocky areas across the Cape, the land may not have been plowed, and it was not entirely stripped of its trees; perhaps it was woodlot or pasture, and was allowed to revert to woods sooner than more easily farmed areas.

Namequoit bog drains into Pah Wah Pond through a culvert under Namequoit Road. Part of this bog was once a commercial cranberry bog, but cultivation has ended, and the bog is now owned by the Orleans Conservation Trust.

The shores of Little Pleasant Bay are studded with large rocks and boulders of various rock types, including the red-brown sandstone best known to the world as brownstone, at least when it is used to build row houses in Brooklyn. Brownstone for construction was quarried in the lower Connecticut River Valley, but these pieces probably came from the Bay of Fundy.

Explore Kent's Point
It is hard to believe that this area is only 27 acres; it has a variety of places to go and provides a sense of quiet (except for powerboats in the river) that is hard to equal in many larger areas. Named trails lead through the woods and along the shoreline; the whole network is shown on a map at the parking area. You can walk all the main trails in less than an hour, but Kent's Point is a place that rewards more leisurely observation. The "Frostfish" for which the cove is named are Tomcod, which spawn in estuaries and rivers in the frosty weather of early winter.

The woods are mostly large Scarlet, White, and Black Oaks, which are shading out the pioneer Bear Oaks, Bearberry, and Pitch Pines. The soil must be rich and moisture-retentive, for Winterberry, viburnums, Red Maple, and Highbush Blueberry are quite common. But even so these woods look quite unlike the richer woods on the Mid- and Upper Cape because of the limited variety of trees and low plants: there are no hickories, American Beech, or Sassafras, no Trailing Arbutus or Lady's Slippers. This paucity suggests that at least some of the land was totally cleared and probably plowed. Species that spread easily have returned; others have not.

The shoreline of this area adds up to almost a mile, and what a lovely mile! You can walk a mile along many stretches of the ocean beach, but a mile of bay shore is unusual. There are salt marshes, rocky beaches, and large glacial boulders draped with rockweed. Ribbed Mussels grow in the peat, and small pockets of sand fill in between stands of *Spartina* and Pickleweed. But there is no sign of Fiddler Crabs; the water must be too cold.

The views from the shoreline and from the end of the point are wonderful. On a clear day you can see south past Pah Wah Point to Little Pleasant Bay and on beyond to Hog Island and Nauset Beach.

There were houses here recently, indicated not only by the road but also by the surviving garden plants and several foundations.

Paddle Little Pleasant Bay

Little Pleasant Bay gives some idea of what heavily used bays like Waquoit and Popponesset were like before there were so many of us on the Cape. Here the bottom is thickly covered with Eelgrass, the water is clear, and no floating mats of algae demonstrate eutrophication. Scallops have all but disappeared from many Upper and Mid-Cape bays, but they still flourish here along with the somewhat less sensitive crabs and clams. That is not to say that there are no problems with nutrients here; this system was rejuvenated after the Chatham break in 1989 when the tidal flow increased. As Nauset Beach lengthens, and development continues to add nutrients to the bay, concerns about eutrophication will grow again.

High on the list of attractive paddling destinations are Sampson and Hog Islands, approximately a mile across the bay. Although you will have no problem paddling against the current, it is strong enough to kick up a bit of a chop when the wind is against it; be aware of the current on windy days. Sampson Island has a flattish top about 50 feet above sea level, covered with Pitch Pine and Bear Oaks, with a few Black Oaks and Black Cherries just reaching tree size. It is a pleasant place for a picnic. The island is surrounded by extensive salt marsh whose winding channels harbor Black Ducks and Great Blue Herons (especially in fall) and shorebirds. Hog Island is a group of small islets connected by sandbars and salt marshes. By the accidents of history (what grew on them when they were separated by rising sea level, what the hogs ate, what seeds birds have brought here since . . . you can probably think of more) they are quite different from each other, and well worth exploring. Expect them to be teeming with migrating land birds in late summer and fall. Flocks of Yellow-rumped Warblers linger into early winter eating the berries of Poison Ivy, Red Cedar, and sumac. Both Hog and Sampson show old, vegetation-covered, wave-cut bluffs on their southeast sides, evidence of erosion by ocean waves before Nauset Beach grew to protect them.

Beyond Sampson and Hog Islands, Pochet and Little Pochet Islands beckon, with Nauset Beach beyond (see site 41). Broad and Pochet Creeks both provide good paddling and attractive views on all sides. In Broad Creek a number of floats mark shellfish aquiculture sites.

You can also paddle up the various tidal arms of The River and explore the more developed shores of Arey's Pond, Kescayo Gansett Pond, and Meeting House Pond, and stop at Kent's Point for a walk.

SITES

43. NAUSET MARSH AND FORT HILL, EASTHAM AND ORLEANS

Moors, Woodlands, Salt Marshes, Salt Water
Paddling, Walking, Birdwatching

PREVIEW

The view of the spectacular Nauset Marsh from Fort Hill is surpassed only by visiting it in person. But while you're on Fort Hill take a walk to explore the fields, and to see the Red Maple swamp. All of this area is in the Cape Cod National Seashore; it is contiguous with the plains of Nauset (site 44).

ACCESS

Fort Hill is at the end of Governor Prence Road, off Route 6. There usually is more room in the first parking lot. You can launch a boat to explore the marshes at either the landing at Hemenway Road or the one at Salt Pond.

GEOLOGY

The low area now occupied by Nauset Marsh, like Pleasant Bay to the south, marks the location of a protrusion of the South Channel lobe of the glacier. All around the marsh are the ice-contact deposits and out-wash plains deposited on and against the ice from the main body of the South Channel lobe to the northeast. The ice-contact deposits are rocky and contain many large boulders. Steep bluffs such as those at Cedar Bank were cut by ocean waves when sea level first rose high enough about six thousand years ago, before Nauset spit formed. The marshes probably began to grow about four thousand years ago, as sea level rose higher and the spit provided protection.

Nauset spit, like all barrier beaches, is a dynamic place, changing as it absorbs the energy of the waves. When Henry Beston spent a year in the "Outermost House" (and wrote his book of the same title) in

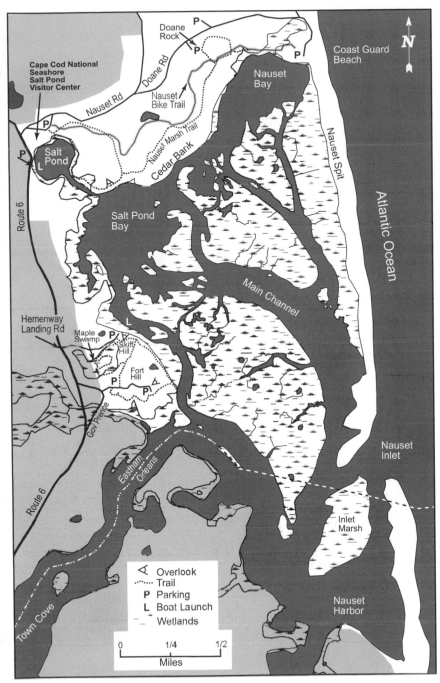

Map 43. Nauset Marsh and Fort Hill

1927, the dunes were as much as 50 feet high. Beginning with the Great Hurricane of 1938 the spit was progressively overwashed, and cuts opened through the dunes that had built up over a hundred years or more. During the blizzard of February 1978 the storm surge rose more than 15 feet above normal high tide. Storm waves advanced across the beach and flattened the dunes, carrying the sand into the bay behind the spit. These aprons of sand are now colonized by Beach Grass, which is trapping sand blown off the beach and beginning the process of building new dunes. Depending on how soon a storm of that magnitude strikes again, these dunes may someday reach their former height, but they have been moved westward, staying in line with the erosion of the bluffs.

HISTORY

In 1605 Samuel de Champlain anchored inside Nauset spit while exploring what was then New France. The map he made of the bay and marshes, though somewhat diagrammatic, is still entirely recognizable. Despite the many changes in the spit, marshes, and inlet in the past four hundred years, he could anchor here today—his small ship probably drew about 5 feet. At high tide in calm weather this would still be the most attractive anchorage between Provincetown and Chatham.

Champlain's map also shows the houses and fields of native peoples all around the shores of Nauset Marsh; the Pilgrims bought corn and beans from this same village in 1622, so this must have been a long-term settlement. These people were the original "Nausets"; all the other Nausets—beach, heights, schools, roads, and marsh—derive their names from them.

Settlers from Plymouth in 1644 founded a town called . . . Nauset. Eventually it was renamed Eastham during political maneuvering in which Wellfleet and Orleans took their leave from the mother town. The salt marsh was a big part of the attraction of this area to early settlers; the Salt Marsh Hay provided needed fodder for livestock. Salt Marsh Hay from Nauset Marsh continued to support dairy herds in Eastham until the end of the 1800s.

In the 1930s and 1940s Wyman Richardson, a physician from Boston, spent time in a farmhouse overlooking Nauset Marsh. His book, *The House on Nauset Marsh*, is a wonderful portrait of the area and even today can serve as a guide.

Lower Cape Sites

Walk the Fort Hill and Maple Swamp Trails

This 2-mile loop trail includes wide vistas of Nauset Marsh, boardwalks through the Red Maple swamp, woods and thickets that attract migrating land birds, and open fields that preserve a sense of the historic farm landscape here. The fields are burned or mowed to prevent trees from taking over. Rock walls, apple trees, and asparagus are evidence of farming here, as are the many old-world plants that the colonists inadvertently brought to North America. Look for the blue flowers of Chicory, the flat white umbels of Queen Anne's Lace, the yellow four-petaled flowers of Mustard, and the brambles of raspberry. More recent arrivals from abroad reflect our changing relationship with the land: they are not food plants but ornamentals escaped from landscape plantings—Honeysuckle, Bittersweet, and Autumn Olive. In summer look for Bobolinks and sparrows in the fields; in fall Yellow-rumped Warblers forage in the thickets.

The Red Maple swamp has a long period of glorious color in the late summer and fall because Tupelos grow here too, along with many plants that grow well in wet soil. Few areas have as many kinds of ferns. The ferns may have become dominant here when the competition of the trees was removed during logging in the swamp.

Skiff Hill

From the Skiff Hill overlooks the tide flats and the marshes open out before you. At low tide this is a likely place for shorebirds. In fact, this site is well known to birdwatchers; you might encounter a flock of them, too, peering through their spotting scopes at a group of Marbled Godwits or Black-bellied Plovers.

At Skiff Hill is a large glacial boulder used by the native peoples— look for the narrow grooves where fishhooks were sharpened and the broad polished areas used for grinding adzes or other blades. This stone speaks not only of the technologies of native peoples but also of the rise in sea level and the growth of the marsh here. When this stone was in use, it was not out in the marsh where the Park Service found it. It was on the upland near the village or encampment beside what was then the estuary. Nor did the rock go down into the marsh; sea level rose, and the marsh grew to keep pace, drowning the upland and overwhelming this stone in a sea of marsh grass. By the time the stone was

SITES

found by the Park Service, it was out in the marsh and not accessible; they moved it uphill to tell its story. Much other evidence of former lives, animal and plant, is buried in the peat of the salt marsh. The marsh may look unaltered, but this stone is a reminder of the changes that have taken place, not just on a geological timescale, but within human history.

Paddle the Marsh

In the Nauset Marsh you must watch the tides—the wide tide flats make paddling difficult at low tide. The marshes are most interesting below midtide, when the banks and flats are exposed and the shorebirds come out to feed. You won't need to worry about the tides if you take to the marshes in a boat that is light enough to carry over whatever flats (mud in the upper bays and sand near the inlet) intervene between you and your goal. If you don't wish to portage, note the state of the tide and plan your trip accordingly. In general, go south if you have midtide and falling (you'll have to wait for rising tide to return); go north if it is rising.

Once you are out in the marsh, the evidence of civilization retreats behind the lanes of water and banks of rustling *Spartina*. A strong west wind may bring you occasional tidings of trucks or tour buses on Route 6, but otherwise you might equally expect to see a Nauset dugout or Wyman Richardson's fishing canoe as a clam digger in a powerboat. Interestingly, the marsh has no mosquito-control ditches. That means that isolated marsh pools exist out in tracts of marsh grass, providing cover for Black Ducks who sometimes spring suddenly into the air before you are aware that they exist. Marshes with a network of ruler-straight ditches look somewhat tamed and domesticated once you've seen Nauset.

From midsummer to late fall the marsh is a haven to the hosts of migrating shorebirds pouring south from their nesting grounds in the far north. Their foraging must have a significant effect on the populations of the small shellfish, amphipods, and worms that are their food—each bird seems to spend every possible moment searching for and consuming the fuel for the next leg of its journey. This flood of birds peaks in late August or early September, but even in late October good numbers of an interesting variety of birds may be found here—many kinds of sandpipers, yellowlegs, Black-bellied Plovers, godwits . . . you'd better check them out for yourself. The Black Ducks are year-round residents; there are few other places where you'll see so many.

The peat of the marsh is riddled with holes made by Ribbed Mussels, and often crowded with Periwinkles and Mud Snails but not Fiddler Crabs—they would have to travel through cold Atlantic water to get here. Abundant shells and clammers suggest that Quahogs and Soft-shelled Clams are common here as are, surprisingly, Lobsters. And that is just a hint at the diversity of life in the marsh—think of it: forty-six species of fish live or feed here.

If you can't get out into the marsh by boat, take the walk along the Nauset Marsh Trail from the Salt Pond Visitor Center to Coast Guard Beach. (See also the plains of Nauset, site 44.)

SITES

44. THE PLAINS OF NAUSET, THE GREAT BEACH, AND NAUSET SPIT, EASTHAM

Woodlands, Ponds, Salt Water, Beach, Dunes

Birdwatching, Walking

PREVIEW

Henry David Thoreau described the plains of Nauset as "desolate," though the wind-driven autumn rain on the day he walked from Orleans to Wellfleet may have had as much to do with the description as the treeless, empty moors. Today the woods hereabouts are thick, and if they hide the wide views of bay, marsh, and moor Thoreau might have had, they provide other points of interest. The walking is pleasant and easy on paved trails, footpaths, and old woods roads. Just to the south, Nauset spit, the interface between the marsh and the ocean, provides all the waves, beach, dunes, views, and sky anyone could wish for—some 2 miles of it. See Nauset Marsh (site 43) for paddling.

ACCESS

Park at the Cape Cod National Seashore Salt Pond Visitor Center, at Doane Rock, at Little Creek Staging Area, at Coast Guard or Nauset Light Beaches (fee in summer), or, for the woods walk, at the sandy turnout where the abandoned Little Creek Road joins Nauset Road just north of Nauset Ranger Station.

GEOLOGY

Thoreau's "Plains of Nauset" are on the outwash plain, which forms the land north and west of Nauset Marsh. A thick bulge of ice protruding from the South Channel lobe of the glacier prevented deposition of sand and gravel here, forming the indentation in the coast that holds the marshes. Irregular ice occupied the area to the north as far as Cable Road, and it was buried by the outwash. When the buried ice melted, the ground above it collapsed, forming this irregular country

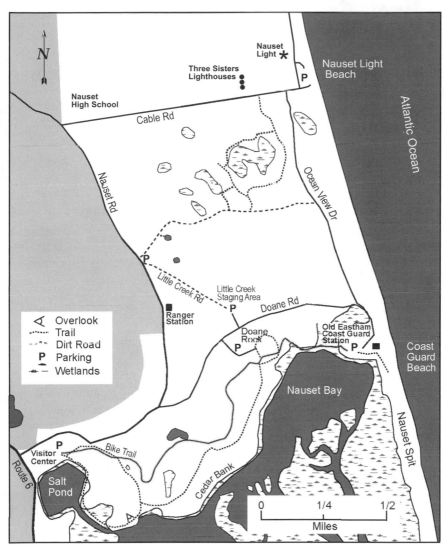

Map 44. The Plains of Nauset, the Great Beach, and Nauset Spit

pitted with dozens of small, closed depressions. There is hardly a flat "plain" surface anywhere.

North of Cable Road the surface is smooth and even, with no depressions. Here the sand and gravel formed a thick deposit; there was no buried ice to interrupt the plain. Within a mile or so of Nauset Light the outwash is rocky and contains many large boulders; to the west, farther from the former edge of the melting ice, there are few boulders, and the sand grain size is much smaller. Doane Rock, one of the largest glacial boulders on the Cape, lies close to Doane Road on the southern edge of the irregular terrain. This boulder, some 45 feet long, melted directly out of the ice of the South Channel lobe and was only partially buried by outwash.

The bluff at Nauset Light Beach shows a good cross-section of the outwash plain in this area. Boulders and lumps of rust-colored, rocky ice-contact debris are surrounded by irregular layers of sand and gravel deposited by the outwash streams. North along the sea cliff, where the outwash was deposited farther from the edge of the ice, there are no boulders, and the outwash is finer-grained and more evenly layered.

HISTORY

Nauset spit has undergone many changes since French mapmaker Samuel de Champlain named it Mallebarre (Bad Bar) in 1605, and even since Henry Beston wrote *The Outermost House* in 1927. Storms have overwashed the spit numerous times, flattening the dunes and carrying away Beston's "Fo'castle." Because there is a constant supply of sand, the spit remains, and with time the wind will rebuild the dunes.

The Coast Guard Station here was manned until the 1950s; its surfmen walked the beach every night, keeping watch for vessels in trouble. The surfmen were no longer needed when radio, radar, and electronic navigation systems helped ships to stay out of trouble, and helicopters and motorized vessels could quickly reach ships needing assistance.

When Thoreau walked across the Nauset plains in the 1850s the area around Nauset Marsh was treeless, and a walker on any high point could see both the Atlantic Ocean and Cape Cod Bay. Even as recently as the 1930s and 1940s, most of the ridges supported only Bearberry and occasional patches of shrub-size Bear Oak. The swales held Pitch Pines and larger Bear Oaks. The older pines in the swales are noticeably larger today than the ones on the ridges. As if farming, wood-cutting, and grazing were not enough to denude the countryside, the area around Salt Pond and along Cedar Bank was a golf course in the early 1900s. Ghosts of the greens can still be seen in the vegetation on the inland side of the Nauset Marsh loop trail. Trees are making a comeback on the Nauset plains, but the woods are still dominated by the first growth of Pitch Pine and Red Cedar, with oaks just reaching tree size.

WHAT'S TO SEE AND DO

Walk the Bay Shores

The Nauset Marsh Trail runs for 2 miles from the Visitor Center to the Coast Guard Station, along the marsh and through the edge of the woods. It joins the paved bike path for the last ¼ mile; another branch loops back through the old golf course. Halfway between Salt Pond and the beach is Doane Rock and the short Doane Homestead loop trail. The woods are pleasant, but the views of the marsh are spectacular. Wyman Richardson's "house on Nauset Marsh" is the one on the hillside behind you at the marsh overlook just east of Salt Pond.

Walk the Beach and Nauset Spit

Nauset spit is a very different place today than in 1927, when Henry Beston spent a year in his small house on the dunes. Not only is his house gone, but the dunes are gone too; both were casualties of the February blizzard of 1978, which also cut Monomoy Island in two. To get an idea of what this area might have been like before the dunes were washed into the marsh, visit Nauset Beach south of the Orleans Town Beach (see site 41). Because there is a constant supply of sand, the dunes here will build up again until a series of large storms occurs at high tide. The processes that built the previous dunes will build new ones, and will continue as long as there is sand, wind, and space to build.

We owe the fact that there are no vehicles on this beach to that February storm as well: it took out the large parking lot and vehicle access road, as well as the remaining beach houses and the jeep trail that served them. The absence of vehicles probably matters to the creatures that live here even more than to walkers—vehicles and their tracks make life hard for Piping Plovers, Tiger Beetles, terns, and many other small beach users.

Both the ocean side and the bay side of Nauset spit are open to walking at most states of the tide, one or the other providing sheltered walking in either easterly or westerly winds. On the bay side note the many chunks of peat and the occasional chunks of concrete and asphalt, testimony to the insistent strength of the ocean waves that ripped them from their origin and deposited them here.

South of the intensively trampled section of the beach near the boardwalk, the wide summer beach retains a record of what has passed over it in the past few days: walkers, winds, dogs, birds, and tides. You

SITES

can determine the direction of the wind that made the ripples in the sand and estimate its strength—the stronger the wind, the coarser the sand grains in the ripples.

If you walk south the 2 miles from the Coast Guard Station to the inlet (map 43) on a sparkling day with gentle winds, or even on a gusty gray day, try to imagine the Coast Guard surfmen who patrolled this beach in the dark every night, no matter the wind or weather. During storms they made three trips each night, rather than the fair-weather two, always ready to warn ships or rescue sailors. Picture them picking their way along through the scud with a flickering lantern or walking on the dunes if the waves covered the beach. Oh, and the spit is a mile shorter today than it was in the 1930s.

The sands in the inlet are always in motion, so the channel is marked with small buoys that are shifted when the channel shifts. Ebb currents carry sand seaward, creating bars in the mouth of the inlet. It is impressive to watch local boats thread the channel when the wind is high. Inside the inlet are other new and shifting sandbars deposited by flood tides, where shorebirds and gulls roost, protected from people and their dogs. Gray and Harbor Seals are sometimes seen here too.

The present inlet was created in the 1970s when the tip of Nauset spit was cut off in an event similar to the 1989 Chatham break. The old tip has migrated westward and forms an islet called (in good Cape Cod naming tradition) New Island. Inlet Marsh (see Nauset Marsh map, site 43) just inside the inlet may have formed in the same way, but long enough ago that it has been colonized by Cordgrass. Terns and gulls nest on this marsh island and will chase you away if you get too close in early summer.

Walk the Woods of Nauset Plain

Wyman Richardson described this walk in *The House on Nauset Marsh.* Although you can't walk his route, because of the trees and underbrush, you can find some of his landmarks. From the Nauset Road parking spot the walk to Nauset Beach through the woods is about 2½ miles round trip. Richardson's "Single Snipe Pond" is in the depression south of the trail just east of Nauset Road (despite what you may have concluded in summer camp, Snipe are real birds). Even in dry seasons there is water in this small pond, and there are White

Water Lilies, so wetland birds such as Snipe are still possible. In several nearby swales Trailing Arbutus (Richardson calls it Mayflower) still grows thickly, though it is not common on the Lower Cape.

The woods are quite young—it was a long time after Thoreau traversed this country before trees reestablished themselves. Few species of trees grow on the ridges between the swales, mostly Pitch Pine and Bear Oak, though both will soon be shaded out by the growing White, Black, and Scarlet Oaks. Much Bearberry and some Broom Crowberry still grow beneath the trees, reminding us that this forest was moor not long ago. Richardson's comfortable "Couch Bush"—springy clumps of either Broom Crowberry or Bayberry—has been shaded out, alas.

Few of the swales have permanent ponds, though many contain vernal pools. Reaching the water is difficult, however, because of thickets of Bear Oak, Highbush Blueberry, and Sweet Pepperbush, all woven together by Greenbrier. The swales have much richer soil than the ridges and support plants that are otherwise uncommon on the Lower Cape, including Beaked Hazel, club mosses, Pipsissewa, Spotted Pipsissewa, and Pink Lady's Slipper.

The trail follows old woods roads, in whose ruts you can see occasional polished and faceted ventifacts. These stones were gradually buried by some fifteen thousand years' worth of fallen leaves, but the soil was eroded after the forest was cut, reexposing the earlier postglacial surface.

45. MARCONI AREA AND THE PLAINS OF EASTHAM AND WELLFLEET

Beach, Woodlands, Moors, Cedar Swamp
Walking

PREVIEW

One of the largest unbroken areas of open space on Cape Cod, the Marconi area stretches from Cable Road in Eastham 5 miles north to LeCount Hollow in Wellfleet, just beyond the northern edge of map 45; it is part of the Cape Cod National Seashore. Trails and old woods roads thread the countryside; some tread gingerly along the top of the 100-foot sea cliff, others make a beeline across flat country, and bits of the Old King's Highway meander like the path it originally was. Here is also an isolated and beautiful section of the Great Beach worth walking either north or south from Marconi Beach. Marconi Station has no beach access, but a trail leads to a boardwalk in a large Atlantic White Cedar swamp, and a viewing platform on the brink of the cliff provides a good view of the ocean and beach to the east and of Wellfleet Harbor and Great Beach Hill to the west, with Cape Cod Bay in the distance (see site 46, Great Island Tombolo).

ACCESS

Park at Marconi Beach (fee in summer) or at Marconi Station, or bike in via the bike path.

GEOLOGY

This entire area lies on the Wellfleet outwash plain, which is about 15 feet higher than the younger Eastham plain to the south and contains more granitic rocks. The outwash plain probably originally extended as much as 3 miles farther east; it has since been eroded by the ocean waves. Today the sea cliff is eroding at an average rate of 3 feet per year.

HISTORY

Thoreau walked through Wellfleet, sometimes on the beach and sometimes near the edge of the cliff, but even though it still looks the same,

Lower Cape Sites

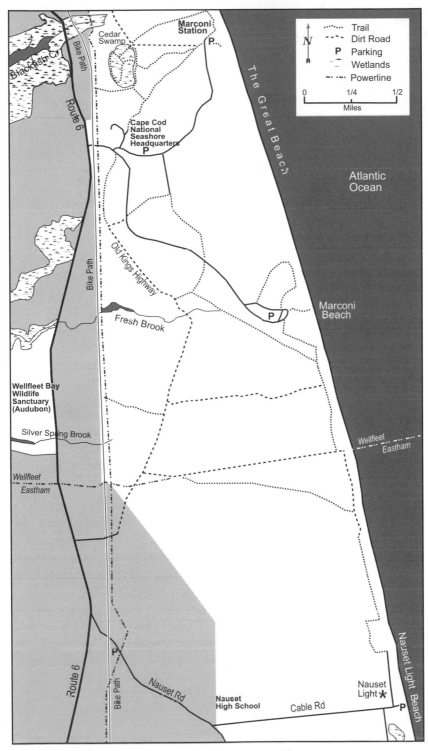

Map 45. Marconi Area and the Plains of Eastham and Wellfleet

this is not the cliff edge, or the beach, that Thoreau walked. They have eroded back some 450 feet since he was here. Erosion all along the cliff proceeds at this rate; it necessitated moving both the Nauset and Highland Lighthouses in the 1990s to prevent them from falling into the ocean.

The first two-way wireless communication between Europe and the United States was achieved in 1903 at Marconi Station. Until the station was closed at the start of World War I, South Wellfleet was a major portal for the exchange of news with Europe. The sand road that is the northern branch of the Cedar Swamp Trail was the access to the wireless station. Only a little remains of the wireless station—the rest has been lost to erosion of the bluffs.

During World War II part of this area, known as Camp Wellfleet, was a training ground for U.S. soldiers.

WHAT'S TO SEE AND DO

Walk the Beach
From Marconi Beach you can walk north to . . . well, however far you want to go. It's 2½ miles to busy LeCount Hollow Beach, 20 to Head of the Meadow Beach in Truro, and 6 more to Race Point. You will have much of the area to yourself. Look for whales offshore in the autumn, and for seals and northern birds such as loons and eiders in fall and winter. After winter storms you may see Gannets and deep-sea birds such as shearwaters close to shore. As you go by, notice the sea cliff, which provides a look at what the Lower Cape is made of.

Walk the Atlantic White Cedar Swamp Trail
This 1¼-mile loop includes a boardwalk through 20 acres of Atlantic White Cedar swamp in a shallow kettle hole. The kettle seems deeper than it is because the approach is down the west-sloping outwash plain from 100 feet elevation at the parking area to 20 feet at the rim of the kettle hole. Coffee-colored, acidic water standing in the swamp creates an environment in which the Atlantic White Cedars can out-compete other trees. Beneath the water, the peat is 24 feet thick, recording the plants of the area (and whatever else blew, fell, or washed in) over the last seven thousand years. Atlantic White Cedars began to grow here about five thousand years ago; generation succeeded generation until the European settlers arrived and repeatedly cut the trees. But

conditions favoring Atlantic White Cedars were not altered, so when cutting ended the cedars reestablished themselves.

As you walk from the cliff edge to the swamp, watch the gradual transition from ground-hugging Bearberry, Poverty Grass, Bear Oaks, and Broom Crowberry through stunted Pitch Pines to progressively taller and more varied trees. The low plants and stunted trees make visible the winds off the ocean—strong, salt-laden, and close to the ground at the brink of the cliff, rising to blow over the heads of the trees that huddle on the slope to the west. As the environment becomes less harsh downslope, Black, Scarlet, and White Oaks begin to grow among the Pitch Pines and Bear Oaks. The younger trees couldn't have started here without the protection of the pioneer forest, but one day they will take over. You can't tell by looking at them, but almost all the Pitch Pines, whether dwarfed or full-size, are about 75 years old.

At the bottom of the slope are Red Maples and Tupelos that make the swamp a glorious place in late summer and fall. Note the other plants that also flourish in this environment: Sphagnum, Sweet Pepperbush, Highbush Blueberry, Leatherleaf, and ferns.

Walk the Woods above the Sea Cliff
In the Wildlife Management Area around Marconi Beach, from the Saturday after Columbus Day to the Saturday after Thanksgiving, the Massachusetts Department of Fish and Wildlife releases farm-raised Quail and Pheasants, and hunters in orange clothes take their guns and dogs and hunt them. That's the downside of the site. The upside is that there are trails and old woods roads across the moors, along the clifftop, and through the woods. It is a place to spend some time.

A good introduction is the 2½-mile loop south along the sea cliff from the southeast corner of the Marconi Beach parking area, west on the old woods road to the Old King's Highway, then north on this former major thoroughfare to a smaller woods road running southeast back toward the parking area. It is a good idea to wear orange if you are walking here during the game-bird hunting season.

Visit the Wellfleet Bay Wildlife Sanctuary
Just west of the Marconi area, this 1,000-acre preserve between Wellfleet Harbor and Route 6 has nature trails as well as an education center and active research programs.

SITES

46. GREAT ISLAND TOMBOLO AND THE HERRING RIVER ESTUARY, WELLFLEET

Salt Water, Salt Marshes, Beach, Dunes, Woodlands
Walking, Paddling

PREVIEW

A tombolo is a barrier beach that connects an island to the mainland—just what we have here at Great Island. This string of wooded islands, dunes, barrier beaches, and salt marshes extends south 2 miles from the mainland and is the protection for Wellfleet Harbor. South of Great Beach Hill the beach tapers down to Jeremy Point, a sandbar that is exposed only at low tide. Between the islands the walking is loose sand, but the views, the beaches, the marshes, and the islands themselves are definitely worth it. Or you can paddle down the estuary and land on a beach, or see it from the water. This area is part of the Cape Cod National Seashore. The Bound Brook Island area is adjacent to the north (see site 47).

ACCESS

Parking and the Great Island trailhead are at the end of Chequesset Neck Road. Light boats can be launched from the sand parking area on the south side of Chequesset Neck Road just west of the Herring River dike (this parking area may be inundated during high moon tides, when parts of the Great Island Trail may also be underwater). For paddling the upper reaches of the river, see Bound Brook Island (site 47).

GEOLOGY

This is probably the most geologically complicated site on the Cape. Both the South Channel lobe and the Cape Cod Bay lobe contributed to its formation. The islands are rocky sand deposited in holes or indentations in the ice of the Cape Cod Bay lobe and contain deposits from both lobes; some parts were deposited as deltas into the Cape Cod Bay lake. The catastrophic drainage of another glacial lake, which formed east of the Lower Cape, may have cut the steep bluffs between

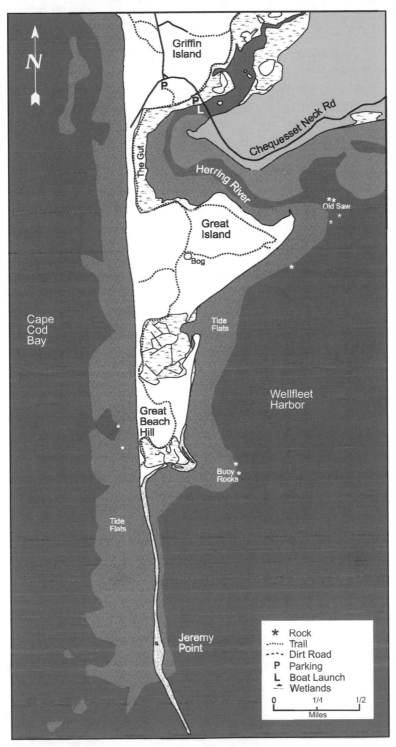

Map 46. Great Island Tombolo and the Herring River Estuary

the islands. At the end of the glacial time Bound Brook Island, Griffin Island, Great Beach Hill, and Billingsgate Island (now just a shoal south of Jeremy Point) were hills of glacial debris high and dry on the continental shelf. The glacial winds blew sand across the land, sandblasting the rocks lying at the surface. These ventifacts can be seen anywhere erosion has stripped away the soil that developed in the intervening fifteen thousand years.

As sea level rose, waves began to reshape the glacial deposits. Until about six thousand years ago northerly winds carried sand south along the Cape Cod Bay shore, building a barrier beach on Billingsgate Shoal, a small moraine to the southwest formed during a minor re-advance of the Cape Cod Bay lobe. Now comes the interesting part: about six thousand years ago Georges Bank, which had been an off-shore island, was finally submerged below sea level, exposing the Atlantic coast of the Cape to waves from the southeast. Those waves moved sand north along the east side of the Cape and began building Provincetown spit north and west from High Head in Truro. As the "fist" at Provincetown grew larger, it protected this shore from north-easterly winds, and the dominant direction of sand flow reversed. Sand began to move northward under the influence of southwest winds, as it does today. The barrier beach was eroded, and the sand moved north to form new spits.

The beach that forms the tombolo has developed in historic times —there were openings between the islands into the 1800s, a fact memorialized by the anachronistic name "The Gut" on the beach that joins Great Island to the mainland. This area is still changing rapidly— Billingsgate Island, which once had houses and a lighthouse, is now just a shoal south of Jeremy Point; the last bit of dry land was eroded away in the 1940s. Jeremy Point was breached in 1933; although the breach has closed, the spit will continue to dwindle because there is no longer a source of sand upwind.

HISTORY

These outposts in the bay were used by the inhabitants, beginning with the native peoples, for fishing and whaling. Very likely trees were cut here to try out the whale oil on the beach. From the mid-1600s to the mid-1700s there was a tavern on Great Island; a plaque marks the spot. This site has been excavated, and some of the artifacts are to be seen in the Salt Pond Visitor Center (see site 43). These islands were appar-

Lower Cape Sites

ently also used as pasture for livestock (Thoreau reports a conversation to that effect) into the 1800s.

WHAT'S TO SEE AND DO

Walk the Great Island Trail
It is 3 miles from the trailhead to the Jeremy Point overlook on Great Beach Hill, and another 1½ miles to the end of Jeremy Point (low tide only). The walk is enjoyable even if you don't go to the end. At high tides higher than 10 feet, the trail along the marsh between Griffin Island and Great Island floods; be prepared to wade, or don't go within an hour of highest tide.

On Great Island the 1-mile loop trail to the tavern site leads you close to the high bluff on the eastern point. From here you have a wide view across the harbor and the hills to the east. The light green water tower on stilts on the eastern horizon is near Marconi Station, less than ¼ mile from the sea cliff, demonstrating how narrow the Cape is here.

The Great Island woods are almost entirely young Pitch Pine, though there are a few surprises, including a small bog in the center of the island that supports Sheep Laurel and cranberries. Even more astonishing are two American Chestnut trees. They are seedlings, not root sprouts, and appear to be thirty or forty years old. It will be interesting to see if the 12 miles that separate them from the nearest Chestnut with blight will protect them.

The 6 miles of empty beach on Cape Cod Bay from the tip of Jeremy Point to Bound Brook Island are interrupted only at Duck Harbor just north of Griffin Island, where there is parking near the beach. Otherwise you will have this beach to yourself and a few like-minded walkers.

Paddle the Herring River Estuary and Wellfleet Harbor
This is a great place for a small boat, with all of the island chain as possible destinations. At low tide wide flats fringe the uplands and the marsh, restricting you to the center of the channel; high tide lets you explore into the marshes. Shorebirds frequent Wellfleet Harbor in both spring and fall migrations. Although you can see them from land, you can often approach closer in a boat.

SITES

47. BOUND BROOK ISLAND TO THE GREAT BEACH, WELLFLEET AND TRURO

*Beach, Dunes, Salt Water, Woodlands, Fresh Water
Hiking, Walking, Paddling*

PREVIEW

The 15-square-mile near wilderness from Bound Brook Island to the Great Beach has only a few hundred houses; the Cape Cod National Seashore stretches from Cape Cod Bay to the Atlantic. True, Route 6 cuts through, and Wellfleet Center is on the southern edge, but this little-known area is mostly open space. Hikes and walks of every description abound, and the ponds and Herring River make for good paddling. This site is adjacent to the Great Island Tombolo (site 46) and Pamet River (site 48).

ACCESS

For the west side of the area park on Griffin Island, at Duck Harbor Beach, or on Bound Brook Island. For Lombard and Paradise Hollows, park off Route 6 at George Nilson Road opposite Snow Pond. For the beaches you can park at Newcomb or Cahoon Hollow Beaches (Wellfleet residents only in summer) or at White Crest Beach (fee in summer). For the ponds there is parking and a boat ramp at Gull Pond, and parking at Great Pond (Wellfleet residents only in summer). Tiny parking areas, too small to show on the map, are at Higgins and Spectacle Ponds. To paddle the Herring River, you can park and launch at the crossing at Bound Brook Island or at the dike at High Toss Road.

GEOLOGY

This area is outwash plain, made of sand and gravel deposited by streams running southwest away from the front of the South Channel lobe of the glacier. Most of the eastern part of the plain was deposited on top of stagnant glacial ice. When the ice subsequently melted, the outwash collapsed, creating the irregular land surface and the many

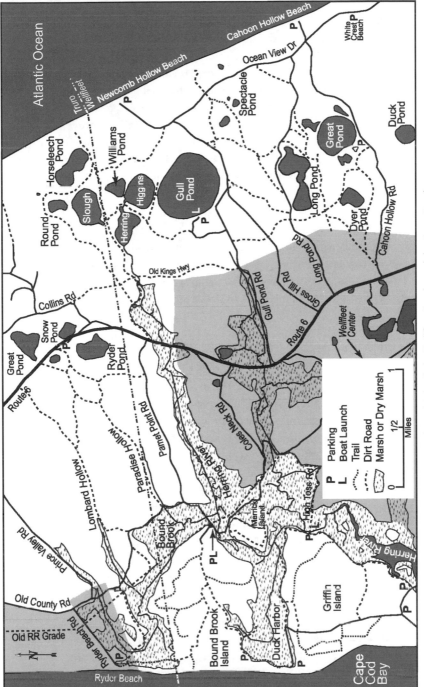

Map 47. Bound Brook Island, the Wellfleet Ponds, and the Great Beach

kettle ponds. These ponds are the archetype of the kettle hole: round, deep, and steep-sided. They are round because pond waves have built barrier beaches along their shores and across indentations. The bluffs above the water are about as steep as sand can stand, and the steep sides continue below the water to depths well below sea level.

Ice from the Cape Cod Bay lobe, to the west, also played a part in shaping this area; it occupied Wellfleet Harbor, preventing the deposition of outwash there. The islands from Bound Brook south to Great Beach Hill (see Great Island Tombolo, site 46) may have been deposited in holes or indentations in that ice, perhaps after the parallel valleys such as Lombard Hollow were first cut.

These parallel valleys appear to have been cut, or at least deepened, by water draining from the lake that formed in late glacial times east of the outwash plains. That lake apparently drained catastrophically, and water rushed west, deepening any preexisting spring-sapping valleys, and perhaps cutting new valleys. The flow from the lake apparently soon abandoned this area and concentrated in the Pamet River Valley.

Duck Harbor was open to Cape Cod Bay until the late 1800s, Bound Brook until the mid-1700s. The growth of the barrier beach closed off those openings (assisted by a small dike at Duck Harbor) in historic times. When that happened, the drainage in the low areas behind the barrier beach reversed—where once the marsh creeks ran west to the bay, water now must make its circuitous way east to the Herring River. The drying of these former marshes was intensified when the Chequesset Neck Road dike was built in 1908 (see Great Island Tombolo, site 46). Because the tides no longer flood and salt these areas, the marshes have dried out and become fresh, and shrubs and trees have taken root. Just inside the barrier beach, where you would expect salt marshes (and where Salt Marsh Hay still grows), shrub thickets now flourish. The growth of the barrier beaches is due to sand moving north along this shore since the development of the "fist" of Cape Cod at Provincetown has protected the area from northeasters (see Great Island Tombolo, site 46, for more details).

HISTORY

Bound Brook may have been named for the fact that it reached Cape Cod Bay right at the boundary between Wellfleet and Truro.

The Atwood Higgins house on Bound Brook Island was built in the early 1700s as a "half house" and was expanded over the years, reflecting the growth of wealth and population in the area. This house is a Cape Cod National Seashore interpretive site; it is open to the public in the summer. The flat parts of the island support only Pitch Pine, showing the ravages of intensive agriculture on the soil.

The railroad was completed to Provincetown in 1873. It linked the Lower Cape towns to the rest of the world, but it cut off large sections of salt marsh, restricting water flow and significantly changing the environment.

The dike at Chequesset Neck Road, at the mouth of the Herring River (see map 46), was built in 1908 with the twin goals of reducing the mosquito population and turning the salt marshes into agricultural land. The project failed in both respects; in fact mosquito populations increased as fish were excluded from the area upstream of the dike. Even worse, the project almost destroyed the Herring run in the river, and the desiccation and decomposition of the salt marsh peat still produces conditions of very low oxygen and very high acidity that have caused major fish kills. More saltwater was allowed to enter the lower section of the river beginning with a reconstruction of the tide gates in 1987. Saltmarsh plants have recovered somewhat in the area just above the dike, but the effect does not propagate very far upstream. The peat in the old marshes will continue to decay in the areas above the reach of tidewater. This decay process will continue to deplete the oxygen in the water, release sulfuric acid into the river, and lower the level of old marshes until salt water is restored to the system. The processes of salt marsh restoration are being studied in the Scusset Marshes (see site 17), and in Hatches Harbor (see site 50). There is hope that a restoration project may be started here.

WHAT'S TO SEE AND DO

Paddle the Herring River
The upper reaches of the Herring River feel like wilderness—obvious signs of modern civilization are quickly left behind. If you launch on the upstream side of Bound Brook Island Road you can paddle the Herring River upstream almost to Route 6, depending on how many trees have fallen across the stream since it was last cleared. This section of the river runs through shrub thickets of Winterberry (glorious in

fall), alder, Poison Ivy, and Bayberry, with a great many Gray Birch rising above them. In summer Swamp Roses, iris, Rose Mallow, Steeplebush, and Meadowsweet decorate the banks, and Watercress sometimes clogs the shallows. In fall migrating songbirds often fill the thickets, foraging for the plentiful berries.

The narrow river channel runs fairly straight through the center of the valley, evidence that, despite appearances, this is not wilderness. The straight channel was dug in the 1930s, in yet another attempt to control mosquitoes. The salt or brackish marshes that became fresh with the 1908 dike were completely dried out and destroyed by the channelization. The valley is now occupied by thin woods and damp thickets; all that remains of the original river are a few patches of cattails and Sphagnum Moss and some shallow dead ends.

From the downstream side of Bound Brook Island Road you can paddle to the embankment at High Toss Road, which you can portage and continue to salt water above the Chequesset Neck Road dike—a total of about 2 miles (for paddling the estuary below the dike see Great Island, site 46). Here too the river has been artificially straightened, leaving great loops of the original channel dry; the banks have been taken over by trees and shrubs. The channel cuts close to both Bound Brook and Merrick Islands, and the differences between the islands are striking. Some large trees overhang the river along Bound Brook Island, all planted species: Black Locust, Norway Maple, and apple, giving evidence of the island's agricultural past. On Merrick Island the big trees are oaks, and the ones at the foot of the slope along the river are quite large, though many show the multiple stems that indicate sprouting from stumps.

Where the bed is wider, the river is trying to redevelop the looping path of the old channel, cutting close first to one bank and then the other. The reestablishment of a more natural channel is a slow process because this is a small river and because constrictions both up- and downstream slow the water, but it is worth noting that channelization did not stop this natural process. In the shallows on the insides of the incipient meanders, banks of Bur Reeds and Water Weed are trapping sediment and beginning to build bars out from the points. The nutritious seeds of the Bur Reed attract Wood Ducks in the fall, but other than ducks, few birds use the river. This is because the acidic, low-oxygen water prevents growth of populations of the invertebrates that are the major sources of food for shorebirds. Some patches of Wild Rice are found here—look for their 4- to 6-foot stalks standing in the water.

Salt water now reaches only a short way above the dike at Chequesset Neck Road, though it must originally have reached at least to the location of Route 6. The Park Service has salvaged the Herring run with an ingenious gate and water bypass where the river leaves Herring Pond. In a labor-intensive process they test the river water and prevent the fish from leaving the pond when water conditions in the river are dangerous to them. The Herring are in a precarious position that will be resolved only by improving the harmful water chemistry with the return of salt water. The Herring have a long trip to their spawning ponds here: more than 5 miles from Wellfleet Harbor. They pass under Chequesset Neck Road, up the lower reaches of the river, and into fresh water near the High Toss Road dike, under Bound Brook Road, up the narrow channel, under the major fill and culverts of Route 6, and on up the valley to Herring Pond.

Go for a Walk or a Hike

A nice introduction to the Bound Brook area is the 3-mile loop via the old railroad bed to Ryder Beach, returning along the beach or across the dry marsh and up onto the island. To the south the railroad grade rapidly becomes overgrown once you cross the Herring River on the old trestle. The many other walks on Bound Brook and on Merrick Island will entice you back. Be sure to check out the fascinating western part of Bound Brook Island, where beach, dunes, upland, and old marsh compete for your attention. The plant community here is unusual: Bearberry (most common in dry, bare sand), Large Cranberries (freshwater bogs), Salt Marsh Hay (yes, salt marshes), Highbush Blueberries, and Beach Plum grow cheek by jowl or even intermixed. These unusual associations result from the recent closing of the barrier beach and the progressive drying of the old marshes. Some plants have persisted despite the changes—Salt Marsh Hay, for instance, originally took root when the area was salt marsh but can survive in the conditions that replaced the tides. Cranberries certainly did not grow in the salt marsh; there must be enough fresh water now to support them, for they not only survive but bear fruit.

Lombard and Paradise Hollows provide an interesting loop trip through deep oak and pine woods. Notice the relatively large oaks in the rich, protected environment of Paradise Hollow. This area is prime deer-hunting territory; best to stay away during deer-hunting season.

Explore the Ponds Afoot or Afloat

Sand roads circle the ponds, giving access to many nice areas as well as the occasional house. Most of the roads are open to vehicles, but there is little traffic. A good introduction to the area is the 2¼-mile loop from the Gull Pond landing via Higgins and Herring Ponds, the Herring River and the Old King's Highway.

Gull Pond is an extraordinarily round pond, but the kettle hole it sits in was not round—Higgins and Williams Ponds are in the same depression and were created when barrier beaches closed across sections of the original larger body of water. The kettle hole occupied by Great Pond was also quite irregular (see fig. 20, page 47). These were large kettle holes; the slope above Gull Pond on the east side rises more than 100 feet from the water surface and both ponds are deep, too—Gull Pond is 69 feet deep, more than 60 feet below sea level, and Great Pond is 59 feet deep.

Its great depth and large area make Gull a two-story pond, with deep cold water that supports trout (stocked) and warmer surface water occupied by fish like bass. A lot of fishing goes on here, both from the shore and from boats, but no boats with combustion engines are allowed. Wellfleet's Herring River runs out of Herring Pond; the Herring also spawn in Williams, Higgins, and Gull Ponds. If natural precipitation doesn't keep the sluiceway between Gull and Higgins Ponds open, it is dug out to allow passage of the Herring fry. The sluice attracts Great Blue Herons, still known locally as "cranes," which may be one of the reasons that most of the fry leave the pond at night. Most of the time the water is low enough that boats must be portaged between Higgins and Gull Ponds. Thoreau commented in the 1850s that gulls congregated on the appropriately named Gull Pond, as they do today. It is not clear what makes this pond more attractive to them than any of the others.

There are twenty ponds in this area, of all varieties—you'll find old cranberry bogs, swimming beaches, wide waters, tiny pools, havens for waterbirds, deep tree-shaded bowls, almost-swamps, and much more. Go look.

Visit the Great Beach

Until the early 1900s most people lived on the more-sheltered bay side of the peninsula and only visited the "Back Side" for the resources the Atlantic shore had to offer. There are some areas of development overlooking the Great Beach, but mostly this area is still empty. This relatively narrow beach is no place to walk during storms, but at other times it is delightful; you will soon leave most people behind and have the beach to yourself.

48. PAMET RIVER AREA AND THE GREAT BEACH, TRURO

Salt Marshes, Dunes, Beach, Fresh Water, Moors
Birdwatching, Walking, Hiking, Paddling

PREVIEW

The low, wet valley of the Pamet River cuts across the Cape from Cape Cod Bay to within a hundred yards of the Atlantic, where it is blocked by low dunes. To the north and south high cliffs face the Atlantic, topped by some of the most isolated and beautiful moors on the Cape. There are many days' worth of exploration here, both afoot and afloat, in beautiful areas that invite return visits. This area is contiguous with Bound Brook Island to the Great Beach (site 47).

ACCESS

Park in the small lot on the west side of the National Environmental Education (NEED) Center at the end of North Pamet Road or at Ballston Beach at the end of South Pamet Road (Truro residents only in summer). Launch your boat at Pamet Harbor for the saltwater portion of the river; for the freshwater section launch down the embankment by the weir east of Route 6 on the east side of South Pamet Road (park on the shoulder west of the road).

GEOLOGY

This area is outwash, deposited by meltwater streams from the South Channel lobe of the glacier. The outwash plain originally extended several miles farther east; it has eroded back to this point since the ocean reached it some six thousand years ago. The major feature here is the Pamet River, a large, flat-floored valley that runs all the way across the Cape. This valley was probably begun by spring sapping: groundwater seeped to the surface in an area now beneath Cape Cod Bay and cut its way eastward. But the Pamet River Valley is quite wide, and curved, and beneath the marshes the bottom is well below sea level. These features suggest that the valley was cut by a large, tem-

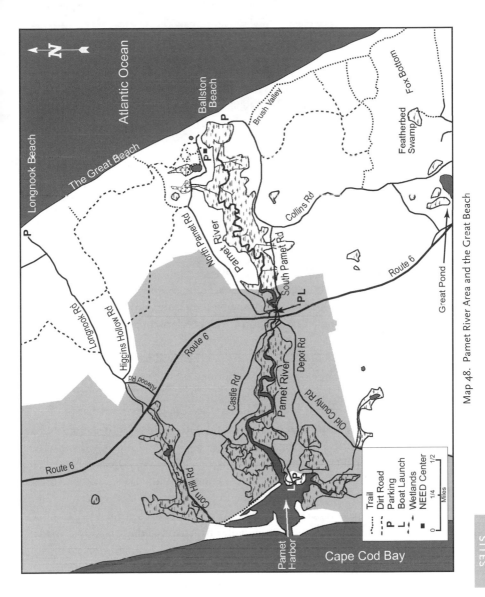

Map 48. Pamet River Area and the Great Beach

porary river formed when the glacial lake to the east drained catastrophically. The rushing waters quickly cut down through the soft
outwash, leaving a wide gash similar to the valley of the Monument
River (now occupied by the Cape Cod Canal, see site 1), which was
cut in the same way.

Since the Pamet River Valley formed, waves have cut away the sea cliffs, eroding the eastern end of the valley and exposing it to the open ocean. That opening is now blocked by a barrier beach and dunes that continually reform when they are breached by storms. There have been numerous washovers here, including those of 1896, 1933, and 1972, during the February gale of 1978, and during Hurricane Bob in 1991.

HISTORY

Pamet Harbor, now silted in, was a significant port into the 1800s, surrounded by wharves, warehouses, fish flakes, and shipyards—the infrastructure of a maritime economy. The town centered on the river, with houses thickly clustered on both sides. An early bridge was located about where Route 6 crosses now, where the valley is narrowest.

WHAT'S TO SEE AND DO

Explore the Moors

A pleasant introduction to the area is the ½-mile round-trip to Bear-berry Overlook just north of the NEED Center, down into the nearby kettle hole, and along the pond. The overlook provides a spectacular 360-degree view of the Pamet River, the dunes and Atlantic Ocean, the hills to the north and south, and the pond and former cranberry bog below. The bogs were abandoned when they were acquired by the National Seashore in 1963.

Both north and south of the river valley are large stretches of open country crossed with old roads and paths. This can be some of the most beautiful walking on the Cape. For a longer hike try the 5-mile loop north on the gravel road just east of the NEED Center to Higgins Hollow Road, across to Longnook Hollow Road, and back via the beach. Or go only partway and enjoy both the tapestry of the hills and the panorama of the Atlantic from one of the several overlooks. To the south the hills provide equally attractive walking on similar roads and trails. In fact you can walk all the way to Gull Pond in Wellfleet via parts of the Old King's Highway and the younger roads and trails. In a few places the lip of the sea cliff dips down, and trails reach the beach. Be careful at the edge of the cliff; it can avalanche unexpectedly.

The small pond just northeast of the NEED Center is deep in a sheltered kettle hole. Its slopes are clothed with Bayberry, blueberries, Beach Plum, and Poison Ivy, which provide food for birds well into the early winter. From the road above you get a grandstand view.

Walk the Great Beach

The narrow beach backed by dunes here on the Back Side gives way both north and south to an equally narrow beach backed by the 100- to 150-foot sea cliffs of Truro. This is an isolated stretch of beach in either direction—almost 3 miles south to Newcomb Hollow in Wellfleet and 2 miles north to Longnook Hollow, with 3 empty miles beyond that to Highland Beach. In heavy weather there is little beach here; waves can wash all the way to the foot of the cliff—beach walking at such times can be hazardous.

In many stretches of the cliff here, especially to the south, thick layers of clay and silt are exposed; they were deposited in the bottom of the glacial lake that formed mostly east of the Lower Cape.

The flotsam on the beach is evidence of the large numbers of fishing boats that work offshore; the floats, lines, and other gear they have lost litters the sand.

Paddle the Pamet

The Pamet River is best explored by small boat. From Pamet Harbor on Cape Cod Bay to Route 6 the tidal river meanders through salt marshes filled with birds. If you launch in the harbor a couple of hours after low tide, you can ride the last of the flood up toward Route 6 and have slack or ebb on the way back down. The salt marshes around the harbor are interesting too.

The section of the river east of Route 6 is fresh water, so there is no tide. Because the groundwater lenses that feed this section of the river are small and low (less than 10 feet above sea level), dry weather can quickly lower the level of the river. The river meanders through the marsh in its almost-level valley, dissolving tannin from the peat in its long, slow course. By the time it reaches Route 6, the river looks more like espresso than water.

The marshes are quite heavily wooded with Winterberry and Bayberry, above the banks of Wide-leaved Cattails. This is probably a recent change—the road embankments have shut out the tides and erased the former gradation from salt marshes in the lower reaches to brackish or fresh water in the eastern section, allowing the woody vegetation to take over. The river alternates between shallow pools and somewhat deeper channels, though the bottom is mucky everywhere. Except in a strong east wind this area is quite sheltered.

49. HIGH HEAD AND HEAD OF THE MEADOW BEACH, TRURO

Woodlands, Swamp, Marshes, Dunes, Beach
Walking, Birdwatching

PREVIEW
High Head is the northernmost end of the glacial deposits on the Cape, edged by old wave-cut bluffs that provide stunning views of the dunes and ocean beyond. There is lots of good walking both on trails and on the beach. Fall is the most beautiful time—the thickets become a rich tapestry of colors, and the bike trail is often deserted, even on weekends. This area is part of the Cape Cod National Seashore.

ACCESS
Pilgrim Heights Road leads to parking and the trailheads for Small's Swamp and Pilgrim Spring Trails. High Head Road gives access to the north end of Head of the Meadow Bike Trail and a sand road across the dunes to the beach. Parking for Head of the Meadow Beach and the south end of the bike trail is at the end of Head of the Meadow Road—in summer the National Seashore (CCNS on the map) charges a fee, and the Truro parking is by resident sticker only. On the south side of Route 6 is parking for the Truro High Head Conservation Area, which has a different view.

GEOLOGY
The uplands here are outwash, the sand and gravel washed away from the front of the South Channel lobe of the glacier by meltwater streams. The trails have cut down through the vegetation and soil, exposing the layer of wind-polished rocks that were created after the glacier melted but before plants anchored the sand. This layer was probably buried more deeply, under a layer of soil, before the early settlers cut the trees.

The bluffs bounding High Head on the north and west were cut by ocean waves after the glacier melted and sea level rose. Georges Bank, to the east, was above sea level and protected the Cape from

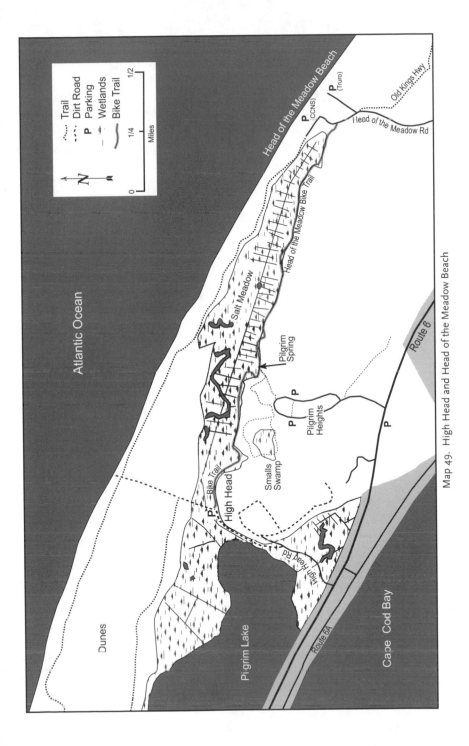

Map 49. High Head and Head of the Meadow Beach

southeasterly swells for a time, so eroded sand moved south alongshore. The sea cliffs had eroded back to this point on High Head when Georges Bank was finally covered by the sea, some six thousand years ago; sand then began to move north alongshore, under the influence of southeasterly winds. The sand that moved north was deposited at the foot of the High Head cliffs, protecting them and beginning the process of building the "fist" of Cape Cod. These old, vegetation-covered cliffs are not as steep as they used to be, nor as steep as those currently being cut by the ocean; they have slumped and slipped until they reached "the angle of repose." Active ocean cliffs, by contrast, are continually cut away at the base, which keeps them steep and prevents the establishment of plants that take longer than Beach Grass to grow.

HISTORY

"Pilgrim Spring" below High Head on the north has been identified by some as the spring encountered by an exploring party from the *Mayflower* in November 1620.

In 1851 "Minot's Gale" breached the dunes at the head of Salt Meadow. This raised concerns of a permanent inlet and the destruction of Provincetown Harbor. To prevent this, dikes were built across Salt Meadow, and Beach Grass was planted to stabilize and rebuild the dunes. The construction of the dike that carried the railroad across the mouth of what had previously been called "East Harbor" completed its transition to "Pilgrim Lake." Over time Pilgrim Lake became fresh water, as did Salt Meadow, which nevertheless retained its old name. The dike and roadbed across the marsh at High Head Road restrict water flow, probably speeding the filling of the marsh.

This area, like most open space on the Cape, is reverting to natural vegetation from agricultural land. The most recent use was the farm of the Small family, who raised cows, corn, and asparagus here until the 1920s. The farm buildings were down in the kettle hole, near the swamp, for protection from the wind. Reminders of the farm are planted apple trees and other domesticated plants, and the worn-out soil.

WHAT'S TO SEE AND DO

Go Walking from Pilgrim Heights

Two loops of improved trail, each about ¾ mile, begin near the interpretive shelter on Pilgrim Heights. The Small's Swamp Trail leads immediately downhill into the kettle hole, which you can see from the edge of the bluff. This wooded swamp is thick with Highbush Blueberries, Winterberry, and Swamp Azalea; it is beautiful in bloom and when the leaves color. The slopes above the swamp are mostly covered in shining Bearberry, though Pitch Pines and Quaking Aspens are creeping in. To the east the trail climbs back up to the heights, giving spectacular views of the Atlantic Ocean, the dunes, and Salt Meadow. Salt Meadow is cut by ditches, perhaps for mosquito control. You can see the paths of the ditches by following the lines of shrubs that have grown up on the higher and drier linear spoil piles.

The Pilgrim Spring Trail provides fewer views; it leads through the brush-choked valley of the spring, where Winterberry, cattails, and ferns give evidence of abundant water. There is a plaque noting the spring and its possible history too.

Head of the Meadow Trail

This paved bicycle trail connects Head of the Meadow Beach with High Head, following the route of the Old King's Highway along the foot of the old wave-cut cliffs. The thickets obscure most potential views of the dunes and marsh but provide a likely place to see small birds, especially in spring and fall. Trailing Arbutus, typical of shaded woods, and Broom Crowberry, which usually prefers bare sandy soils, grow in unlikely fellowship in the mowed verge.

Hawk Watch in Spring

Pilgrim Heights has long been known as a place to see migrating raptors from mid-April to late May. They fly north along the ocean cliff, so they are close and at eye level as they pass High Head. The Wellfleet Bay Wildlife Sanctuary (see map, site 45) has conducted hawk watches there in spring, sometimes seeing as many as two hundred raptors on a favorable flight day. Sharp-shinned Hawks are the most common raptors seen here, but fourteen species have been identified and counted, including Bald Eagles and Northern Goshawks.

Head of the Meadow Beach

At the eastern end of the bike trail, Head of the Meadow Beach has all the attractions of the Atlantic shore. Dunes rise as high as 50 feet, and the beach here, behind its offshore bars, is splendid. A trail leads north from the north end of the parking lot along the edge of the marsh. Highland Beach is about ½ mile south; beyond that it is about 3 miles to Longnook Beach (see site 48).

50. PROVINCELANDS AND THE GREAT BEACH, PROVINCETOWN

Salt Water, Beaches, Dunes, Woodlands, Ponds, Bogs
Birdwatching, Walking

PREVIEW

In Provincetown the Great Beach on the North Atlantic stretches for 5½ miles of severe beauty, backed by the Provincelands, a wild country of dune, woods, bogs, ponds, and sand. Although parts of this area can be crowded in summer, especially on weekends, the vast majority of the crowd is concentrated in narrow zones close to their vehicles. If the bicycle traffic is not too heavy, the bike trail is good walking. Sand roads and footpaths lead to many less-visited areas. This area is part of the Cape Cod National Seashore. Walkers should be aware that vehicles are permitted on most of the Great Beach from April 15 to November 15.

ACCESS

Park at Race Point Beach or Herring Cove Beach (fee in summer), at Provincelands Visitor Center, at the Beech Forest, off Route 6 opposite Snail Road, or off Provincelands Road. Many areas can be reached via the bike trail.

GEOLOGY

Geologically speaking, Provincetown is young, even by Cape Cod standards. All of Provincetown, actually the entire area west of High Head in Truro (see site 49), was created in the last six thousand years—some twelve thousand years after the glacier melted. Currents moving north along the shore began to build this sandy land once Georges Bank, which had been dry land, was finally covered as sea level rose to within 50 feet of today's level. Provincetown is built on nothing but sand—clean, mobile sand—that has been washed and winnowed out of the glacial deposits in Wellfleet and Truro by waves and wind.

Lower Cape Sites

SITES

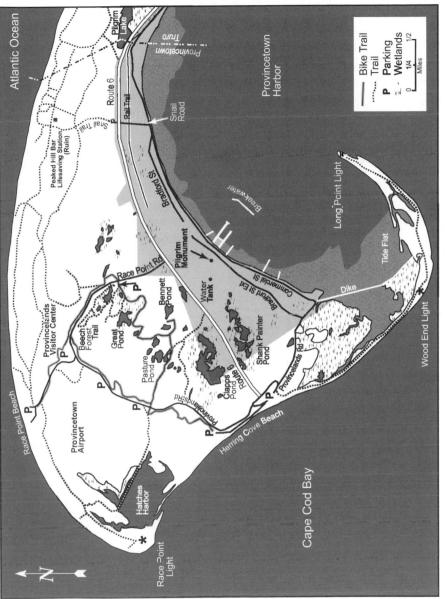

Map 50. Provincelands and the Great Beach

The foundation of the Provincelands was a sand spit, similar to Sandy Neck (see site 21) or Nauset Beach (site 41) that began building west in the lee of the northern end of the Cape six thousand years ago. But at that time glacial deposits extended about a mile farther northeast, so the original spits began in areas that are now well offshore. Over the past six thousand years the cliffs have eroded, and sand has built north and west, eventually creating all of Provincetown. The eastern side of the old sand spit has eroded too, in line with the cliffs; waves and currents keep soft, sandy shorelines smooth. That is why the spit northeast of Pilgrim Lake and Salt Meadow (see site 49) is so narrow—the waves and currents have eroded the old seaward portion, as the cliffs that allowed it to form have themselves been eroded.

Today Race Point continues to build slowly westward as sand eroded from the beach and sea cliffs is deposited on the end of the spit. The westward construction is slow because Race Point is being built into deep water—300 yards west of the shore the water is almost 200 feet deep—and because strong currents around the point move some of the sand south to form Wood End and Long Point, which are also building out into deep water.

In the Provincelands, dunes dominate the landscape, forming steep-sided hills that rise above the low-lying valleys between them. These valleys formed between successive sand spits and dune ridges as the spits built west. Although they are close to sea level, the valleys contain freshwater wetlands, as they have for some thousand years since sea level rose high enough to raise the groundwater table into the sand deposits. This rise in the groundwater may have contributed to the growth of vegetation that stabilized the dunes, leading to the forested sand hills encountered by the Pilgrims.

HISTORY

Provincetown Harbor was the first anchorage of the *Mayflower* in 1620. Although the Pilgrims reported good soil and well-wooded uplands, they ultimately opted for Plymouth over Provincetown. But farmers and fishermen returned ere long, and within a hundred years they had stripped the dunes of trees and shrubs in the process of cutting wood and clearing fields for farming. Once the forest was cleared, the soil quickly eroded, and the unanchored dunes started to move into the harbor and town. The potential burial of the town was eventually prevented by planting Beach Grass on the dunes and a windbreak of various trees around the town; you can still see the evidence in the numbers of introduced trees that occur here and nowhere else on the Cape. Nevertheless some of the dunes are quite active and are encroaching on woods, ponds, and bogs in several places.

WHAT'S TO SEE AND DO

Walk the Beaches

From the remains of the old Peaked Bar Lifesaving Station close to the Truro town line to Race Point and south to Woods End and Long Point, there is a great deal of beach to explore. In summer Herring Cove and Race Point Beaches are jam-packed, but other seasons and other areas invite those looking for less-human nature. The Provincetown Atlantic beach can be a bit disorienting at first—it runs east-west. If you are looking for miles of unobstructed walking, this is a good place. Vehicles are allowed in much of this area, though the area west from High Head is closed from April through the third week in July. Nevertheless, at times the beach can be a lonely place, with only the birds for company. Birdwatching is good in many seasons, especially after northeasters, when oceanic birds such as shearwaters, Gannets, and Razorbills can be seen from shore.

Explore the Dunes

For the determined walker the dunes of the Provincelands offer almost endless possibilities. Trails (many are soft sand, hence the need for determination) and sand roads cross the area, providing access to this varied land of live sand, natural cranberry bogs, tough shrubs, and trees—and wind, almost always wind. Try to stay on the trails and off the vegetation that anchors the sand, for damage to the plants means damage to the dunes. Inholdings of private property exist in the area, one of the reasons for the roads and the vehicles on them. A good introduction is the 1½-mile walk to the beach and back from the Snail Trail parking area. Be sure to check out the bogs among the dunes here, with their many wetland plants.

Explore the Beech Forest Area

The 1¼-mile Beech Forest Trail is a nice introduction to this extraordinary place. Here in a deep defile between two old sand dunes lies a shallow pond surrounded by forest (the Beeches are as much as 120 years old and may have sprouted from much older root systems).

Other such ponds and forests must lie buried beneath some of the active dunes. In addition to the large American Beech trees, the woods include Red Maple, Gray Birches, Tupelo, and Sassafras. This is a famous birdwatching locale, especially in spring, when great numbers of migrating warblers can often be seen in the thickets, resting and eating for the next leg of their trip north. The pond is very shallow, as you can see from the Water Lilies, Pickerelweed, and Bur Reed emerging from the water. As you walk around the pond and on the loop to the north, notice how suddenly you move from one environment to another where the conditions change—old stable dune, moving dune, swamp, open water. On the west side of the pond an active sand dune is burying the old forest. The dune supports mostly Pitch Pines and other such barren-sand pioneers, though Sphagnum Moss grows incongruously in one area, presumably wicking water upward through its buried stems. Here in the middle of the woods you can often hear the surprising sound of the foghorn 2 miles away on Race Point.

The segment of the bike path between the Beech Forest and Provincelands Road is particularly interesting, passing close to a number of small ponds, along some abandoned cranberry bogs (note the straight ditches), and through the varied woods that have resulted from clearing, planting, and dune movement.

Explore Hatches Harbor
The dike across Hatches Harbor, which allows you to reach the dunes and the beach from Provincelands Road, was built in the 1930s for mosquito control. Not only was the project a failure at mosquito control—it excluded the fish that eat mosquito larvae—but it destroyed 100 acres of productive salt marsh. In 1999 the Park Service began a project to restore some of that lost marsh. They have increased the size of the culverts to allow the tides to enter the former marshes, which are now dominated by Phragmites. The culverts have gates that are being opened a little more each year for a five- to ten-year period to make a gradual transition to tidal conditions. It will be interesting to see how the restoration area reacts, and to watch for the reestablishment of saltwater species.

The area between the dike and Provinceland Road has some prolific wild cranberry bogs.

On an easterly wind you could paddle here from Herring Cove Beach and explore the shallow harbor by boat.

LIST OF BIRDS REGULARLY SEEN

In this list of birds regularly seen on Cape Cod, related birds are grouped, and groups are in a more or less standard taxonomic order. Most field guides to birds are organized along these lines. To break the list up and make it easier to find the bird you are looking for, large groups of related birds are designated with headings; smaller groups have no headings. Abundance is shown as C (common), U (uncommon), and R (rare) for the indicated habitat and season.

Name	Habitat	Abundance	Season
Red-throated Loon	Bays/sounds	U	Winter
Common Loon	Bays/sounds	C	Year-round
Pied-billed Grebe	Ponds/marshes/bays	U	Year-round
Horned Grebe	Ponds/bays/sounds	U	Winter
Red-necked Grebe	Bays/sounds	R	Winter
Northern Fulmar	Ocean/open bays	R	Fall/winter
Cory's Shearwater	Ocean/open bays	R	Fall/winter
Greater Shearwater	Ocean/open bays	R	Fall/winter
Sooty Shearwater	Ocean/open bays	R	Fall/winter
Manx Shearwater	Ocean/open bays	R	Fall/winter
Wilson's Storm-Petrel	Ocean/open bays	R	Fall/winter
Leach's Storm-Petrel	Ocean/open bays	R	Fall/winter
Northern Gannet	Ocean/open bays	C	Fall/winter/spring
Great Cormorant	Ponds/bays/sounds	U	Winter
Double-crested Cormorant	Ponds/bays/sounds	C	Spring/summer/fall

Herons and Related Birds

Name	Habitat	Abundance	Season
American Bittern	Marshes	R	Year-round
Great Blue Heron	Wetlands/ponds	C	Year-round
Great Egret	Wetlands	U	Summer
Snowy Egret	Marshes	C	Summer
Little Blue Heron	Marshes	R	Summer
Tricolored Heron	Marshes	R	Summer
Cattle Egret	Marshes/grass	R	Spring/fall

Name	Habitat	Abundance	Season
Green Heron	Wetlands	R	Summer
Black-crowned Night-Heron	Ponds/marshes	C	Year-round
Yellow-crowned Night-Heron	Ponds/marshes	R	Summer
Glossy Ibis	Marshes	R	Spring/summer
Swans, Geese, and Ducks			
Mute Swan	Ponds/bays/sounds	C	Year-round
Snow Goose	Ponds/bays/sounds	R	Winter
Brant	Bays/sounds	C	Winter
Canada Goose	Ponds/bays/sounds	C	Year-round
Wood Duck	Swamps/ponds	U	Year-round
Northern Shoveler	Bays/ponds/marshes	R	Summer/fall
Green-winged Teal	Bays/ponds/marshes	C	Summer
Blue-winged Teal	Ponds/marshes	C	Summer
Harlequin Duck	Bays/sounds	R	Winter
Black Duck	Wetlands	C	Year-round
Mallard	Ponds/marshes	C	Year-round
Gadwall	Ponds/marshes	U	Year-round
American Widgeon	Wetlands/bays	U	Year-round
Eurasian Widgeon	Wetlands/bays	R	Fall/winter
Northern Pintail	Bays/marshes	U	Year-round
Canvasback	Bays/marshes	C	Winter
Redhead	Ponds/bays	U	Winter
Ring-necked Duck	Coastal ponds/bays	U	Winter
Greater Scaup	Ponds/bays	C	Winter
Lesser Scaup	Ponds/bays	U	Winter
Common Eider	Bays/sounds/ocean	C	Winter
King Eider	Sounds/ocean	R	Winter
Oldsquaw	Bays/sounds	C	Winter
Black Scoter	Bays/sounds	C	Year-round
Surf Scoter	Bays/sounds	C	Year-round
White-winged Scoter	Bays/sounds	C	Year-round
Common Goldeneye	Ponds/bays	C	Winter
Barrow's Goldeneye	Ponds/bays	R	Winter
Bufflehead	Ponds/bays	C	Winter

Birds Regularly Seen

Name	Habitat	Abundance	Season
Hooded Merganser	Ponds/bays	U	Winter
Common Merganser	Ponds/bays	C	Winter
Red-breasted Merganser	Ponds/bays	C	Winter
Ruddy Duck	Ponds/bays	U	Winter

Raptors

Name	Habitat	Abundance	Season
Turkey Vulture	Soaring	U	Spring/summer/fall
Bald Eagle	Shores/soaring	R	Winter
Northern Harrier	Marshes	U	Year-round
Sharp-shinned Hawk	Woods/thickets	C	Year-round
Cooper's Hawk	Woodlands	R	Year-round
Northern Goshawk	Irregular	R	Fall/winter/spring
Red-shouldered Hawk	Woods/swamps	R	Year-round
Broad-winged Hawk	Woods	U	Summer
Rough-legged Hawk	Open country	U	Winter
Red-tailed Hawk	Woods/marsh	U	Year-round
Osprey	Marsh/bay/soaring	C	Spring/summer
American Kestrel	Forest edge/fields	U	Year-round
Merlin	Woods	R	Spring/fall
Peregrine Falcon	Open country	R	Migrating
Ring-necked Pheasant	Fields/marshes	U	Year-round
Ruffed Grouse	Woods	U	Year-round
Northern Bobwhite	Woods/fields	C	Year-round
Wild Turkey	Woods/fields	U	Year-round
Clapper Rail	Marshes	R	Year-round
Virginia Rail	Marshes	R	Year-round
Sora	Marshes	R	Summer
American Coot	Ponds/marshes/bays	U	Fall/winter/spring
Common Moorhen (Gallinule)	Ponds/marshes/bays	R	Summer/fall/winter

Shorebirds

Name	Habitat	Abundance	Season
American Oystercatcher	Shores/tidal flats	U	Summer
Piping Plover	Shores	C	Summer
Semipalmated Plover	Shores/tidal flats	C	Summer
Killdeer	Fields/shore	U	Year-round

Name	Habitat	Abundance	Season
Black-bellied Plover	Shores	C	Spring/fall
Lesser Golden Plover	Shores	U	Spring/fall
Whimbrel	Shores	U	Late summer
Willet	Marshes/shores	U	Summer
Greater Yellowlegs	Marshes/shores	C	Spring/fall
Lesser Yellowlegs	Marshes/shores	U	Spring/fall
Solitary Sandpiper	Shores	U	Spring/fall
Spotted Sandpiper	Shores	C	Summer
Upland Sandpiper	Fields/meadows	U	Spring/summer
Short-billed Dowitcher	Shores	C	Migrating
Long-billed Dowitcher	Shores	R	Late summer/fall
Common Snipe	Marshes	U	Year-round
Woodcock	Woods/swamps	U	Summer
Ruddy Turnstone	Shores	C	Winter/migrating
Sanderling	Shores	C	Year-round
Hudsonian Godwit	Shores/marshes	U	Summer/early fall
Marbled Godwit	Shores/marshes	R	Summer/fall
Purple Sandpiper	Rocky shores	R	Winter
Dunlin	Shores	U	Winter
Stilt Sandpiper	Shores	U	Fall
Buff-breasted Sandpiper	Shores	U	Fall
Red Knot	Shores	C	Migrating
Semipalmated Sandpiper	Shores	C	Migrating
Western Sandpiper	Shores	U	Summer/fall
Least Sandpiper	Marshes/shores	C	Migrating
White-rumped Sandpiper	Shores	U	Summer/fall
Baird's Sandpiper	Shores	R	Fall
Pectoral Sandpiper	Shores	R	Fall
Wilson's Phalarope	Ocean/open bays	U	Late summer/fall
Red Phalarope	Ocean/open bays	R	Spring/fall/northeasters
Red-necked Phalarope	Ocean/open bays	U	Spring/fall/northeasters

Gulls and Related Birds

Name	Habitat	Abundance	Season
Pomarine Jaeger	Ocean/open bays	R	Fall/northeasters
Parasitic Jaeger	Ocean/open bays	U	Fall/northeasters

Name	Habitat	Abundance	Season
Common Black-headed Gull	Bays/shores	R	Winter
Laughing Gull	Shores	C	Summer/fall
Bonaparte's Gull	Shores	U	Fall/winter
Ring-billed Gull	Ponds/shores	C	Fall/winter/spring
Iceland Gull	Shores	R	Winter
Herring Gull	Ponds/shores	C	Year-round
Great Black-backed Gull	Shores	C	Year-round
Lesser Black-backed Gull	Shores	R	Winter
Glaucous Gull	Shores	R	Fall/winter
Black-legged Kittiwake	Bays/shores	C	Fall/winter/spring
Arctic Tern	Beach/bays/sounds	U	Summer
Sandwich Tern	Beach/bays/sounds	R	Summer
Forster's Tern	Beach/bays/sounds	U	Fall
Common Tern	Beach/bays/sounds	C	Summer
Least Tern	Beach/bays/sounds	C	Summer
Roseate Tern	Beach/bays/sounds	U	Summer
Black Tern	Shores	R	Late summer
Black Skimmer	Coastal ponds	R	Late summer
Dovekie	Ocean/open bays	R	Winter
Razorbill	Ocean/open bays	U	Winter
Common Murre	Ocean/open bays	R	Winter
Thick-billed Murre	Ocean/open bays	U	Winter
Black Guillemot	Ocean/open bays	U	Winter
Atlantic Puffin	Ocean/open bays	R	Winter
Rock Dove	Fields/bridges	C	Year-round
Mourning Dove	Woods/fields/yards	C	Year-round
Black-billed Cuckoo	Thickets	U	Summer
Yellow-billed Cuckoo	Thickets	U	Summer

Owls

Name	Habitat	Abundance	Season
Barn Owl	Towns/woods	R	Year-round
Short-eared Owl	Marshes/dunes	R	Summer
Snowy Owl	Open areas	R	Winter
Eastern Screech Owl	Woods/swamps	U	Year-round
Great Horned Owl	Woods/fields	C	Year-round

Name	Habitat	Abundance	Season
Long-eared Owl	Woods/trees	R	Year-round
Northern Saw-whet Owl	Woods/conifers	R	Year-round
Whip-poor-will	Woods	U	Summer
Common Nighthawk	Open areas	R	Summer
Chimney Swift	Flying	C	Summer
Ruby-throated Hummingbird	Flowers/gardens	C	Summer
Belted Kingfisher	Ponds/wetlands	U	Year-round
Red-headed Woodpecker	Woods	R	Fall/winter/spring
Red-bellied Woodpecker	Woods	R	Year-round
Downy Woodpecker	Woods	C	Year-round
Hairy Woodpecker	Woods	U	Year-round
Northern Flicker	Woods/lawns	C	Year-round
Yellow-bellied Sapsucker	Woods	R	Winter

Flycatchers

Name	Habitat	Abundance	Season
Olive-sided Flycatcher	Woods	R	Spring/fall
Eastern Kingbird	Wood margins/fields	C	Summer
Western Kingbird	Wood margins/fields	R	Fall
Great Crested Flycatcher	Open woods	C	Summer
Eastern Phoebe	Woods/marshes/yards	U	Summer
Willow Flycatcher	Woods	R	Summer
Alder Flycatcher	Woods	R	Migrating
Least Flycatcher	Woods	R	Migrating
Eastern Wood-peewee	Woods	C	Summer
Horned Lark	Fields/shores	C	Year-round
Tree Swallow	Fields/marshes	C	Summer
Bank Swallow	Near water	U	Summer
Northern Rough-winged Swallow	Banks near water	C	Summer
Barn Swallow	Buildings/fields	C	Summer
Cliff Swallow	Woods/open areas	R	Spring/fall
Purple Martin	Woods/open areas	R	Summer
Blue Jay	Woods	C	Year-round
American Crow	Woods/fields	C	Year-round
Black-capped Chickadee	Woods/thickets	C	Year-round

Name	Habitat	Abundance	Season
Tufted Titmouse	Woods	C	Year-round
Red-breasted Nuthatch	Conifers	U	Winter
White-breasted Nuthatch	Woods	U	Year-round
Brown Creeper	Woods	U	Year-round
House Wren	Woods/thickets	U	Summer
Carolina Wren	Woods/thickets	C	Year-round
Winter Wren	Woods/thickets	R	Winter
Marsh Wren	Marshes	U	Year-round
Golden-crowned Kinglet	Conifer woods	C	Fall/winter
Ruby-crowned Kinglet	Conifer woods	U	Fall/winter
Blue-gray Gnatcatcher	Woods/thickets	U	Summer
Eastern Bluebird	Wood margins/fields	R	Year-round
Wood Thrush	Moist woods	U	Summer
Gray-cheeked Thrush	Woods	R	Spring/fall
Swainson's Thrush	Woods	U	Spring/fall
Veery	Moist woods	R	Summer
Hermit Thrush	Conifer woods	R	Winter
American Robin	Fields/woods	C	Year-round
Gray Catbird	Thickets/woods	C	Year-round
Northern Mockingbird	Thickets/woods	C	Year-round
Brown Thrasher	Thickets/woods	U	Year-round
Water Pipit	Fields	R	Spring/fall
Cedar Waxwing	Woods	U	Year-round
Northern Shrike	Marshes/thickets	R	Spring/fall
European Starling	Fields/woods	C	Year-round
Red-eyed Vireo	Woods	C	Summer
White-eyed Vireo	Woods	R	Summer
Solitary Vireo	Woods	R	Spring/fall
Warbling Vireo	Woods	R	Spring/fall
Philadelphia Vireo	Woods	U	Late summer

Warblers

Name	Habitat	Abundance	Season
Blue-winged Warbler	Woods	R	Summer
Golden-winged Warbler	Woods	R	Late summer
Tennessee Warbler	Woods	U	Spring/fall

Name	Habitat	Abundance	Season
Orange-crowned Warbler	Brush/woods	U	Migrating
Nashville Warbler	Woods	U	Spring/fall
Northern Parula Warbler	Woods/swamps	C	Summer
Black-and-white Warbler	Woods	C	Summer
Black-throated Blue Warbler	Thickets	U	Spring/fall
Chestnut-sided Warbler	Shrubs/thickets	R	Summer
Blackburnian Warbler	Woods/thickets	U	Spring/summer
Yellow-throated Warbler	Woods/thickets	R	Spring/fall
Yellow-rumped Warbler	Thickets near water	C	Fall/winter
Magnolia Warbler	Woods	C	Spring/fall
Cape May Warbler	Thickets	C	Spring/fall
Black-throated Green Warbler	Thickets	C	Spring/fall
Prairie Warbler	Low in woods	C	Summer
Bay-breasted Warbler	Woods	U	Spring/fall
Blackpoll Warbler	Conifers	C	Migrating
Pine Warbler	Woods/pines	C	Year-round
Palm Warbler	Woods/field margins	C	Spring/fall
Prothonotary Warbler	Woods/thickets	R	Spring/fall
Worm-eating Warbler	Woods/thickets	R	Spring/fall
Yellow Warbler	Moist woods	C	Summer
Kentucky Warbler	Woods	R	Spring/fall
Connecticut Warbler	Woods	R	Fall
Mourning Warbler	Woods	R	Spring/fall
Ovenbird	Woods	C	Summer/fall
Northern Waterthrush	Woods	U	Spring/fall
Common Yellowthroat	Thickets/marshes	C	Summer
Hooded Warbler	Woods	R	Spring/fall
Wilson's Warbler	Woods	U	Spring/fall
Redstart	Forest understory	C	Summer
Canada Warbler	Woods	U	Spring/fall
Yellow-breasted Chat	Thickets	R	Year-round
Rose-breasted Grosbeak	Thickets/woods	U	Summer
Scarlet Tanager	Woods	U	Summer
Northern Cardinal	Woods	C	Year-round

Name	Habitat	Abundance	Season
Blue Grosbeak	Woods	R	Spring/fall
Indigo Bunting	Thickets/woods	R	Summer
Rufous-sided Towhee	Woods	C	Year-round
American Tree Sparrow	Thickets/fields	U	Winter
Chipping Sparrow	Wood edges/fields	C	Spring/summer
Clay-colored Sparrow	Fields	R	Fall/winter
Vesper Sparrow	Fields	R	Summer/fall
Lark Sparrow	Fields	R	Fall
Savannah Sparrow	Fields	C	Year-round
Grasshopper Sparrow	Fields	R	Migrating
Sharp-tailed Sparrow	Marshes	C	Year-round
Seaside Sparrow	Marshes	U	Year-round
Field Sparrow	Fields/woods	U	Year-round
Song Sparrow	Thickets/marshes	C	Year-round
Lincoln's Sparrow	Moist thickets	U	Migrating
Swamp Sparrow	Bogs/marshes	U	Year-round
White-throated Sparrow	Thickets/brush	C	Winter
White-crowned Sparrow	Woods/thickets	U	Winter
Fox Sparrow	Thickets/brush	U	Winter
Dark-eyed Junco	Woods/thickets	U	Winter
Lapland Longspur	Fields/beaches	U	Fall/winter/spring
Snow Bunting	Fields/dunes/beaches	U	Winter

Blackbirds and Orioles

Name	Habitat	Abundance	Season
Red-winged Blackbird	Wetlands	C	Spring/Summer/Fall
Eastern Meadowlark	Fields	U	Year-round
Bobolink	Fields	U	Summer
Rusty Blackbird	Swamps	U	Winter
Brown-headed Cowbird	Fields/woods	C	Spring/summer/fall
Common Grackle	Fields	C	Spring/summer/fall
Orchard Oriole	Orchards/woods	U	Summer
Northern Oriole (Baltimore)	Tall trees/woods	C	Summer
House Finch	Woods/thickets	C	Year-round
Pine Siskin	Conifer woods	U	Winter
American Goldfinch	Woods/thickets	C	Year-round

Name	Habitat	Abundance	Season
White-winged Crossbill	Conifers	R	Winter
Pine Grosbeak	Conifers	R	Fall/winter
Evening Grosbeak	Conifers	C	Winter
Common Redpoll	Fields	R	Winter
Purple Finch	Woods	U	Year-round
House Sparrow	Towns/farms	C	Year-round

Birds Regularly Seen

ACKNOWLEDGMENTS

During the course of a three-year project covering the entire Cape, more than 5,000 road miles, and hundreds of miles of trails and waterways, I have enjoyed the advice, assistance, and company of many helpful people. I am immensely grateful to them all.

Dick Backus, Molly Cornell, Dave Crary, Mario DiGregorio, Fred Dunford, Jennifer Gaines, Maggie Geist, Anne Giblin, John Hobbie, Aimlee Laderman, Evelyn Martin, Chris Neill, Tim Parshall, Pam Polloni, John Portnoy, Rob Thieler, Sarah Twichell, Dave Twichell, Ivan Valiela, Dave Whittaker, and Chris Weidman generously gave technical information and advice on everything from *Ammophila* to zooplankton. Lee Baldwin, Richard Carey, Bobye Coyle, Sue Donovan, Barbara Dougan, Shelley Fenily, Pam Goguen, Tom and Ginny Gregg, Darcy Karle, Natalie Mariano, Bill Meyer, Betsy Morris, Nancy Soderberg, Zoltan Szego, Gene Valli, and numerous others in libraries and town offices helped find information, books, and maps and provided many kinds of valuable help and support. Molly Cornell, Pam Goguen, Archana Joshee, Vicky Lowell, Ashley Meyer, Audrey Meyer, and Gary Schwarzman covered many miles of trail or water with me, adding both pleasure and their own unique perspectives. Thanks to Tucker Clark, Becky Lash, and Patrice Buxton for their ongoing encouragement and careful reading of the manuscript, and to Will Hively for meticulously riding herd on the details. And special thanks to Gary for his sharp eye and critical and independent judgment, and for his forbearance and constant support.

I especially appreciate the time, thought, and expertise of the reviewers who cast their careful eyes over the science in the book. Mario DiGregorio reviewed the botany; Jim O'Connell and Rich Williams reviewed the geology at late and early stages respectively. Jerry Melillo reviewed the entire book with special attention to ecology and climate, and Dave Whittaker did the same for marine biology. They made many helpful suggestions and did not press me too hard to include more details from their own areas of interest. Whatever faults remain, whether of omission or commission, are mine, and probably reflect basic character flaws; the reviewers did their best to correct them.

B.C.S.

SUGGESTED READING AND RESOURCES

Books

Cape Cod. 1865. By Henry David Thoreau. Many later editions.
The original Cape Cod nature narrative provides historical perspective and interesting commentary on the Mid- and Lower Cape.

The Outermost House. 1928. By Henry Beston, Ballantine Books.
The classic account of a year on Nauset Beach. Wonderful descriptions of the beach and its inhabitants. Makes clear how much has changed and yet how much is unchanged.

The House on Nauset Marsh. [1947], 1997. By Wyman Richardson. Countryman Press.
Wyman Richardson loved the Nauset Marsh and the surrounding country. With this book you can follow his walks and paddles and find many of the same delights.

The Run. 1959. By John Hay. Doubleday.
The title refers to the Stony Brook Herring run in Brewster. Hay follows the fish, birds, and people that congregate at the run from early spring to late fall.

A Beachcomber's Botany. 1968. By Loren C. Petry. The Chatham Conservation Foundation, Inc.
Covers the plants of dunes, beaches, and salt marshes. It is informative and detailed but dry—as dry as Cape Cod sand, which the beautiful drawings evoke on every page.

Life and Death of a Salt Marsh. 1969. By John and Mildred Teal. Ballantine Books.
An in-depth consideration of salt marshes, written for the layman; Cape Cod marshes are well covered.

The Flora of Cape Cod. 1979. By Henry K. Svenson and Robert W. Pyle. Cape Cod Museum of Natural History.
A list of the plants found on the Cape.

A Vanishing Heritage: Wildflowers of Cape Cod. 1989. By Mario DiGregorio and Jeff Wallner. Mountain Press. Out of print.
Beautiful photographs and knowledgeable text make this an important addition to a Cape naturalist's library.

Birding Cape Cod. 1990. Cape Cod Bird Club and Massachusetts Audubon Society.
A guide to the best spots to see birds on the Cape, with extensive notes on what you may find, and when.

Cape Cod and the Islands, the Geologic Story. 1992. By Robert Oldale. Parnassus Imprints.
Oldale is the geologist who made the geological maps of Cape Cod. This book contains detailed geological information.

Secrets in the Sand: The Archaeology of Cape Cod. 1997. By Fred Dunford. Parnassus Imprints.
Dunford, archaeologist at the Cape Cod Museum of Natural History, reports on his archaeological investigations on the Cape.

In the Footsteps of Thoreau—25 Historic and Nature Walks on Cape Cod. 1997. By Adam Gamble. On Cape Publications.
Detailed hiking directions for many walks and hikes on the Mid- and Lower Cape; focuses on areas traversed by Thoreau.

Paddling Cape Cod. 2000. By Shirley and Fred Bull. Backcountry.
Advice and detailed launch and route directions for thirty-one paddling tours on the Cape.

Maps

For more detail than this book provides, the best maps are the topographic maps made by the United States Geological Survey. They are generally available at sporting goods stores. The following quadrangles cover the Cape:

Chatham	Monomoy Point	Sagamore
Cotuit	North Truro	Sandwich
Dennis	Onset	Wareham
Falmouth	Orleans	Wellfleet
Harwich	Pocasset	Woods Hole
Hyannis	Provincetown	

INDEX